MODERN INVENTORY OPERATIONS

Methods for Accuracy and Productivity

MODERN INVENTORY OPERATIONS

Methods for Accuracy and Productivity

Jan B. Young

Catalyst USA, Inc.

VNR VAN NOSTRAND REINHOLD
New York

Library of Congress Catalog Card Number
ISBN 0-442-23979-3

Printed in the United States of America

Van Nostrand Reinhold
115 Fifth Avenue
New York, New York 10003

Chapman and Hall
2-6 Boundary Row
London, SE1 8HN, England

Van Nostrand Reinhold
102 Dodds Street
South Melbourne 3205, Victoria, Australia

Nelson Canada
1120 Birchmount Road
Scarborough, Ontario M IK 5G4, Canada

16 15 14 13 12 11 10 9 8 7 6 5 4 3 2 1

Library of Congress Cataloging-in-Publication Data

Young, J.B. (Jan B.), 1943-
    Modern inventory operations: methods for accuracy and
 productivity / J.B. Young.
        p.   cm. — (Automation in manufacturing)
    Includes bibliographic references and index.
    ISBN 0-442-23979-3 : $49.95
    1. Inventory control. I. Title. II. Series.
TS160.Y68   1991
658.7′87—dc20   90-40998
                                                              CIP

To Vic and Margaret, Tom and Alice, and, of course, Mary

It is one thing to show a man that he is in error, and another to put him in possession of the truth.

All men are liable to error; and most men are, in many points, by passion or interest, under temptation to it.

Essay Concerning Human Understanding
John Locke (1632–1704)

Nine times out of ten . . . there is actually no truth to be discovered; there is only error to be exposed.

Prejudices, Third Series
Henry Louis Mencken (1880–1956)

Table of Contents

Preface

The science of inventory control is not new. Bob Cratchit undoubtedly had responsibility for keeping track of Scrooge & Marley's stock in trade. And long before Charles Dickens created his Victorian characters, unnamed clerks probably kept records of Hannibal's elephants and Amenhotep's palm frond fans. But modern day inventory control is different. We struggle with problems that are, in many respects, far more complex than the ancients ever imagined.

First, modern day businesses are bigger. A typical manufacturing company today handles upwards of 20,000 distinctly different items including raw materials, purchased and manufactured parts, subassemblies in many stages of completion, and finished goods ready for shipment to customers. A large distribution warehouse can have over 200,000 items.

Second, products are more complex. A Roman chariot was built from basically two raw materials (wood and iron) and could be assembled from approximately 50 parts. Since part interchangeability was never an issue, there was no point in stocking parts; repairs were made directly from the raw materials. The Roman chariot maker probably had no more than 20 or 30 inventory items to control, and even the Pharaoh's inventory manager probably never controlled more than a thousand.

Third, labor costs have risen dramatically over the last few millennia. Slave labor is gone (at least in most places), and we are faced with greatly increased control and material handling costs.

And, finally, competition has arrived. Vastly improved communications and transportation technologies have benefited the consumer by bringing head to head companies that are physically thousands of miles apart. We now have to control both investment and labor costs to survive. We must provide a quality product at competitive prices, and we must deliver when the customer needs it.

These factors first came into play during the industrial revolution, but were not significant economic forces until the early part of the 20th century and were not recognized as potent forces until the middle part of the century. The commercial availability of practical computers starting in the early 1960s made automated systems possible, and the continuing decline of computing cost per transaction since the early 1970s has made increasingly sophisticated transactions possible. Competitive pressures have converted possibilities into requirements, to the point that companies which cannot support accurate inventories are now at a distinct disadvantage. Today's customers expect service and no longer accept the excuse that "the computer goofed."

The principles underlying accurate inventories are straightforward and easily understood. In a phrase, the way to achieve accurate inventories is to stop allowing errors to occur. The application of this principle is the most difficult part. It can get especially complicated when the environment is complex.

Many books and articles have been written which explain the need for accurate inventory records and bemoan industry's inability to provide them. If any have been written which explain in detail how to achieve accuracy, they are well hidden. A few systems houses have made a living providing high-accuracy inventory control systems, but it has otherwise been a do-it-yourself world.

This book was written to fill that vacuum. With it, the reader should gain an understanding of the principles involved and benefit from the author's experience as a participant in the design of high-accuracy inventory control systems for more than 40 companies over the past six years.

ORGANIZATION OF THIS BOOK

Modern Inventory Operations is divided into three parts. Part 1 covers fundamental subjects that are too often misunderstood. How inventory records are kept and why they go wrong may seem obvious to some. The pluses and minuses of the various methods used to correct errors are a little less obvious. Proper methods for measuring inventory accuracy are even more sophisticated. This book will not be well understood, and the principles presented are not likely to be properly applied, by those who do not have a working knowledge of these basic subjects.

Part 2 describes methods used to achieve accurate inventories. Because inventory record keeping is almost always a function of material handling, the techniques often relate closely to the material handling methods used and sometimes depend directly on equipment and procedures. Part 2 covers both universally applicable techniques and a wide range of specialized topics. The reader is asked to pick out those items having application to his or her situation.

Part 3 is addressed to the system designer. Because operations managers must live with the systems designers' work, they should also be interested in the problems and opportunities cataloged here. Super-accurate inventory systems do not, of course, just happen. They require an uncommon degree of attentive and intelligent design.

Examples

Unless otherwise noted, the examples used throughout this book are hypothetical. Hypothetical examples can be constructed to focus on a single problem or situation at a time while remaining realistic and believable.

Complexity

Some readers may be concerned about the amount of detail and the number of possible solutions offered in this book. They may quickly conclude that there has to be an easier way and that it simply isn't worth the expense.

No one should represent accuracy as cheap. However, readers should be assured that many companies have found the techniques and methods described in this book to be worth the cost. And, it should be remembered that this book is designed to cover a wide variety of products, warehouse configurations, material handling methods, and management strategies. No company will need to do everything. Most will require only 25–50% of the material.

For the reader with minimal prior knowledge of the subject, the best approach may be to begin with principles. Read Chapters 1 through 5 and 8 through 10, concentrating on the overall picture without worrying about detailed techniques. Next, reread Chapter 5 in detail: the concept of validation is probably the most important subject in the book. Then read Chapters 10 through 15, concentrating on the details where they seem germane to your business. Finally, read Chapter 16 to see how one company actually uses these techniques to run a business in which inventories are so accurate that cycle counters sometimes go weeks without finding any errors at all.

ACKNOWLEDGMENTS

This book is mostly the result of my experience as a system designer at Catalyst USA, Inc. I would be remiss if I did not acknowledge the value of that experience and offer my thanks to the company's management for consenting to the project and cooperating with me in a variety of ways.

Thanks are also due to a number of people who helped. George Howe and Dennis Templar, in particular, spent many hours reading the draft and gave me many detailed and helpful suggestions. Steve Halula, Jim Stowers, and Bob Hayden also contributed from their knowledge and experience.

Finally, the assistance of Ken Pagel and Bob Hall at Grote Manufacturing was crucial. They shared their experience with their system and gave me permission to write about it. Grote Manufacturing's willingness to be part of this project speaks well of the company, both as a manufacturer and as a corporate citizen.

Part 1

FUNDAMENTALS

1

Why Accuracy Is Important

PERPETUAL INVENTORY RECORDKEEPING FUNDAMENTALS

Most businesses require a continuing flow of materials and supplies. To avoid disruption of that flow, most make an effort to keep track of the amounts of each item on hand. In small businesses with small amounts of inventory, it is often sufficient for a human to remember approximate inventory records. When the human thinks that supplies may be getting low, he or she can walk to the stockroom and check. Even a moderately industrious person can effectively control several dozen items this way.

However, as the amount of inventory increases and as the rate of material flow into and out of stock increases, it becomes more and more difficult for a human to remember even approximate inventory balances. Some form of recordkeeping is needed to supplement the human mind. Regardless of whether the records are kept on file cards or in a computer, these basic methods involve three steps:

1. When material is received and added to the inventory, a new inventory balance is calculated by adding the receipt quantity to the prior on-hand balance.
2. When material is withdrawn from the inventory, another new balance is calculated by subtracting the quantity withdrawn from the quantity on hand prior to the withdrawal.
3. From time to time, for a variety of reasons, it may be found that the recorded on-hand balance differs from the quantity actually on hand. In these cases, the records are updated by adding an adjustment to the on-hand balance or subtracting an adjustment from it, as necessary.

These three steps can be combined into a single equation, called the "perpetual inventory equation." It looks like this:

$$COH = POH + R - I \pm A$$

In this equation, COH is the current on-hand balance, POH is the previous on-hand balance, R is the quantity received, I is the quantity issued, and A is the quantity of the adjustment.

The Manual Perpetual Inventory System

In most businesses it is normal for several people to be involved in the keeping of inventory records. Often the clerical job of doing the arithmetic and writing the results on file cards is separated from the material handling jobs of placing items on shelves, removing them when they are needed, and performing occasional counts to verify the recorded balance. In a typical manual system, material handlers move material into and out of the warehouse and create written records (called transactions) as they work. Periodically, the transactions are turned over to a clerk for posting to ledger cards.

Often, different people will perform the same jobs on different shifts. Sometimes one group will be responsible for receiving material and putting it away, while another will be responsible for withdrawing it. And, of course, over time there will be turnover of personnel, requiring that new people be introduced to the system.

When things go right, manual perpetual inventory records can, in fact, be an efficient way for businesses to assure that they have the materials they need. Unfortunately, this method of keeping inventory records, simple as it may seem, is vulnerable to a long list of possible problems. For instance:

1. Material handlers can accidentally move the wrong material.
2. The right material can be moved, but it can be moved to the wrong place. In larger stockrooms, material in the wrong place is effectively lost because the time required to find it is prohibitive.
3. The quantity of parts moved can be wrong.
4. If the quantity of parts moved is right, it can be recorded incorrectly, or either the part identity or the new location of the parts can be recorded incorrectly.
5. The clerk who copies the transaction record onto the file cards can select the wrong card.
6. The numbers can be copied incorrectly.
7. The arithmetic can be done incorrectly.
8. The results can be recorded incorrectly.

And these are only the most obvious of the things that can and often do go wrong. Material handlers also forget to create transactions. Transactions are lost. Clerks accidentally make double postings or forget to post transactions. Or, for instance, suppose a withdrawal is made and then the remaining inventory is recounted. If the recount is posted before the withdrawal, the end result will be a recordkeeping error. It is essential that the withdrawal be posted to the inventory record before the recount if the books are to be right. Timing, therefore, can be an important consideration.

Still more complex problems can occur in a manually posted inventory system. A company in New York once ran out of an expensive, critical raw material that had a very short shelf life. More was ordered, but when it arrived and was put away, it's storage location was incorrectly recorded and it couldn't be found. Still more was ordered, but the supplier was now out of stock. Then the inventory manager found that the original shortage had been caused by an inventory recordkeeping error and, in fact, there had been material on hand all along. But, by this time the original stock was out of date and, by the time the second shipment order could be found, it too was useless. The net result was a shortage that lasted several weeks when, in fact, there never had really been a shortage at all. Even this is only a sample of the complex problems that can occur. But it makes the point. Manual inventory systems are vulnerable to error and, in general, are unreliable.

The Computerized Inventory—In a Batch Environment

The next step up from a clerk-and-cards system is computerization in a batch environment. Batch inventory systems simply automate the clerical portion of the inventory system. Material handlers still manually record the receipt and shipment of material for central processing. But, the written transactions are keyed and electronically posted to records inside a computer. There is little or no change in data gathering and material handling procedures.

The main advantage associated with a batch inventory system is the creation of a central database that can be used in a variety of ways by different departments. Batch computerization also eliminates almost all arithmetic errors, although arithmetic errors are usually a small contributor to the overall error rate, even in manual systems. The net effect is that little is done to improve accuracy. In fact, experience shows that such systems typically achieve accuracies of between 50 and 85 percent when the people involved are conscientious and are trying to do a good job.

The worst part of the batch computerization story, however, is that when an inventory error occurs, it affects a central database and often has broad ramifications. These ramifications are explored in the next section.

THE EFFECTS OF INACCURATE INVENTORY DATA

Impact on Systems That Use Inventory Data

The importance of inventory accuracy has long been underestimated. The cost to business of inaccurate inventory records can be immense, particularly when the term "cost" is taken in the broad sense, including more than just out-of-pocket expense. It is far more than just the cost of finding the inventory errors and correcting them. It involves virtually every aspect of every department.

For instance, production planning systems like Material Requirements Planning (MRP) and Manufacturing Resource Planning (MRP II) are affected. An inventory error that understates inventory will cause reorders to be placed too soon. The result is excess inventory, shortages of storage space, and unnecessary costs and investment. When inventory errors overstate the quantity on hand, the result is often delayed reorders, shortages, expediting, and late deliveries to customers. Late deliveries and other forms of poor customer service tend to drive customers away, of course. Lost opportunity costs can be significant, sometimes driving a company out of business.

Both MRP and MRP II depend on accurate inventory records to work correctly. Neither will pay its own way unless it can work with an accurate on-hand balance for every item in the bill of material. In fact, because these planning tools tend to replace manual judgment with computer programs, the presence of bad inventory information may result in a situation that is worse than under the manual system. Many MRP installations have failed for this precise reason. Distribution Requirements Planning systems (DRP) are similarly affected by inaccurate inventories. DRP, like MRP, assumes that the inventory data used is correct and its tolerance for error is nearly zero.

But the impact isn't limited to planning systems. Financial systems, for instance, are affected when inventory errors occur. Since inventory is an asset, general ledger software usually reflects the on-hand balances in the company's books. When the on-hands are wrong, the ledger is wrong and the company's profit is misstated.

Order entry systems are still another example. Modern order entry systems often calculate product availability taking into account existing stocks, allocations or reservations, and, sometimes, the future flow of product into inventory. If current on-hand balances are overstated, availability will be overstated and customers will be given promised shipment dates that cannot be met. Further, when on-hands are overstated, resupplies of finished goods from the factory will be delayed, making the shortage situation worse. On the other hand, when inventories are understated, customers are told that product will be shipped later than it could be. This makes the business less competitive and reduces the chance of getting orders. To lose an order because the product isn't in stock is one thing; to lose the order because you didn't know you had the material is another entirely.

Impact on Users

When inventories are wrong, systems are affected. But more important, people are affected in their daily working lives. The production control office, for instance, is responsible for planning production and measuring accomplishments against its plan. When a delay occurs, it is usually production control's job to find a way out of the mess.

Production control is directly and immediately affected when inventories are wrong. Material Requirements Planning determines when replacement stocks should arrive, attempting to consume and minimize inventory. If inventory runs out before it should, a shortage occurs and someone is likely to be in trouble. If inventory is actually higher than the records show, an unnecessary investment has been made and one of the major benefits of MRP has been lost. And, of course, there is the risk that someone will intentionally increase safety stock levels to cover a history of inaccuracies.

The expediting workload can become enormous. Production plans become obsolete with each shortage and must be redone frequently. The demand for real-time production planning systems is due, at least in many businesses, more to the need to correct for internal problems than to the need to accommodate customer order changes. And those internal problems, more often than not, revolve around inventory errors.

The purchasing department is also directly affected when inventory errors occur. Errors in raw material and purchased part inventories cause emergency orders to be placed, wasting inordinate amounts of the buyer's time. Inventory errors in work-in-process and finished goods also affect the buyers. Emergency manufacturing orders consume parts and material more quickly than planned, requiring still more emergency purchase orders to be placed. Inventory errors can also place an undue emphasis on vendor delivery cycles, sometimes causing buyers to choose vendors more for their speed than for the quality or price of their products. When inventories are accurate, deliveries can be more accurately planned and emphasis on vendor selection can be adjusted.

The sales and marketing departments also suffer when inventories are wrong. They are the front line troops who have to explain to irate customers why deliveries are late and why substitute materials were used. The company with a record of missed deliveries is at a significant competitive disadvantage when bidding against a company that has proven itself reliable.

In a manufacturing company, the shop ultimately foots the bill for many of the costs of inaccurate inventories. Overtime needed to squeeze emergency orders through is only the tip of the iceberg. Extra work-in-process means a more crowded shop and more material handling labor to get at pallets buried under others. Extra machine setups are required to accommodate emergency orders and reduced lot sizes. The shop becomes harder to keep clean and safe. Morale declines as overtime demands increase. And both personnel plans and vacation schedules are disrupted.

The stockroom or warehouse becomes less efficient. Warehouse people spend more time searching for lost items and less time doing productive work. Shortages must be recorded, back orders increase, and expediting becomes a critical function. Physical inventories are required more often and cycle counting frequency must be increased.

Quality control suffers when emergency jobs must be inspected quickly, often under pressure to accept the product despite minor flaws. Product that has been temporarily "lost" may be obsolete when it is found or may have been damaged through excessive handling. As a result, added inspections are needed and reworked parts must be inspected again.

Even the engineering department is affected. When inventory errors occur, samples and test units are hard to get. Consultations with QC are needed to re-solve problems. And the engineering change process can be made significantly more complex than necessary. Product changes are often orchestrated to syn-chronize the introduction of new parts with the use-up of old parts. If, however, the engineering department is misinformed about the number of old parts on hand, much of the point of change control is lost unless extraordinary efforts are made.

Impact on the Business

Eventually, it all boils down to an adverse effect on the business in one or more of three forms:

1. Poor customer service is one of the ultimate results of the shortages that occur when inventories are wrong. Either shipment promises are missed or lead times are overstated. The costs associated with poor customer service cannot be stated in dollars. But, as any sales man-ager will testify, they are very real and very large.
2. Unnecessary inventory investment results from incorrect production and purchase plans made by the material planners when inventories are understated (i.e., when the system records show that there is less material in stock than there really is). And, whether records are un-der- or overstated, production planners quickly learn that inaccura-cies exist. Their response is usually to increase the size of safety stocks. Increased safety stocks, of course, translate directly into un-necessary inventory.
3. Reduced production efficiency is the third adverse effect. Inventory inaccuracies cause emergency orders that are less efficient to place with vendors and less efficient to manufacture. Overtime, extra mate-rial handling, unnecessary machine setups, and poor morale in the shop all play a part.

SOLVING THE PROBLEM—PREREQUISITES

It is, in fact, possible to create and maintain perpetual inventory records that are as high as 99.9 percent accurate by location. A few companies are doing it today. While these companies have invested, some of them heavily, in systems and equipment, financial returns have often been dramatic. And, in many cases, pro-ductivity gains have accompanied improvements in accuracy to shorten the pay-back period even more.

Computer-Based Inventory by Location

Computers have become so ubiquitous that it is easy to forget that many smaller businesses operate successfully without them. As noted, accuracy and productiv-ity are possible in small businesses and in small stockrooms in larger businesses without much trouble. All it takes is an employee with the time and the dedication to do the job. But, as businesses get larger, the amount of activity in the stockroom and the amount of bookkeeping required soon surpass the ability of a person to control it.

Absolute accuracy requires that a human devote his or her entire attention to each transaction, one at a time. Even though the human might be able to update ledger cards at the rate of two or three a minute, continuous work at that pace cannot be done without having the job become routine and mechanical. Attention will wander and errors will creep in. In fact, for many people, the practical limit to the amount of activity that can be handled in an 8-hour shift with perfect accuracy could be as low as 100 transactions.

Most companies, therefore, need computer-based inventory systems and computerization should be considered a prerequisite for inventory accuracy and productivity. Although computerization does not, itself, provide accurate inventory records, the machines do arithmetic flawlessly, eliminate other problems such as illegible handwriting, and make possible the sheer volume of calculations necessary with no degradation of internal accuracy.

In the early days of computer-based inventories, many systems kept only a four-wall inventory. Four-wall inventories are those which record only the on-hand balance within a building or in a department or, so to speak, within the four walls. For several reasons, four-wall inventories simply do not work. When, for instance, a cycle counter is instructed to count and verify the inventory of a part, he or she must be able to locate the parts to count. If the inventory is four wall, the cycle counter has a big job, just to find the parts to count. On the other hand, if the cycle count is to take place within a single bin, finding the material is easy.

Therefore, not only is a computer-based inventory system a prerequisite to accuracy and productivity, it must be one that keeps track of the quantity on hand and its actual, physical location in the plant. Physical locations must be tracked in enough detail so that material can be found with reasonable ease.

Business Size

For the smallest businesses, this book is unnecessarily complex. Ledger cards and manual recordkeeping can be done accurately if the people involved are given the right training and motivation and if they are given the time required. Experience has proven, however, that beyond a certain point, manual solutions simply do not work and something else is required.

Lock the Stockroom

The introduction of material requirements planning to the manufacturing industry in the early 1970s raised the visibility of inventory accuracy problems for the first time. At first technicians, and later production control people, came to recognize the importance of accuracy. The nearly universal solution to accuracy problems was to limit access to inventory to a select group of people and make those people responsible for keeping accurate records.

Inventory managers were (and often still are) measured on the efficiency with which they handle inventory and on the number of shortages that occurred. Production supervisors, however, were measured on production efficiency and on the degree to which schedules were met. It was, therefore, of little interest to production whether or not inventory records were correctly kept. They wanted only to assure that they had the material they needed to keep the factory running without a moment of lost time. Instances of production people "stealing" inventory (withdrawing it without authority and without recording the withdrawal) were commonly considered an important factor. "Lock the stockroom to keep production out," was the common cry of inventory managers.

There has never been an advantage to limiting access to inventory other than the fact that people cannot be held responsible for the job of keeping accurate records unless they are given the control necessary. The locked stockroom was and is an important control mechanism.

There has always been, however, great value in assuring that inventory transactions are properly recorded. Ideally, businesses will operate in an atmosphere in which people routinely and accurately record their transactions and can take what is needed when it is needed. Properly designed systems, operating with accurate data, should predict the shop's requirements and should provide the required material with only occasional need for emergency withdrawals. When emergency withdrawals are required, they should be made through the inventory system, using material selected and allocated by the system, with proper audit trails kept.

It is also important to remember that sophisticated inventory systems assign random storage locations when material is put away. The employees, therefore, do not often know where to find things. This makes it much harder for the "midnight requisitioner." If the system is up and running, it is easier for people to use it than it is for them to go around it.

It is a fundamental assumption of this book that inventory will be handled by trained employees who follow management's rules for recording their transactions. If it is necessary to provide walls, fences, and locks, to achieve this goal, so be it.

The Solutions

The following chapters explain how superaccurate inventories are possible. Hardware and software are both involved, but the most important ingredient is an understanding of the importance of accuracy and of the techniques used to achieve it. While there certainly could be ways of keeping accurate inventories that are not reflected in this book, the methods and techniques presented here are proven and known to work.

One more point: The sheer magnitude of the solutions to some of the problems presented in this book may be daunting. If so, think about dividing the problem into pieces and concentrating first on those that have the highest payback ratios. Each element of an inventory accuracy project should be justifiable within itself. Inventory accuracies, after all, don't have to be 100 percent accurate. They only have to be accurate enough to successfully compete.

2

How Inventories Go Wrong

Paper-driven batch computer systems have been the most common form of inventory recordkeeping for nearly two decades. The flow of information through one such system is diagrammed in Figure 2.1.

1. As purchase orders are placed, they are keyed and a file of open orders is maintained. In many instances, the system uses this file to print the purchase orders that are mailed to vendors.
2. Either copies of the purchase order or specially designed worksheets are printed and filed on the receiving dock. These copies tell the people who work in receiving what should be in each shipment when it arrives. Some systems delay the printing of the documents until the shipment is at the door or is soon to arrive.
3. Arriving material is counted and recorded on the receiving dock. Written receipt records are carried or sent to the office for key entry into the inventory system. Within the system, the data is used to relieve purchase orders and update on-hand balances.
4. Following receipt, a material handler (shown as a lift-truck driver in Figure 2.1) is assigned to put the material away. The material handler knows approximately where the material should be kept, finds an open space for it, puts the material in that space, and records where it was put. The put-away record is then keyed, allowing the system to update its inventory.
5. Customer orders are also received and keyed. Most paper-driven systems print a pick list shortly before the order is to be shipped. Pick lists are usually organized in an efficient sequence for picking and

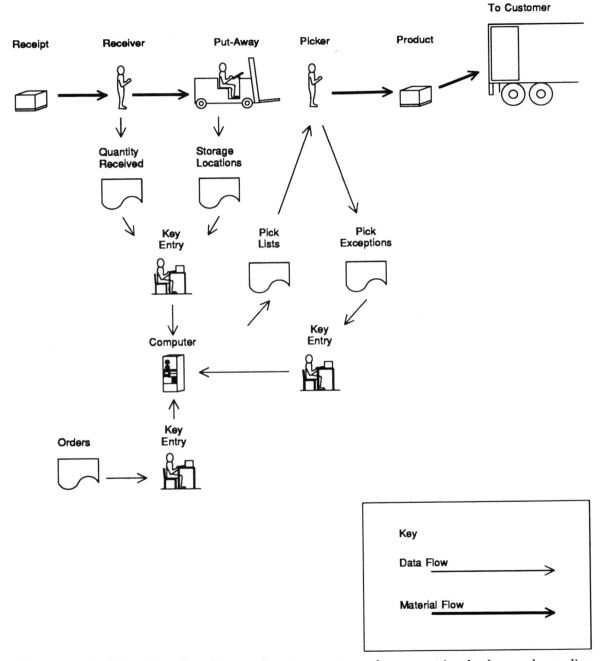

Figure 2.1. Traditional data flow. Common inventory systems of years past involved manual recording of information on paper and key entry after the fact. These systems have proven themselves unresponsive and inaccurate.

often include the locations from which the material is to be picked. They are delivered to a supervisor who divides them up among the pickers.

6. Each picker then moves through the warehouse, taking material from the shelves and either packing it for shipment or stacking it on a pallet. Problems such as insufficient inventory or an incorrect part number are noted on the pick list. One copy is attached to the shipment; another is returned to key entry where exceptions are entered into the computer. The computer uses this information to deduct from the inventories, for billing, and for the printing of freight manifests and bills of lading.

Sources of Errors

Paper-driven, computerized systems like the one described above have been successful in industry, at least to the extent that they have been very widely used. These systems have made possible large distribution facilities that handle thousands and thousands of items. They have contributed significantly to the ability to serve customers with a wide range of products and have allowed faster shipments at much lower costs.

However, paper-driven systems have major problems. Most of these problems relate directly to the number of hands through which information flows and the number of times that information must be copied, keyed, printed, read, and understood, as shown in Figure 2.1. There is, of course, a cost incurred every time the information is handled. And there is a probability that errors will be introduced. Even if the chance of error is small, when thousands of transactions are performed each day and millions each year, the laws of probability make it clear that errors will occur. Since errors tend to accumulate in inventory systems, the eventual result is inaccurate inventories.

To illustrate this compounding of little errors into big inaccuracies, a computer simulation was written by the author that provided the numbers in the example below.

Imagine a factory that employs 10 full-time material handlers. Also, imagine that each of these material handlers creates an inventory transaction (a put-away, withdrawal, or a move) every 30 seconds, 8 hours a day, 5 days a week. This implies 48,000 transactions each week. If the material handlers are 98 percent accurate in following instructions and reporting results to the system, 960 errors are generated each week (2 percent of 48,000). And, because inventories are perpetual, another 960 locations go bad each week.

If there are 20,000 storage locations in the factory and if a physical inventory is performed only once a year, the physical inventory will find about 18,200 locations, or 91 percent of the inventories, to be incorrect. (The number of incorrect locations is not simply 960 times the number of weeks in a year because some incorrect transactions will be posted against already incorrect locations.)

If this factory should employ a cycle counter to locate and correct inventory errors, the situation improves a little. Suppose the cycle counter is able to count, verify, and update the records on a location in 5 minutes. This means that he or she will count 12 locations an hour, or 480 a week. The cycle counter results in an improvement in inventory accuracy. But, at the end of a year's operations, the number of errors still stands at 12,700, or 63 percent incorrect. Again, the number of corrected inventories is less than the number of locations counted because some counts are made at already correct places.

In fact, additional variables such as the accuracy of the cycle counters and the physical inventory takers should also be taken into account. When this is done, the simulation hints that it could be necessary to perform cycle counts as fast as inventory is handled if an overall accuracy level of 95 percent is to be maintained. That is to say, if 500 inventory transactions are recorded daily and 500 locations are cycle counted daily, inventory accuracy is likely to stabilize in an acceptable range.

The key to accuracy, therefore, is a matter of locating sources of error and eliminating or minimizing them. If, for instance, the factory in the simulation could handle inventory transactions with 99.95 percent accuracy, inventory accuracy levels by location would remain above 95 percent for the entire year, even without a cycle counter. With one cycle counter on the staff, transaction accuracy could fall to 99.92 percent while still maintaining 95 percent overall. But even this level only allows 8 errors in every 10,000 transactions. Since each movement transaction is handled at least three times, the accuracy required at each step to achieve 8 errors in 10,000 transactions is something less than 3 errors in 10,000 transactions. This means that only about 15 errors per week are permitted at the stated transaction rate of 48,000 per week. The individual material handlers and key entry operators can each, therefore, afford only about one error per week.

Studies have been performed that estimate typical manual data entry error rates at about 1 in every 400 characters.[1] Even if a transaction is only 25 characters long, the job of achieving 99.92 percent accuracy in a paper-driven system is clearly impossible. Error rates for bar-code entry, on the other hand, are often quoted at 1 per 3 million characters, which translates to accuracies in excess of 99.999 percent for 25 character records.[2] Bar codes are not the total answer, but the numbers give a hint that they can be an important part of the solution.

The list of possible sources of error in paper-driven systems is very long. For instance:

1. The initial, or beginning, balance can be wrong. Physical inventories are notoriously inaccurate.
2. Working from documents, the receiver, the put-away person, or the picker can misread part identities or quantities.
3. The receiver and picker must count items and can miscount.
4. Counting done by the receiver and picker can be recorded incorrectly or can be recorded against the wrong line on either the receiving work sheet or the pick list.

[1]Michaels, Eugene S. (Bell Labs), "Qwerty versus Alphabetic Keyboards as a Function of Typing Skills," *Human Factors*, Vol. 13, no. 5, 1977, pp. 419–426.
[2]Allais, David C., *Bar Code Symbology: Some Observations on Theory and Practice*, Intermec Corporation, 1982.

5. The picker can misread the picking location number.
6. The material handler can record the wrong storage location.
7. Any of the recording done by the receiver, the material handler, or the picker can be illegible.
8. Any of the transactions can be lost or misplaced as they travel between the users and the computer.
9. Any of the transactions can be keyed incorrectly.

Errors of this kind are not the only errors that can affect accuracy. In the daily rush to get the product made, it is understandable, if not desirable, that some employees will concentrate on the work and leave the recordkeeping for later. When transactions are delayed, inventory records get out of date and are, in fact, wrong. This would not be a significant problem if the paperwork were eventually to catch up. But, in most businesses, there is a continuing stream of delayed transactions. So the inventories (and therefore the balances used by material requirements planning and distribution requirements planning) are continuously wrong. For most purposes, in most companies, delays are as bad as errors.

Traditional Database Design

Database design for location-by-location control over inventories also affects the accuracy of inventory records. Figure 2.2 diagrams the traditional database layout that was once thought right for inventory control. Although this design is now widely considered inadequate, many older systems based on it remain in use.

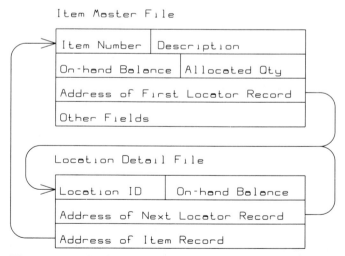

Figure 2.2. Traditional inventory file structure. Many older inventory systems support less-than-complete file structures that, in turn, limit the flexibility of the warehouse. In this example, no method of recording empty storage locations is shown, making automated assignment of locations to arriving material impossible.

As shown in the figure, traditional inventory control systems are based on an item master file with a location detail file chained to it. The item master file is usually keyed by item or part number. The location detail file may be keyed by location ID (location number) or may be without keys. Both files often contain many fields in addition to those shown in the figure.

Even more primitive inventory systems have been written and remain in use that keep the inventory balances on the item master file and carry at most one location number for each item. These systems offer no hope of achieving any reasonable level of accuracy and, therefore, are ignored here.

More Sources of Errors

Traditional file structures offer opportunities for subtle kinds of errors that may not be clear from examination of the data flow diagram in Figure 2.1. For instance:

1. The record layouts shown are not designed for real-time processing and thus do not show in-transit quantities. If, for instance, a pallet of product X is being moved from point A to point B at the same time that a cycle counter is counting item X, the cycle counter might double count the in-transit pallet or miss it altogether. Either will result in an error being inserted in the inventory records.
2. Allocations are done by product rather than by location. If a product can exist in more than one location, employees must record the actual location(s) affected every time material is moved. This recording activity offers additional opportunities for error.
3. In a typical implementation, new location detail records are created as product arrives and old records are deleted as it is shipped. Because there is no permanent record of the locations that physically exist, there is nothing to keep material handlers from recording nonexistent locations. When erroneous locations are keyed and reported, the person who is to retrieve the material is left with no idea where to look for it. The material has been lost and the inventory records are in error.

IMPROVED DATA FLOW

Many of the sources of error that were noted in the traditional approach to inventory system design can be eliminated. There are a variety of ways to improve accuracy. Many of them will be discussed in detail in Part 2 of this book. Figure 2.3 diagrams one method that eliminates errors by eliminating paperwork and manual recording. This example uses portable terminals connected to the inventory control system via a radio link.

The concept behind Figure 2.3 is that every material handler in the plant is given a radio terminal. All material movements are scheduled by the computer

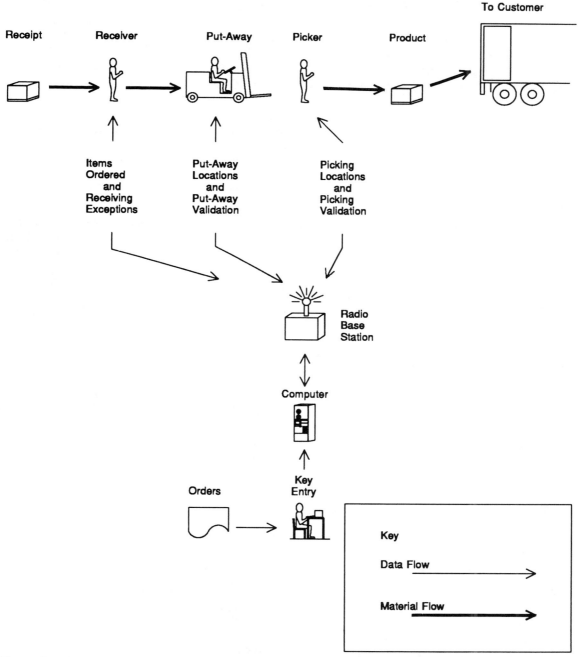

Figure 2.3. Improved data flow. In a more modern inventory system, virtually all paperwork and manual handling of information is eliminated using bar codes and portable radio-linked computer terminals. Accuracy and efficiency are significantly improved as a result.

and, with proper controls, are dispatched to material handlers one at a time. The material handler responds to each computer-generated request for material movement by scanning a bar code on the material (or on a rack or bin). Only in rare instances, must a material handler key data.

For instance, Figure 2.3 shows a picker who receives pick lists one line at a time via the radio terminal. The picker executes each pick as it is presented and confirms by reading a bar code on the bin. Key entry is needed only if the bin does not contain the expected quantity of parts. And, if inventory records are accurate, the number of exceptions will be small. Paperwork and delays have been eliminated. Key entry relating to the picking function has been minimized. The result is error-free work and, therefore, error-free inventories.

Improved Database Design

Figure 2.4 shows an improved database design. Like the data flow shown in Figure 2.3, this database has been structured to allow added error checking as data is received. The result is lower error rates and more accurate inventories. In the

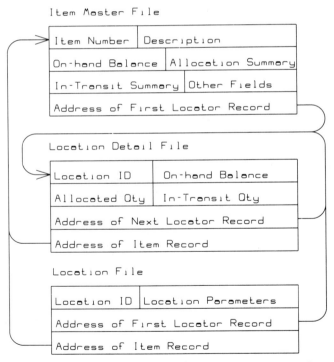

Figure 2.4. Improved inventory file structure. Modern file structures provide a place for information about locations as well as items and inventories. The structure shown also accommodates mixed items and an unlimited number of locations for any item.

figure, inventory records are kept on a location detail file. This file is accessible either through the item master file or through a separate location file. As in-transit inventory field is provided and allocations are done by location with only a summary allocation kept at the item level. As material movements are dispatched, the inventory in the source location is reduced, but the inventory in the destination location is not increased. Instead, the in-transit balance is used to temporarily hold the quantity of material being moved until the movement is reported complete. The database is thus closely tied to the physical movement of material and truly reflects item status.

Errors that Can Still Occur

The techniques embodied in Figures 2.3 and 2.4 represent a major step forward in achieving accuracy. They are capable of preventing the great majority of inventory errors and, properly applied, can result in accuracies in excess of 99 percent. However, it should be recognized that they are not adequate to completely eliminate errors. For instance, factories and warehouses using these techniques will still experience, to some degree, the following kinds of errors:

1. Receiving. Because the receiving department must still manually identify product and count it, receiving remains an area of exposure. Although techniques exist that can minimize the frequency and impact of receiving errors, it remains a critical operation. When receiving is done well, everything else becomes much easier.
2. Key entry of shortages. Until the day arrives when it is possible to have perfectly accurate inventories, shortages will occur. Whenever a shortage does occur, parts must be manually counted and the actual quantity must be keyed. The counting and key entry are another source of possible error.
3. Sabotage and pilferage. Employee sabotage is, thankfully, rare. And pilferage is controllable, at least to a degree. Well-designed history files can, over time, lead to the capture of the saboteur or thief and his or her dismissal. In addition, techniques exist (described in Chapter 14) that can make pilferage harder and less attractive to most employees.
4. And, finally, companies may choose to ignore good inventory control practices when the cost of achieving a high level of inventory accuracy is not covered by the benefits. In these cases, of course, errors and a certain level of inaccuracy are judged acceptable.

3

Inventories in Different Industries

Modern, on-line inventory systems receive most of their input from and direct most of their output to the hourly workforce. These systems control and direct a significant number of people, representing a significant labor cost. Therefore, to be successful, they must be designed to achieve high levels of productivity along with high levels of accuracy. The details of the products being stocked, the layout of the facility, the material handling methods used, and other factors thus become important design considerations.

For instance, imagine a business that distributes industrial goods nationally. The customers pay for the freight and are, therefore, allowed to specify the carrier. Since different trucking lines pick up at different times of the day, it makes sense for this business to schedule its order picking in waves timed to have the goods ready for loading when each carrier arrives. Now imagine the system that controls inventory for this business applied to a business that makes home deliveries of, for instance, appliances. The home delivery business ships on its own trucks, with each truck routed over a different group of destinations each day. A system that tries to organize picking by carrier would at best be difficult to use and at worst would be entirely unmanageable.

So, inventory systems differ from industry to industry, from business to business, and even from department to department within a business. An understanding of similarities and differences between industries gives perspective and can be a useful source of ideas to the system designer.

SIMILARITIES AMONG INDUSTRIES

Almost every business has inventory to manage and control. Some have only small inventories and can succeed with only informal controls. But the list of industries with major investments in inventory is surprisingly long. It includes, for instance:

- Manufacturing of all kinds including machinery and equipment, textiles, clothing, food, furniture, electrical and electronic equipment, building materials, paper and paper products, automotive products, and many more.
- Distribution including not only manufacturers and wholesalers but also large retail chains with company owned distribution centers. Inventory control may be more important in distribution than in any other industry. Distributors usually invest a larger percentage of their total assets in inventory than do other industries.
- Insurance companies keep large inventories of supplies including forms and other office supplies. Some of the larger insurers also keep inventories of office furniture and equipment for local sales offices and even stocks of materials to be flown to disaster areas when the need arises. The largest insurers have company owned networks of distribution centers.
- The transportation industry includes airlines, railroads, and bus and truck lines. Most of these businesses keep substantial stocks of spare parts and equipment in addition to fuel, lubricants, forms, and supplies.
- The health care industry, particularly hospitals, keeps an ever-increasing range of pharmaceuticals, instruments, and supplies. Inventory control in the health care industry requires particular rigor when controlled substances and life- or health-supporting equipment or pharmaceuticals are involved. It is especially well suited to the techniques used to achieve high levels of accuracy.
- Government, especially the military, has vast stocks of everything from weapons and ammunition to food and clothing, all of which must be tracked and controlled. The broad diversity of materials handled may complicate system requirements and make the achievement of accuracy particularly difficult.
- Utilities inventory equipment, parts, and supplies, typically at central depots with distribution to local stockrooms.
- Even the religion "industry" has inventory. Many central church organizations have distribution centers that ship publications and office and religious supplies around the world. Some of these distribution centers are larger and more complex than many manufacturing warehouses.

Throughout all of these diverse institutions, there are major areas of commonality. Some of the most important are described in the following sections.

Receiving

Warehouses and stockrooms all receive material. All but the smallest of them have a formal receiving process in which arriving material is checked against an open order and is either accepted into the inventory or turned away.

Receipts from vendors are almost always verified against a copy of a purchase order. Controls often exist to prevent the receipt of material earlier than specified or in quantities exceeding those ordered. Net receiving information is sent back to the purchasing department where it is used to close out orders and authorize payment of invoices. Internal receipts are often handled less formally. In some cases manufacturing or warehouse transfer orders are used simply to notify the receiver that something is coming. In other cases, material is simply accepted without advance notice and regardless of quantity or timing.

Almost all stockrooms and warehouses also receive items from the people they ship to. These customer returns are sometimes preauthorized on a document called a return authorization. In other cases, returns are simply accepted.

Physical facilities and handling methods used by receiving departments differ from one business to the next, of course, but the common elements of work are remarkably similar:

- Identify the source.
- Identify the order number.
- Verify that the order exists.
- Verify that the order is due.
- Verify the piece count against the carrier's freight bill.
- Identify the item.
- Verify that the item appears on the order.
- Count the quantity received.
- Verify that the quantity received is not greater than the quantity ordered.
- Record the quantity received.
- Label or otherwise identify the receipt.
- Transmit receipt information to the purchasing and accounts payable departments or systems.

Additional receiving tasks found in many (but not all) receiving operations include:

- Identification and recording of lot numbers and/or serial numbers
- Repackaging and/or repalletizing
- Freight bill entry

Quality Control

Incoming inspection processes are performed by almost all warehouses and stockrooms. In some cases they are formal and in others, informal. Informal inspection can be as simple as instructing the receiver to open and look at anything that appears damaged on the outside. Problems can be brought to the attention of the receiving supervisor. Informal inspection procedures can work well for inventory facilities that receive product only from internal sources and in facilities that have relatively low receiving volumes, uncomplicated products, and few receipts.

Most larger facilities, however, operate with more formal inspection procedures which consist of:

- Drawing samples to be inspected and moving them to an inspection area.
- Establishment of a "hold" on the material received to prevent use of the material until inspection is complete.
- Testing the sample. Tests consist of a wide variety of measurements, inspections, and analyses. Some tests are destructive and some are not.
- Upon completion of the tests, either release the hold on the material or reject it. If the material is rejected, a disposition must be determined and carried out.
- When tests are nondestructive, sample units must be moved to stock. In some instances it is necessary that they be merged with the original lot; in other cases they can simply be stored in a convenient location.
- Throughout the process, sample numbers, serial numbers, and lot numbers may be tracked.
- And, throughout the process, records are kept for later analysis.

Put Away

Received material must be put away. Although handling methods and storage devices vary from place to place, the basic steps required are almost universal:

- A storage location must be selected. Selection can be made by the inventory control system, by a supervisor, or by the material handler who puts the material away. When material handlers select locations, they often do so according to a prespecified scheme. The warehouse or stockroom, for instance, may be divided into zones or areas and the material handlers directed to put certain materials in certain areas.
- A material handler must be assigned the put-away task. The assignment may be made prior to selecting a storage location or after the selection is done.
- The material must be physically put away.
- The storage location must be recorded and the fact that the material has been put in it must be confirmed. In some businesses, confirmation occurs by default (i.e., it is assumed unless notification to the contrary is received).

Rewarehousing

In addition to receiving and disbursing material, stockrooms move material about within their borders. These moves can occur for a variety of reasons that vary from business to business and depend on the physical arrangement of the storage space. Reasons for internal movement include the consolidation of like product to free up storage locations, the replenishment of forward picking areas, and the rearrangement of stock to improve efficiency.

Miscellaneous Items

Even in this age of computerization, businesses generate great quantities of paper. Storage of these records is often a problem. It is a rare manager who can look at a large warehouse or stockroom and not see the possibility of storing things other than product in it.

The term "miscellaneous items" refers to items stored in a company's warehouse that are not part of the normal product. In addition to records, examples of miscellaneous items include furniture, office supplies, marketing supplies, maintenance supplies, and obsolete tooling. These items are usually characterized by being slow moving, by their absence from the bill-of-material and item master files, and by lack of a formal scheme of identifying numbers. However, because they consume space and can be lost if their storage location is improperly recorded, they must be included in the inventory system's database.

Order Management, Picking, and Shipping

The outbound side of a stockroom or warehouse is much more likely to be unique to the needs of the business than is the inbound side. The fact that many businesses receive in bulk and ship individual items means that the preponderance of the warehouse labor dollar is spent on picking and shipping. Much more attention, therefore, is often paid to efficiency on the outbound side. As a result, material handling equipment is more complex and both picking and shipping methods are more sophisticated. There are, however, still a number of basic processes that apply to almost all businesses:

- Orders from customers must be entered, credit must be approved, and when supplies are short, priorities must be assigned. Manufacturing orders and orders for transfers between warehouses must be entered (or generated by a computer system).
- Once a base of outbound orders has been established, the sequence of picking and shipping must be determined. Some businesses print pick lists for distribution by a supervisor or dispatcher in whatever sequence he or she sees fit. Other businesses use a computer to divide the work into batches (or waves) and schedule them based on, for instance, the expected departure times of various carriers.
- The allocation (or reservation) of material is best done after orders have been sequenced for picking. That way, material needed for an order to be shipped now will not be allocated to an order for next week. The selection of picking locations is an integral part of allocation when allocation is done in the computer at the location level.
- Personnel are usually assigned to pick and pack orders after the loca-

tions are selected and after pick or packing lists have been prepared. Pick lists can be printed on paper or can be electronic.

- The actual picking consists of taking parts or pallets of parts from storage devices. The methods used to control the picking process differ greatly from one business to the next.
- If an order is assigned to several pickers, the items picked by each of them must be physically gathered and packed for shipment.
- Completed shipments must be sorted by carrier and staged pending the carrier's arrival. Upon arrival of the carrier, they must be loaded and shipping paperwork must be completed.
- And, finally, the completed work must be reported to the inventory system so it can relieve its records. Confirmation must also be passed to the order tracking system for posting against orders and to the accounts receivable system, which prints invoices and accepts payments.

These are the greatest areas of commonality between inventory facilities and, therefore, between inventory control systems. While there are businesses that do not perform one or more of these functions or that perform them in ways other than that described, the exceptions are few or represent special cases. The best inventory control systems address all of these areas of commonality and address them more or less as described here.

DIFFERENCES BETWEEN INDUSTRIES

There are also major areas of diversity from one industry to the next and even from one business to the next within a single industry. Examples follow.

Cross-Docking

Many warehouses and some manufacturing facilities cross-dock receipts when there are existing customer or outbound transfer orders for them. The term "cross-docking" means movement of the material directly from receiving to shipping without ever putting it away. The intent is to reduce material handling labor and cost and to improve customer service by shipping more quickly.

Work-in-Process

In some businesses, inventory outside the stockroom must be controlled. The term "work-in-process" is a convenient handle for this inventory. In a manufacturing business, work-in-process is inventory that is being processed or assembled and that is temporarily associated with a work center rather than a storage location. Or, work-in-process can be inventory that has been shipped to an outside vendor for processing and is associated with the vendor rather than a storage location.

The existence of work-in-process inventory can greatly complicate the installation of inventory systems, particularly if it is necessary for the systems to track and control floor stock and a large number of point-of-use storage facilities. Because this inventory is spread throughout the plant, many more remote system terminals are necessary and much additional cabling is needed. More important, however, is the fact that many additional people are likely to be picking and withdrawing materials. Training, therefore, becomes even more critical. Chapter 10 includes a more detailed analysis of inventory systems in a work-in-process environment.

Bills-of-Material and Assembly Operations

The existence of bills-of-material and assembly operations is the hallmark—almost the definition—of manufacturing. Inventory control is complicated by the fact that parts change identity and quantities can be decreased (and occasionally increased) as material moves through the plant.

The inventory control system must also recognize that some bills-of-material do not involve assembly and that some items in the bills have no physical reality. The classic example is the wheelbarrow, which is stored as a pallet of wheels, a pallet of handles, and a pile of barrows. When the customer orders a wheelbarrow, the inventory control system must be able to allocate handles only if the wheels are in stock and wheels only if the barrows are in stock. All three parts must be picked and shipped. The system must be able to ignore the fact that the wheelbarrow itself is never received, handled, or shipped. In fact, it does not exist until the customer assembles it.

Multiple Stockrooms

Some businesses have more than one stockroom within a single building. Others have multiple stockrooms in separate buildings. In some cases the separate buildings are within a single facility, in other cases they are separated by a few miles, and in still other cases they are separated by hundreds of miles.

The existence of multiple stockrooms must be known when the inventory control system is designed. Three factors are important:

- The methods used to ship between stockrooms
- The strategy defined for determining which items are to be stored in which stockroom
- If the same items are stored in more than one stockroom, the methods used to decide which orders are picked from which stockroom

Check-Out, Check-In

Manufacturing toolrooms need the ability to check tools out to employees and then check them back in. The logic required to keep accurate tool inventories is also applicable, in some instances, to product. The entertainment industry, for instance, operates much like a large video store. Films and tapes are checked out when shipped to television stations or movie theaters and are checked back in upon return.

Material Handling Methods

Probably the single most significant difference between inventory systems lies in the design of a facility's handling systems. In manufacturing applications, this includes the handling of material into, through, and out of the shop. Picking, sortation, packing, and shipping usually offer the most complexity and the most variation. The list of equipment and the combinations in which it can be applied is limited only by the imagination of the plant's engineers and management. For example:

- To speed picking, many warehouses and some manufacturers create "forward" picking areas and replenish these locations from "reserve" stock. This creates a need to define and execute replenishment moves. Since every move is a potential source of inventory error, it also creates a need for the inventory system to control the moves.
- Picking methods can vary from the simple to the incredible. At one extreme, a lift truck driver can simply move pallets to the shipping area. At the other extreme, parts can be picked to a take-away conveyor with transactions communicated to the picker through radio terminals or through a network of small computer displays known as a "pick-by-light" system. The take-away conveyor can then pass through a packing station to a conveyor sortation system or through a tilt-tray sorter to an outbound trailer.
- When picking is divided into zones, orders are often split among zones for picking. The picks must then be brought together for packing. Consolidation methods range from serial picking of the orders into a common shipping container (each picker does his or her share and passes the order along to the next person in sequence) to complex staging and sorting arrangements.
- Shipment methods also differ substantially from one inventory facility to the next. Logic required to organize material for shipment on a company owned truck route is significantly different from that required for United Parcel shipments, for example.

And, these are only the most commonly found areas of difference between inventory systems in different industries and businesses. Others include serial number and lot tracking, assembly and loading of shipments in the proper sequence for delivery by a route truck, the efficient handling of sales promotions, special provisions for the handling of high value and dangerous products such as drugs, chemicals, explosives, and weapons, and the need to segregate products like foods into different storage environments such as a freezer or a cooler. The way inventory control and material handling managers are measured and their performance judged is one major factor causing these differences. The nature of the product and the methods chosen to handle it is another.

PROCESS DIFFERENCES

Even within the confines of the manufacturing industry, there are differences between businesses that need to be reflected in the inventory system. For example, some businesses build products in batches or jobs while others operate continuous processes. Job shops tend to authorize work in the form of work orders, with each work order specifying the item and quantity to be built and the date on which the work should be completed. Continuous process shops, on the other hand, tend to work from production schedules that define the quantity of each product to be made in a specific period of time, often a week. Job shops tend to pick all the material required for a job at one time and deliver it to the shop before work starts. Continuous production shops, however, prefer to flow material from the warehouse to the production floor. The inventory system must be adapted to work with the scheduling technique in use.

Some manufacturing businesses assemble products from components, others fabricate products from raw materials, and still others do both. Where assembly is done, there is often a need for the inventory system to have access to the bill-of-material file, which lists the component parts used to make a product. Often assembly bills are multilevel and contain "phantom" items. (A phantom item is one that has no physical reality, but is included in the bill-of-material for the convenience of the users. Phantom items also have some specific purposes in other systems.) On the other hand, a pure fabrication business can operate without a separate bill-of-material file simply by listing the raw material used for each item on the item master file.

Build-to-order businesses also differ significantly from build-to-stock ones. When products are built to order, there are many one-time items that may or may not explicitly appear on the item master file. The inventory system must be able to recognize these items and manage their movement from the shop through the finished goods stockroom to shipping and to assure their shipment is on time to the right customer.

4

How to Measure Accuracy

Publicly owned companies are required to keep financial records in a relatively standard way so stockholders can read financial reports with reasonable assurance that profits are profits and losses are losses. Further, it is required that an independent auditing firm review the bookkeeping methods and testify annually to the appropriateness and fairness of the reports.

The value of inventories is a major item on the annual financial report of most companies. Any misstatement in inventory will directly affect profit. If an error overstates inventory, costs will be understated and profit overstated until the error is found and corrected. Then the correction will result in a reduction in the previously reported profit. If a similar error understates inventory, profit is understated at first, with the correction later resulting in an increase. Naturally, both internal and external auditors are vitally interested in inventory record accuracy.

INVENTORY ACCURACY DEFINED

Before inventory accuracy can be measured, it has to be defined. For the purposes of this book, and for the purposes of inventory control managers and systems, an inventory record is accurate if the corresponding storage location contains all of the correct part numbers and if a physical count of the parts agrees precisely with the recorded quantities. In addition, if material is accounted for by job, the recorded job numbers must be correct and the quantities allocated to each job must total to the actual quantity on hand. If any single element of data is not in agreement with the record, the record is incorrect. Inventory accuracy is the percentage of locations for which the records are correct by the above definition.

Accuracy on a location-by-location basis is important because material handlers are required to find the material when told what location it is in. If, in a large inventory facility, material is stored somewhere other than the recorded location, the effort required to find it can be so great that the material might just as well not exist. Four-wall inventories are useful to the bookkeeping department; they are nearly worthless to the people who actually handle the stock.

An accuracy tolerance can be allowed when counting the content of a storage location that contains a bulk material such as a fluid or a powder. These materials sometimes stick to the sides of their containers, and may be subject to evaporation and other losses. Further, it is often impossible or impractical to measure quantities to enough significant places to prevent little errors from accumulating into larger ones. See Chapter 15 for a discussion of the special problems encountered when handling fluids in bulk.

In some instances, an accuracy tolerance can also be allowed when dealing with low-cost, physically small items like fasteners. As with fluids, it may be impractical to count these items precisely, even with the most accurate electronic scales. However, for most items, the definition of inventory accuracy assumes a zero tolerance for counting and identification errors.

WHY MEASUREMENT IS IMPORTANT

Surprisingly few companies actually measure the accuracy of their inventories. If inventory accuracy is stable and the records are known to remain accurate, measurement can be infrequent and, therefore, inexpensive. If, however, record-keeping methods change often or if personnel turnover is high, more frequent measurement is needed. Management needs to have a handle on the level of record accuracy so that it can take action when the level is unacceptable or when a downward trend becomes evident. Without measures, management is blind, assumptions are made, and problems are ignored until they grow to the point where they do real harm.

HOW TO MEASURE

The annual physical inventory is typically not a valid measure of accuracy for two reasons. First, as discussed in Chapter 2, the annual physical inventory itself is almost always inaccurate and can introduce more errors into the inventory records than it removes. The result is that it represents a biased and inaccurate measurement. And second, physical inventories are usually done too infrequently to serve as a reasonable measure of accuracy. Good inventory management demands a fresh measure of accuracy at least quarterly.

Many companies no longer do physical inventories because they have proven to themselves and to their auditors that these inventories are not needed. For these companies, the annual physical inventory is simply not available as a measure of accuracy. Cycle counting, when done by well trained employees in a "do-it-right" atmosphere, may be management's only real handle on inventory accuracy.

Basic Measurement Techniques

Cycle counting programs are closely related to quality inspection programs that draw samples from the parts on, for instance, a pallet. The quality of the parts in the sample is measured and is used as an indication of the quality of the entire group. Similarly, cycle counters can sample the inventory and use the accuracy of the sample as an indicator of overall accuracy.[1]

The techniques required to measure inventory accuracy can, therefore, be adapted from ones used by quality control, which, after all, has been measuring the accuracy of the production workforce for years. The only extension is to use the techniques to measure the accuracy of the material handlers.

Inventory accuracy should be measured by randomly selecting a number of storage locations and sending a cycle counter to verify that these locations contain exactly what the inventory control system says they contain. It is important to note that random selection of the locations to be cycle counted is important. Statistical sampling theory requires this randomness. None of the methods and techniques presented here are valid if they are applied to a nonrandom group of locations.

The number of locations to be cycle counted each time period (day, week, or month) are shown in Table 4.1. Very precise measurements require huge samples. But reasonably accurate measurements require only modest samples. If accuracy is believed to be 70 percent, and needs to be confirmed within ± 10 percent, the required sample size is only 189 counts. If accuracy is 98 percent and needs to be confirmed within 10 percent (i.e., that accuracy is greater than 88 percent), only 18 counts are required.

The degree of precision defined for this formula accounts for variations in measurement because the process is based on sampling techniques. The sample chosen, being random, may not truly represent the overall accuracy. The degree of precision does not, unfortunately, account for errors made by the people doing the cycle counting. Sampling theory assumes that inspectors and cycle counters do not make mistakes. So, they must be well trained and motivated to work carefully. Any excess emphasis on speed in cycle counting will tend to reduce its precision in unpredictable ways.

Inventory stratification, also known as "ABC analysis," may affect the way inventory accuracy is measured, since accuracy goals can properly be a function of inventory class. Suppose a business is maintaining 99.5 percent accuracy for A items, 95 percent accuracy for B items, and 90 percent accuracy for C items. If the measurements are to reflect actual accuracy within ± 2 percent, then a

---

[1] For those who wish to pursue the theory and practice of statistical sampling in more detail than is shown in this book, the following book is highly recommended: Crow, Edwin L., Frances A. Davis, and Margaret W. Maxfield, *Statistics Manual,* New York: Dover Publications, 1960.

TABLE 4.1.   NUMBER OF COUNTS REQUIRED TO MEASURE INVENTORY ACCURACY
WITHIN A SPECIFIED TOLERANCE

Expected accuracy	Tolerance									
	1%	2%	3%	4%	5%	6%	7%	8%	9%	10%
99.9	90	22	10	6	4	2	2	1	1	1
99.8	180	45	20	11	7	5	4	3	2	2
99.7	269	67	30	17	11	7	5	4	3	3
99.6	359	90	40	22	14	10	7	6	4	4
99.5	448	112	50	28	18	12	9	7	6	4
99.4	537	134	60	34	21	15	11	8	7	5
99.3	626	156	70	39	25	17	13	10	8	6
99.2	714	179	79	45	29	20	15	11	9	7
99.1	803	201	89	50	32	22	16	13	10	8
99.0	891	223	99	56	36	25	18	14	11	9
98.5	1,330	332	148	83	53	37	27	21	16	13
98.0	1,764	441	196	110	71	49	36	28	22	18
97.5	2,194	548	244	137	88	61	45	34	27	22
97.0	2,619	655	291	164	105	73	53	41	32	26
96.5	3,040	760	338	190	122	84	62	47	38	30
96.0	3,456	864	384	216	138	96	71	54	43	35
95.5	3,868	967	430	242	155	107	79	60	48	39
95.0	4,275	1,069	475	267	171	119	87	67	53	43
94.0	5,076	1,269	564	317	203	141	104	79	63	51
93.0	5,859	1,465	651	366	234	163	120	92	72	59
92.0	6,624	1,656	736	414	265	184	135	103	82	66
91.0	7,371	1,843	819	461	295	205	150	115	91	74
90.0	8,100	2,025	900	506	324	225	165	127	100	81
85.0	11,475	2,869	1,275	717	459	319	234	179	142	115
80.0	14,400	3,600	1,600	900	576	400	294	225	178	144
75.0	16,875	4,219	1,875	1,055	675	469	344	264	208	169
70.0	18,900	4,725	2,100	1,181	756	525	386	295	233	189
65.0	20,475	5,119	2,275	1,280	819	569	418	320	253	205
60.0	21,600	5,400	2,400	1,350	864	600	441	338	267	216
55.0	22,275	5,569	2,475	1,392	891	619	455	348	275	223
50.0	22,500	5,625	2,500	1,406	900	625	459	352	278	225

random sample of 112 A item locations, 1069 B item locations, and 2025 C item locations must be drawn and those locations must be counted. It might also be decided that the measurements for B and C items need be less accurate than those for A items, limiting the total number of counts required to obtain a measurement. Clearly, as the number of levels of stratification increases, the amount of counting required goes up and the cost of measuring goes up.

Some people are surprised to find that the sample size required to measure accuracy is not a function of the number of parts or locations in an inventory class. This is because the technique assumes a homogeneous population of inventory records and because samples are drawn randomly. The amount of salt in seawater can be determined as easily from a cupful as it can from a tank car full.

Table 4.1 is calculated from Equation 4.1, below, which may be used in its place if, for instance, the number of locations to be counted is to be determined by the inventory system. The number of locations to be cycle counted each time period depends on the number of independent measurements management wants during that period. And, for each measurement, it depends on the precision with which management wants accuracy measured. Suppose, for example, management decides that a fresh measurement of inventory accuracy is needed for each of three product lines each week. This means that three samples must be drawn weekly, each random but limited to locations containing parts for one of the three product lines. During the week, these locations will be counted and the counts compared to the inventory records. At the end of the week, the number of counts made for each product line will be divided into the number of locations found to be in error in each sample. The result will be an estimate of the inventory accuracy for that product line:

$$\text{Inventory accuracy} = \frac{\text{number of errors found}}{\text{number of counts made}}$$

If more than one error is found in a location, the location is considered to be in error and the two errors count only once.

The number of locations to be counted in each of the samples should be a function of two things: the expected level of inventory accuracy and the desired counting precision. Well-established sampling theory provides the following equation:

$$N_C = \frac{\text{EIA} \times (1 - \text{EIA})}{(P/3)^2} \tag{4.1}$$

N_C, the number of counts required in a sample, is calculated from the expected inventory accuracy (EIA) and the precision required (P). Both are expressed as decimals (i.e., 3 percent is 0.03) for calculation purposes. It is interesting to note that the more accurate inventories are, the fewer counts it takes to prove them accurate. And, the number of counts required to achieve a measurement goes up with the square of the required precision.

So, for example, imagine a business that feels that it needs a fresh measure of inventory accuracy each month. If that business feels that it has 95 percent accuracy (maybe demonstrated by an earlier measurement) and if it requires that measurements be accurate within ± 2 percent, the number of counts required is:

$$N_C = \frac{.95 \times (1 - .95)}{(.02/3)^2} = 1069$$

Thus 1069 counts must be performed each month. If the 1069 counts are performed and 50 errors are found, the overall accuracy may be estimated at something between 93.3 and 97.3 percent, slightly better than the first estimate. (The calculations are as follows: 50 errors divided by 1069 locations sampled is a 4.7

percent error rate, or a 95.3 percent accuracy rate. Given that the measurement is ± 2 percent, accuracy is known to be between 97.3 percent and 93.3 percent.)

And, once again, it is important to understand that the equation will not produce valid results unless random locations are counted. Locations that are cycle counted for other reasons (such as the discovery of an error or the scheduling of an item for routine periodic cycle counting) should not be included in accuracy measures because they introduce biases. Other circumstances may limit the usefulness of the equation and expert statistical help may be advisable before relying on it heavily.

Recalculating Confidence

Inventory accuracy sample sizes are calculated based on an expected level of accuracy. Initially, the expected level of accuracy is probably a guess, made by someone knowledgeable. After some experience has been gained, expected levels should be reasonably well known. However, there can be times when the expectations are not borne out by the results of the sample.

Whenever locations are cycle counted and inventory accuracy is calculated, the results should be compared with the value of EIA used to determine the sample size. If the first estimate differs from the value of EIA by more than a small amount, the formula used to select the sample size should be worked backward to calculate the actual tolerance level achieved. In other words, having obtained an estimate of the inventory accuracy, the actual precision available from this estimate should be calculated from:

$$P = 3 \times [(IA \times (1 - IA)] / N_C{}^{0.5} \tag{4.2}$$

In this equation, P is the precision, as defined previously, IA is the actual inventory accuracy that resulted from the sampling, and N_C is the number of counts performed.

If, for instance, a company estimates its inventory accuracy at 95 percent and wants to sample within ± 2 percent, the proper sample size is 1069 as calculated previously. If, however, the cycle counters find 125 errors in the 1069, the result of their work is an accuracy estimate of 88.3 percent. Then, the precision of the 88.3 percent estimate can be calculated as:

$$P = 3 \times [(.883 \times (1 - .883)] / 1069)^{0.5} = 0.0295, \text{ or } 2.95 \text{ percent}$$

This means that the company knows for sure only that its inventory accuracy is somewhere between 85.35 and 91.25 percent. If a tolerance level of 2 percent is important, a new sample size must be calculated using Equation 4.1 with an estimated accuracy of 88.3 percent. The results of this calculation will require that additional locations be randomly selected and cycle counted. Following the completion of these cycle counts, it will be possible to calculate a new estimate that, if close to 88.3 percent, will be accurate within the original 2 percent tolerance.

CONTROL CHARTS

Now that a sample has been drawn and a measurement obtained, the next step is to decide what to do with it. One can, of course, make immediate judgments about the quality of the inventory records, but it may be even more useful to look at a series of measurements over time. A statistical technique known as the control chart is valuable.

The concept of a control chart is simple. Its purpose is to detect changes in an ongoing, stable situation. The chart is simply a graph with inventory accuracy on the vertical axis and time periods on the horizontal axis. A horizontal line across the center of the chart defines the desired or expected accuracy. A second line, called the lower control limit, defines the point at which action should be taken.

Figure 4.1 shows a sample control chart for a hypothetical company that has historically been achieving 97 percent inventory accuracy. This company mea-

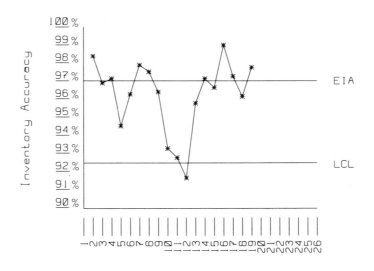

EIA · EXPECTED INVENTORY ACCURACY

LCL · LOWER CONTROL LIMIT

Figure 4.1. Control chart. A control chart is a device for managing random fluctuations in a measurement. In the instance shown, inventory accuracy is tracked over time. The measurement performed in week 12 is below the lower control limit, indicating that a problem is likely to exist beyond the variations normal in measurement.

sures accuracy weekly to within ± 2 percentage points by doing 655 counts each week as specified in Table 4.1. Management often examines the control chart looking for either of two things:

1. One or more samples below the lower control limit of 92.3 percent. If such a sample exists, there is a likelihood that inventory accuracy has actually slipped.
2. A consistent downward trend. Obvious trends indicate the possibility that inventory accuracy is currently slipping.

The chart in Figure 4.1 shows a downward trend beginning in week 8 and culminating in week 12. The measurement plotted for week 12 is below the lower con-

TABLE 4.2.   CONTROL LIMIT SPACING (EXCLUDING THE CONFIDENCE FACTOR) AS A FUNCTION OF INVENTORY ACCURACY AND SAMPLE SIZE

Expected accuracy	Sample size								
	10	15	20	25	30	35	40	45	50
99.9	1.0	0.8	0.7	0.6	0.6	0.5	0.5	0.5	0.4
99.8	1.4	1.2	1.0	0.9	0.8	0.8	0.7	0.7	0.6
99.7	1.7	1.4	1.2	1.1	1.0	0.9	0.9	0.8	0.8
99.6	2.0	1.6	1.4	1.3	1.2	1.1	1.0	0.9	0.9
99.5	2.2	1.8	1.6	1.4	1.3	1.2	1.1	1.1	1.0
99.4	2.4	2.0	1.7	1.5	1.4	1.3	1.2	1.2	1.1
99.3	2.6	2.2	1.9	1.7	1.5	1.4	1.3	1.2	1.2
99.2	2.8	2.3	2.0	1.8	1.6	1.5	1.4	1.3	1.3
99.1	3.0	2.4	2.1	1.9	1.7	1.6	1.5	1.4	1.3
99.0	3.1	2.6	2.2	2.0	1.8	1.7	1.6	1.5	1.4
98.5	3.8	3.1	2.7	2.4	2.2	2.1	1.9	1.8	1.7
98.0	4.4	3.6	3.1	2.8	2.6	2.4	2.2	2.1	2.0
97.5	4.9	4.0	3.5	3.1	2.9	2.6	2.5	2.3	2.2
97.0	5.4	4.4	3.8	3.4	3.1	2.9	2.7	2.5	2.4
96.5	5.8	4.7	4.1	3.7	3.4	3.1	2.9	2.7	2.6
96.0	6.2	5.1	4.4	3.9	3.6	3.3	3.1	2.9	2.8
95.5	6.6	5.4	4.6	4.1	3.8	3.5	3.3	3.1	2.9
95.0	6.9	5.6	4.9	4.4	4.0	3.7	3.4	3.2	3.1
94.0	7.5	6.1	5.3	4.7	4.3	4.0	3.8	3.5	3.4
93.0	8.1	6.6	5.7	5.1	4.7	4.3	4.0	3.8	3.6
92.0	8.6	7.0	6.1	5.4	5.0	4.6	4.3	4.0	3.8
91.0	9.0	7.4	6.4	5.7	5.2	4.8	4.5	4.3	4.0
90.0	9.5	7.7	6.7	6.0	5.5	5.1	4.7	4.5	4.2
85.0	11.3	9.2	8.0	7.1	6.5	6.0	5.6	5.3	5.0
80.0	12.6	10.3	8.9	8.0	7.3	6.8	6.3	6.0	5.7
75.0	13.7	11.2	9.7	8.7	7.9	7.3	6.8	6.5	6.1
70.0	14.5	11.8	10.2	9.2	8.4	7.7	7.2	6.8	6.5
65.0	15.1	12.3	10.7	9.5	8.7	8.1	7.5	7.1	6.7
60.0	15.5	12.6	11.0	9.8	8.9	8.3	7.7	7.3	6.9
55.0	15.7	12.8	11.1	9.9	9.1	8.4	7.9	7.4	7.0
50.0	15.8	12.9	11.2	10.0	9.1	8.5	7.9	7.5	7.1

TABLE 4.2. (CONTINUED)

Expected accuracy	Sample size									
	60	70	80	90	100	110	120	130	140	150
99.9	0.4	0.4	0.4	0.3	0.3	0.3	0.3	0.3	0.3	0.3
99.8	0.6	0.6	0.5	0.5	0.5	0.4	0.4	0.4	0.4	0.4
99.7	0.7	0.7	0.6	0.6	0.6	0.5	0.5	0.5	0.5	0.5
99.6	0.9	0.8	0.7	0.7	0.6	0.6	0.6	0.6	0.5	0.5
99.5	1.0	0.9	0.8	0.8	0.7	0.7	0.7	0.6	0.6	0.6
99.4	1.0	1.0	0.9	0.8	0.8	0.8	0.7	0.7	0.7	0.6
99.3	1.1	1.0	1.0	0.9	0.9	0.8	0.8	0.7	0.7	0.7
99.2	1.2	1.1	1.0	1.0	0.9	0.9	0.8	0.8	0.8	0.7
99.1	1.3	1.2	1.1	1.0	1.0	0.9	0.9	0.8	0.8	0.8
99.0	1.3	1.2	1.1	1.1	1.0	1.0	0.9	0.9	0.9	0.8
98.5	1.6	1.5	1.4	1.3	1.2	1.2	1.1	1.1	1.0	1.0
98.0	1.9	1.7	1.6	1.5	1.4	1.4	1.3	1.3	1.2	1.2
97.5	2.1	1.9	1.8	1.7	1.6	1.5	1.5	1.4	1.3	1.3
97.0	2.3	2.1	2.0	1.9	1.8	1.7	1.6	1.5	1.5	1.4
96.5	2.5	2.3	2.1	2.0	1.9	1.8	1.7	1.6	1.6	1.5
96.0	2.6	2.4	2.3	2.1	2.0	1.9	1.8	1.8	1.7	1.6
95.5	2.8	2.6	2.4	2.2	2.1	2.0	1.9	1.9	1.8	1.7
95.0	2.9	2.7	2.5	2.4	2.2	2.1	2.0	1.9	1.9	1.8
94.0	3.2	2.9	2.7	2.6	2.4	2.3	2.2	2.1	2.0	2.0
93.0	3.4	3.2	2.9	2.8	2.6	2.5	2.4	2.3	2.2	2.1
92.0	3.7	3.4	3.1	2.9	2.8	2.6	2.5	2.4	2.3	2.3
91.0	3.9	3.5	3.3	3.1	2.9	2.8	2.7	2.6	2.5	2.4
90.0	4.0	3.7	3.5	3.3	3.1	2.9	2.8	2.7	2.6	2.5
85.0	4.8	4.4	4.1	3.9	3.7	3.5	3.3	3.2	3.1	3.0
80.0	5.4	5.0	4.6	4.3	4.1	3.9	3.7	3.6	3.4	3.3
75.0	5.8	5.4	5.0	4.7	4.4	4.2	4.0	3.9	3.7	3.6
70.0	6.2	5.7	5.3	5.0	4.7	4.5	4.3	4.1	3.9	3.8
65.0	6.4	5.9	5.5	5.2	4.9	4.7	4.4	4.3	4.1	4.0
60.0	6.6	6.1	5.7	5.3	5.0	4.8	4.6	4.4	4.2	4.1
55.0	6.7	6.2	5.7	5.4	5.1	4.9	4.6	4.4	4.3	4.1
50.0	6.7	6.2	5.8	5.4	5.1	4.9	4.7	4.5	4.3	4.2

Expected accuracy	Sample size									
	200	250	300	350	400	450	500	550	600	650
99.9	0.2	0.2	0.2	0.2	0.2	0.1	0.1	0.1	0.1	0.1
99.8	0.3	0.3	0.3	0.2	0.2	0.2	0.2	0.2	0.2	0.2
99.7	0.4	0.3	0.3	0.3	0.3	0.3	0.2	0.2	0.2	0.2
99.6	0.4	0.4	0.4	0.3	0.3	0.3	0.3	0.3	0.3	0.2
99.5	0.5	0.4	0.4	0.4	0.4	0.3	0.3	0.3	0.3	0.3
99.4	0.5	0.5	0.4	0.4	0.4	0.4	0.3	0.3	0.3	0.3
99.3	0.6	0.5	0.5	0.4	0.4	0.4	0.4	0.4	0.3	0.3
99.2	0.6	0.6	0.5	0.5	0.4	0.4	0.4	0.4	0.4	0.3
99.1	0.7	0.6	0.5	0.5	0.5	0.4	0.4	0.4	0.4	0.4
99.0	0.7	0.6	0.6	0.5	0.5	0.5	0.4	0.4	0.4	0.4
98.5	0.9	0.8	0.7	0.6	0.6	0.6	0.5	0.5	0.5	0.5

(Continued)

TABLE 4.2. (CONTINUED)

Expected accuracy	Sample size									
	200	250	300	350	400	450	500	550	600	650
98.0	1.0	0.9	0.8	0.7	0.7	0.7	0.6	0.6	0.6	0.5
97.5	1.1	1.0	0.9	0.8	0.8	0.7	0.7	0.7	0.6	0.6
97.0	1.2	1.1	1.0	0.9	0.9	0.8	0.8	0.7	0.7	0.7
96.5	1.3	1.2	1.1	1.0	0.9	0.9	0.8	0.8	0.8	0.7
96.0	1.4	1.2	1.1	1.0	1.0	0.9	0.9	0.8	0.8	0.8
95.5	1.5	1.3	1.2	1.1	1.0	1.0	0.9	0.9	0.8	0.8
95.0	1.5	1.4	1.3	1.2	1.1	1.0	1.0	0.9	0.9	0.9
94.0	1.7	1.5	1.4	1.3	1.2	1.1	1.1	1.0	1.0	0.9
93.0	1.8	1.6	1.5	1.4	1.3	1.2	1.1	1.1	1.0	1.0
92.0	1.9	1.7	1.6	1.5	1.4	1.3	1.2	1.2	1.1	1.1
91.0	2.0	1.8	1.7	1.5	1.4	1.3	1.3	1.2	1.2	1.1
90.0	2.1	1.9	1.7	1.6	1.5	1.4	1.3	1.3	1.2	1.2
85.0	2.5	2.3	2.1	1.9	1.8	1.7	1.6	1.5	1.5	1.4
80.0	2.8	2.5	2.3	2.1	2.0	1.9	1.8	1.7	1.6	1.6
75.0	3.1	2.7	2.5	2.3	2.2	2.0	1.9	1.8	1.8	1.7
70.0	3.2	2.9	2.6	2.4	2.3	2.2	2.0	2.0	1.9	1.8
65.0	3.4	3.0	2.8	2.5	2.4	2.2	2.1	2.0	1.9	1.9
60.0	3.5	3.1	2.8	2.6	2.4	2.3	2.2	2.1	2.0	1.9
55.0	3.5	3.1	2.9	2.7	2.5	2.3	2.2	2.1	2.0	2.0
50.0	3.5	3.2	2.9	2.7	2.5	2.4	2.2	2.1	2.0	2.0

Expected accuracy	Sample size									
	750	1000	1250	1500	1750	2000	2000	5000	8000	10000
99.9	0.1	0.1	0.1	0.1	0.1	0.1	0.1	0.1	0.1	0.1
99.8	0.2	0.1	0.1	0.1	0.1	0.1	0.1	0.1	0.1	0.1
99.7	0.2	0.2	0.2	0.1	0.1	0.1	0.1	0.1	0.1	0.1
99.6	0.2	0.2	0.2	0.2	0.2	0.1	0.1	0.1	0.1	0.1
99.5	0.3	0.2	0.2	0.2	0.2	0.2	0.1	0.1	0.1	0.1
99.4	0.3	0.2	0.2	0.2	0.2	0.2	0.1	0.1	0.1	0.1
99.3	0.3	0.3	0.2	0.2	0.2	0.2	0.2	0.1	0.1	0.1
99.2	0.3	0.3	0.3	0.2	0.2	0.2	0.2	0.1	0.1	0.1
99.1	0.3	0.3	0.3	0.2	0.2	0.2	0.2	0.1	0.1	0.1
99.0	0.4	0.3	0.3	0.3	0.2	0.2	0.2	0.1	0.1	0.1
98.5	0.4	0.4	0.3	0.3	0.3	0.3	0.2	0.2	0.1	0.1
98.0	0.5	0.4	0.4	0.4	0.3	0.3	0.3	0.2	0.2	0.1
97.5	0.6	0.5	0.4	0.4	0.4	0.3	0.3	0.2	0.2	0.2
97.0	0.6	0.5	0.5	0.4	0.4	0.4	0.3	0.2	0.2	0.2
96.5	0.7	0.6	0.5	0.5	0.4	0.4	0.3	0.3	0.2	0.2
96.0	0.7	0.6	0.6	0.5	0.5	0.4	0.4	0.3	0.2	0.2
95.5	0.8	0.7	0.6	0.5	0.5	0.5	0.4	0.3	0.2	0.2
95.0	0.8	0.7	0.6	0.6	0.5	0.5	0.4	0.3	0.2	0.2
94.0	0.9	0.8	0.7	0.6	0.6	0.5	0.4	0.3	0.3	0.2
93.0	0.9	0.8	0.7	0.7	0.6	0.6	0.5	0.4	0.3	0.3
92.0	1.0	0.9	0.8	0.7	0.6	0.6	0.5	0.4	0.3	0.3
91.0	1.0	0.9	0.8	0.7	0.7	0.6	0.5	0.4	0.3	0.3
90.0	1.1	0.9	0.8	0.8	0.7	0.7	0.5	0.4	0.3	0.3

TABLE 4.2.   (CONTINUED)

Expected accuracy	Sample size									
	750	1000	1250	1500	1750	2000	2000	5000	8000	10000
85.0	1.3	1.1	1.0	0.9	0.9	0.8	0.7	0.5	0.4	0.4
80.0	1.5	1.3	1.1	1.0	1.0	0.9	0.7	0.6	0.4	0.4
75.0	1.6	1.4	1.2	1.1	1.0	1.0	0.8	0.6	0.5	0.4
70.0	1.7	1.4	1.3	1.2	1.1	1.0	0.8	0.6	0.5	0.5
65.0	1.7	1.5	1.3	1.2	1.1	1.1	0.9	0.7	0.5	0.5
60.0	1.8	1.5	1.4	1.3	1.2	1.1	0.9	0.7	0.5	0.5
55.0	1.8	1.6	1.4	1.3	1.2	1.1	0.9	0.7	0.6	0.5
50.0	1.8	1.6	1.4	1.3	1.2	1.1	0.9	0.7	0.6	0.5

TABLE 4.3.   CONTROL LIMIT CONFIDENCE FACTOR VALUES

Factor value	Confidence that a point below the control limit is not caused by random variation (%)
0	50.0
0.1	54.0
0.2	57.9
0.3	61.8
0.4	65.5
0.5	69.1
0.6	72.6
0.7	75.8
0.8	78.8
0.9	81.6
1.0	84.1
1.1	86.4
1.2	88.5
1.3	90.3
1.4	91.9
1.5	93.3
1.6	94.5
1.7	95.5
1.8	96.4
1.9	97.1
2.0	97.7
2.1	98.2
2.2	98.6
2.3	98.9
2.4	99.2
2.5	99.4
2.6	99.5
2.7	99.7
2.8	99.7
2.9	99.8
3.0	99.9

trol limit, indicating a problem. Judging from the later measurements, management found the problem and fixed it.

Control charts are easy to construct. The only technical point is the placement of the lower control limit, which may be calculated from Tables 4.2 and 4.3. Begin by selecting a value from Table 4.2 based on the expected inventory accuracy and the size of the samples used to measure accuracy. Then select a value from Table 4.3 and multiply the two values together. The result is the space between the inventory accuracy line and the lower control limit line on the control chart, stated in percentage points.

The control limit confidence factor in Table 4.3 is derived from the statistical notion of a normal curve. In essence, to determine a value, the user of a control chart must first decide how much time should be spent on wild goose chases. Because samples are randomly chosen, there is always the possibility that results aren't representative of real life. Therefore, it is necessary to consider the possibility that an unusually low measurement is, in fact, only normal day-to-day variation in the measurements themselves.

If, for instance, a person wishes to be 90 percent sure that a low measurement truly represents a problem before he or she spends the time to investigate, the factor value used should be approximately 1.3. The hypothetical company whose control chart is illustrated in Figure 4.1 chose a factor of 0.7 from the table, which gives them a 25 percent chance of chasing a wild goose but also gives them a lower probability of missing a real problem.

Those who wish to write software to prepare control charts need to know the underlying mathematics. The lower control limit is spaced from the expected value of accuracy according to Equation 4.3:

$$S_{\text{CL}} = F \times \sqrt{[\text{EIA} \times (1 - \text{EIA})] / N} \qquad (4.3)$$

Where S_{CL} is the control limit spacing, F is the control limit confidence factor (discussed below), EIA is the expected inventory accuracy, and N is the sample size.

All terms to the right of the equals sign excepting F are included in Table 4.2. The calculation of values for F is complex and beyond the scope of this book, so Table 4.3 should be stored in the inventory system and used as is.

Part 2

TECHNIQUES AND TECHNOLOGIES

5

Validation, the Foundation of Accuracy

Imagine a business with a completely static inventory. The warehouse is reasonably full, but nothing moves. There are no employees. Customers don't buy and no orders are placed with vendors, so the dock doors have been bricked up. The product just sits there week after week and month after month. If this warehouse were carefully inventoried so beginning inventories were 100 percent correct, how difficult would it be to keep accurate records in the future?

Of course, the data processing manager of this hypothetical warehouse would have to assure that backup copies of the inventory database and the software used to access it were made and safely stored away. Over the years, he or she might even have concerns about degradation of the media on which the backups were kept. But beyond those relatively simple problems, keeping accurate inventories would be a snap.

Such a business couldn't be profitable, of course. But the example illustrates an important point: Inventory movement is the source of essentially all error. Once inventory records are correct, they are unlikely to go bad until something moves. Therefore, if inventory movement can be controlled, inventory accuracy can be controlled.

Of course other sources of error do exist. For instance, the possibility always exists that a program bug could introduce errors into the inventory or cause it to be reported incorrectly. Or media degradation could cause the computer to read an inventory incorrectly from the disk. Or a fire could completely destroy all copies of the inventory database. In the warehouse, someone could steal something, or an erroneous cycle count could affect a previously accurate inventory. But on an ongoing day-to-day basis, for all practical purposes, errors are introduced only when material is moved.

There are two kinds of inventory movements: automated and manual. The distinction is important because accuracy requires different techniques for different kinds of movements. People make errors and, therefore, systems must prevent or at least detect the errors. Machines make errors too but much less often. Frequently machine errors are so rare that they can be ignored. The objective, after all, is to achieve adequate accuracy, not perfection.

Automation is becoming more common; one of the contributing reasons is the resulting reduction in errors. But most material movements in most businesses are still done by people. This situation is likely to continue for many years because automation is expensive and isn't fully applicable to all situations.

The major challenge in the design of superaccurate inventory systems, therefore, is to detect and compensate for human error (and sometimes for some forms of human malfeasance). There is a way to do this that is applicable in one form or another in almost every situation. The technique is called "validation."

CONCEPTS

Validation is the verification, through the collection of independent data, that an inventory movement was performed correctly. The independent data is compared to the record of the work that should have been done and discrepancies are singled out for correction.

The correction process may be done by any of a number of methods, but two things are critical: (1) the system must demand positive correction of apparent errors and must refuse to default unless specifically instructed to do so, and (2) the system must track detected errors and continue to present them until positive correction is received.

For example, suppose a box is to be stored on a shelf and a person is assigned to the task. Validation of this movement can be achieved by identifying both the box and the shelf with bar-coded labels. The person first scans the bar code on the box and then the bar code on the location where the box is to go. The identifying numbers for the box and the location are compared by the computer system to expected values. If they match, the inventory is then assumed to be in its proper place and records are updated by the system. If they do not match, the likely reason is either that the person selected the wrong box, placed it in the wrong location, or both. The inventory control system, detecting this error, initiates the correction.

Correction might, for instance, be done by placing a hold on both the planned storage location and the storage location in which the box was actually put. Then, the inventory control system might schedule a cycle count of the two locations involved and update its records based on the results of the cycle count. Or a supervisor might be called in to determine what actually happened. Or the error might be presented to the material handler, allowing him or her to correct it on the spot.

In this example, the independent data collected consists of the two bar code scans. The data is said to be independent because, unlike key entry, it is relatively independent of human action. It is important that the information used for validation be removed from the control of humans to the extent possible to eliminate errors.

Bar code error rates are very low, and they make it impossible, for all practical purposes, to cheat. Bar coding, therefore, is an effective way of gathering independent data for validation, but it is not the only possible way. See Chapter 7 for more information about alternative technologies.

Various forms of validation can work on line or off line (in real time or not). There are advantages and disadvantages to either method, as shown in the following examples.

Example 5.1. All-manual data collection using central key entry. All-manual validation is not often implemented. But, to demonstrate that it is possible, the following method is illustrated. All-manual validation may be appropriate in special cases that rule out the use of equipment. Extremely cold food freezers, for instance, play tricks with printed circuit boards. All-manual validation may also be appropriate in companies that are unable to finance the purchase of hardware but can provide the labor necessary. Some firms operating off shore with very low labor rates may fall into this category.

In an all-manual shop, validation of a material movement might be accomplished as shown below and in Figure 5.1.

1. When movements are required, a computer system, clerk, or supervisor creates a document specifying the part number and quantity to be moved and both its current location and its destination.
2. Working from this document, a material handler does the move. On making the pickup, the material handler records the part number of the material stored in the location immediately to the right of the material moved. Upon dropping the material off, the material handler again records the part number of the material immediately to the right of the material moved.
3. If the material is either picked up or dropped off at the end of a row, procedures require the material handler to note that fact instead of recording a second part number.
4. The document is then turned in for key entry. The key operator keys all part numbers, the source and destination locations, and the quantities.
5. The inventory control system next cross-checks the source and destination locations by verifying that the parts stored in the next location are correct.
6. If either of the verifications do not check properly with data on file, the inventory control system considers the movement to have been made in error. It then places a hold on the affected location(s) and prints a notification for either the supervisor or a cycle counter. The affected locations will then be double-checked to assure that the inventories are correct before additional movements are allowed.

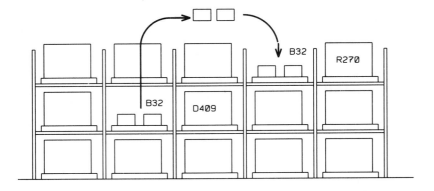

Figure 5.1. All-manual validation. Accuracy depends not on bar coding, but on validation. This example illustrates an all-manual, non-bar-coded (but labor intensive) method of validation.

This process is, obviously, very labor intensive. In special circumstances, however, it can be appropriate. It can result in extremely accurate records when the procedural details are carefully thought out and enforced. Examples 2 and 3 below describe equally accurate methods that involve much less labor.

It should be noted that the process described does not validate the part number moved. Part number validation could be added to the process by, for example, providing the material handler with a set of scales and requiring that the load be weighed. Given a validated quantity being moved and knowing the part being moved, it would be possible to catch at least some part identification errors. However, part number validation is not included in the procedure because the inventory is presumed to be accurate. Therefore, validation of the source location also validates the part number. There is, therefore, no chance that the right storage location will be selected, but the wrong part will be moved. (Assuming that only one part is stored in a location.)

Example 5.2. Paper-driven off-line data collection. The labor required for validation can be substantially reduced by mechanizing. One way is to use portable transaction terminals with bar code scanners attached. These devices are typically about the size of a large paperback novel. They usually have alphanumeric keyboards with several function keys, a one- or two-line display, and ports for communication with a bar code scanner and a host computer. Figure 5.2 shows generally what these devices look like.

The off-line data collection example also assumes that storage locations are labeled with bar-coded labels. Figure 5.3 shows one example of such a label. Portable terminals are, in themselves, computers. They require software and have the flexibility to be used in many ways. For instance:

1. When movement is required, a system, a clerk, or a supervisor creates a document like the one in Example 1, but it includes bar codes. Figure 5.4 illustrates one possible design.

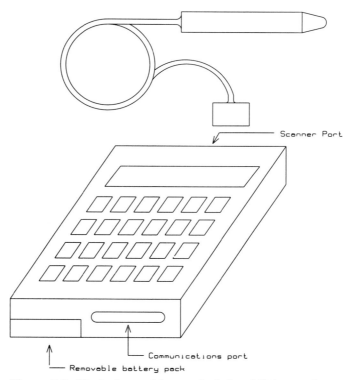

Figure 5.2. Typical portable terminal. In addition to the example shown, off-line portable terminals are available with full alphanumeric keyboards. Support for laser scanners is also possible but usually involves a larger unit or an external battery pack to provide the additional power required.

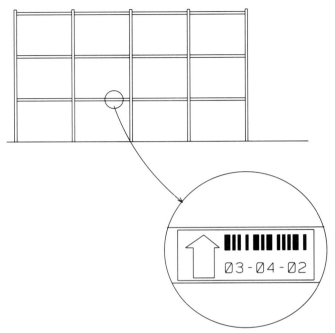

Figure 5.3. Typical location labeling. Location labels must be physically tough to last through many scans and the abuse that is normal in the warehouse. Their design must also make it clear which label relates to which location.

2. Working from this document, a material handler performs the move. The material handler begins the day with the portable terminal by scanning his or her ID badge and keying a password. The terminal stores this information and appends it to every transaction performed. Next the material handler scans three bar codes that appear on the printed document. These scans load the source location, the quantity, and the destination location for the first transaction into the terminal.

3. The material handler moves to the source location and scans its label. The terminal compares the value found in this scan with the value received from the scan of the transaction document. If the two match, the material handler is given the okay to proceed. If they do not match, the location scanned is stored and the material handler is told to correct his or her error or to press a key indicating that the source location is to be overridden.

4. After the pick has been made, the material handler keys the quantity actually moved. The system allows a default to the quantity scanned from the document. If the quantity keyed matches the quantity

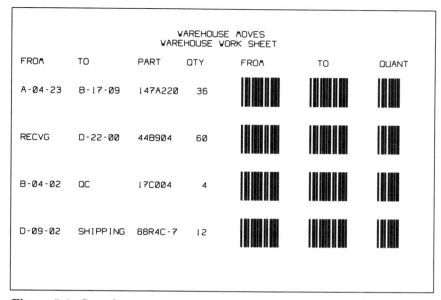

Figure 5.4. Sample transaction document for use with a portable terminal. This document is one way that an inventory system can communicate with a material handler using a portable, off-line terminal. The material handler scans the bar codes on the sheet and then collects confirming information as the work is done. Only when the terminal is uploaded to the inventory system is the database updated.

scanned, the material handler is given a second okay to proceed. If there is a mismatch, the material handler is warned and must rekey the quantity or override the default.

5. Upon delivery of the material to its destination, the material handler is once again required to scan the location label. The terminal compares the scanned value with the expected value and, once again, warns the material handler if necessary.

6. Periodically (probably several times each shift), the material handler turns the "used" terminal over to a clerk and picks up a fresh one to begin the cycle again. The clerk connects the terminal to the inventory computer through a device called a "dump port" and instructs it to dump its record of completed transactions. The inventory computer uses these records to: (a) delete records from its pending transaction file, (b) update inventories, (c) add to a file of open errors, and (d) credit the material handler with the work accomplished and the errors committed.

7. The used terminal's memory is cleared, its battery is recharged if necessary, and it is reissued to another material handler.

8. Several times a day, a clerk or supervisor checks the system's file of

open errors, assigns cycle counters to verify the actual content of the locations involved, and enters any needed adjustments. This process also clears outstanding errors from the file.

This process is much less labor intensive than the first example. Bar codes can be read much more quickly than part numbers can be determined and recorded. Most important, the terminal validates immediately so errors are discovered within seconds of the time they are made. Immediacy allows errors to be corrected on the spot and provides psychological benefits.

On-Line Validation

If there is a flaw in the use of portable terminals for validation, it lies in the fact that they are off line. Material is allocated (or reserved) for movement and transaction documents are printed. The documents are batched and given to material handlers. And only after the material handler has completed a batch and the terminal has been uploaded to the inventory system can allocations be relieved and inventory made available.

Suppose, for instance, an inventory facility has 10,000 pallets of material and is operated by 10 lift-truck drivers, each of whom handles 50 pallets per hour, or 400 pallets per day. If movements are printed and given to the drivers in 2-hour batches, the time between the allocation of material for movement and its release will average 3 hours (1 hour average waiting time between the printing of a transaction and its assignment to a driver, plus the 2 hours the driver will spend making the moves called for in the batch). At 50 pallets per hour, and 10 drivers, this means that 1500 pallets, or 15 percent of the total inventory will be continually reserved and unavailable.

In most real warehouses the ratio of material handlers to storage locations is usually less than 1:100, as shown in this example. But, Just-in-Time concepts and the importance of high turnover rates are driving industry to maintain higher and higher levels of activity. As the level of activity increases, the amount of inventory tied up by off-line validation increases. With this, the incentive to go on-line increases. Example 5.3 resolves this problem.

The problems associated with off-line validation of material movement can be resolved by validating on-line. In most cases, this is done using a portable terminal that communicates with the inventory control system using radio frequency (RF) transmission as shown in Figure 5.5. Terminals that communicate via RF are generally available in two forms. One is intended for hand-held use. It looks like an off-line terminal but is slightly larger to accommodate a radio transceiver and additional batteries and has an antenna. The other is designed for semipermanent mounting to a vehicle and is powered from the vehicle's batteries or alternator. Figure 5.6 is a drawing of a typical vehicle-mounted terminal.

Example 5.3.   Hi-tech. Using RF terminals, movements are controlled and validated as follows:

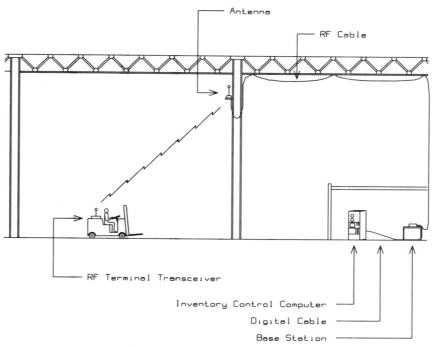

Figure 5.5. RF terminal connectivity. This example shows the RF base station inside the computer room. In fact, it is often (but not always) better to mount it in the warehouse closer to the antennas.

1. All movements are either computer generated or key entered into the inventory control system. The system places the movements in a queuing system.
2. A material handler begins the day by scanning an ID badge and keying a password into his or her RF terminal. The information is passed to the inventory control system over the RF link. The system grants (or denies) access and links the material handler's ID to the terminal ID. As transactions are completed, the system notes each one with the ID of the person who did the work.
3. The inventory control system examines its queues and selects the first transaction to be performed by the material handler. The selection process will vary but can include consideration of the material handler's location, the type of vehicle being used, the type of work assigned to the material handler by a supervisor, and the priority and age of the transactions currently in the queue. The inventory system transmits the first source location to the material handler's radio terminal, where it is displayed.
4. The material handler moves to the source location and scans its label.

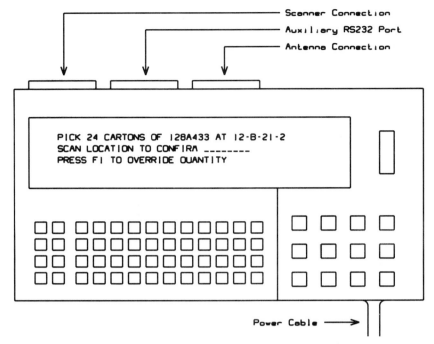

Scanner Connection
Auxiliary RS232 Port
Antenna Connection

PICK 24 CARTONS OF 128A433 AT 12-8-21-2
SCAN LOCATION TO CONFIRM _____
PRESS F1 TO OVERRIDE QUANTITY

Power Cable ⟶

Figure 5.6. Typical vehicle-mount RF terminal. Vehicle-mount RF terminals have the advantage of being powered from the vehicle's battery. They can, therefore, support higher power displays and laser scanners.

The inventory control system compares the value found in this scan with the expected value. If the two match, the material handler is told the quantity to pick. If they do not match, the location scanned is stored and the material handler is told to correct his or her error or to press a key indicating that the source location is to be overridden.

5. After the pick has been made, the material handler keys in the quantity actually moved or accepts the quantity scanned from the transaction document. If the quantity keyed matches the quantity scanned, the material handler is given the destination location. If there is a mismatch, he or she is warned and given a chance to override or to correct the error.

6. Upon delivery of the material to its destination, the material handler is once again required to scan the location label. The inventory control system compares the scanned value with the expected value and, once again, warns the material handler if necessary. On completion, the inventory control system updates its database by relieving the allocation and in-transit quantity, altering inventory balances, and crediting the material handler with both the work accomplished and the errors committed.

These three examples illustrate some of the ways that inventory movements can be achieved with very high accuracy rates. There are, of course, many other ways to validate. For instance:

1. Portable terminals are actually capable of much more than the second example credits them for. For instance, a task list can be generated by the inventory control system and downloaded to an off-line portable terminal. Assuming adequate memory and appropriate software, the material handler can then be on-line with the portable terminal. Paper transactions need no longer exist. And all of the interactive processing in the third example can occur, with one exception: The inventory system's database updates must still rely on an upload from the terminal and will be delayed.

2. When shipments are picked from a rack or shelving to a take-away conveyor, validation can be done by a laser scanner mounted beside the conveyor. For example, pickers can apply labels to boxes as they are picked. The labels can constitute the pick list, provide a bar code for validation, and provide enough information in the bar code to control conveyor sortation.

The concept of validation can be applied to more than simple movements from point A to point B. All kinds of material handling tasks, cycle counts, and even physical inventories can be validated. The more broadly validation is applied, the more accurate will be the resulting transactions. And, the more accurate the transactions, the more accurate will be the inventory records that depend on those transactions.

Validation, just like the proofreading of a letter, easily removes the vast majority of human errors. The concept is simple: Each material handling task is assigned to a specific employee. That employee is required to return confirming, or validating, information as the task is completed. Only after the loop has been closed are final changes made to the database. Bar code technology is often employed for the collection of validating information, but other methods exist.

The concept of validation is simple. Unfortunately, complexities abound in its application. These complexities are addressed in Chapters 8 through 15.

PREREQUISITES

Before validation can be accomplished, several conditions must be met. Although some of these prerequisites are obvious, some are not. First, validation requires that the inventory control system know about each material movement before it is made. The system must know the identity of the material to be moved, where material is to be moved from, and where it is supposed to go. This means the system must either generate or be told about every material movement.

Under most circumstances, modern inventory systems generate movements as a by-product of other work. For example, the inventory control system may be given list of customer orders. It then knows what must be moved to the shipping dock. If that same system allocates inventory, it knows the source location. The system is then able to define and validate picking and shipping. This implies, of course, that inventory information is stored on a location-by-location basis and that the system selects picking locations. The selection of locations by a computer leads into a host of other considerations that will be explored later.

Under some circumstances, even in the most completely computerized operation, people will define material movements. If, for instance, the roof begins to leak, the stock locations under the leak will have to be emptied. A supervisor can make these miscellaneous movements though verbal instructions to a material handler. The material handler can move the stock without benefit of system control and adjustments can be posted to the inventory records. There is, in this case, no validation. The supervisor risks inserting material handling and adjusting errors in the inventory.

Or, the supervisor can give verbal instructions and repeat those instructions to the inventory system. When the movement is made, the actual work done can then be validated against the supervisor's input. This method, however, leaves open the possibility that the supervisor will make a mistake in entry. If, then, the material handler does the job correctly, the system will detect an error that is not actually an error and the business will pay the cost of running it to ground.

A better way is for all movements to be controlled through the system. When the leak is discovered, the supervisor tells the system what movements should be made, and the system directs the material handler and validates his or her work. While it is still possible that the supervisor will make an error, validation has protected the integrity of the inventory records. The inventory may end up in the wrong place, but at least the system knows where it is and can find it quickly and easily.

Discipline is the second prerequisite of validation. For example, a practical inventory system must include a way to move material without validation so work can continue when equipment is down. The danger is that supervision will allow employees to use this backup path as a temporary expedient, particularly if it is more efficient for them to do so in the short term. And expedients, of course, have a way of becoming permanent.

The inventory software can contribute to discipline by making the backup paths harder and slower than the preferred method. But, the conscious reduction of productivity, even under special circumstances, is poor practice. A better way is to run a disciplined shop.

Two things are fundamental to discipline: a system that is truly easier to use than to ignore and a workforce that really understands how to use it. The topics of system design and training are covered in Chapters 17 and 19, respectively. As a third prerequisite, validation requires a systems approach to design and implementation. One often cannot implement portions of an inventory system and achieve accuracy. Errors made in portions of the system that have not been implemented will destroy the accuracy of the portions that are in use. In this context, the idea of a systems approach implies a very careful and very thorough system design. Much attention must be paid to the methods and procedures used by material handlers and supervisors.

The fourth prerequisite to validation is financial investment. Although this book includes all-manual examples, few companies will be willing to pay the labor costs involved. The examples are intended for illustrative purposes only. Few companies achieve high levels of inventory accuracy without major expenses for both hardware and software. The dollars can be big but so can payback.

Because accuracy costs money, it requires management support. Like discipline, management support is talked and written about a great deal but is rarely defined or explained. Management support, for the purposes of this book, consists of an understanding on the part of top management of the problem, the solution, and the costs and benefits. Systems and operating managers know that they have top-level management support when they get a business plan that does not conflict with the project, when they get approval to invest in the necessary hardware and software, and when adequate staff is assigned to the project in a timely fashion.

PROBLEMS

Validation is the single most important technique used to achieve accuracy. It is not, however, a panacea. Several problems such as the following are not solved by validation:

1. Intelligent malfeasance. Validation does not prevent material handlers (or supervisors) from purposefully creating inventory errors, should they be inclined to do so. A lift-truck driver, for instance, when told to put a pallet in location X, can place it in location Y, drive to location X, and validate. Nothing prevents this. However, if audit trails are kept by the system, it won't be long before the driver is pinpointed and appropriate action taken.
2. High speed operations. Some operations, such as high speed picking, rule out validation because of the labor cost of even the most automated form of validation. In most of these cases there are other ways of achieving at least some of the accuracy offered by validation.
3. Adjustments. After-the-fact adjustments by supervisors and clerks cannot be validated because they involve no physical movement of material or even the presence of a person in the stockroom. Proper system designs can minimize adjustment errors.

These problems and others are addressed in the chapters that follow.

6

Automatic Identification

Inventory control systems require the frequent identification of things to the computer. For instance, to record the movement of a pallet of material from one point in the facility to another, three identifications must be made: the material being moved, its source or origin, and its destination. In large warehouses and distribution centers, tens of thousands of identifications can be needed each day.

Inventory accuracy, as we have seen, requires achieving extremely high levels of transaction accuracy. Many businesses have found that mechanizing the identification of things such as products and locations to the system helps substantially in the achievement of the necessary levels of accuracy. Machines, particularly electronic ones, are capable of the accuracy and reliability required. Humans are not, at least not without expensive checking and double-checking. Automatic identification, therefore, is important to inventory accuracy and productivity.

In addition to achieving accuracy, automatic identification is often justified by labor cost savings. Under some circumstances (e.g., scanners beside conveyors), automatic identification can happen without labor cost. In most other cases, automatic identification is faster than manual identification and keying. In only a few instances does automatic identification actually increase cost.

The possible forms of automatic identification are almost numberless, given the imagination of an industrial designer and the possible number of devices that have been built and tried. Most companies, however, are unlikely to be interested in designing and building their own equipment. Proven, serviceable equipment is readily available in the market.

BAR CODING PRINCIPLES

Bar coding is the most widely applied of the automatic identification technologies. Bar code technology is well developed, the equipment required to print and read bar codes is inexpensive, and the resulting reliability and accuracy are extremely high. A bar code is a series of light and dark printed bars. The pattern of the bars is preestablished to represent alphabetic and numeric characters in any of a number of standard schemes. When a wand or a laser beam is run across the bars at a constant velocity, light is reflected from the bars and spaces in a series of pulses that can be electronically detected and converted into the appropriate characters. Figure 6.1 illustrates this process.

Self-checking methods are built into many of the various standard coding schemes to assure that the pattern detected is valid. Added checking can be and often is done in applications programs. The result is an error rate that often approximates 1 misread character in 3,000,000. Using this error rate, and assuming a 12-character bar code, the implied error rate for the entire field would be on the order of magnitude of one error in 250,000 symbols read. This might translate to one or two errors per year in many businesses, an entirely acceptable rate.

Because bar code symbols are printed, they are not easily updated. Bar codes, therefore, are most applicable when the information to be encoded does not change rapidly. Things that can be readily identified with bar codes include: prod-

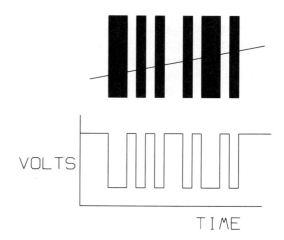

BITSTREAM   1 00001 001 00

Figure 6.1. Decoding a bar code. Bar code scanners use photocells to distinguish between dark and light areas. Voltage levels (as shown) or voltage durations make up binary 1s and 0s to form the message.

ucts (a bar-coded label might be attached to a pallet or preprinted on the product or its carton), storage locations (often labels are attached to the rack or bin), employees (the bar code is usually on an ID badge or card), vehicles, tote pans, etc. In all these cases, the information contained in the bar code is constant and unvarying; it serves to identify one particular item or kind of item among many similar ones without ambiguity and with only a small chance for error.

For the same reason, bar codes are not normally used to encode information that changes frequently. For instance, it would be difficult to use bar codes to store the quantity held in a bin or the job currently being run on a machine. Instead, most systems use bar codes to identify the bin or the machine and retrieve the on-hand balance or the current job from the system's database.

Bar codes date back into the early 1950s or late 1940s. Their first large-scale application was in railroad car identification. A program was sponsored by the American Association of Railroads in 1960, with Sylvania Manufacturing (now a part of GTE) producing the equipment. The railroad car identification project ultimately failed because the bar codes were not able to withstand the wear and lack of maintenance that railroad equipment is subjected to. The idea, however, was a good one and made a good test bed for bar coding as a concept. Industry has gained a great deal as a result.

In 1970 the Uniform Code Council was formed and the UPC became a reality. It is intended specifically for retail sales applications but has possible uses wherever retail products are handled. Bar code development accelerated in the 1970s and 1980s. In 1974, the now-popular Code 39 was developed. In 1982 the Department of Defense adopted bar coding standards. In 1983 the American National Standards Institute accepted bar coding. And since that time developments have occurred at an ever-accelerating pace.

This book is about inventory accuracy and, therefore, only covers bar coding in a minimal amount of detail. However, a fundamental understanding of bar codes is critical to their successful implementation. And bar codes are critical, in most cases, to the achievement of inventory accuracy. The system designer must be able to specify equipment that will work together when installed. Printers, for example, must print bar codes that can be read, and scanners must be capable of reading the bar codes printed. Sales people's claims are a good starting point, but few companies can allow success or failure of a system investments to hinge on the accuracy of those claims.

BAR CODE SYMBOLOGIES

The manner in which bars and spaces are organized to represent characters is called a "symbology." There are literally dozens of symbologies, some of which have fallen into disuse, others of which were never particularly popular, and a few of which represent the mainstream of modern use. The codes most commonly used, of course, are those for which equipment is most readily available and most reasonably priced. So, except for unusual situations, most companies should limit their application to one of these codes: Code 39, Interleaved 2 of 5, and the Universal Product Code (UPC).

Code 39

Code 39 is so named because a single character is represented by nine elements, three of which are always wide. (An element is either a bar or a space.) A narrow space always separates the characters. Figure 6.2 shows the Code 39 code configuration.

Although it is rarely done, it is possible to read bar codes manually. When doing so with Code 39, one first reads the five dark bars and converts them into 1s and 0s based on their width. Next, one reads the four spaces and similarly converts them into 1s and 0s. The nine resulting binary digits are then translated into characters using Figure 6.2. It should be noted that the character shown in Figure 6.2 as an asterisk (*) is actually a start-stop character that is displayed as an asterisk by convention.

PATTERN	BARS	SPACES	CHAR	PATTERN	BARS	SPACES	CHAR
	10001	0100	1		11000	0001	A
	01001	0100	2		00101	0001	N
	11000	0100	3		10100	0001	O
	00101	0100	4		01100	0001	P
	10100	0100	5		00011	0001	Q
	01100	0100	6		10010	0001	R
	00011	0100	7		01010	0001	S
	10010	0100	8		00110	0001	T
	01010	0100	9		10001	1000	U
	00110	0100	0		01001	1000	V
	10001	0010	A		11000	1000	W
	01001	0010	B		00101	1000	X
	11000	0010	C		10100	1000	Y
	00101	0010	D		01100	1000	Z
	10100	0010	E		00011	1000	-
	01100	0010	F		10010	1000	●
	00011	0010	G		01010	1000	SPACE
	10010	0010	H		00110	1000	*
	01010	0010	I		00000	1110	$
	00110	0010	J		00000	1101	/
	10001	0001	K		00000	1011	+
	01001	0001	L		00000	0111	%

Figure 6.2. Code 39 configuration. Code 39 is a widely used alphanumeric bar code symbology. The patterns of wide and narrow elements are separated by narrow spaces and both started and terminated by the "*" character to make a complete bar code.

Code 39 is notable as being the most commonly used code that can encode alphabetic characters. Other newer and less well-known codes capable of handling alphanumerics are Code 49 and Code 128. Code 39 has been adopted as standard by the Department of Defense (Logmars), by the Automotive Industry Action Group (AIAG), and by other groups and standards organizations. The popularity and standardization of Code 39 is important to the individual user because it means that the code is well established, that printer and scanner vendors are familiar with it and have proven equipment that works with it, and that software vendors know its features and shortcomings well. When an established standard can be used, of course, costs, risks, and lead times are all reduced.

Interleaved 2 of 5

The Interleaved 2 of 5 symbology is also very popular. It differs from Code 39 in a number of respects, but only two differences are important from the user's viewpoint. Interleaved 2 of 5 allows the coding of only numeric values. Interleaved 2 of 5 is significantly more compact than Code 39 because each character is represented by five elements, two of which are wide. Therefore, at a given density, it consumes only $\frac{5}{9}$ of the space of Code 39. (The fraction is approximate because start and stop characters are different.)

The word "interleaved" means that the bars and spaces used to represent the characters are interleaved. In other words, the digits are represented in pairs by a group of 10 bars and spaces. Five bars represent the first character; the intervening five spaces represent the second. The code is described in Table 6.1 and the idea of interleaving is illustrated in Figure 6.3. One implication of interleaving is that only an even number of digits can be represented in an Interleaved 2 of 5 symbol. If one wishes to encode the number 531, for instance, the code must actually contain the characters "0531."

TABLE 6.1.   INTERLEAVED 2 OF 5 CODE

Character	Code
0	00110
1	10001
2	01001
3	11000
4	00101
5	10100
6	01100
7	00011
8	10010
9	01010
Start	110
Stop	101

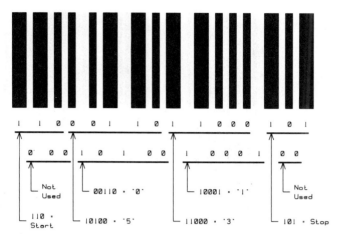

Figure 6.3. Interleaved 2 of 5 example. Interleaved 2 of 5 code works much like Code 39, but the elements are interleaved as shown in this example. Interleaved 2 of 5 is, therefore, limited to codes that contain an even number of characters.

Universal Product Code

The Universal Product Code (UPC) was developed specifically for retail use and has seen little use outside of retail warehouses and stores. UPC codes, however, can also be used within a company where it makes sense to do so.

There are several variations on the original concept, but the most commonly encountered UPC symbol (version A) consists of two halves separated by a pair of narrow bars. Each half of the symbol consists of six numeric characters. The first symbol encodes the product classification number and the number assigned to the product's manufacturer by the Uniform Code Council. The second symbol contains a five-digit number assigned by the manufacturer that identifies the specific item plus a one-digit check character. A sample UPC appears in Figure 6.4.

Each of the 12 characters is composed of seven elements. Bars, however, need not be separated from each other by spaces, and spaces need not be separated by bars. The individual elements are grouped into what appears to the eye to be two bars and two spaces of variable width. Readers interested in the details of the construction of UPC codes, should contact the Uniform Code Council.

The UPC specification includes both parity checking and a check digit. (Definitions of both terms appear on the glossary.) As a result, it is highly reliable. However, the fact that the Uniform Code Council issues company identifiers limits the code's usefulness to its original intent: identification of a product and its manufacturer.

Figure 6.4. Sample UPC code. The ubiquitous UPC code was designed for and is most commonly used in retail applications.

Other Codes

Although Code 39, Interleaved 2 of 5, and UPC are the most commonly found symbologies, they are far from being the only ones in existence. Some other codes are important because they are new and their popularity is growing. Others are technically past their prime but are still found in older applications:

EAN and JAN. The European Article Numbering symbology is like the Universal Product Code but was developed for use in Europe. EAN includes both the manufacturer and product numbers (as in the UPC code) and a country code. It is actually a superset of UPC. The Japanese Article Numbering (JAN) symbology is similar.

Codabar. Codabar was designed to tolerate the inaccuracies inherent in early printers. Each character consists of four bars and three spaces; a single narrow space separates characters. Numeric characters consist of two wide and three narrow bars. Other characters (there are 14 of them, including 7 alphabetics) consist of three wide bars and no wide spaces. But, the width of the wide bars and spaces varies to provide a constant character length. Codabar, therefore, is complex to print. Most codabar use is in older applications. Few new codabar installations are now being made.

Code 2 of 5. Code 2 of 5 is different from Interleaved 2 of 5. It encodes all information in the width of the bars, using narrow spaces to separate all bars. Each character is represented by five bars. Four bars each represent a value: 1, 2, 4, and 7, respectively. The fifth bar contains parity. Two bars are always wide and three narrow. If one of the first four bars is wide, its value is the character encoded and the fifth bar will be wide. If two of the first four bars are wide, their values are added to determine the character and the fifth bar will be narrow.

This code is the same code as that used in Interleaved 2 of 5 (see Table 6.1). Because Code 2 of 5 does not encode information in its spaces, it results in relatively less dense symbols than some other codes. Therefore it is not often used.

Code 11. Code 11 gets its name from the fact that it allows 11 characters to be encoded—the 10 digits and the dash (hyphen). Like Interleaved 2 of 5 and (noninterleaved) 2 of 5, Code 11 encodes each character in five elements. But, unlike those codes, Code 11 uses three bars and two spaces for each character, separating the characters with a single narrow space. Code 11 therefore carries the density of Interleaved 2 of 5 without its requirement that an even number of digits be encoded. However, Code 11 is not considered to be a self-checking code because a single printing defect can transpose one character into another. A user-supplied check digit, therefore, is mandatory and two check digits are often used.

Plessy. The Plessy code was developed in England in 1971 and has seen extensive use in libraries. It encodes each character in four bars and four spaces, with each bar and space pair being either wide and narrow or narrow and wide to encode a single bit. In addition to the wide and narrow encoding, Plessy code specifies that 1 bits use a four-unit wide bar and a one-unit wide space, while 0 bits use a two-unit wide bar and a three-unit wide space. Thus a measure of self-checking is imposed. Plessy is another primarily numeric code. It is relatively low density and, therefore, is used only in special circumstances. Variations on the Plessy code are known as the Anker and MSI codes.

Telepen. The Telepen symbology encodes the full 128-character ASCII set. Telepen consists of two separate character sets. It uses special characters to allow switching between the sets in mid-symbol. Characters are encoded in 16 elements, all of which are the same width, but each of which can be either a bar or a space. In the first character set, the 16 elements represent a single ASCII character. In the second, they represent two numeric characters.

Telepen is self-checking only through a check character. Since it offers no density advantage over Code 39 or (in its second character set) over Interleaved 2 of 5, it has not been widely applied. Its only significant advantage is it's ability to encode some characters that code 39 cannot. (The ASCII 128 character set includes the 10 digits, all 26 alphabetic characters in both upper- and lowercase, a variety of special characters such as punctuations and signs like $ and #, and a group of 32 nonprinting characters that have special functions for the control of printers and other devices. Examples of these 32 special characters are the carriage return, form-feed, backspace, end-of-text, and others.)

Code 128. Code 128 is a more recent and more dense symbology, able to encode all 128 ASCII characters. It is the symbology used in the UPC case code and, therefore, is important in inventory control. Characters in Code 128 consist of three bars and three spaces, with their widths distributed to encompass a total of 11 elements. Code 128, however, is not self-checking and is difficult to print to specification. Users considering it, therefore, should verify that all of the printers to be used can, in fact, produce symbols that can be successfully read.

Code 93. Code 93 was introduced in 1982 as a high-density alternative to Code 39. Code 93 uses three bars and three spaces with a total width of nine elements to encode the same 43 characters as Code 39. Because Code 93 is not self-checking, it uses two check characters as does Code 11.

Code 49. The Code 49 symbol consists of a "stack" of between two and eight rows, each composed of 18 bars and 17 spaces. All 128 ASCII characters are represented. Code 49 was developed to allow the encoding of large volumes of data in a relatively small space. A single 8-row symbol may consist of as many as 49 alphanumeric characters or 81 digits. Check characters and control characters are included. The control characters allow users to scan the individual rows in any sequence, relying on the scanner to arrange them properly.

Code 49 is quite new, having been introduced in 1988 by Intermec. It has the advantage of allowing the complete 128 character set to be encoded at high density with high reliability, but the disadvantage is that multiple scans are required to read a symbol. The popularity of Code 39 probably means that Code 49 will mature into a specialized symbology, useful in some circumstances but not as a general-purpose tool.

One might ask why so many symbologies exist. The fundamental answer is competitive pressure. Most of these symbologies (UPC is a notable exception) have been developed and introduced by the manufacturers of bar code equipment, primarily as a way to sell more equipment. Each code, having been developed at a different point in time, represents a different state of the art and a different trade-off in conflicting desirable features.

OTHER BAR CODE SPECIFICATIONS

The technology of bar coding goes beyond the selection of a symbology. A number of other concepts and terms should be understood by people proposing or using bar codes. The most important of these follow.

Encoding Methods

Note that the bar code shown in Figure 6.1 uses a wide element to represent 1 and a narrow element to represent 0. This is called module width (MW) encoding. Code 39 is a module-width code. Other codes, UPC being the most notable example, do not have wide or narrow elements but use dark bars to represent 1 and light bars to represent 0. When several 1s appear side by side in a code, the congruence of the bars appears as a wide bar but is actually several normal bars together. The use of dark bars to represent 1 and light bars to represent 0 is called "non-return-to-zero" (or NRZ) encoding.

Bidirectionality

Bar codes are bidirectional, which means they can be scanned in either direction. When wand-type scanners are used, bidirectionality is important because some people will prefer to scan from right to left and others from left to right. With moving-beam laser scanners, however, scans are usually done by oscillating light beams. The beams move so quickly that bidirectionality is almost inconsequential.

Bidirectionality is accomplished within the scanner. When a scan fails to decode, the sequence of the bits is reversed and the decoder makes a second try. All modern bar codes are bidirectional.

Narrow Bar Width

The width of a narrow bar (or space) as printed is a key consideration in the design of labels and the selection of symbologies. Each printer and each scanner has a minimum and maximum narrow bar width. Long-range laser scanners require very large symbols and, therefore, very wide narrow bars. Wands, however, can be purchased that have very small apertures to read very fine symbols. At least within a system, the specifications of all printers and all scanners should overlap, and the greater the degree of overlap, the better.

Bar Ratio

Wide bar and space widths are usually not cited in bar code specifications. Rather, it is conventional to specify the narrow bar width and ratio of the wide bars to the narrow ones. (Even though some symbologies such as UPC do not have a fixed ratio.)

Most of the figures in this book are drawn with a 2:1 bar ratio for simplicity. The figures, however, are only examples. In real life, ratios should be set according to industry standards or according to the specifications for the printers and scanners in use. In practice, some experimentation may be required. Ratios of either 2.5:1 or 3:1 often work well when dot matrix printers are used.

The narrow bar width, the bar ratio, and the number of characters to be encoded, when taken together, determine the size of the symbol. For instance, if 12 characters are to be encoded in Code 39 with a narrow bar width of .020 inch and a ratio of 3:1, the calculations are:

1. Each character in Code 39 consists of three wide and six narrow elements plus a space called an intercharacter gap. The intercharacter

gap, which is normally the same width as a narrow bar, serves to separate the characters.

2. Therefore, each character will consume the equivalent of 16 narrow bars (3 times 3 plus 7), or 0.320 inch.
3. There are 14 characters to be encoded, 12 user-defined characters plus the stop and start characters. The overall length, therefore, is 4.480 inches.
4. There is no intercharacter gap following the final character, so one narrow bar width may be subtracted, making the actual symbol length 4.460 inches.
5. When comparing the symbol with the available space for it, "quiet space" (a blank white area) must be allowed on either end of the symbol. Assuming a quiet space equal to 10 narrow bars (20 is preferable), a quarter inch of space must be allowed at each end. Therefore, the total free space on the label must then be at least 4.960 inches long.

Bar Height

Bar height may be a matter of specification for industry-standard labels. In other cases, however, height is not so much a function of the symbology in use as it is a matter of readability and cost. Generally, the height of the bars should be between 25 and 100 percent of the length of the complete symbol. Short bars are harder to scan because more precise scanner and symbol alignment is required. Tall bars require larger and more expensive labels, the cost of printer maintenance goes up, and printers fail more often.

Density

Density is a measure of the amount of information that can be encoded in a given space. Density can be particularly important when labels are designed to fit a particular object. Code 39, although one of the most popular codes, is also one of the least dense. Other codes, such as Interleaved 2 of 5, can encode many more characters in the same or less space.

Density is measured in characters represented per linear inch of bar coding (always at a specified narrow bar width). The term "density" is also used in a more general sense. Low-density bar codes are normally considered to be those with narrow bar widths greater than 0.012 inch. Medium-density codes are those with narrow bar widths between 0.008 and 0.012 inch. And high-density codes are those with narrow bar widths less than 0.008 inch. These numbers, however, are more a matter of opinion than of specification and should not be taken to be definitive.

Self-Checking

Figure 6.5 shows several kinds of printing defects. All modern symbologies have built-in structure that allows scanners to isolate and reject defects. This prevents

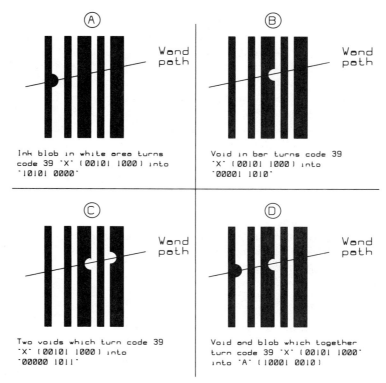

Figure 6.5. Bar code printing flaws. The best bar code symbologies are designed to allow detection of printing and scanning errors. In the examples given, only one of the four errors will go unnoticed by the decoding algorithm.

errors from entering the inventory system and contaminating the database. For instance, Figure 6.5A shows and ink blob located between two bars in such a way that it converts a narrow bar and wide space into a wide bar and narrow space. Therefore, what should have been a Code 39 X, decodes as 10101 0000 and not as it should have. Code 39, however, was designed to recognize the possibility of this happening. Because there is no character corresponding to 10101 0000, the scanner can easily recognize the existence of an error and can refuse to accept the scan. Figure 6.5B illustrates a similar error based on a printing void in a bar. Again, the decoded result will not translate into a valid Code 39 character.

The situation becomes more complex when two printing defects occur together. Figure 6.5C shows two voids, both of which are encountered by the scanner. Again, the decoded result is not a valid character. But, Figure 6.5D shows a combination of a void and an ink blob, so placed that when both are scanned, the Code 39 X becomes a Code 39 A. Of the four examples shown, only this last one represents a problem from the viewpoint of the application system.

Code 39 is considered to be self-checking because it is adequately structured to allow the scanner to detect at least some errors. Most self-checking codes use this principle or a similar one. Others (like UPC) have built-in check digits for greater self-checking strength. Users can also add check digits where necessary. No symbology provides a 100 percent accurate scan rate. The demonstrated capability of Code 39 is about one error in 3,000,000 characters scanned. This seems adequate for most applications. In instances where still higher reliability is desired, however, the application system can add its own check characters.

In addition to the structure of the symbology, the ability to sense defects is partly dependent on the electronics of scanner, partly on decoding software, and partly on the user's application.

BAR CODE PRINTERS

Successful use of bar codes in an inventory system (or in other systems) depends heavily on the printing technology used. Inappropriate printers lead to poor read rates and to additional errors. Therefore, a brief outline of the available printing technologies is appropriate in this book.

Formed Character Printers

Formed character printers, often called drum impact printers, consist of a drum with raised characters and bars around its edge. The drum is rotated and a hammer mechanism is used to force the ribbon and paper against it as the appropriate character passes the trigger point (see Figure 6.6). Most of these printers move the paper perpendicular to the drum axis. Multiple lines of print and multiple bar codes are produced by increasing the height of the drum, by raising more than one row of symbols and/or characters on its circumference, and by providing separate hammers at each level.

While formed character printers can create reasonably high-quality images, they are relatively slow and noisy. Further, their design reduces flexibility in label design and size. And, drum printers are generally not designed to print interleaved symbologies or symbologies in which the size of the character varies from one to the next.

Dot Matrix Printers

Dot matrix is probably the most popular bar code printing technology. In a dot matrix printer, a "head" contains anywhere from 9 to 24 pins (or wires) and a mechanism for firing and retrieving each of them separately from the others. The head is moved across the page and the pins are fired as each crosses a point on the page where ink is required. As the pin is fired, it impresses the ribbon against the page, which rests on a platen (see Figure 6.7).

A variation on dot matrix technology uses several heads and hundreds of pins mounted on an oscillating bar perpendicular to the direction of travel of the paper. All of the heads print simultaneously, each covering a portion of the page. These so-called shuttle matrix printers offer significantly higher throughput and are capable of printing much higher volumes of labels than single-head printers.

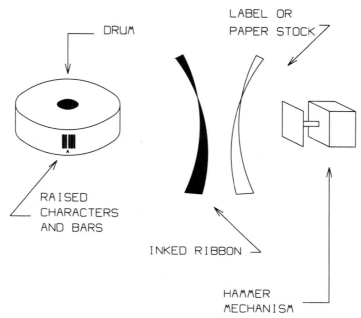

Figure 6.6. Formed character printing. Formed character printers use raised characters and bars on a rotating drum. The media receives an impression when a hammer mechanism forces it against the drum.

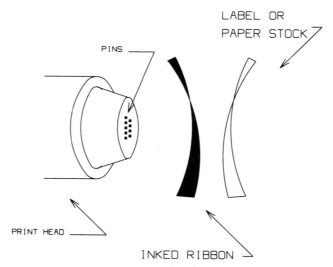

Figure 6.7. Dot matrix printing. Dot matrix printers are the most commonly available ones. Any graphics-capable dot matrix printer can be used to print bar codes if supporting software is available.

Dot matrix printers are both electrically and mechanically complex and might not be a good printing option if it were not for their popularity and flexibility. The huge volume of dot matrix printers that have been sold in recent years has prompted development and investment in the technology. As a result, the disadvantage of complexity has been overcome and dot matrix reliability is now as good as or better than simpler equipment. Inventory system designers should consider using dot matrix printers.

The flexibility of dot matrix printing technology comes about because dot matrix printers are capable of printing any shape in any location on the page. All decisions about the size and location of the bar code symbol and of any accompanying text, boxes, etc., are made in the software. Few physical limits (other than the printer's resolution) exist.

Although dot matrix printers have many advantages as bar code printers, they are susceptible to some problems. Failure of a single pin, for instance, may result in unreadable symbols. If a pin fails intermittently, the problem may not even be noticeable, except as a decrease in read rates. Ribbons and paper can also be problems. Too-fresh ribbons produce smeary codes and the ink tends to spread, widening the bars and narrowing the spaces. Worn-out ribbons print with inadequate contrast and can leave voids.

Direct Thermal Printers

Both direct thermal and thermal transfer printers are a form of matrix technology. Direct thermal printers use a special paper stock that darkens when heat is applied. The paper is passed under a print head which applies hot wires to the paper, darkening the paper in the appropriate places to produce an image (see Figure 6.8). Direct thermal printers make very high-contrast labels that look excellent and usually scan easily. The high-quality appearance of direct thermal labels, however, may not always translate into good scanning properties. The use of presensitized paper in direct thermal printers is a drawback. Not only is the paper more expensive than common paper stock, it can also fade. If direct thermal bar codes are used in applications where they will be exposed to sunlight or heat, special high-temperature paper must be used.

Thermal Transfer Printers

Thermal transfer printers (illustrated in Figure 6.9) work much like direct thermal printers except that the ink is carried in a separate temperature-sensitive ribbon and transferred to normal paper by selectively heating areas of the ribbon. Like direct thermal printers, thermal transfer printers make a high-quality, high resolution image at moderate speeds with excellent edge definition. Both direct thermal and thermal transfer printers are often designed with zero tear-off dimensions, making them excellent for use in demand-printing situations where labels are to be printed one at a time. The zero tear-off dimension allows a completed label to be removed from the printer without disturbing the next one on the roll and without wasting one.

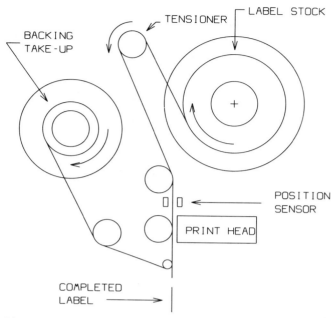

Figure 6.8. Direct thermal printing. Direct thermal printers produce very high-contrast bar codes that usually read easily. The symbols, however, tend to fade in sunlight and over long periods of time.

Ink Jet Printers

Ink jet printers use a liquid ink rather than a ribbon. As shown in Figure 6.10, the ink is forced under pressure from a nozzle through a charging tunnel, which gives it an electrical charge. The droplets then pass through deflector plates that are also electrically charged. The plates, in effect, "steer" the droplets onto a path that puts them in the right place on the paper.

Ink jet printers have the advantage of being mechanically simple, reliable, and very quiet. However, the technology has only recently been developed to the point where they work well and bar code firmware is not readily available for them. Ink jet printing is a technology to watch in the years to come.

Laser and Electrostatic Printers

When very large quantities of labels are required and when they cannot be printed on a printing press, laser and electrostatic printers are an option. Working much like photocopiers, these printers use a transfer drum to capture an image. The drum passes under a toner (ink) applicator and picks up toner in the places required to make an image. It then carries the toner to the paper and transfers it to create the image. The toner is later fixed in place with an application of

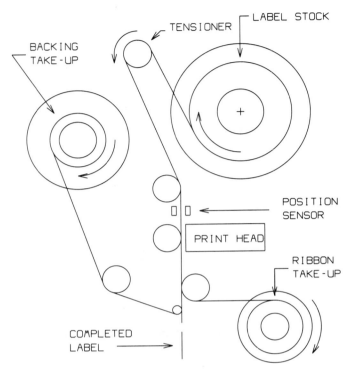

Figure 6.9. Thermal transfer printing. Thermal transfer printers create an image by transferring ink from a ribbon to the label media by heat. Contrast and edge definition are usually very high.

heat (see Figures 6.11 and 6.12). Laser printers place the image on the drum using a laser and a moving mirror; electrostatic printers use a character generator.

Although they are relatively expensive, laser and electrostatic printers can create large numbers of bar codes quickly. Because the images are controlled by software (and firmware), they are flexible. If necessary, each label can be different. Printing processes such as lithography and offset can produce large volumes of labels at lower cost but are limited to exact copies of a single label.

BAR CODE SCANNERS

Like printers, bar code scanners are important to the application of bar codes. Scanners must be matched to the codes to be read, must be reliable, and, if hand held, must be convenient to use and tolerant of human failures. A complete bar code reading system can be thought of as consisting of the four parts shown in Figure 6.13: the scanner, the decoder, a terminal, and the host computer. Available equipment often packages more than one of these parts in a single unit. For

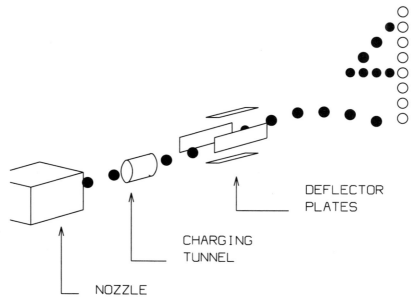

Figure 6.10. Ink jet printing. Ink jet printers literally throw droplets of ink onto the paper. They are very quiet in operation but do not always produce acceptable bar codes because edge definition may not be adequate.

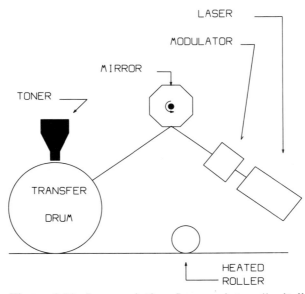

Figure 6.11. Laser printing. Laser printers "write" on a rotating transfer drum with a laser. The drum picks up toner (ink) in the places touched by the laser and transfers the toner to the labels where it is fixed by a heated roller.

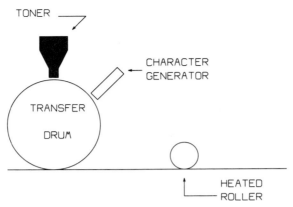

Figure 6.12. Electrostatic printing. Electrostatic printers directly generate charged areas on a rotating transfer drum. The drum picks up toner (ink) in the places touched by the laser and transfers the toner to the labels where it is fixed by a heated roller.

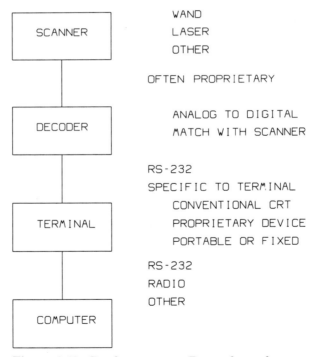

Figure 6.13. Reader systems. Bar code reader systems generally consist of four parts: a scanner, a decoder, a terminal, and a host computer. As purchased, these four parts may be packaged separately or in a single unit, depending on the manufacturer.

instance, a scanner and a decoder may be packaged together into a device that communicates via ASCII characters on an RS232 line. Or, the terminal and decoder may be packaged together into a portable unit with a keyboard and ports for the scanner and for communications with a host computer. Regardless of packaging, all four must be present to form a functioning bar code reader system.

The function of the scanner is to detect the presence of a symbol and to capture the pattern of bars and spaces in the form of an electrical signal. Analog scanners pass the electrical signal to the decoder with amplification but without other processing. Digital scanners convert the signal from an analog wave form to a digital signal before passing it to the decoder.

The decoder's job begins with the conversion of the signal received from the scanner to digital form (if necessary). The decoder then decides which symbology is in use by attempting to decode the digital signal using several different symbologies. Although many decoders "autodiscriminate" between a number of symbologies, some are able to deal with only one. Finally, the decoder detects errors in the scanning of the symbol, determines which characters it contains, and passes the resulting character string to the terminal.

The communication protocol used between the scanner and the decoder may be proprietary. Communication between the decoder and the terminal may be RS232 asynchronous or may be specific to the terminal. Decoders are sometimes connected to terminals in parallel with the keyboard using devices called "wedges." When this is done, the application program does not know whether the arriving data was keyed or scanned. Keyboard parallel scanners do not require the writing of separate programs to handle them, but they limit systems by not allowing the different actions to be taken for different data entry methods.

The terminal receives a decoded character string from the decoder, processes it as determined by the application, and passes it on to the computer. Processing in the terminal might, for instance, consist of displaying the character string and offering the user an opportunity to accept, reject, or modify it. The terminal may also provide for key entry, log on and log off, and other application-oriented functions.

There are numerous types of scanners. Many scanners that appear different on the outside are, in fact, very similar on the inside. The three most common types of scanners are wands, hand-held lasers, and fixed-location lasers.

Wands

A bar code wand is a hand-held device typically between 6 and 7 inches long and about an inch in diameter. As shown in Figure 6.14, it has a hole in one end through which the bar code is detected and a cable for connection with the decoder on the other end. Some bar code wands have decoders built into them and communicate directly with a terminal.

Power enters the wand through the cable and is fed to an emitter that generates light. The light is focused on the aperture (the hole in the wand's tip) where it reflects off the symbol. The reflected light is converted into an electrical signal by a detector and the signal is fed to an amplifier (and in some wands is decoded).

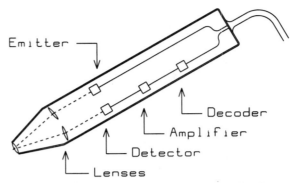

Figure 6.14. Wand bar code scanner. A wand scanner consists of an emitter, a system of lenses, and a detector that gathers the emitted light reflecting from the surface of the symbol. The signal put out by the detector is usually (but not always) amplified and decoded within the wand itself.

The wand is hand held like a pencil and is brought into contact with a bar code symbol. As it is drawn across the symbol, the amount of light reflected varies as the aperture passes over bars and spaces. This causes the electrical signal generated by the detector to vary and allows the decoder to determine the content of the symbol.

Wands are simple and reliable devices. They are inexpensive but have two drawbacks. First, a certain degree of technique must be learned to effectively use a bar code wand. The wand should be held at an angle to the symbol; not perpendicular to it. And the user must learn to move the wand smoothly through the entire symbol at an appropriate speed. Both the wand angle and the speed required vary from manufacturer to manufacturer. Although most specifications allow broad tolerances, users generally need instruction and some practice before they can reliably read symbols on the first pass.

The second drawback of wands as bar code scanning devices is the requirement that they must contact the symbol to be read. Contact scanning is not a problem in some applications, but in others, it can be. For example, the driver of a lift truck who uses a wand must dismount or, at the very least, must maneuver the lift truck to read the bar code on a pallet. This takes time, energy, and money. Wands, therefore, are most often used at desk-type workstations.

One error often made when specifying bar code wands is the selection of an incorrect aperture size. In general, aperture sizes should be no larger than the narrow bar dimension. When aperture sizes are larger than the narrow bar dimension, the wand "sees" more than one bar at a time. Since it averages the reflectance of the symbol, larger apertures tend to reduce the effective contrast between bars and spaces and therefore tend to create no-reads. On the other hand, aperture sizes that are too small tend to pick up more printing defects than a larger aperture would. Therefore they, also, are less reliable. One implication of the need to select an appropriate wand aperture size is that it is not practical to use a single wand to read both high- and low-density bar codes. So, to the extent possible, businesses should standardize on a single density for all bar codes in a plant or at least in an application.

Hand-Held Lasers

A second very common bar code scanning device is the hand-held laser. As shown in Figure 6.15, the hand-held laser is a device shaped roughly like and about as big as an oversized pistol. These devices are, in fact, often called laser guns. The hand-held laser consists of a small, low-powered laser that generates a beam of light when the trigger (not shown in Figure 6.15) is pulled. The light beam is reflected off a rotating mirror, which causes it to sweep from side to side through an arc of about 5 degrees. When the light beam strikes a bar code symbol, the reflected light forms a pattern that can be detected, amplified, and decoded in a manner very similar to the wand.

In addition to the moving-beam variety (shown in Figure 6.15), fixed-beam

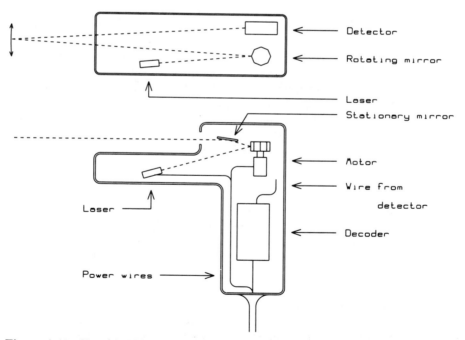

Figure 6.15. Hand-held laser scanner. Hand held laser scanners direct a beam of coherent laser light across the symbol, moving it from side to side with a rotating mirror. (Some hand-held lasers omit the mirror and require the user to move the beam manually.) Light reflected from the symbol is detected and decoded to determine the significance of the symbol.

hand-held lasers are also available. These devices are similar but omit the rotating mirror and rely on the operator's wrist action to draw the laser beam across the symbol. Being simpler, fixed-beam hand-held lasers are less expensive than moving-beam ones but rely more on operator skill. Therefore, they require more training and practice and have lower first time read rates.

Hand-held lasers are more expensive than wands. But, they are easier to use and require less training. And, they do not require contact with the symbol. Effective scanning distances between the laser and the symbol range from a few inches to approximately 4 feet. It should be noted, however, that scanning distances in excess of 20 or 24 inches (depending on the manufacturer) requires higher levels of power and lower-density symbols. At extreme ranges, symbols must be very large, possibly larger than the space available for them. And, large symbols take longer to print, requiring more printers for a given application.

Hand-held lasers can work well in an appropriate application, but two additional drawbacks should be noted. First, they require more power than wands. Therefore, in portable applications the user must deal not only with the additional bulk of the scanner but often must also deal with additional batteries. And second, lasers are affected by their surroundings, particularly by ambient light. Hand-held lasers may not function well outdoors on a bright day. They may also suffer from conflicts with certain kinds of indoor lighting that are strong in their particular spectrum. Sodium vapor lighting, for instance, can conflict with lasers operating in the 820-nanometer range. When designing systems that use hand-held lasers, it is wise to verify that existing light fixtures do not conflict with the specific laser to be used.

People encountering laser scanners for the first time are often concerned about safety issues. Although employees should be cautioned about directing the beam into an eye, safety has not been a problem in existing applications. The beam is not powerful enough to do much damage, and it moves too fast to allow people to look into it for any period of time.

Fixed-Location Lasers

A third common type of scanner is the fixed-location laser. These devices are similar to hand-held lasers but are packaged in a box designed to be bolted or clamped beside a conveyor to read bar codes as objects pass. Internally, these scanners are much like hand-held scanners, so Figure 6.16 concentrates on the environment in which one might be used, rather than its construction.

Fixed-location lasers, like hand-held ones, are noncontact scanners. They are designed to work at a specified distance from the symbol to be read (the optical throw) within a specified tolerance (the depth of field). They also require that the symbols be perpendicular to the laser beam within a specified maximum angle (the skew angle). Most require a sensor such as a photocell to detect the presence of an object to be scanned.

Some fixed-location lasers, like hand-held ones, are unidirectional, which means that the beam oscillates left to right, but not up and down. Other fixed-location

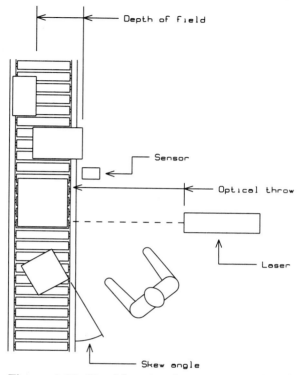

Figure 6.16. Fixed-location laser scanner. Fixed-location laser scanners work internally much like hand-held lasers (see Figure 6.15) but often include more than one set of rotating mirrors to allow the beam to be moved in two-dimensional patterns. These devices are designed to work at a particular optical throw (within a depth of field) and with a maximum skew angle. They are usually turned on and off by a separate sensing device.

lasers, unlike hand-held ones, are omnidirectional. Several rotating mirrors are used to move the beam in complex two-dimensional patterns. The result is that symbols no longer require exact orientation. The distinction is important when bar-coded labels are applied by hand.

Fixed-location scanners vary greatly in cost, with cost increasing as pattern complexity (and, therefore, first-time read rates) increases. Cost also increases with increased power (which translates into increased optical throw) and increased tolerances for skew angle and depth of field. All fixed-location scanners are more expensive than hand-held ones. But, because they do not need an operator, they may be less expensive in total.

Other Scanners

Other scanning technologies exist but are of minor importance in comparison. Examples are charge-coupled diode (CCD) scanners and a variety of optical scanning systems.

Some devices that appear to be different technologies are simply different packages. Slot readers, for instance, are devices that allow bar-coded documents such as employee ID badges to be read by passing them through a slot. Most slot readers are electrically equivalent to wands.

CHOOSING A BAR CODE TECHNOLOGY

With bar coding as complex as it is, the selection of a technology is a tough decision, particularly for those who are inexperienced. For example, the desirable properties of a bar code symbology are:

- A large character set
- High reliability
- High tolerance for printing defects
- Wide availability of printing and scanning equipment
- Abilities proven through a large number of successful implementations over several years

The decision-making process can be simplified, however, by leaning on the experience of others. Unless there is specific reason to the contrary:

- Use a single symbology in all applications.
- Adhere to existing practices and proven industry standards.
- If no industry standard exists and if no alphanumeric characters are to be encoded, use Interleaved 2 of 5.
- Or, if space exists for large symbols and if alphanumeric characters must be encoded (as is often the case), use Code 39.
- When equipment is purchased from more than one source, always witness tests that demonstrate compatibility between the printers and the scanners.

The selection of printing and scanning technologies can also be simplified with a few broad guidelines. Unless there is reason to the contrary:

- When volumes are large and symbols are identical, use a specialty printer for the lowest-cost label.
- When large volumes of unique symbols are required, consider laser printers to take advantage of their flexibility.
- When labels are to be produced on demand (one at a time), consider either direct thermal or thermal transfer printers because they are often designed for demand printing.
- Otherwise, consider dot matrix technology as a low-cost and high reliability option.

And, for scanners:

- Consider fixed-position lasers where operatorless operation is possible or where they can be configured to work with an operator, as in a grocery-store check-out lane. Use more expensive omnidirectional lasers only where they are cheaper than reliable label orientation.
- Use wands when contact reading is possible because they are less expensive and more reliable than hand-held lasers.
- Otherwise, use hand-held lasers.

OTHER IDENTIFICATION TECHNOLOGIES

Bar codes are the most commonly used automatic identification technology. But they are neither the only technology nor are they applicable in every circumstance. For instance, bar codes are useful in most environments but not in all. They can be coated to resist dust, dirt, and mild chemicals. They are relatively impervious to light, electromagnetic interference, and shock. But they do not survive extremely harsh conditions. High-temperature heat treating processes, chemical baths, and long periods of outdoor weathering will destroy bar codes printed on paper. Bar codes are available etched into metal and ceramic materials that can withstand far more abuse than paper and plastic but still are sensitive to abrasion, strong chemicals, and extremes of temperature. Bar codes also are impractical where the symbols will be covered by painting or packaging operations. And, in some applications, there is simply no place to put a bar code.

Optical Character Recognition

Optical character recognition (OCR) is the direct interpretation of human-readable characters by a scanning device. The most popular method uses one of several type fonts designed specifically for OCR use. OCR is a printed medium and, therefore, shares many of the characteristics of bar codes; information encoded must be relatively stable and must be protected from environmental extremes. The major advantage of OCR over bar coding is the elimination of separate machine-readable and human-readable symbols. This advantage can be important when limited space is available as, for instance, on a retail price tag.

The technology of optical character recognition has improved in recent years. While first time read rates have improved significantly, they remain below those of most bar codes. Generally, this is because scanner alignment requirements are harder to meet and because OCR does not contain the redundancy of bar codes. OCR is, therefore, more sensitive to dirt and wear than bar codes. Further, OCR's alignment needs rule out operatorless operation. And, OCR printing and reading equipment is only slightly less expensive than bar code printers and readers.

OCR scanners also exist that are capable of reading typeset and ordinary computer-printed pages and even hand printing. These devices, compared to bar coding and even to the scanning of OCR fonts, are slow and highly error-prone. They are not recommended for automatic identification use in inventory systems.

Radio Frequency Identification

Radio frequency identification (RFID) uses devices called RF tags that communicate via radio waves with a transceiver and then to the inventory system (see Figure 6.17). An RF tag is a silicon chip that can absorb energy from a radio field and use that energy to make a low-power radio transmission. Simple tags can transmit a unique serial number programmed into the tag as part of its manufacture. More sophisticated tags can update an internal database and rebroadcast variable information. These tags often require an external power source.

RF tags can be packaged in a variety of ways. They can be glued to surfaces, encapsulated in packaging materials, or even buried in a concrete floor. Properly packaged, they can be impervious to almost all environmental considerations except extreme heat. Because RFID is applicable in extreme environments, it attracts interesting applications.

A veterinarian can implant a glass-encapsulated RF tag about the size of a grain of rice under the skin of a pet. Animal shelters, using an RF scanner, can electronically read the RF tag's serial number and the animal's owner can be quickly located. Because the microchip is under the animal's skin, it can't be lost and won't be noticed by thieves. The result: pets saved, less hassle for the shelters, and less trauma for pet owners.

The U.S. Fish and Wildlife Service injects more than 50,000 RF tags into salmon as they are released into the Columbia River each year. At key points in the river, the salmon are forced to swim through pipes to circumvent dams. An-

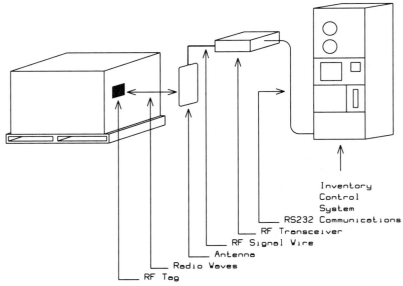

Figure 6.17. RFID connectivity. RFID systems operate much like RF terminals but communicate with an RF tag rather than a human-operated terminal.

tennas wrapped around the pipes allow computers to track the migratory patterns of the salmon.

Washington D.C.'s National airport has replaced a card-based security system with RF tags. RF tags are now fastened to the frames of official vehicles and antennas are buried in driveways. A computer reads the tags and controls vehicle gates, providing access and logging movements. Drivers no longer need come to a full stop, and problems with lost access cards have been solved. Further, drivers need not roll windows down to gain access in bad weather.

Chrysler attaches RF tags to the frame of the cars it builds, uniquely identifying each vehicle as it moves down the assembly line. Body parts, paint colors, and trim items are automatically matched by computers and process controllers. The RF tags pass through the paint and final trim shops and are then removed just before shipment and reused. The system was justified based on increased accuracy and reduced clerical labor (*Auto ID News,* February 1989).

In an inventory application, RFID has several possibilities. For instance:

- RF tags can be attached to the product with antennas located at strategic points throughout the facility. The tag serial number can then be used as the identifier for the product. As material is moved from place to place, the computer is notified automatically. In particular, product moving on conveyors can be detected and identified at checkpoints.

  As one example, imagine a conveyor sortation system that delivers material to loading doors. As each product is picked, the picker identifies it to the system, places an RF tag on the material, and sends it on its way. The conveyor first passes an antenna, which causes the tag's serial number to be read. The serial number is then sent to the inventory system, which uses it to locate the specific pick and thus the customer's order and the loading door. The product next enters the sortation system, eventually emerging at a loading door where it passes another antenna. The second antenna reads the serial number again and the inventory system verifies that the product has arrived at the correct door. The result: virtually 100 percent protection against sorting errors.

- RF tags can be applied to carriers such as totes or pallets instead of product. When the carriers are reused rather than being shipped to the customer, this eliminates the need to recover the tags before shipment for reuse.

- In another example, RF tags can be buried in the floor (concrete can be poured over them since they require no power source) and antennas mounted on lift trucks. The antennas can be connected through radio modems to the inventory system or can be operated through the auxiliary port of a radio terminal. When, for instance, a drive-in rack is used, the tags can automatically report the lift truck's location to the inventory system. The result: hands-off validation of put away and pick operations (see Figure 6.18). Note that this example depends on

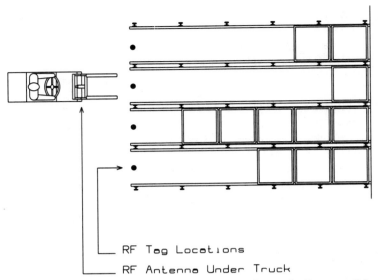

Figure 6.18. Using RFID with a drive-in pallet rack. One possible use for RFID tags is the validation of material movements in a drive-in rack. RFID tags can be buried in the floor as shown in the figure and an antenna can be mounted on or under the lift truck. This provides the basic mechanism to detect the truck's location and determine whether or not material is being handled as specified.

some rather sophisticated programming and on fairly exact placement of the tags in the floor. While workable for a drive-in rack, it would be difficult to apply to open floor storage because nothing would prevent a lift truck driver from driving across many tags to reach the assigned location.

- Or, RF tags can be attached to people, laminated, for instance, into ID badges. If an antenna is then placed at a doorway, the computer system can be notified as people move from room to room. This application of RFID can be particularly useful when security is a problem as, for instance, in drug companies and military contractors.

RFID systems vary from manufacturer to manufacturer in several ways. One of the most important variables is the maximum allowed distance between the RF tag and the antenna. Distances up to 30 inches may be achievable under some circumstances, but many RFID systems require the antenna to be much closer. This is particularly important to material handling and inventory systems since it implies more exact alignment between the antenna and the tag than one might assume.

Probably the most important disadvantage of RF tags is their cost. While RF tag reader costs are similar to the cost of high-quality bar code readers, the tags themselves typically cost 20 to 50 times the cost of a printed bar code symbol.

RF tags, therefore, are best used in circumstances where they can be recovered and reused, rather than being shipped to the customer as are many bar codes.

Magnetic Strip

Magnetic strips, either on cards or mounted to a surface, are an interesting alternative to bar codes. The advantages of magnetic strips are their resistance to dirt and wear and their independence of any light source. Magnetic strips are also impossible to photocopy and have a much higher information density than do bar codes. Disadvantages are relatively costly encoding and reading equipment and media and a sensitivity to strong electromagnetic fields.

Magnetic strips have been used successfully in ID badges and in labor-reporting job cards. They are less useful in cases where the mixing of media is important such as, for instance, the need to print a bar code on a packing list. Magnetic strips also need physical contact between the strip and the reader.

Magnetic Ink Character Recognition

Although not strictly optical, a technology known as magnetic ink character recognition (MICR) can be thought of as a special subset of OCR. MICR is widely used by the banking industry to identify and sort canceled checks. Because almost all available MICR equipment is designed specifically for check handling, the technology has seen little application elsewhere.

The Cauzin Strip

Relative to bar coding and other automatic identification methods, the Cauzin strip is a new development. Although similar to bar coding in some respects, the Cauzin strip is capable of information densities of 150 to 1000 characters per square inch. It can encode the full 256 ASCII character set, graphics, and almost anything a user might want to represent. As a printed technology, it can be produced on demand, photocopied, or preprinted on a printing press.

Figure 6.19 shows a small portion of a sample strip, much magnified. Real strips are about an inch wide and many inches longer. The strip is essentially a grid, consisting of black and white squares. Each column on the grid represents a character. The grid locations are divided into pairs with each pair assuming a binary value (1 or 0). The binary 1 is represented by a black square over a white square; the binary 0 by a white square over a black one. Additional rows provide parity checking. Rows on the top and bottom (the "rack" and "checkerboard") are for reader alignment. A header on the left end of the strip (as shown in Figure 6.19) carries density information for the reader.

Cauzin strips can be printed on most printers and are read with optical readers. Unlike bar codes, the technology is patented and users must purchase licenses for access to it. The most important aspect of the Cauzin strip from the viewpoint of an inventory control system is its ability to handle large amounts of information in a small space. For instance, in a critical lot-tracking situation, the entire

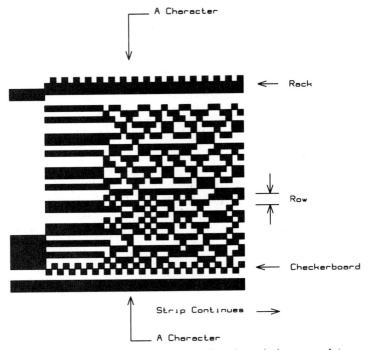

Figure 6.19. The Cauzin strip. The Cauzin strip is a proprietary technology capable of handling very high-information densities. This illustration is much enlarged.

history of a production lot could be printed in strip form and stored with the material. Should field problems arise, remote devices could read the complete service history and make it available to the service person.

The biggest drawback to the Cauzin strip is that it must be removed from the object it identifies and placed in a scanner to be read. This means that strips can be misplaced or lost, adding a potential source of error into the inventory system. Further, in inventory systems, there is only an infrequent need to encode this much information.

APPLICATION

Automatic identification is best applied as a replacement for the keyboard when fixed, known data is to be entered. Automatic identification has two major benefits:

1. When properly applied, near-zero transaction error rates can be achieved and near-perfect inventory accuracy can be supported.
2. In most cases where the data is to be entered repetitively, automatic

identification is less expensive than key entry. This is particularly true when operatorless equipment can be used.

Automatic identification in inventory systems can be summarized in two major application categories:

1. Attended. The primary attended application of automatic identification is the validation of material movements. Secondary applications are the identification of work arriving at a work station, the identification of containers, vehicles, and other objects, and the identification of people (at log-on time).

2. Unattended. Unattended automatic identification applications usually involve conveyor systems. In these cases, arriving materials are identified and the inventory system uses the identity of the material to determine how it should be processed or routed through the conveyors. Other applications of unattended automatic identification are rare.

Automatic identification and validation are the two most important techniques for achieving accurate inventory records. Properly applied, they can eliminate essentially all opportunity for error in the preparation, execution, and recording of inventory transactions.

7

Alternatives to Automatic Identification

Many businesses run into situations where automatic identification is neither desirable nor feasible, yet where accuracy is essential for inventory purposes. Examples of these kinds of situations include:

1. Products being processed through operations where automatic ID devices—even RF tags—will not survive. Examples include extreme heat or cold, high chemical concentrations, painting operations, and others. Also included in this category are operations where automatic ID devices are not allowed because of the possibility of contamination. Some drug and integrated circuit manufacturing processes fall into this category.
2. High-speed picking operations. In these operations, pickers need both hands for picking and have little time to handle bar code scanners and read bar codes to validate picks.
3. Products stored or processed in locations which are not under the company's direct control. Examples include public warehouses and manufacturing operations performed at a vendor's plant. In both cases, the owner of the material is not in a position to implement validation or automatic identification.
4. Fluids emerging from a refinery or processing facility at, for instance, a packaging machine. If the fluids are incorrectly identified, the resulting inventory records will be wrong. Yet there is no way to put a label on them before they are packaged.

There are also requirements in virtually every inventory system for the entry of nonidentification information. Examples include:

1. Counts. It is generally good practice to design both material handling and inventory systems to minimize the need for employees to count product. At times, however, counting is unavoidable and must be entered by production workers and material handlers.
2. Codes. Inventory systems often require information that is entered in coded form. One example might be the reason code entered when product is substituted.
3. Test results, such as those arising from a quality control inspection. While entry of test results might not be considered to be an inventory system function, accuracy is affected when results are entered incorrectly. Therefore, entry methods are of interest to inventory systems designers and users.
4. Account numbers, job numbers, and a host of other miscellaneous information must be entered from time to time. Accuracy is the byword. The methods used can have a real impact on the overall accuracy of the system.

Although bar code menu sheets can sometimes be used to enter nonidentification information, there are other times when the number of possible values is simply too numerous to list. In these cases the use of automatic identification is almost always ruled out. Yet, the achievement of inventory accuracy makes it necessary that the data be entered with high levels of accuracy. What, then, are the alternatives? There are five. Ranked approximately in order of desirability, they are:

1. Avoid data entry altogether. In some cases identification may not be necessary. For instance, parts might be carried through a degreasing operation on an overhead conveyor. If the parts are loaded onto the conveyor with validation, the inventory system can be certain of their identity and sequence. If the system tracks them through degreasing, identification as they leave is unnecessary because the conveyor is known to enforce departure in the same sequence as arrival.

   An inventory system, therefore, should never ask for data that it already has unless there is a possibility that the data could be wrong or obsolete. Deciding where the system can be certain of accuracy and where doubt exists can be a difficult design issue. Often, as in the case of the degreaser, the answer involves the physical make-up of the processes and material handling equipment.
2. Use automatic identification methods at a later time or in a different place. High-speed picking, for instance, lends itself to this approach in some cases. When a conveyor system is used to take completed picks away from the picking area, pick lists can be printed on label stock along with bar codes that identify the pick. The pickers pick the quantities shown on each label and attach the label to the product. The completed pick is then conveyed past a laser scanner that reads the previously attached product ID label and the pick label.

Once the two labels are read, the order is retrieved from the system's database. A check is made by the system to verify that the material ordered is, in fact, the material that was picked. If the pick was made correctly, it is then validated and the information collected can be used to control the conveyor sortation system. If an error was made, the product can be sent to a reject chute and the pick can be put back on file for another attempt in a later picking wave.

Similarly, the movement of material within a public warehouse or a subcontractor's plant generally cannot be tracked using automatic identification methods because the equipment and training required are not present. These facilities, however, can be treated like "black boxes" by the inventory system. In other words, the entire facility can be handled as though it were a single, large storage location with the ability to handle unlimited quantities of an unlimited number of items. Movements of material to these facilities are validated as they are loaded onto the outgoing trailer. Movements of material coming back are validated upon return.

3. Get the required data from another source. In some circumstances, the data required can be gotten reliably from another system or another piece of equipment. For instance, unless refineries are small, they are probably operated by process control computers or programmable controllers. The device that controls the pumping of material probably knows what it is handling. Changes to its software and a communications line between it and the inventory system can eliminate the need for automatic identification of the material. Or the process controller can be programmed to print bar-coded labels for the material being filled. These labels can then be used to identify material to the inventory system.

   Production and material handling counts can sometimes be obtained from other sources. For instance, the counting of small parts can be automated with electronic counting scales. Or production equipment may be operated by a process control computer that can provide the quantity produced. Or an existing shop floor data collection system may be able to provide adequately accurate count information. The use of equipment interfaces to obtain reliable information is discussed in more detail below.

4. Have a human enter the data through a nonkeyboard technology. Several technologies exist that can effectively replace keyboards with devices that achieve high accuracy rates. The entry of the codes might, for instance, be done with a touch screen. These technologies are described in more detail later.

5. When absolutely necessary, key the data using key entry methods specially designed for accuracy. In most businesses, the entry of test results and information such as account numbers will be through a keyboard because no better method can be found at a reasonable

price. Intelligent design of key entry facilities can go a long way toward accuracy in keying.

MACHINE INTERFACES

Interfaces between inventory systems and a variety of other intelligent devices are a rich source of reliable information for an inventory system. These interfaces are most useful in the tracking of work-in-process and in-transit inventories.

Over the years, attempts have been made to connect business applications directly with production and material handling equipment. One way to make these interconnections is through a device called an analog-digital (A/D) converter. An A/D converter is a circuit board that reads electrical signals (voltages or current flows generated by a machine), converts the signals into digital values, and places the digital values in memory for access by the processor. While attempts to communicate with production equipment via A/D converters have been successful in some instances, many businesses have found that:

1. General purpose computers are not always appropriate in the real-time atmosphere of the shop. There are two reasons: (a) Physical survival is problematic when a computer is placed outside the protected environment of the computer room, and (b) response times are not always adequately reliable and consistent when other software is competing for resources in a multiprogramming system.
2. The skills required to write and maintain the software necessary are different from those required to write and maintain business applications. These skills can be hard to come by and hard to keep.

Because these difficulties exist, most connections between inventory systems and real-world devices are now being written for special-purpose process control computers known as programmable logic controllers. The programmable logic controllers handle interface work and assume responsibility for some of the control requirements. They free the inventory system from the need for high-speed on-line monitoring of equipment and thus greatly simplify programming.

Programmable Logic Controllers

Programmable logic controllers are becoming more and more common in the manufacturing and distribution industries. These devices are actually general-purpose computers that have been modified for their intended use. (In this chapter the term "programmable logic controller," or PLC, is used instead of the equivalent term "programmable controller" to avoid confusion between PC as an abbreviation for personal computer and PC as an abbreviation for programmable controller.) Specifically, the changes made to PLCs are intended for:

1. Survival in the industrial environment. Dust and dirt are assumed to be present. Conditions are not always stable. Mechanical vibration

and electro-magnetic interference can be present. Humidity and temperature ranges can be significant.

2. Ease of use by plant electricians and technicians. Interfaces for connecting devices are part of the machine and conform to building codes. Hardware is modular. Self-diagnostic circuits are included. Software programming uses electrical conventions.

3. Real-time operation. Although most programmable controllers are single programming (one program at a time), their special-purpose software makes them fast enough to keep up with events in the real world.

Typical PLC applications include material handling and process operation. Material handling applications include conveyors, carousels, automated storage and retrieval system (AS/RS) machines, and automated guided vehicle (AGV) systems. Process applications include the operation of machine tools, pumping, plating, painting, cutting, wrapping, blending, treating, and packaging systems. The PLC excels where input from real-world sensors must be blended with input from a user or from another computer system with outputs going to various devices and actuators. Feedback transactions are also often generated and transmitted back to the user or host computer. Many PLC systems are capable of communicating with other computers either synchronously or asynchronously and can handle either the ASCII or the EBCDIC character sets.

Figure 7.1 shows an example of the use of a programmable logic controller in a very simple conveyor sortation system. Product is assumed to be bar coded. It is loaded on the left end of the conveyor and is carried to the right. The product first passes a sensor that detects its presence and raises (or drops) a voltage on the line to the PLC. The PLC recognizes the voltage change and passes a signal (usually an asynchronous message) to the bar code scanner, which turns itself on and looks for a recognizable bar code. If the scanner finds a bar code within a fixed period of time, it decodes the symbol and passes the decoded value back to the PLC. The PLC then reports to the inventory system that it is now sorting a particular item. Or, if the scanner is unable to find a bar code, it passes a message to the PLC to the effect that it was unable to find anything. When no-reads occur the PLC might inform the inventory system, or it might select its own programmed-in default.

The inventory system then decides which lane the product should be sorted into. This decision might involve a look-up in a file of products that are planned for loading onto the conveyor system. It might involve calculations based on the space available in the various lanes. Or it might involve entirely different logic, based on the application. In any event, when the lane has been selected, the inventory system responds to the PLC with the product's identification and the selected lane number. The PLC adds that product to a stack, or work queue.

Some time later, the product will pass the next sensor. If it is to be diverted into lane 1, the PLC will wait a predetermined amount of time and then signal the air cylinder that operates the diverter at lane 1, causing the product to be diverted. Or, if the product is not intended for lane 1, the PLC will simply note

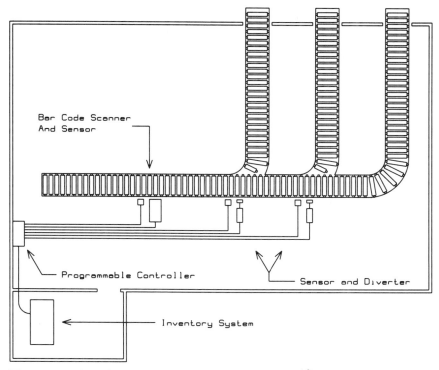

Figure 7.1. Simple conveyor sortation system. Programmable logic controllers are used for a variety of interfaces between equipment and inventory systems. In this example, a bar code identifying material is read as the material passes the scanner. The inventory system determines which lane the material should be put on and the programmable logic controller operates the diverters as necessary to put it there.

the product's passage and wait for it to show up at lane 2. When the product is eventually diverted to the proper lane, the PLC will remove it from its work queue and inform the host computer that it has sorted the item.

This PLC application seems so simple that it may be hard to understand why a specialized computer is required to implement it. In most real-life cases, however, conveyor sorters routinely handle hundreds of items simultaneously and manage dozens of divert points. The added complexity of real-time tracking of all these things makes the need for the PLC more obvious. And, even in this simple example, the PLC is likely to pay for itself in reduced programming and testing costs and in increased reliability.

In addition to conveyor systems, PLCs are often employed as machine and machine center controllers. Information of interest to an inventory control system can often be drawn from these PLCs with very high reliability. But, the inventory system designer should make a detailed review of the operations controlled by the PLC to assure that the PLC's programming is capable of handling exceptions and unusual situations adequately. In some cases a supplementary inventory system terminal might be advisable.

For example, a manufacturer of small capacitors had an automated assembly machine operated by a PLC. The machine did its own setup and, therefore, knew the part number being built. Since it controlled the assembly of each piece and even tested the completed product, it was able to keep accurate count of both good production and scrap. However, the machine operator also spot-checked the machine's output and would occasionally reject units for problems that the machine could not detect. Missing or illegible part number stamps on the capacitor cases were one of the causes.

This particular operation was never integrated into a superaccurate inventory system. Had it been, however, it would have required both an interface to the machine's PLC and an inventory control terminal to allow the operator to override or change the PLC's production counts. Another design might have called for a button for the operator to push when rejects were found. The PLC could have sensed the button and made its own adjustments prior to communicating the counts to the inventory system.

More detailed information about the capturing of production counts appears in Chapter 9.

Scales

Accurate counting of small parts is often a problem. Bored material handlers make estimates instead of actually counting or, even if they do count, often make mistakes. Further, the counting of small parts is time consuming and expensive.

Many small parts counting problems can be solved with electronic counting scales. These scales can be strategically placed in key locations throughout a stockroom, warehouse, or plant and can transmit counts directly to the inventory control system. Accuracies on the order of one part in a thousand are generally achievable when part weights are consistent from item to item. This is, of course, much better than is possible with manual counting. And the direct communications link eliminates the possibility of key entry errors. For example, see Figure 7.2., which shows a small stockroom that uses an electronic counting scale to assure accuracy in receipts and disbursements.

In the figure, most of the stockroom is devoted to inventory stored in bins, on shelves, or in drawers. One corner, however, makes up the working area. It consists of a receiving area large enough to accept incoming pallets through a lift-truck-sized door and a counting and disbursing area. The counting area is equipped with an inventory system terminal, a bar code wand, and an electronic counting scale, wired to the inventory system. A section of shelving for return-to-stock items separates the two working areas.

The receiving area is not a true receiving area because incoming material has already been processed through the plant receiving area. It is, therefore, identified and has been counted. The purchase order has been checked, and accounts payable has been notified of the receipt. The stockroom receiving area is actually only a depalletization point.

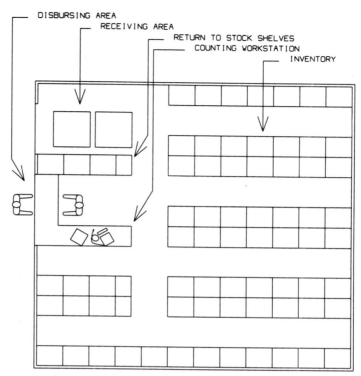

Figure 7.2. Small parts stockroom illustrating the use of electronic counting scales. Electronic counting scales can increase accuracy dramatically when small parts must be counted. This figure illustrates their use in the small, self-contained stockroom.

When material arrives, a stockkeeper scans the bar-coded label on each receipt using a portable terminal (not shown in the drawing). The bar code contains a receipt number and a storage location number within the stockroom. The portable terminal displays the storage location on its screen. The stockkeeper then puts the material away and validates the put-away by scanning the bar-coded label on the storage location. The portable terminal compares this location number with the one first scanned and complains (with a beep) if they differ. When errors occur, the stockkeeper is allowed to move the material to correct the error and may then rescan the location label. Several times each shift the stockkeeper connects the portable terminal with the inventory system using an interface cable in the counting area and uploads the put-away information. This makes the newly received inventory available for picking.

Employees wanting to withdraw material arrive at the stockroom with bar-coded work orders. One possible work order design is shown in Figure 7.3. This document is divided into three parts. The top part describes the order, displaying the order number, the item being built, the quantity to be built, the planned start

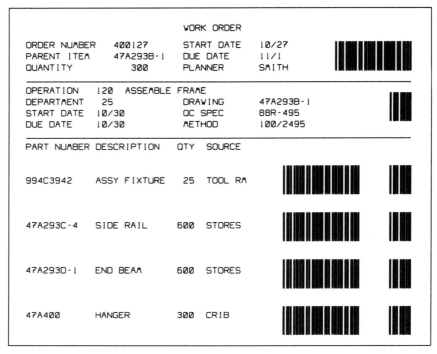

Figure 7.3. Sample work order document. Work orders comprise the basic form of communication between shop planners and the operating people. This design also includes the bar codes required to control the movement of material from the stockroom to the shop floor.

and due dates for the order, and the name of the planner. It includes a bar code containing the order number. The second part of the work order describes a single operation, in this case a main frame assembly. The operation number and description, department number, start and due dates for the operation, and references to the drawings, quality control specifications, and method documentation are included. The bar code in the second part of the work order contains the operation number.

The third and final part of the work order lists the component parts, tools, and fixtures required. Each is specified with a part number and description, the quantity required to complete the work order, and a source. The source column lists only the stockroom or warehouse from which the material is to be obtained, not the specific location. Each item required to complete the work order is accompanied by two bar codes. One bar code contains the location from which the items should be picked and the other contains the quantity.

When an employee arrives with a work order, the stockkeeper in the stockroom in Figure 7.2 uses a portable terminal to scan all the bar codes in sequence, top to bottom and left to right. Each bar code contains a prefix character as well as the data, so the portable terminal can recognize out-of-sequence scans and take exception to them. When scanning is complete, the portable terminal discards locations that are not in that particular stockroom, sorts the picks in location sequence, and displays the location number of the first pick. The stockkeeper moves from one bin to the next, picking material and validating the picks by scanning the bar codes on the location labels. As each pick is validated, the portable terminal displays the location of the next one. Where quantities are small, the stockkeeper counts as picking is done and takes only the exact quantity required. Where quantities are large (possibly greater than 10 pieces), the stockkeeper does not count but simply takes "enough."

Next, the stockkeeper moves to the counting area. Large-quantity parts are placed on the counting scale one at a time. The bar code wand attached to the inventory system is used to scan the work order and operation numbers along with the specific item bar codes. The inventory control system displays a screen that tells the stockkeeper how many parts to add to or subtract from the scale. The quantity on the scale is adjusted until this screen shows zero. The parts are then disbursed to the requester.

Later, when the portable terminal is uploaded to the inventory system, the parts are deducted from the on-hand quantity and allocations are relieved. Leftovers from the counting process are either put into temporary places in the return bins to be returned to stock later or are returned immediately. In either case, their return is validated with the portable terminal to assure that they are returned to the correct location and are not lost in the wrong bin.

Other orders are generated by the inventory and production control systems. These orders are downloaded to a portable terminal and can be prepicked and staged waiting for pickup.

Figures 7.2 and 7.3 illustrate only one possible use of electronic scales. The design is heavily influenced by the need for the stockkeeper to carry material to the scale. However, the example could have been taken one step further with a portable scale. All that would have been required would have been a power source for the scale (batteries), a means of moving it (a cart), and a communications method (through an auxiliary port on the portable terminal).

Electronic noncounting scales can also be used to obtain counts if container tare weights and part unit weights are known. Typically, if a tote of mixed parts is picked in a stockroom, the gross tote weight can be compared to a calculated value and counting problems can be detected within about 5 percent of the weight. While this level of accuracy might not be as high as some might wish, it is adequate to catch many errors and can be another contributor to overall inventory accuracy.

Other Counting Methods

Other accurate parts counting technologies exist. One company makes large quantities of kits for customer assembly. Each of the kits contains precisely counted quantities of many small parts. This company has developed its own automated high speed packing and counting equipment. Parts are dropped from vibrator bowls through a detector-counter into a plastic bag.

Unitization is another effective way of obtaining accurate counts. Unitization is the packaging of material in standard quantities, usually called "unit loads." When a tote, box, or pallet contains a known quantity, material handlers can simply count the unit loads and multiply by the unit load quantity. This is much faster and much more accurate than counting by hand. Some companies go so far as to design special carriers or tote inserts to handle products. Each insert is shaped for a single product and will handle only a specific number of them. These companies also often require that every time materials are moved, partial pallets be combined to make full pallets and that partial totes be combined to make full totes. Material handlers, therefore, know that every movement contains no more than one partial pallet and no more than one partial tote. Inventory and shop floor control systems allow for the direct entry of the number of full pallets, the number of full totes on the one partial pallet, and the number of pieces contained in the one partial tote. This allows the system to do the calculations, simplifying the material handler's job and improving accuracy even further.

Vision Systems

Vision systems have potential as parts counters although they are usually best applied to more sophisticated problems where counting is only a portion of the job. For example, Figure 7.4 shows a top and side view of a parts counting application in which parts are classified by size as well as counted. Two video cameras view objects passing on a conveyor. One camera takes a top scan. The other sees the objects from the side. Both video images are fed to an analyzer, which measures the height, width, and length of the objects, classifies them, and transmits their size to the inventory system.

Vision system technology is still evolving. Far more complex and more general in scope than bar coding, machine vision systems are used most often for parts sorting and classifying, inspecting, and positioning. Some machine vision systems in some circumstances can even read and decode bar codes and human-readable characters. Machine vision systems are not of primary importance to inventory systems or to the achievement of inventory accuracy. But, the technology is available and has enough unique characteristics to be worth remembering.[1]

NONKEYBOARD DATA ENTRY

If a machine interface is either impractical or uneconomic in a particular application, it falls to a human to enter data into the inventory system. Under many circumstances, keyboards are the most labor intensive and error-prone method

---

[1]More information about the growing technology of machine vision can be fond in Zuech, Nello, *Applying Machine Vision,* New York: John Wiley & Sons, 1988.

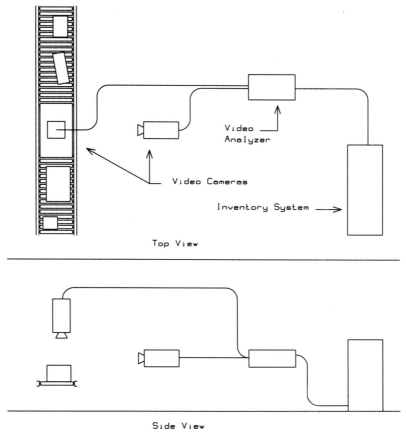

Figure 7.4. Machine vision application. Machine vision is a relatively new technology with possible significant application in inventory systems.

available. But, they are only one of the possible data entry methods. Several others deserve consideration.

Mark-Sense

Mark-sense is a technology in which printed forms are used. A grid of boxes is printed on the form, usually in gray or blue ink. Each row of boxes represents one character of the alphabet or one numeric digit; each column represents one character in a message. The characters that will make up the message are indicated by blackening the appropriate boxes with a pencil. Completed forms are then passed through a reader that optically senses the blackened boxes and deciphers the data. Mark-sense technology is often used by educational institutions for testing purposes. Figure 7.5 shows a mark-sense inventory withdrawal form as one example of its possible use.

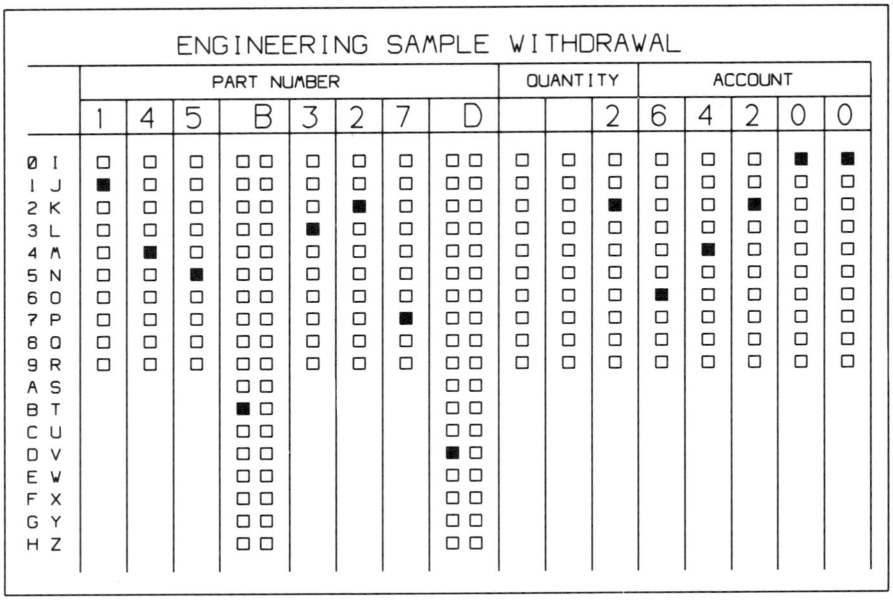

```
 ENGINEERING SAMPLE WITHDRAWAL
┌──────────────── PART NUMBER ────────────────┬── QUANTITY ──┬──── ACCOUNT ────┐
│  1   4   5   B   3   2   7   D  │       2  │  6   4   2   0   0  │
```

Figure 7.5. Mark-sense withdrawal form. Mark-sense forms like the one illustrated can be effectively used to control some kinds of withdrawals and other material movements.

Mark-sense is a fully mature technology. Readers and forms are relatively inexpensive and training requirements are minimal. Because the key entry step is eliminated, data accuracy levels tend to be higher than with manual handwrite-and-key systems. However, the time required to fill out a mark-sense form is greater than that required to simply handwrite information.

There is a story—probably apocryphal—that the first push-button telephones were designed with their keypads upside down (compared to 10-key adding machines) to reduce the rate at which skilled users could enter phone numbers. According to the story, the first generation of touch-tone equipment couldn't keep up with the fastest users and, as a result, all telephones now have upside down keypads. In some sense, mark-sense data entry achieves accuracy in the same way; the user is slowed down by the marking process and is, therefore, more careful and more accurate.

Voice Recognition and Speech Synthesis

Typically these two technologies are applied together to provide two-way spoken communication. The advantage is that they allow humans and machines to communicate through natural spoken language. Both accuracy and productivity can be high. In a typical application (see Figure 7.6), an employee communicates with the inventory system through a headset. Spoken words are detected by a microphone and carried down a cable to a battery powered transmitter worn on the

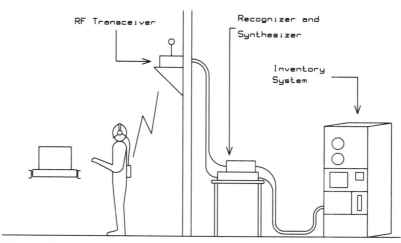

Figure 7.6. Use of voice communications. Person-to-computer voice communication has the advantage of leaving the person unburdened with equipment. Both hands and both eyes remain free for the job, while data can still be recorded in a natural and easy-to-learn way.

employee's belt. From there they are transmitted to a transceiver and passed to the voice recognizer. The voice recognizer separates and identifies individual words and passes them to the inventory control computer in the form of ASCII character strings. The inventory system processes the information as necessary and responds to the employee by passing one or more ASCII character strings to a voice synthesizer. The synthesizer converts the character strings to analog signals that are carried to the transceiver on a cable and transmitted from there to the employee.

Speech synthesis and voice recognition are separate and distinct technologies, working in entirely different ways. Either can be used without the other, but if voice recognition is used alone, some method of feedback to the employee is required. This feedback can be accomplished through a screen, a system of beeps transmitted to the employee, colored lights, or a variety of other methods. Speech synthesis, however, is often a good solution.

Speech synthesis is the simpler of the two technologies. One method allows entire messages to be prerecorded in digital form and "played" (actually reconstructed) on command from the computer. Another method involves the true synthesis of speech. In this method, the actual words to be spoken are passed to the synthesizer as a character string. The synthesizer retrieves sounds from its database according to the characters seen and applies a series of rules to modify the sounds, making them into intelligible speech. While the "prerecorded" method produces a higher quality result, true synthesis offers more flexibility and reduces the time required to set up the system. The performance of many true synthesizers can be enhanced by spelling messages phonetically or, at times, even by misspelling them.

There are two basic kinds of voice recognizers: speaker dependent and speaker independent. Both kinds begin with a digitized version of the electrical impulses generated by the microphone. Speaker-independent recognizers match the pattern of the speech with standard patterns to identify words to be passed to the computer. Speaker-dependent systems also match patterns. But rather than matching against standard voice patterns, they match against prerecorded samples spoken by the individual whose voice is being recognized. Because differences in pronunciation, rhythm, tone, and inflection between people are taken out of consideration, speaker-dependent systems use simpler pattern matching algorithms. They are, therefore, faster and more reliable than speaker-independent systems and can support much larger vocabularies.

Speaker-dependent voice recognition is the better developed and more popular technology, even though it requires that each user "train" the recognizer. Training of the recognizer generally requires that the individual repeat a phrase three to five times into a microphone and then key the matching message or code. The recognizer averages the samples it has received and stores the resulting pattern along with the code for future use.

Inventory systems can, in some instances, turn the need to train voice recognizers into an advantage. First, there is no necessary connection between the spoken words and the characters the recognizer sends to the computer. Therefore message data can be simplified, message lengths reduced, and computing resource requirements limited. For instance, the message, "I just closed the door," might be used on a shipping dock. Through the voice recognizer, this message could be converted to "14." The 14 could, in turn, be the address of a table entry that tells the system what action to take.

Another advantage of voice recognition is language independence. Neither the voice recognizer nor the synthesizer care whether the word "yes" is pronounced "yes," "si," "ja," "oui," or even "da."

Speaker-dependent voice recognition can also provide a measure of security. If logon is accomplished through the recognizer, only those people who have had the opportunity to train the recognizer will have patterns on file that match their voices. Only these people, then, will be allowed to sign onto the system.

Touch Screens

Touch screens are CRT display screens that are made sensitive to the touch of a finger. For instance, imagine a menu displayed on a touch screen. When a user touches one of the options, the touch screen device senses the presence and location of the finger, enabling the software to identify the option touched and proceed with its execution.

Touch screens are most commonly implemented as shown in Figure 7.7. A normal screen is surrounded by a special bezel (the frame around the front edge of the cathode-ray tube). On two adjoining sides of the bezel, infrared light emitters generate invisible light beams. On the other two sides, collectors gather that light. When a finger touches the screen, at least two of the beams are interrupted and, therefore, light ceases to reach two of the collectors. The controlling electronics detects the changes and converts them into the coordinates of the point

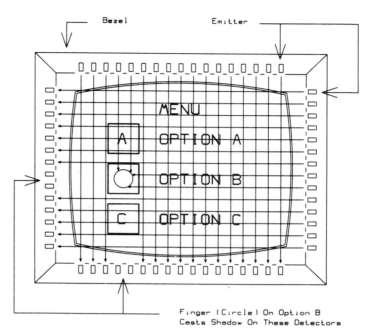

Figure 7.7. Touch screen construction. Touch screens work by sensing the shadow of a person's finger on the screen. The shadows are usually cast in infrared light and, therefore, are not visible to the naked eye.

touched. The coordinates are passed to the computer, which translates them into an action command.

The real value of touch screens lies in their ease of use. Little or no training is required and accuracy is more likely to result than with keyboards. There are, of course, additional hardware and software costs that must be balanced against the benefits of touch screens. But, in appropriate applications, the costs are minor compared to the benefits.

In inventory systems, touch screens are best used when employees must choose among a limited set of options, as in a menu. At times, numeric entry can be done efficiently with an on-screen keypad. If the user's eyes are already focused on the screen, a touch screen keypad will probably be faster and more accurate than one on a keyboard. In general, it is not advisable to mix touch screens with keyboards because the user looses both time and accuracy when switching modes. The size of the touch points on the screen should be kept as large as possible and dead space should be allowed between them to minimize false selections.

As an example, touch screens might be useful in a UPS manifesting operation. Parcels might arrive at the shipping workstation on a conveyor and be slid onto a scale by the operator. If the shipping label contained the destination zip code in bar code form, an overhead laser scanner could read it while the scale transmitted the weight to the manifesting computer. The operator then need only select the special services required (i.e., oversize, COD, etc.) and key any amounts neces-sary (such as the COD amount). The selection of special services would be nearly an ideal application for a touch screen. And, unless a very large number of COD parcels are handled, COD amounts could also be entered through the touch screen.

EFFECTIVE KEY ENTRY TECHNIQUES

Some inventory data simply must be keyed. Key entry is notoriously inaccurate, but a close investigation of keying methods and accuracies discloses that some things are easier to key than others. Also, intelligent system design can simplify the process for users, substantially reduce error rates and thereby contribute to the overall level of accuracy.

Based partly on human psychology and physiology, and partly on computer technology, here is a list of ideas for improving key entry accuracy:

1. The guiding principle is to make it easier for the user to be right than to be wrong. At every step in the system design process, questions should be asked about possible errors, how they can be prevented or their probability reduced, and how they can be detected and corrected once made.

2. Consistency of data entry methods from screen to screen within a system and even across systems is important. Which key does the user push to blank out a field? Which key is a destructive backspace and which is nondestructive? Which key signals completion of a field or a screen? Which summons help? Confusion and frustration lead to errors.

3. Screen presentations also need to clearly state what's expected of the user. Field lengths, where fixed, should be shown. The user should know in advance of keying whether numeric or alphanumeric data is required. Colors and image reversals can help measurably.

4. Numeric data should be subjected to value and/or range checks in real time. The checks should be made immediately after completion of the field or no later than upon completion of the screen. Error mes-sages must be clear and unambiguous. In some critical cases, several nested range checks may be indicated with the severity of the error message and the amount of work required to override dependent on which limits were exceeded.

   For instance, a review of past inventory transactions might reveal that 95 percent of all transactions are for less than 10 pieces. If that were the case, key entered quantities from 1 to 9 might be accepted without question. Quantities between 10 and 20 might be accepted after presenting the message "Are You Sure the Quantity Is Right (Y/N)?" and receiving a positive response. Quantities greater than 20 might be also involve an inventory look-up to assure that adequate inventory is on hand. And quantities over 50 might require entry of an authorization code by a supervisor. This technique can, of course, be refined by making the range limits a function of the item number and, possibly, the stockroom, the job, and other factors.

5. Alphabetic data, where possible, should be verified against tables of preestablished values. If a material handler, for instance, moves a pallet to work center 42 in department F, the system should verify that department F exists and that it includes a work center 42. And this verification should be done while the user is still at the keyboard. In some circumstances, it may be possible to go further, verifying not only the existence of the department and work center but also the reasonableness of moving a particular kind of material to it. If, for instance, electronic circuit boards are delivered to the foundry, there is the strong possibility that a mistake has been made somewhere.

6. Default values are a double-edged sword and deserve special attention during system design. In some cases, the presentation of default entries that can be accepted by users simply by pressing the enter key can significantly improve accuracy and eliminate errors by suggesting an appropriate response. In other cases, defaults simply give the user an easy way out and encourage the entry of erroneous data.

   For instance, imagine a receiving dock where incoming material is counted and the counts are keyed. If an item is known to be shipped by the vendor in unit loads, the entry screen might allow a user to key the characters "FP" for full pallet or to enter a quantity when a partial pallet arrives. This technique eliminates the need to count most parts and eliminates counting errors without unduly tempting the receiving operator.

   As an example of the poor use of defaults, imagine a cycle counting operation in which the quantity entry field defaults to the on-hand balance. The counter will be sorely tempted to simply press Enter, avoiding the work of actually counting parts and knowing that the odds are favorable.

7. Codes, such as a quality control reject reason code, can be most accurately entered by uncoupling employees from the codes themselves. A screen of code descriptions can be displayed with a moving reverse-color bar. The user can move the bar to the description required and press Enter much more accurately (and more quickly) than he or she can enter a code. When the list of possible entries is long, a search facility may be required to help the user locate the desired one. Or, in some cases it may be possible to structure the list of entries in a hierarchy or order the list by frequency of use.

8

Inbound Operations

At first glance, accurate inventories appear easy to achieve. Material movements are the key. Control them, validate that they are done properly so errors cannot enter the inventory balances, and the result is accuracy. While the concept is simple, its application is not. Special considerations and requirements abound. Many of these special requirements result from the need to maintain a high level of productivity. Others result from physical constraints. Still others are caused by business considerations. The most common of these special requirements are discussed in this chapter and the two that follow. Few businesses will require all of the techniques described and the reader should select those that are of value and ignore the rest.

RECEIVING

In a very real sense, the receiving function is the most important one in an inventory facility when accuracy is considered. If receipts are made accurately and reliably, a foundation is established on which all other functions can lean. But, on the other hand, if errors are made in receiving, the work of all other functions is made more complex, more difficult, and more error prone. As a result, inventory accuracy becomes harder to achieve throughout the business.

Receiving's responsibility is assumed to end with the creation of loads of received material that have been accurately identified and counted and are ready to be put away. These loads may be in the form of pallets, cartons, totes, or containers of any kind. Some receiving departments are also responsible for the put-away of newly received stock, but this book considers put-away separately.

Traditional Receiving Operations

Receiving procedures vary from company to company based on a number of factors. Product size and value, carriers, the presence or absence of serial and/or lot numbers, requirements for product inspection, and other factors all play a part in shaping day-to-day receiving operations. This variation aside, traditional receiving usually involves several steps, each with some risk of error. In many businesses, these steps include:

1. Unloading of the trailer. The unloaded material is typically staged on the receiving dock floor.
2. Identification of the vendor and order, often done from the bill of lading, a packing list, or even a shipment label.
3. Verification that the items were, in fact, ordered.
4. Count of parcels, pallets, and other containers and inspection for external damage.
5. Verification that the items and quantities shown on the packing list are correct and that all material said by the vendor to be present is, in fact, present.
6. Inspection of the material to ensure that specifications have been met.
7. Palletization, sorting, or repackaging as required in preparation for putting the material away.
8. Staging the material in preparation for putting it away.
9. Notification to material handlers that the material can be put away.

Throughout this process, data can be recorded in several ways, the most common being handwritten notations on the packing list. The marked-up packing lists are then delivered to an office where they are keyed, constituting "receipt" of the material.

There are three key points in the receiving process. The first is the point at which receiving personnel decide that the carrier has met its obligations, the bill of lading or manifest is signed, and payment of the freight bill is authorized. The second key point occurs when the receivers decide that the vendor has met its obligations and generate the transactions necessary to authorize invoice payment. And the third is the point at which materials are added to the inventory and made available for allocation and use. Each of these key decision points involves a degree of risk.

Unless otherwise provided for, the receiving company usually bears risk of loss on incoming shipments. This means that failure on the part of receiving personnel to note missing parcels or take exception to external damage can weaken the company's case when a freight claim is filed. In some cases, in fact, this failure can eliminate all possibility of recovery from either the carrier or the vendor. Further, the counting done as parcels are unloaded from the trailer may be the only count performed on the receipt. If this is the case, an error made here will directly affect inventory accuracy because the erroneous count will eventually become the quantity put away.

The point at which receiving personnel decide that the vendor has met its obligations is often considered to be the point at which materials are "received." This is generally the point at which the materials should be added to inventory and reflected on the company's books. Risks at this point include incorrect part number identification, incorrect counting, and, if inspection is done, improper inspection. Any of these errors will result in an inventory error and a matching reduction in inventory accuracy.

Of all these risks, experience indicates that the most significant lie in the identification and counting of parts. Once the receiving department has properly identified and counted a pallet, has labeled it accurately, and has correctly established it in the inventory system's database, the rest of the organization can use the information with assurance that it will be right. The entire job of accurate inventories then becomes possible.

Access to Order Information

The first step in the development of an accurate receiving subsystem is to provide the receivers with on-line access to information about inbound orders. While most receiving departments already have a tub file of order copies, on-line access is important because it allows interaction between the receivers and the database. The system can edit and verify entries immediately. Problems, which are sure to occur, can be solved on the spot while the receiver's attention is still focused on the order being received. And, most important, when the receiver's attention turns to the next order, all of the required recordkeeping can be complete.

Many businesses prefer to operate their shop floor data collection and inventory systems on dedicated computers. This protects the shop and the warehouse against mainframe downtime and most variations in response times. When receiving's software runs on a distributed computer, the need for on-line access to the orders implies a download of the orders from the system that maintains them to the inventory system. Also implied is an upload communicating actual receipts back to the host so orders can be closed and bills paid. These communications can be on-line. Typically, however, it is as effective and significantly less costly to batch information at each end of the communications link and transmit it several times each day.

For many businesses, the receiving department will require information about all kinds of pending receipts: purchase orders, manufacturing orders, customer return authorizations, and inbound transfers from other plants or divisions. Because different kinds of receipts are handled differently, data requirements differ. Generally, the information required for purchase orders includes the order number or return authorization number, the vendor number, the vendor name, and the carrier name or number. In addition, for each item ordered, the item number, quantity ordered, anticipated arrival date, the vendor's part number, and the QC inspection requirements must be known.

Information must be available for all work orders (or shop schedules) that affect inventory. In most businesses, this means the entire work order file. The information required for each order usually consists of the order number, the planned start and completion date, and the item numbers and quantities required for all needed component parts. Work order information is also required for the picking and delivering of parts to the shop prior to the start of the order. See the discussion of picking and shipping in Chapter 10 for more information.

Even if formal receiving processes are not used on manufacturing completions, work order information is still required for the assignment of storage locations and the allocation of materials to customer orders. But the work order information need not necessarily be available in advance. Instead, it can be picked up as product is completed and accepted.

For inbound transfer orders and customer return authorizations, the data requirements are similar. They include an order or authorization number, a source plant or warehouse or a customer number, and a carrier name or number. For each item, the item number, and quantity, is necessary. An anticipated arrival date is useful.

The data requirements listed here assume that the receiving portion of the inventory system also has access to a part master file and, probably, to a vendor file, a department file, and a plant file. (An alternative method excludes access to these files and provides the necessary data as part of the transmission of each order.)

When an inventory system is not distributed (i.e., when it runs on the same computer as the purchasing and manufacturing systems), the download can be eliminated and direct access to database provided. But, whenever systems work simultaneously with the same files, care must be taken that only one program at a time attempts to update a single record. Record locking may be built into a database manager. But, if it is not, some other form of protection must be provided.

Electronic Transmission of Packing Lists

Standards for electronic data interchange (EDI) have been developed and are maintained by the American National Standards Institute. These standards are the basis for computer transmission of documents between businesses. Documents supported by the standard include purchase orders, invoices, remittance advices, price lists, quotations, shipping schedules, shipment notices, receiving advices, and more. Standards for new documents are being added periodically.

While EDI offers the promise of important savings to many businesses, it affects inventory accuracy only on the receiving dock. The shipment notice is a packing list transmitted electronically from the shipper to the receiver. Once received, it can serve to replace or to supplement access to purchase order data. From the viewpoint of the receivers, the major advantage of an electronic shipping notice over a purchase order copy is that only the items actually shipped will appear. There are, therefore, fewer exceptions to enter and labor costs will be lower.

Electronic shipping notices should, for security reasons, be verified against the open purchase order file before receiving personnel are allowed to use them. This verification can be done as part of the inventory system or it can be done elsewhere.

Order Identification

After the physical unloading of a trailer or rail car, the first step in most receiving processes is to identify the vendor and the purchase order number. Because shipping labels and packing lists vary from vendor to vendor, there can be no fixed method established. Most shipments will arrive clearly marked but some won't. The inventory system can assist in this process by providing reasonable search and inquiry capabilities.

For instance, imagine a parcel that has just arrived and is completely devoid of markings. The receiver verifies that it is addressed to the company and wasn't incorrectly delivered by the carrier. He or she then opens it and examines the content. Finding no paperwork, the receiver is faced with a search of the open order file based on the minimal information on hand. This information is limited to:

1. The date of receipt
2. The carrier
3. An approximate description of the material received
4. And, probably, the return address of the shipper

Many inventory systems provide search and inquiry capabilities based on these four elements and, sometimes, on combinations of them. Receivers may enter ranges of dates, carrier names, an optional vendor name, and one or more key words describing the material in the shipment. The inventory system then searches its purchase order file and displays a screen of orders that match. The receiver is allowed to scroll up and down through the display and, if necessary, to redefine the search criteria to widen or narrow the search. When the appropriate order is found, the receiver then selects it by placing the cursor on it and pressing the enter key. With, at times, the assistance of a supervisor, this process should allow receivers to identify order numbers quickly, easily, and accurately in almost every case.

In addition, from time to time there will be material arriving for which there is no purchase order. The material may not have been ordered, the order may have been canceled after shipment, or it may be that the purchase order simply has not yet been created. The handling of these orders is largely a matter of policy. Some inventory systems allow the receiver to create "dummy" purchase orders and then receive unidentifiable parts against them. Other inventory systems allow the creation of "dummy" purchase orders but restrict the ability to supervisors or other specifically authorized people. Some businesses simply refuse to accept material for which there is no order on file. In these instances, the carrier is instructed to return the material to the shipper and (usually) no formal records are kept.

Preparatory Steps

After identification of the order or orders to be received, two preparatory steps are usually required before the actual receiving process can begin. These steps can legitimately take several forms, but the most common are the entry of freight bill information and exceptions and the printing of receiving worksheets.

Freight bill information to be entered usually includes the actual carrier, number of shippable pieces (boxes or pallets), weight, and terms (prepaid or collect, usually). In addition, exceptions such as variances between the bill of lading and the actual receipt or external damage to one or more of the pieces must be recorded.

Worksheets can look like the sample shown in Figure 8.1. The figure assumes

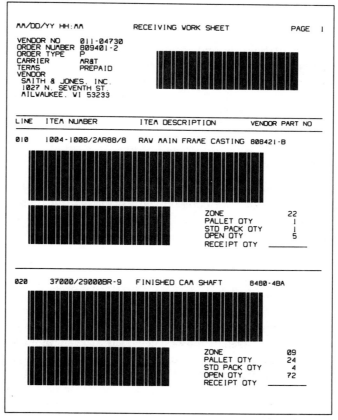

Figure 8.1. Receiving worksheet. This receiving worksheet is designed for both speed and accuracy when material arrives without vendor-applied bar codes. The bar codes illustrated point out what happens when item numbers are long: The bar codes must become correspondingly long.

the use of dot matrix printed Code 39 bar codes and long part numbers (up to 20 characters). The result is large bar codes. Compare this sample with the sample work order shown in Figure 7.3. That design assumes more modest part number sizes (eight characters) and higher density printing such as might be achieved by a laser printer. The differences are in the amount of white space on the page, the number of detail lines on a single sheet, and the amount of printing time required to produce the report.

The receiving worksheet should bear the order number, part number, part description, and the open order quantity. All but the description should be contained in bar codes. If the vendor's part number is available, it should also be included. Other useful information that can be added includes the vendor's address, the requested carrier, and freight terms. Items that are immediately required in production or on the shipping dock can be highlighted, allowing them to be expedited and avoiding the need to either put them away or to pick them immediately.

The receiving worksheet is used in the receiving staging area as a guide to the actual identification and counting of the material. Portable terminals can be used to collect data or counts can be handwritten on the worksheet for later key entry. However, accuracy suffers whenever handwriting is required.

In some operations where many small parts are received, workstations can be set up that allow incoming materials to be conveyed past the receiver. This arrangement can significantly reduce labor costs.

Parts Identification

The actual receiving process begins when the receiver opens the receipt and scans the order number bar code on the worksheet. Next, the receiver identifies and, if necessary, sorts the parts. Many will be labeled, but in isolated cases, identification will be a problem.

Imagine, for instance, a purchase order for 1000 each of two different o-rings. If a partial shipment is made of, say 600 of one type and 1000 of the other, and if the shipment arrives without the proper labels, how is the receiver to know which o-ring is which?

The answer may not be simple. Receivers can be given access to product specifications, drawings, and even photographs to handle unusual problems. In the most extreme cases, it may be necessary to telephone vendors or to obtain technical help from quality control or engineering. In less extreme cases, however, the product description and both the company's part number and the vendor's part number will normally be adequate. The receiver then identifies the parts to the inventory system by reading the corresponding part number and quantity bar codes from the worksheet.

Counting

Next, the receiver must count the parts and decide whether or not the quantity actually received is the same as the quantity on the worksheet. This is where standard packaging and standard pallet quantities are most useful. If, for instance, a receiver knows that the bearings being received are packed in cases of 12, it is a simple matter to count 16 cases and multiply by 12. Counting 192 individual bearings is a lot more work and is much more susceptible to error. This is why the receiving worksheet in Figure 8.1 includes both a standard package quantity and a standard pallet quantity. Better yet, the receiver can enter the number of full pallets, full cases, and loose pieces received. When the system does the calculations, error rates are further reduced.

In some businesses it may also be valuable to provide counting scales in the receiving area. When connected to the inventory system, the scales can eliminate all or almost all of the need to count products and key the results. Both counting and keying errors are eliminated and inventory accuracy is improved.

Sorting and Preparation for Put-Away

Following identification and counting, one or more additional steps may be required before the job is complete and the receipt can be put away. They are:

1. Most businesses that produce serial-numbered product capture the serial numbers at the time of shipment. Some businesses, however, need to capture serial or lot numbers as product arrives. The receiving subsystem used by these companies should recognize when serial numbers should be recorded and should prompt for them at the appropriate time. Generally the part master file is the appropriate place to store a "serial number capture required" flag or a "lot number capture required" flag. And, generally, the serial and lot numbers are best captured during the receiving process, immediately after entry of the quantity received for each item.

   High-accuracy capture of serial and lot numbers is generally practical only when vendors put bar coded labels on their products. Lacking bar codes, manual key entry is necessary. Inventory systems that support key entry of serial and lot numbers should be designed to be flexible when errors are found as material moves through the facility.

2. Many businesses inspect arriving materials. Generally inspections are based on a sample, drawn from the receipt either by a QC person or by the receiver. But sometimes inspections are 100 percent (i.e., not based on a sample), and sometimes inspections are not done. Inspection can legitimately be skipped for vendors and items with a demonstrated history of quality performance.

   When a sample is required and when it is to be drawn by receiving personnel, it can be most accurately and efficiently drawn as the receipt is made ready for put-away. The worksheet, for instance, could specify that an inspection is required based on a part master flag and the worksheet itself could show the number of pieces required by the inspectors. If, however, the sample size varies with the lot size, the quantity to be sent to QC cannot be precalculated because the actual receipt quantity is not known at the time the worksheet is printed. Therefore, the worksheet must show the basic information required so the receiver can calculate the sample size.

One advantage of an on-line receiving process using, for instance, radio terminals, is that these calculations can be done by the system. The receiver is saved both time and errors. Samples are sometimes drawn by the inspection department because, for instance, of a special need for randomness. In these cases, the entire receipt is often routed to the inspection department or is set aside in a holding area pending the sampling.

Once the need for an inspection has been identified and the sample size has been calculated, the receiver must repackage the receipt for internal transportation. Most companies will move the sample itself to an inspection area and put the remainder of the receipt into stock under an inspection hold. Inspection holds are computer-based flags that prevent the material from being used until the inspectors approve it. They are described in more detail under the heading "Quality Control" later in this chapter.

Samples, once drawn, are moved either to the inspection area or to a holding location. The samples are inventory, no different from the material to be put away. The movement to inspection, therefore, should be controlled and validated, just like the movement into the stockroom or warehouse.

3. Another receiving function that may be required is sometimes known as cross-docking. If there are any past due customer orders for the item being received, the receipt can be moved directly across the facility from receiving to shipping, saving both time and labor.

The software required to achieve cross-docking with reasonable response times can be complex. The implication is that every receipt involves an inquiry into the open customer order file. When open orders are found, the allocator must be run to allocate the material to the order. Other processes are required to control its movement, packing, and shipment. Because the amount of computing involved is significant, systems often take short cuts. One reasonable short cut, for instance, is to keep a back-order flag on the part master. This flag would be turned on whenever back orders exist for an item. Its existence eliminates the need to inquire into the customer order file for every receipt but does so at the cost of complicating the software.

When a number of short cuts have been taken, the result can be reasonable response times in receiving, but the software becomes hard to debug and hard to maintain. Some companies, therefore, simply bypass the problem by assuming that all arriving material will be put away in stock and then picked to an order.

Cross-docking is also greatly complicated when several customer orders are to be filled from a single receipt with the remainder going into stock. The process of breaking down a receipt into multiple shipments is best done in the picking area where facilities exist to support just that kind of work. Cross-docking is, therefore, of greater value to companies that buy and sell products on a one-for-one basis than it is to companies that break bulk.

4. Many inventory systems are designed around the concept of unit load "license plate" labels. These labels are typically simple, bearing only the pallet's or carton's identifying number in both human and machine-readable form. A sample license plate label is shown in Figure 8.2.

The license plate label serves the same purpose as an automobile license plate; it identifies the object it is attached to. If it is necessary to get detailed information about a license plated unit load, the retrieval is relatively fast because the license plate number tells the computer exactly where to find the data.

When license plate labels are used, the receiving process is the ideal place to apply them. At the same time, the database connection between the license plate and the material it represents can be established. This is generally best done by requiring that the receiver scan the license plate bar code at an appropriate point in the receiving process.

5. The receiving process may also involve notification of the appropriate personnel that material has arrived. Notifications are best handled entirely within the inventory system, both because of labor cost and of the potential for error.

Figure 8.2. Unit load license plate. Unit load license plates in many inventory systems consist of nothing but a serial number in human-readable and bar code form. This allows them to be preprinted (at lower cost than if they were printed on-line) and makes them very flexible in use.

6. And, as a final step in the receiving process, a material handler must be notified that the material is ready to be taken to a storage location, to inspection, or directly to the shop. The movement functions themselves are discussed in more detail in Chapter 9.

Intercompany Labeling Standards

Much of the labor and potential for error inherent in the receiving process can be completely circumvented. And business is moving in the right direction to do it. What may be the ultimate in receiving processes depends on shipping labels, applied by the shipper and scanned by the receiver. Companies that ship products to other companies usually have computer systems with reasonably accurate knowledge of the content of each shipment. If these shippers were to label materials with the appropriate data in bar codes, the receiving companies could do their receiving with a simple scan.

The automotive industry has established a nonprofit organization known as the Automotive Industry Action Group with the purpose of establishing standards that promote just this kind of intercompany communication. The AIAG has written pioneering standards that cover a variety of communications and most important, establish a universal shipping label. These standards are available to all and are practical for use in almost any manufacturing business.

A sample of the AIAG standard shipping label appears in Figure 8.3. It is not an address label for use by the carrier. Rather, it is specifically designed to speed the receiving process. It allows for bar coding of the part number, vendor number,

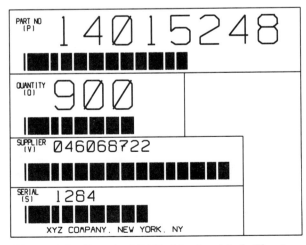

Figure 8.3. Sample AIAG shipping label. The Automotive Industry Action Group shipping label design is widely accepted within the automotive industry and is often used in other industries as well.

and quantity of material on a pallet or in a container. The AIAG standard specifies that the part number and vendor number used are to be assigned by the customer. A field known as the serial number field is assigned by the vendor and used for its internal tracking purposes. Another label (not illustrated) identifies loads of mixed product. Each item in a mixed load must also be labeled with a shipping label.

Using AIAG or similar shipping labels, the receiving process can be reduced to the following elements:

1. The receiver scans, in any order, the bar codes appearing on the label.
2. The receiving subsystem sorts out the bar codes (each has in built-in identifier so the computer knows which is which) and verifies that each item is on order from the vendor in the quantity stated.
3. The system next verifies that a sampling has been performed on this vendor and that its labeling has been found to be accurate.
4. Finally, the system decides where the material should go within the plant.
5. And the receiver moves to the next pallet.

The major automotive manufacturers are now insisting that most of their vendors label shipments with AIAG standard shipping labels. Because there are so many automotive suppliers, the AIAG standard shipping labels are becoming widely known and accepted. Even if a company is not in a position to demand standard labels on its receipts, it is worth asking vendors for them. More and more companies are doing it; more and more vendors are supplying them even if they do not advertise the fact.

Companies outside the automotive industry should determine whether standards have been set by a group representing their industry. If so, those standards should probably be used in place of the AIAG standards. But, lacking an industry organization and standards body, the AIAG standards may be an excellent route.

Parcel Carrier Receipts

In many businesses, receipts that arrive via parcel carriers such as the U.S. Postal Service, the United Parcel Service, Roadway Parcel Service, and Federal Express are a problem. Mail and parcels are often received in a mail room, separate from the receiving dock. Material receipts may be indistinguishable from correspondence. The frequent result is direct delivery to the requester who may or may not follow established receiving procedures.

In cases where mail room receipts are a problem, one solution might be to direct all vendors to make shipments to the attention of receiving. Parcels received can then be easily diverted to receiving for processing, or a small receiving operation can be established within the mail room. If an internal delivery destination code is added to the purchase order or the receiving worksheet, the receiving department will know how to handle these receipts.

Mail room and receiving procedures should recognize that some mail and overnight delivery parcels are urgent. Provisions should be made for expediting them.

Example 8.1. All-manual data collection using central key entry. Usable methods for accurate all-manual receiving depend heavily on the nature of the product being received and the type of material handling in use. This example assumes a palletized product that is handled entirely by conventional lift trucks. It also assumes that some receipts are of less than pallet quantities and other receipts are more than a full pallet.

The all-manual receiving operation is based on purchase order copies that are made at the time purchase orders are placed and stored in vendor name sequence in the receiving office. As shipments arrive, receivers are assigned to unload the trailers. Without knowing the content of the shipment, the receivers physically sort the material by vendor, count the number of pieces from each, and record their counts on a preprinted form. This form, together with the packing lists, is then turned in to the office where a clerk compares it with the driver's bill of lading. Assuming that the number of pieces matches the bill of lading and assuming that the receivers have noted no external damage, the bill is signed and the driver is allowed to leave. The first step has thus been validated by comparing the piece count made by the receiver with the bill of lading. The comparison is valuable because the receiver does not know how many items are supposed to be in the shipment when the count is being made. The clerk completes the first part of the receiving operation by keying required information from the freight bill.

The clerk next pulls two copies of the purchase order from the file. One copy is retained in the office with the packing lists and the second copy is given to the receiver. The office copy of the purchase order is kept to ensure that paperwork does not get lost.

The receiver uses the purchase order, together with experience and, when necessary, assistance from a supervisor to identify and count the material received. No order quantities appear on the receiver's copy of the purchase order because the carbon paper between copies is not inked in the quantity column. Since the packing lists are in the office, the receiver is again counting blind.

The receiver counts everything in the receipt, repalletizing as necessary. Completed counts are handwritten on the purchase order copy. The receiver also completes a three part put-away form for each pallet or, in the case of multiitem pallets, for each item on the pallet. The form provides space for entry of a part number, a quantity, and the receiver's initials. Two copies of the form are placed with the material for use during the put-away process. The third copy of the form is turned in to the clerk together with the purchase order copy bearing the summary counts. The clerk then compares the packing list with both of the receiver's counts and identifies exceptions.

Exceptions are handled by the supervisor, who must be called in whenever a packing list is found to be in error. The supervisor either recounts the relevant portion of the receipt personally or assigns another receiver to make another blind count. Eventually, the supervisor determines the final, accurate total and records it on the purchase order copy. This final total is then keyed by the clerk for entry into the inventory system.

To ensure accurate key entry, the inventory system verifies order numbers, part numbers, and quantities. The order numbers and part numbers are required to be on file. The quantity must be equal to the order quantity within a tolerance. If an order is expected in several shipments, the quantity must be within a tolerance of the quantities due and overdue. Receipts above the tolerance are accepted only if a supervisor submits a separate transaction that repeats the order number, part number, and quantity. This duplication acts like a countersignature on a large bank check. It validates the correctness of a number that might otherwise be an error.

Daily, as a final verification that receipts have been properly recorded, the inventory system prints a variance listing. This report lists only items for which the receipt quantity differed from the order quantity, but it lists all of them, regardless of tolerances. The report is printed in order number sequence with only one order on a page. The receiving clerk is required to match this paperwork with the bill of lading copy, the packing lists, the put-away forms, and the two receiving purchase order copies. The clerk staples all of this paperwork into a single package and, after comparing the computer's variance report with the other counts, initials, dates, and files the package. These files are kept for a period of 6 months. Auditors visit the receiving department at random times to verify that the receiver has properly compared quantities and initialed the documents.

While the procedure outlined in this example is labor intensive, as are all such manual procedures, it does provide the necessary checks and balances to ensure accurate receiving. Order and part numbers are verified with the purchase order, the packing list, and the receiver's experience. Quantities, the most vulnerable point, are rechecked several times and even the key entry function is verified after the fact. Most important, the people doing the work are required to commit themselves to the accuracy of their individual tasks by initialing and dating their paperwork. The combination of motivation and validation, when backed by responsible supervision, will produce excellent results.

Example 8.2. Paper-driven off-line data collection. Paper-driven, off-line receiving systems are considered optimum in many instances. They can be highly accurate yet do not involve the complexities and costs of on-line software. Receiving typically begins with the delivery of the shipping papers (bills of lading or manifests) to the receiving office. A clerk identifies the arriving orders through an on-line CRT. He or she keys freight bill information into the system (including the carrier, the number of pieces in the shipment, the freight charges, terms, and other information), connects an off-line bar code terminal to a nearby computer port, and downloads the orders to the terminal while a worksheet is being printed. Personnel are assigned to the receiving operation and given both the portable terminal and the worksheet.

As the shipment is unloaded, pieces (shipping containers) are counted and each item in each shipping container is identified based on its description and on the receiver's experience. The items are sorted and labeled with a simple license plate label bearing only a serial number in bar-coded and human-readable form (Figure 8.2). As each item is identified, the corresponding bar codes on the worksheet are scanned, together with the license plate bar code. When shipments involve more than one purchase order, the scanning includes the order number bar code for each item as well as the part number and quantity bar code. When a shipment involves only a single order, the order number bar code need be scanned only once. After scanning the bar codes for each item, the terminal displays the item number and quantity, and the receiver visually verifies it and presses a key to proceed to the next item.

On completion of the unloading, counting, and identification process, the terminal displays the total number of pieces received for each order. The receivers compare this total with the bill of lading, sign for the receipt, and the driver is released. The portable terminal is then returned to the clerk, who reconnects it with the inventory system and uploads the actual receipt information. The inventory system handles all remaining paperwork and uses the license plate label to identify the material as it is put away in the warehouse.

Example 8.3. Hi-tech. Because radio terminals are typically small-screen devices, they are less than ideal in some instances. This hi-tech receiving example uses a mixture of radio terminals and CRT workstations to take advantage of the strengths of the two technologies.

The receiving process begins, as always, with the arrival of a trailer and the accompanying bill of lading or manifest. When loads arrive that bear vendor applied labels, no office work is required other than entry of the freight bill information. The supervisor assigns personnel to unload the trailer and supplies the personnel with radio terminals. As each item is unloaded, all labels are scanned and, when the unloading process is complete, the receiving process is likewise complete. The inventory system reports a count of the pieces received, this count is compared with the bill of lading, and the delivery person leaves.

Naturally, from time to time external damage will be apparent and from time to time bill of lading piece quantities will disagree with the counts performed as the product is unloaded. In these instances, human judgment is required and a supervisor is called in. The inventory system supports the inquiry tools required to locate problems and allows adjustments and corrections to be made to its database.

When product arrives that is not prelabeled, the process changes, becoming akin to the paper-driven, off-line example above. As in that example, a clerk is responsible for identifying orders and printing receiving worksheets. The radio terminals are used to read bar codes from the worksheets as the product is handled. License plates are applied, and their bar codes read. The most important change from the off-line receiving process is the elimination of the need to pass orders to and from a portable terminal. Instead, order information and actual receipt data are exchanged over the air in real time. As a result, labor is saved and the material is available for put-away or use faster.

PUT-AWAY

Put-away is the process by which material is moved from the receiving dock to its immediate destination. The term originated in the distribution industry in which almost everything received is put away in the warehouse. Today, however, it can be properly used in all kinds of business, including those that move material directly from receiving to the manufacturing floor and the shipping docks.

This discussion assumes that there are people called material handlers who are responsible for moving material out of the receiving area. The arrangement is a common one. Firms that require the receivers to do their own put-away should be able to adjust the procedures easily.

Busy receiving docks can be messy places. Typically they consist of several staging areas, each filled with pallets of material undergoing receipt. Some products are neatly stacked, others are torn apart for counting. Some pallets are labeled, some are not. The first task of the material handler assigned to put-away, therefore, is to locate material that is ready to go.

There are two ways to signal a material handler that product is ready to be moved out: Either the product can be segregated in an area set aside by the receiving department for completed work, or the pallets can be labeled as they are completed. Or, of course, a combination of the two methods can be used.

Setting product aside has the advantage of allowing the receiving dock to be cleared more quickly after a receipt has been completed. It also makes the material handler's job easy. Anything in the completed work area is eligible for put-away. No searching is required. On the other hand, the completed work area itself consumes space and it consumes that space whether it is full or empty. And the use of a completed work area requires that the receivers be responsible for moving material to it from the staging areas.

The fundamental advantage of labeling product as a signal to the material handler is that the label can do double duty. It can and should also bear a bar code that identifies either the material in the unit load or the location to which the load should be taken. Some mechanized receiving departments do not have the problem of determining which loads are ready for put-away because all loads are complete by the time they reach the end of the process. These are special cases that are not treated here.

When the material handler selects a load to be taken away from the receiving department, the next job is to identify where it must go. Manual systems often do this with handwritten labels on the load. Automated systems also use labels but have bar codes on them. Some businesses simply establish warehouse zones and require the material handler to locate a storage space for the product in or near the appropriate zone.

There are a number of strong arguments for the preselection of storage locations by the computer system and against allowing the material handler to select the location. These arguments and the logic required to efficiently select storage locations are discussed in Chapter 11. For the moment, suffice it to say that computer selection of storage locations is highly desirable.

When the receipt's destination has been selected by the inventory system, the material handler must identify the load to the computer so the computer can respond with the storage location. There are three reasonable ways to do this:

1. The storage location can be encoded in a bar code on a label and placed on the pallet to be stored. A simple bar code scanner can then read the label and display its content to the material handler.

2. If pallets bear serialized license plates, the license plate number can be used as an indirect reference to the storage location. For example, a list of pending put-aways could be loaded into the memory of a portable off-line terminal. The material handler would then use the portable terminal's scanner to scan the license plate. The terminal, having received the license plate number, could look up the storage location in its file and display it.

3. Or, if radio terminals are being used, the license plate number can be transmitted to the inventory system. The inventory system can then refer to its own files to determine the storage location and transmit the location back to the radio terminal for display. If the software is fast enough, the storage location can even be assigned at the time pallets are selected for put-away.

Having received the location where the pallet is to go, the material handler takes it there. He or she then puts the material away or delivers it as necessary and validates that it has been properly stored. Validation, as described in Chapter 5, usually consists of the scanning of a bar-coded label on the storage location or at the destination point. The inventory system compares the scan with the intended destination and is thus able to detect errors and prompt the material handler to correct them.

QUALITY CONTROL

Quality control considerations are germane to the subject of inventory accuracy because quality problems can affect both inventory accuracy and operating efficiency. Some companies impound all new receipts in a quality hold area until inspections have been completed. This time-honored method can do an excellent job of preventing the picking of flawed material. But now all receipts must be physically handled through the QC area. Labor costs, losses, and accuracy problems are thus increased.

Other companies, recognizing the material handling costs involved, try to control the movement of problem material by applying special labels. Material handlers are instructed not to pick or use material bearing those labels. But most have found that the system is not foolproof. The labels have a way of getting lost, resulting in the use of the material. And, more important, unless separate actions are taken to inform the computer of the problem, it will have no way of knowing that the material is unusable. Material requirements planning, therefore, will plan a lower level of production than it should and, sooner or later, unnecessary shortages will occur.

The best way to handle quality inspections and rejects in almost all businesses is to make the inventory system aware of quality problems and to program it to act accordingly. This includes both preventing the use of the material and keeping adequate records so material requirements planning can do its job properly. The feature required in the inventory system is called a "hold."

Holds and Releases

There are five different kinds of holds; all relate in one way or another to quality. Some are applicable in many businesses, others are more specialized. Each inventory system designer must decide which are necessary and which are not. Regardless of which ones are chosen, it is important that each be implemented as a separate field on the database and that it be fully independent of the others. It should be possible, in other words, to place all five holds at one time on a specific pallet or item and to release all of them in any sequence.

In addition to recording and tracking holds, the inventory control system must react to them. The basic purpose of a hold is to allow the material to be moved to a storage location but to prevent its use so long as there is doubt about its quality. Then, when the doubt has been removed, the hold is removed and the material is immediately available for use without moving it again.

If any holds are "on" for a particular item, the system must continue to track the associated inventory but must not allow it to be used. Allocation, movement between locations in either the warehouse or the factory, movement between the warehouse and the factory, and picking for shipment are all affected. The system must prevent the mixing of material on hold with material not on hold. Some reports, such as inventory value and space utilization, must continue to include material on hold. Other reports, such as a marketing availability report, should exclude it. Still other reports may include some held material and exclude others. The interface between the inventory control system and material requirements planning is an example of this last case.

Few inventory systems have control at a level below that of the storage location and part. Therefore, unless a reliable method of identifying individual parts is adopted, holds must apply to all material of a single part number in a storage location. Exceptions might exist when serialized product is handled and when the inventory control system tracks each serial number separately.

With the exception of the receiving hold, which is released automatically by the system, all holds should be releasable only by authorized personnel. In some businesses, the ability to release a manually created hold is limited to the person who initiated the hold.

The five holds are for receiving, incoming inspection, process inspection, inventory accuracy, and shelf life.

Receiving Holds

Businesses with complex receiving operations and high material turnover may find it impossible to store receipts on the receiving dock even for the length of time it takes to unload a trailer and verify the correctness of the bill of lading. These businesses can, at times, have great difficulty contesting bills of lading and can suffer shipping losses at their own expense as a result. One solution is a receiving hold, automatically applied to all receipts as they arrive and automatically relieved when the receipt has been fully reconciled. Like other holds, the receiving hold prevents the use of material while it is in force.

Incoming Inspection Holds

Most companies exempt some products from some vendors from incoming inspection, while requiring sample inspections of others and 100 percent inspection of the rest. The inventory system should know the current inspection requirements for each part or item. Using this information, it should automatically place incoming inspection holds on arriving material when necessary.

The existence of an incoming inspection hold on a receipt should not prevent the material from being put away in the warehouse. It may also be desirable to design the inventory system to allow the movement of material on hold from one storage location to another within the warehouse. The incoming inspection hold, however, like all other holds, should prevent its allocation or use until the quality organization removes the hold.

Depending on business needs, the sample may need to be merged back in with the main body of the lot after inspection is complete. When the inventory system selects storage locations, however, the amount of software required to do this can be significant. System designers and those who specify system requirements should verify that there is a real need for this before proceeding. Most companies simply treat the inspection samples as new, relatively small receipts that do not require inspection themselves. The samples, therefore, can be stored anywhere in the warehouse that makes sense according to the existing rules for putting things away.

In-Process Inspection Holds

In-process inspection holds function like incoming inspection holds but can either be applied automatically or manually. As parts, subassemblies, and finished items are completed in the shop, the inventory system checks its files for a code that indicates that an inspection is required. If it finds that code, it places an automatic in-process inspection hold on the completed material. This does not necessarily prevent movement of the material into the warehouse; it should, however, prevent its allocation or use until released by QC. In addition, random QC checks can result in the manual application of in-process inspection holds at any point.

Inspectors should be allowed to establish in-process inspection holds for a single item in a single location, for all locations containing a specified item in a specified department, or for all locations containing the item plantwide. In addition, where lot control is a consideration, the inspector should be allowed to determine which lot(s) will be held or specify that all lots are to be held.

Whenever an in-process inspection hold is manually established, the inventory system should request entry of the hold type and both reason and responsibility codes. More data can be gathered as necessary. For the sake of accuracy, it is a good idea to allow the use of bar codes to identify items or lots to be held.

Some businesses have more detailed requirements. For example, inspectors, supervisors, or managers may need to be able to locate and place holds on all product within the facility that contains one or more specific lots of a subassembly. Or a business may want to be able to hold only the material that has passed through a certain operation or material that has not passed through that operation. Requirements like these are generally specific to the business and normally must be designed and programmed separately for each case.

The in-process inspection hold also serves as a "miscellaneous" or "management" hold function in many businesses.

Inventory Accuracy Holds

An inventory accuracy hold is a hold automatically placed on an individual storage location whenever an inventory error is reported. The existence of the accuracy hold causes a cycle count to be made of that location on a priority basis and prevents, in the interim, any other movement into or out of the location. Completion of the cycle count or a supervisor's override is required to release the hold.

The accuracy hold is important to the inventory's accuracy because it simplifies the job of tracking down problems. Just as the police line prevents the public from interfering with the investigation of a crime, the accuracy hold keeps employees at bay until the problem can be defined and resolved.

Shelf Life Holds

When products have defined shelf lives, the inventory system should track product age and place an automatic shelf life hold on expired material. A shelf life hold can reasonably allow movement of the material within the facility but should prevent allocation or picking for either shipment to customers or for assembly into a higher-level product.

Shelf life considerations can get complicated. Shelf lives are often a function of storage temperature. For some products, the effect of storage temperature can be important enough to warrant programming the inventory system to take it into account. One way of implementing temperature sensitive shelf lives might be to start each fresh product with an arbitrary value of, say, 10,000 units. Each day the shelf life consumed could be calculated based on that day's storage temperature. When the remaining balance reaches zero, a shelf life hold is placed on the material and it can no longer be used.

Other Quality Control Needs

In addition to holds and releases, most quality control organizations also need the ability to make dispositions and to write scrap and rework orders. Many manufacturing planning and work order systems support these functions. When they are properly interfaced, there is no need to duplicate them in the inventory system. But nonmanufacturing companies such as wholesalers and distributors usually build all required quality functions into the inventory system. In either event, proper performance of these systems affects inventory accuracy and thus bears discussion here.

Material placed under an incoming inspection hold or a work-in-process hold should be automatically added to a prioritized inspection list. Priorities should be established by the inspector or by an inspection supervisor. The inventory system should be able to direct inspectors to the material's location and should support the drawing of samples and the moving of those samples to the inspection area. Like all other material handlers, the inspectors should be required to validate as they draw samples and to validate again as they enter test results. Test result entry should include a pass or fail indication and, in some businesses, may include numeric test results that the inventory control system can pass to a quality analysis system.

When a sample passes inspection, the inspector should specify the number of units from the sample that are to be returned to stock and the number to be scrapped (assuming some tests to be destructive). Next, the inventory control system should generate a move transaction to return the good units to stock and should print an identifying label for the units. The move transaction should be queued for assignment to a material handler, or the inspector can be required to move the material. In either case, movement of the good units should be validated, as are all movements of material. The inventory hold should be released on all portions of the receipt except for the scrap.

Like the good material coming out of inspection, scrap should be moved to a storage location but one separate from the good material. At the same time, the inventory control system should generate a transaction to be passed to the financial system to charge it to the appropriate account. When the scrapped material is ultimately disposed of, a movement transaction should be created to physically remove it from the building and the inventory simultaneously.

When a sample fails inspection, the inventory control system should update a status code on the hold to indicate inspection failure. It should also transfer the sample from the inspector's work queue to a work queue for the material review board (MRB). But the hold on the material should not be released. The MRB will eventually decide to use the material as is, scrap it, rework it, or, in the case of purchased material, return it to the vendor. Rework may include sorting, with portions of the material undergoing further rework, scrapping, return to the vendor, or use as is. Entry of the MRB's decision into the inventory control system should, like all quality related information, be restricted to authorized QC personnel.

If the material is to be used as is, the information entered into the inventory control system and the processing done by the system is the same as if the sample had originally passed. In addition, an authorization code or MRB case number may be useful to allow future reference to the decision.

If the material is to be returned to the vendor or sold for scrap, a shipment order must be created. This shipment order can be structured like a customer order with a name and address and a list of the items and quantities to be shipped. It should also include an authorization code or MRB reference plus, if applicable, the vendor's return authorization number for the shipping label and packing list. Vendor return shipment orders should be encoded to allow the allocation processor and other parts of the inventory control system to override existing holds. Once the order is in place, it will be treated just like all other outgoing orders; the material will be picked, packed, and shipped using normal validation procedures to ensure accuracy.

If the material is to be reworked, a manufacturing rework order is created. Like the vendor return shipment order, manufacturing rework orders override holds, allowing the material to be moved into the factory. A special routing may be required. And most rework orders will include an inspection after completion, which will cause the reworked parts to be put in stock under an automatic in-process hold after the rework is done.

9

In-Plant Operations

The control of material movement within an inventory facility is as critical to inventory accuracy as the control of receipts and shipments. The movement of a pallet from point A to point B will not, in itself, affect the four-wall on-hand balance of the product. But if the wrong material is moved or if the right material is put in the wrong place, an inventory error will occur. The eventual result will probably be a shortage, expediting, missed schedules, and many of the other bad things that can happen when inventories are wrong.

Some manufacturing companies have work-in-process or shop floor control systems that track inventory as it moves through the factory. Other companies design their systems differently, concentrating all responsibility for inventories in a single inventory control system. The techniques used to keep accurate work-in-process inventories are not significantly affected by this difference. For the sake of consistency, therefore, this book blurs the line between shop floor control and inventory control by making the assumption that all relevant functions are handled in a single inventory system. The reader should understand that this is not necessarily a recommendation that a single system be responsible for all inventory throughout the plant.

Figure 9.1 shows a schematic floor plan of a manufacturing facility with an attached warehouse. The arrows illustrate the kinds of material movements that can occur within the warehouse, from the warehouse to production, between work centers in production, and from production back to the warehouse. Movements from receiving into the warehouse and to production are discussed in Chapter 8; movements from production and the warehouse to shipping are discussed in Chapter 10.

As was the case in the preceding chapter, few of the techniques described are essential to all businesses. The reader must pick and choose based on the product

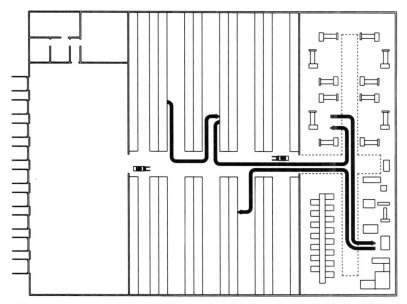

Figure 9.1. Types of internal movements. There are four types of material movements internal to an inventory facility: within the warehouse, from the warehouse to the shop, between locations in the shop, and from the shop to the warehouse.

being handled, the handling methods in use, and management's strategies for buying, manufacturing, storing, selling, and shipping product.

MOVEMENTS WITHIN THE WAREHOUSE

Material is moved from place to place within the typical warehouse for a variety of reasons. Some movements are planned; others occur at random. Each kind of movement has its own set of rules and needs different software than the others. The movements can be generally classified into consolidations, rewarehousing, replenishment, and miscellaneous moves.

Consolidations

Consolidation is the combining of material from several partly filled storage locations into a single one to make space available for new material. Opportunities for consolidation occur whenever a number of partly full storage locations contain the same part. Frequent consolidation in some businesses can spell the difference between stacking things in the aisles and having enough space to run an efficient business. In almost any business, consolidation can reduce the effort required to manage the inventory and, therefore, can improve productivity.

In theory, if materials are used on a first-in, first-out basis (FIFO) and if most receipts are full pallet loads, there should be few partly filled locations in the warehouse. In practice, however, the problem is rarely this simple. Vendors ship partial pallets. Quality control draws samples and returns them to stock. Losses and damage occur. And FIFO rules are sometimes violated. Some businesses have more need for control than others, but experience says that even with the best controls in place, partly filled locations will occur and warehouse space utilization will suffer as a result.

Computer identification of consolidation requirements and complete automation of the process seems attractive at first. Unfortunately, the software required is complex and, therefore, expensive. Imagine an instance in which three locations exist, each with a capacity of 100 parts. Location A contains 40, location B contains 50, and location C contains 60. Should location A be consolidated into B or into C? The inventory system is ill equipped to decide since the answer may depend on things that it is not aware of. Location B might require the use of high-reach equipment or might be in a very busy part of the warehouse. Or, if the product typically moves in full pallet quantities, it might be a good idea to build a full pallet by combining A and C. Programming all possible contingencies is difficult, even for this relatively simple example.

Most inventory systems leave consolidation decisions to a supervisor but provide the supervisor with assistance in the form of a consolidation opportunity report. A sample of such a report appears in Figure 9.2. This report is fundamen-

```
                  Consolidation Opportunities                Page 001

                              Location    Content
   Part Number    Location    Capacity    Cube     Opportunities

   247A113        04-12-31-02   80640       3125    ×
                  02-04-02-03   80640       8422    × ×
                  04-04-16-05   80640      24120    × × ×
                  01-09-17-01   80640      28300    × × × ×
                  02-04-01-05   80640      30245          × ×
                  01-01-03-04   80640      31665             × ×
                  02-14-30-02   80640      48952               ×

   8R-147         03-02-44-02   80640        590                    ×
                  03-01-05-01   40320       3854                  × ×
                  03-03-03-01   80640       8815                 × × ×
                  03-01-03-05   24200      10140                 × × ×
                  03-02-13-05   80640      29852               ×     × ×
                  03-11-26-02   80640      38520   ×                      ×
                                80640      39210   ×

   806AN14B       12-04-02-04   80640       8582   ×
                  01-11-03-01   80640      27300   × ×
                  02-03-01-01   80640      36127   × × ×
                  05-01-02-02   80640      40212       ×
```

Figure 9.2. Consolidation opportunities report. This report is used to combine existing materials in storage, creating empty locations that can be used for other purposes.

tally a list of items containing details by location. Only partly filled locations are listed. Only items with two or more partly filled locations are shown, sequenced in descending order by the number of partly filled locations to put the best opportunities at the top of the report. Within an item number, locations are sequenced by on-hand quantity.

On the right side of the report are 10 columns of asterisks. Each location listed (except the last one for each item) starts a fresh column of asterisks with the column extending through all of the succeeding locations that could be consolidated into the first. Thus, on the sample report, the very first column of asterisks at the top of the page tells the reader that locations 02-04-02-03, 04-04-16-05, and 01-09-17-01 can all be consolidated into 04-12-31-02. A supervisor can scan the columns, select the longest rows of asterisks, verify that the consolidation movements make sense, and instruct the inventory system to perform them. No manual calculations are required and the value of the consolidation effort is immediately obvious in terms of the number of locations that will be made available.

Mathematicians will immediately note that this method is far from optimal. Experience, however, says that it works in practice because it brings human judgment into the picture. Nothing prevents the supervisor from ignoring a consolidation opportunity if there is reason to do so. And nothing prevents the supervisor from creating a new arrangement. All the information required to do so is available on the report.

In some businesses it may be important to avoid mixing product of differing ages and product belonging to different lots. Figure 9.2 ignores these considerations, but they are easily accommodated. If, for instance, FIFO is a consideration, the locations can be listed in FIFO sequence instead of being in sequence by the on-hand quantity. The column of asterisks, then, can be stopped when either the allowable difference in FIFO ages is exceeded or when the top location is at capacity.

One final concern is the speed and accuracy with which the supervisor can convert decisions into transactions to be executed on the warehouse floor. An excellent method is to provide the consolidation opportunity report on a screen and allow the supervisor to select locations for consolidation by moving the cursor to them and pressing a key. As each movement is defined, consolidation opportunities for the item affected can be recalculated and redisplayed. Location numbers won't be typed incorrectly, and the entire job can be completed in only a few seconds per item.

Rewarehousing

Rewarehousing is the movement of material within an inventory facility to improve efficiency. For instance, the physical segregation of fast-moving items from slow movers is common. The time material handlers spend traveling from location to location is unproductive. This segregation, often called "demand storage," improves productivity by minimizing the amount of time material handlers spend traveling and maximizing the time they spend picking and putting away product.

But, demand patterns change as time goes by. The Christmas item that belonged in the fast-moving area in October no longer belongs there in January. Demand can shift from less than case quantities picked from the forward picking area to full case quantities picked (in some businesses) from reserve. So, it is necessary to rewarehouse occasionally if operations are to remain efficient.

Rewarehousing is generally driven by an inventory report that lists opportunities. A typical report program might calculate the actual velocity of an item and compare it to the intended velocity of the area in which it is stored. When an apparent mismatch is found, the system might search for an alternate location in a more appropriate area. It could then list both the present and proposed locations on the rewarehousing opportunity report (see Figure 9.3). As with the consolidation opportunity report, it would be up to a supervisor to approve the rewarehousing movements. Upon approval, the inventory system could generate the transactions required to execute them, dispatch the transactions to material handlers, and validate the results.

The calculation of velocity is important to the concept of rewarehousing. Velocity, for this purpose, should be a measure of the number of times the product is handled each week, month, or year. Manufacturing systems deal with a similar concept known as the ABC class. ABC classification considers the dollar value of an item as well as the quantity handled to determine the degree of planning and control effort that should go into the item. Rewarehousing, on the other hand, is

				Page 001
	Rewarehousing Recommendations			
Item Number	Current Location	On-Hand	Velocity	Proposed Location
14F802-5	12-02-14-03	4523	12.6	04-12-18-02
14F802-9	12-21-03-04	302	8.1	04-09-11-01
14F808	12-14-20-01	38	16.3	04-01-13-04
14F883	12-06-04-02	10429	21.0	06-02-08-03
14F940-8	04-03-04-01	2590	32.3	05-02-02-01
14R303	01-04-02-01	289	20.7	12-14-20-01
15A140-9B	08-13-32-03	3957	4.4	08-12-02-03
17R763	12-06-23-04	32	19.0	04-15-12-04
24F404	04-01-09-03	107	36.4	12-05-09-01

Figure 9.3. Rewarehousing opportunities report. This report lists items in inventory that are stored in the wrong place.

concerned with material handling costs alone and the dollar value of the item is irrelevant. ABC class, therefore, should not be used for rewarehousing unless there is no other measure available.

Replenishment

One of the manifestations of demand storage is the idea of forward picking. Forward picking is an area of the warehouse that is set aside for the picking of less-than-pallet quantities. The amount of space devoted to each item is usually relatively small. Businesses that break bulk (i.e., those that sell in quantities smaller than they buy in) often find that order picking is the single largest element of labor cost. By concentrating most order picking in a small area, pickers can pick faster and these companies save more than enough labor to pay the cost of replenishing the forward picking area.

A forward picking area can get material directly from the receiving department and the manufacturing facility. But in general, most material will first flow through a reserve storage area. Replenishment is the transfer of material from reserve to a forward picking area in support of the order picking process.

Most businesses define two separate kinds of replenishment, regular and emergency. Regular replenishments are usually triggered when the stock in a forward picking area drops below an established replenishment point. Emergency replenishments occur when the stock drops to zero. In both cases, the stock level used to trigger replenishment is usually the "available quantity," the on-hand balance plus any material in-transit to the location less any planned movements out of the location.

Regular replenishments are normally defined as part of an off-line task, run once or several times each day. A warehouse or stockroom planner begins the process by selecting the replenishment option from an inventory system menu. The inventory system reviews the forward picking location and compares the quantity available in each location with that location's replenishment point. When a location is found that is in need of replenishment, the system calculates the replenishment quantity and determines the picking location. The material movement required is then presented to the planner on a screen for change or approval.

In other inventory facilities, the periodic replenishment of forward picking locations may be less desirable. In cases where customer orders are entered a day or more before picking, the inventory system can use them to predict needs for the following day. Using this prediction, it can net against actual inventory in forward picking. Replenishment transactions can then be generated only for those items that will otherwise run short. This method has the advantage of some visibility into the future. Replenishment moves are not made if the material will not be used. However, it has the drawback of requiring that all replenishments for an entire day's worth of picking be defined at once. Because no location will be replenished more often than once a day, each forward picking location must be sized to handle the maximum possible amount that could be picked in a day. The periodic replenishment method (above) allows replenishments to be made several times each day and replenishes only what will physically fit into the forward picking location.

Emergency replenishments, on the other hand, are usually built automatically by the inventory system as part of the allocation of orders. With each allocation, the system calculates the available quantity and, if it turns out to be less than zero, a replenishment quantity is determined and the source location for the replenishment is selected. When an emergency replenishment is defined, the inventory system should verify that no regular replenishments are in progress. If any are found awaiting action, they should be converted to emergencies (and their quantities adjusted as necessary). Or, if a regular replenishment is in progress, the emergency replenishment quantity should be reduced by the amount of the regular replenishment.

Regular replenishments are often controlled by a planner to allow the inventory facility to manage its workload. Many warehouses and stockrooms choose to pick at certain times of the day and replenish at other times. Emergency replenishments, on the other hand, are considered to be true emergencies; orders exist and have been allocated for more material than is available in forward picking. Therefore, immediate action must be taken to move more material into the forward picking area so pickers do not run out of stock. In contrast to regular replenishments, therefore, inventory systems generally do not require a planner's approval of emergency replenishments. If the forward picking locations have been sized properly in relation to the throughput of each item and if regular replenishments are done frequently, there will be few emergencies.

The calculation of replenishment quantities is usually the same for both emergency and regular replenishments. As long as the move from reserve to forward picking is to be made, there is no reason why the quantity moved should not be as great as possible. Therefore, the replenishment quantity is usually the difference between the available quantity and the capacity of the location. The available quantity and the location capacity can be stated in terms of pieces, cubic measure, or weight, depending on the product. For most products, however, the use of cubic measure is common. This measure does not require the recalculation of location capacity every time a different part is assigned to a forward picking location.

The replenishment quantity is generally calculated when the need for a replenishment is found but is often altered as part of the process of selecting the locations from which the replenishment will be picked. If, for instance, the replenishment quantity turns out to be 102 pieces, and the product is palletized in quantities of 100 to each pallet, there is great benefit in reducing it by two pieces. On the other hand, if the replenishment quantity is 142 and there is both a full pallet and a partial pallet of 38 pieces in reserve, most supervisors would prefer to bring both pallets forward. Therefore, the replenishment quantity cannot simply be rounded down to the nearest full pallet quantity. In fact, modern inventory systems are more complex. The discussion of location selection logic in Chapter 11 includes a description of one effective way that replenishment quantities can be manipulated to advantage.

Miscellaneous Moves

In addition to consolidation, rewarehousing, and replenishment, inventory systems should allow the movement of just about anything from almost anywhere to almost anywhere else. Inventory supervisors will always need the flexibility to do what the situation dictates.

Miscellaneous moves are usually defined by a supervisor who scans or keys the source location, the quantity to be moved and, optionally, the destination location. This information is then converted into a transaction for execution by a material handler. If the destination location is not specified by the supervisor, the system must locate and assign one, displaying it for the supervisor's approval before proceeding.

MOVEMENTS FROM THE WAREHOUSE TO PRODUCTION

There are two commonly used ways of determining when material needs to be moved from storage into the manufacturing operation. Using distribution parlance, they can be called "pull" and "push."

The term "pull" means that material is moved to the shop when production requests it. Production, in other words, calls on the inventory system for delivery of material as necessary. The inventory system has no prior knowledge of what will be required or when.

The pull system has several advantages. First, since material is not delivered in advance, it requires the storage of much less material on the production floor. This reduces clutter, allows more compact arrangement of the production facilities, minimizes material handling costs, and maximizes inventory flexibility since material is not allocated to a job until the last possible moment. Second, the pull distribution method is simpler to program and implement, at least in the inventory system. And, third, the pull system easily accommodates variations in the manufacturing process that may require a little more or a little less material than planned.

The pull system is appropriate under certain circumstances such as when deliveries to production must be made quickly, multiple deliveries will be required for the completion of a work order, and precise coordination of deliveries with usage will be important. On the other hand, the need for storage space in production will be limited and material in the shop will turn over quickly.

"Push" means that material is moved to production in response to a prearranged plan such as a production schedule or a work order. Push is appropriate where delivery times are long and where all the material required for a work order can be delivered at once. Temporary storage must be provided in production for material that has been delivered but has not yet been processed.

Some businesses use a method that is partly pull and partly push. The material required is all delivered at one time and may even be prepicked and staged before delivery. But, nothing is delivered until production requests it. This method is partly pull because nothing happens until manufacturing requests it and partly push because the quantities are preplanned and everything is picked and delivered at once. The push method is traditional and is still appropriate in many businesses. The pull method has recently been gaining in popularity with increased emphasis on Just-in-Time concepts.

Push Methods

Use of the push method of moving material into the production area assumes that the inventory system has some advance warning of the work that the shop will be doing. The inventory system needs this information so it can pick and prepare materials for delivery on a planned basis.

In most job shop businesses, advance notice comes in the form of manufacturing (or work) orders. Each work order must contain:

1. An order number to identify it separately from all others
2. The number of the item to be made or assembled under this order
3. The quantity that will be made or assembled
4. Either a start date or a due date

In addition, the inventory system needs access to the list of component parts and items that will be required to complete this order, the list of operations that are to be performed, the work centers at which each operation will be done, and a definition of which components will be required at which work center. The inventory system also needs either access to the planned start dates and times for each operation or the ability to calculate them. Other information that may be required includes expected scrap amounts by operation and tooling requirements.

Inventory systems that run on the same computer as the manufacturing planning system can sometimes share the manufacturing system's database. Others will require that the orders be downloaded to them from the manufacturing planning system. Many inventory systems require that the component list and delivery information be downloaded with each order.

Other businesses, often process-oriented ones, do not control their production with shop orders but use an assembly or production schedule instead. To the inventory system, the production schedule and the shop order are one and the same. Both define what will be made and when it will be made. And, from that definition, the inventory system can deduce the materials and parts that will be required, where they will be required, and when they will be required.

Pull Methods

With pull distribution of materials into production, the inventory system needs a way to find out what is needed and when. One way of communicating needs, is to use two containers for each item required in production. Both containers are marked with the item number and quantity that they should contain. One container is full of parts and is used by the production operators while the other, empty, is returned to the stockroom for a refill. When the full container becomes empty, the production operator swaps containers and the cycle repeats itself.

This is the kanban concept. The word "kanban," is Japanese for "visible record." It refers specifically to the card that Toyota attaches to containers to document the item and quantity required. The kanban concept has become popular in connection with Just-in-Time manufacturing. The idea of a kanban, however, need not be limited to cards or to containers. The only requirements are to inform the inventory system of the items and quantities required and the places where they are required. Kanbans can, indeed, be cards attached to containers. When a card is delivered to the inventory office, a clerk can scan its bar code, informing the inventory system that a delivery to manufacturing is required. Or the scanners can be located in manufacturing, eliminating the need to deliver the cards. In fact the cards themselves can be eliminated. An expediter can be equipped with a radio terminal. The expediter walks the aisles looking for low inventories. When something is found that needs replenishment, he or she scans the label on the shelf or bin. The result is a requirement to pick and deliver one standard quantity of that item.

Another way is to treat point-of-use stores and floor stock as forward picking areas. Material handlers supply the production operations from the point-of-use storage areas. As material is withdrawn, the material handler scans the bin or shelf label and keys the quantity taken. In some circumstances, counting scales can provide direct input of the quantity, or the material handler can simply take a prepackaged quantity. The system then decrements the inventory in that location and applies its normal replenishment logic to determine when more should be brought from the reserve stocks in the warehouse.

The treatment of point-of-use stores as forward picking areas is often particularly useful for low-cost, bulk items like fasteners. But, the additional staging step means additional material handling and additional delay from the receiving dock to the point of use. The added costs of any staging areas or point-of-use stockrooms should be weighed against their benefits.

How Much Control?

Figure 9.4 shows a simple assembly operation with the material flow required to support it. In this example:

1. Both big boxes and little boxes are delivered from the main warehouse to a point-of-use stocking area along the wall.
2. They are each dispensed in pallet quantities to separate work stations on the assembly line. At each work station, two pallets are kept. One pallet is for the assembler's use; the other is for use when the first runs out.
3. The first assembler places large boxes on the line.
4. The second assembler places a small box inside each large box.
5. The third assembler removes the assemblies from the end of the line and palletizes them.
6. The completed assemblies are then taken directly to the main warehouse for storage and disbursement to other departments.

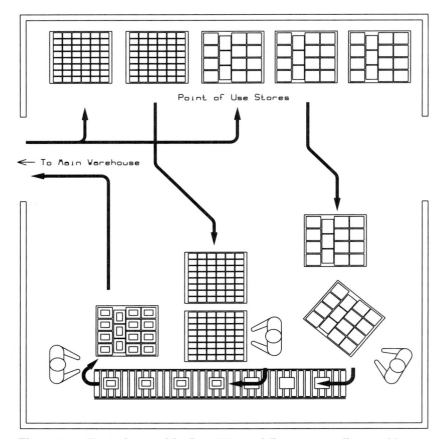

Figure 9.4. Typical assembly flow. Material flow in a small assembly operation involves movement from the warehouse or from a prior operation, point of use storage, on-line storage, work-in-process, and movement of the completed items to the warehouse or the next operation.

An inventory control system (or the work-in-process portion of a shop floor control system) is responsible for tracking this inventory. The question is, how much control should be exercised?

For example, the inventory system can simply issue product as it leaves the main warehouse and rereceive it as it returns. Product in the point-of-use stock area, in-transit, and on the line would not then be part of the inventory. Or, control could be retained over the point-of-use stock area. Material could be removed from the books when it is delivered to the assemblers and they are reintroduced as pallets are completed at the end of the assembly line. Or, even more detailed control could extend to the pallets at the line. Single items could be issued from the inventory as the assemblers remove them from the pallets and they are reintroduced into the inventory as individual completions occur. System cost, operating cost, and inventory accuracy will all be affected by the strategy used.

When deciding how much control to exercise over work-in-process inventory, remember that the real trade-off is between the cost of capturing information and doing without that information. If the location of each item is known precisely, people can find things quickly and easily and the flow of work is only rarely interrupted. If, however, the business can run smoothly with only approximate knowledge of where parts are now located, system cost and material handling labor can be reduced.

In some cases an appropriate compromise between control and cost might be reached by retaining control by location over material to the point where unit loads are broken down. In Figure 9.4 this means controlling the point of use storage area by pallet and by location but considering the pallets at the assembly line to be "in production." Location control is relatively simple for the full pallets. It becomes more complicated when dealing with single items.

MOVEMENTS BETWEEN WORK CENTERS AND TO THE WAREHOUSE

The destination of material leaving a work center is normally specified on the material routing. If the inventory system is provided with access to routings, validation of proper delivery is possible. It should always be possible for a shop scheduler or supervisor to override the material's destination.

Regardless of the material's destination, product movements out of a work center are triggered by completions. In this instance, the key to inventory accuracy lies in accurate capture of the quantities, item numbers, and order numbers involved.

When a load is ready to be moved from one work center to the next or to the warehouse, a signal of some kind should be passed to the inventory system. The inventory system should use this signal to dispatch a material handler to the pick-up point and post the completion quantity to the work center's records. If the destination is a storage location under the inventory system's control, it must also assign storage space and must handle instances in which no space is available.

The completion signal should specify the completing work center and the quantity to be moved. If the inventory system is designed to know which product is being run in each work center, no further input is required. Otherwise the signal must also specify the work order or schedule number and, optionally, the item number.

Item and order identification are most accurately done with bar codes. Barcoded completion documents can be printed along with or as part of the work order itself. AIAG labels, if used internally in the plant to identify product, provide all of the information required. The completing work center can be identified by the inventory system automatically if each is equipped with a terminal of its own. Or, bar codes can be used if work centers share terminals.

Determination of the quantity completed and ready for movement is a more complex problem. By far the most accurate method and the one requiring the least labor involves unit loads. If every load of an item contains only a precisely known quantity, personnel need only indicate to the system whether or not the load is full. Only the last load leaving an operation will be partly full and only this load will require counting. Or, if container tare weights are known accurately in advance or if the items can be weighed without the container, a counting scale can be used.

When items simply cannot be built into precise unit loads, either for economic or physical reasons, it may be necessary to fall back on either a manual count or on a mechanical or electrical counter on a conveyor or machine. In either case, accuracy will be compromised. The situation determines which of these methods will produce the fewest errors.

Machine-based counting has the potential for accuracy, but the facilities must be carefully designed to assure that only good pieces are counted and that all good pieces are counted. Setup scrap, routine losses, and inspection pieces must all be accurately accounted for and must be excluded from the machine's counts. In some businesses, the fact that production people are measured almost entirely on output means that machine counts that are not under the employee's control will be more accurate than those that can be altered. When the cost of the counting equipment and communications with the inventory system are considered, it may simply not be worthwhile.

Manual counts, however, are notoriously inaccurate, although proper personnel training and motivation can help. Improvement in manual counting results from an independent, validating count from another employee. Validating counts can be provided by the material handler who moves the load away from the work center or by the person who receives the load in the next one.

Work order completions involve some additional processing. The last load completed from a work center is likely to be partly full. In this instance, the inventory system should require a count and should not accept a standard unit load quantity unless it is confirmed by the production employee. In addition, left over materials must be returned to inventory, and scrap and losses must be accounted for.

Scrap and loss accounting can be relatively simple if financial management and the quality control department do not require extensive analysis. It can work this way: The inventory system should track material issues to each work order and should record accurate completions. Both numbers are kept accurate through validation. As the work order is closed, the system should explode the completions to determine the quantity of each component that was actually consumed in the manufacture of good product. Returns to stock are accurately counted, put away, and validated for the work order. Then, the quantity issued less the sum of the quantity used and the quantity returned is chargeable to the scrap and loss account.

EXECUTING MATERIAL MOVEMENTS

All internal material movements consist of two parts: a pickup and a drop-off. The proper validation of these two parts is essential to inventory accuracy.

People, after all, make mistakes and when mistakes are made and are not caught and corrected, the result is inaccurate inventory.

The picking of material in the warehouse for delivery to a work center often involves more than simply pulling a pallet for delivery. Warehouse labor tends to be heavily concentrated in picking, so elaborate schemes are often implemented to maximize productivity. Specialized equipment is often used. The material picked for a work order may pass through as many as a half-dozen hands before reaching the production area. In fact, the process of picking material for work orders is so much like the picking of customer orders that discussion of it is deferred to Chapter 10.

Regardless of the source of the material, when a material handler picks up material for internal delivery, the immediate concern is identification of the material. If the material is improperly identified, it will most likely be delivered to the wrong place. As a result, the inventory will be incorrect and labor will have been wasted. There are several methods that can be used to validate proper pickup of material:

1. Some pickups are made from locations that can contain only one load. If the pickup location selected by the material handler is known to be correct and if the inventory in that location is known to be accurate, the load picked up must be the one desired and no further validation is necessary. One example might be a pickup from a single-pallet storage location. If the content of the location is known and accuracy is known to be high, the pickup can be validated by scanning a bar code attached to the location. Another example might be a pickup from a work center that is running a known part. Validation of this pickup can be made by scanning a nearby bar code. Again, if there is no room for error, no further validation is required.

2. Other pickups are made from locations that can contain more than one load, leaving the possibility for error open. Examples include staging areas, receiving docks, work centers that make several items at once, and work centers that change over from one item to the next in a short period of time. (The last example requires validation because the material handler might arrive late and find several loads of different items waiting to be moved.) In these cases, often the best solution is to identify the product with a bar-coded label or tag.

3. Manual load identification is more practical in some businesses than in others and, in some circumstances, may be the only feasible method. Take, for example, the product that passes through an acid etch, a wash, a paint booth, and a dryer on a conveyor. If several products are intermixed on the conveyor and then sorted out by hand at the unloading station, there may be no reasonable alternative to manual identification[1]. In these cases, it is best where possible to ar-

---

[1] Actually, even this case has a solution, although it is complex. If the material arriving at the etch, wash, paint, and dry station is accurately preidentified, the people loading the conveyor could scan

range for the identification to be made separately by two people and cross-checked by the inventory system. The person unloading the conveyor, for instance, could identify the pallet to the inventory system and then the material handler could be required to reidentify it.

These methods assume that material handlers are moving precounted loads of material. In some instances it may not be feasible or economic to precount the material. If inventories are to be kept at all, counting in some form is necessary. Either the material handler can be charged with counting, or arrangements can be made for counts to be performed later at the material's destination. If the system assigns storage locations, counts are required in advance because the quantity being moved is one of the data elements used in location selection. The counts must then be made either by the people working at the pickup location or by the material handler. On the other hand, if the pickup location is an unstaffed machine and the destination is staffed, counting at the destination may be the only sensible alternative. In either case, the techniques of unit loading and counting scales should be used where possible to assure accuracy.

In all cases, regardless of who does the identifying and counting, the next person to handle the material in a production environment should be asked to verify both quantity and identity. When errors are made, they are best found and corrected as quickly as possible.

The drop-off portion of an internal movement of material is simpler than the pickup portion. The major concern at drop-off time is to assure that the material has been delivered to the proper location. In almost all instances, this is best done with bar-coded location labels on every individual storage location, at every machine or work center, and at all in-between staging locations. When the material handler delivers the material, these locations can be scanned, giving the inventory system an error-free record of where the material was placed. As a bonus, the system can then identify instances in which the material was put in the wrong place and can take action to have the problem corrected.

DATABASE CONTROL OVER MOVEMENT

In a large, modern inventory facility, a great deal of material is in constant motion. If control over material in motion is lost, coordination between people, productivity, and inventory accuracy will suffer. An efficient way is needed to track material while it is being moved and being processed in the factory.

There is no single best way to control material in motion. Any competent designer with experience in the design of real-time databases can develop a suitable

---

and remove identifying bar codes as they load parts. The scanner could be connected to a programmable controller that would keep track of the items on the conveyor in the same sequence in which they were loaded. As parts emerge, the programmable controller could drive a bar code printer to produce new labels in the right sequence for application to the parts as they are unloaded. Real complications, however, surface when one considers the number of things which can go wrong. Imagine what must be done when the conveyor breaks down and product is offloaded from the middle of it.

architecture. The example below, however, is proven and can serve as a source of ideas for even the most experienced (see Table 9.1). The table gives a view of a portion of an inventory control database for a manufacturing business. It is designed for a flat file manager rather than a relational database manager to make it as broadly applicable and as easily understood as possible.

The material movement cycle begins when a work order is established and components are allocated for it. During allocation, the pending-picks quantity on the item/location record is increased by the quantity required for the work order to record the allocation and reserve the material. Also, records are added to the item/operation/component/pick file and chained to the item/operation/component record to reflect the planned picking and speed access into the database later.

At some later time, a request is made by manufacturing for a component item to be applied to a particular work order and operation number. The inventory system retrieves the necessary item/operation/component detail record and follows the chain into the item/operation/component/pick file to find a location from which the material can be picked. Sometimes more than one picking location is required. But, for the purposes of this example, it is assumed that only one is necessary.

Then the inventory system reserves storage space at the destination end of the move. If the work center is linked to several storage locations, one of these locations is chosen using the work center/location file and using dimensional data for both the item being moved and the location itself. The reservation is accomplished by increasing the "inbound moves" quantity on the destination item/location record.

Next, the inventory system investigates the path that the material must follow to get from the chosen picking location to the work center that needs it. It retrieves the location/location record for the picking location and the work center at which the operation is to be performed. (Work centers are linked to locations on the work center/location file.) The location/location file, also known as the plant map, accommodates instances in which movements must be broken down into pieces. Suppose, for instance, an elevator move is required to get from location A to location B. If the elevator itself is designated as location C, a record on the plant map would appear on the file listing A as the from-location, B as the to-location and C as the intermediate location. In addition to elevator moves, the plant map can accommodate instances where material must be passed from one type of vehicle to another and similar interruptions in the flow of material. For the sake of the example under discussion, assume that the elevator move is required.

The inventory system then places a movement transaction in the work queue file. The item number and quantity were specified by manufacturing, the to-location was found in the plant map, and the from-location is the picking location itself.

Through some mechanism—possibly a radio terminal—a material handler is assigned the job of picking the material and moving it to the elevator. His or her identification is noted on the work queue. Then, when material pickup is validated, two things happen. First, the picking item/location record's on-hand bal-

TABLE 9.1.   DATABASE LAYOUT FOR MOVEMENT CONTROL

File	Field Name	Description
Work order	Order number	Order number or schedule number
	Item number	Parent item
	Quantity ordered	Quantity to be made
	Quantity in-transit	Quantity completed but not yet received in the warehouse
	Quantity complete	Quantity received in the warehouse
	Due date	Date order must be complete
Item/operation (routing)	Item number	Parent item
	Operation number	What work will be done
	Work center	Where the work will be done
	Production group	Flow of material
	Start date	Start date required for this operation
Item/operation/ component	Item number	Parent item
	Operation number	What work will be done
	Component item	Order line number
	Quantity per	Quantity required per unit completed
	Quantity required	Quantity required in total
	In-transit to mfg.	Quantity issued but not yet received in manufacturing
	Quantity issued	Quantity received in manufacturing
	In-transit to whse.	Quantity returned but not yet received in the warehouse
	Quantity returned	Quantity received in the warehouse
Item/operation/ component/location	Item number	Parent item
	Operation number	What work will be done
	Component item	Order line number
	Location	Where the material will be gotten
	Quantity required	Quantity required in total
	Record type	A delivery or a return
	In-transit to mfg.	Quantity issued but not yet received in manufacturing
	Quantity issued	Quantity received in manufacturing
	In-transit to whse.	Quantity returned but not yet received in the warehouse
	Quantity returned	Quantity received in the warehouse
Item master	Item number	Part number (parent or component)
	Description	Item description
	Item	Dimensions of the unit itself
	Weight	
	Length	
	Width	
	Height	
	Standard Case	Dimensions of the standard case package
	Quantity	
	Weight	
	Length	

TABLE 9.1. (CONTINUED)

File	Field Name	Description
	Width	
	Height	
	Standard Pallet	Dimensions of a pallet of the product
	Quantity	
	Weight	
	Length	
	Width	
	Height	
Work queue	Transaction number	For tracking and auditing purposes
	Transaction type	Put-away, move, pick, etc.
	Item number	Item number to be moved
	Quantity	Quantity to be moved
	From location	Location to move from
	To location	Location to move to
	Destination	Ultimate location
Location	Location	Identifier of a specific storage location
	Function	Reserve stores, forward pick, staging area
	Device	Rack, floor storage, bin, shelf, etc.
	Dimensions	Dimensions of the location
	Weight limit	
	Depth	
	Width	
	Height	
Item/location	Item number	Key field
	Location	Key field
	Quantities	
	On hand	Amount physically on hand
	Pending picks	Amount reserved for an order
	Outbound moves	Amount committed to moves out of this location exclusive of orders
	Replenish (reg.)	In-transit replenishments (normal priority)
	Replenish (emerg.)	In-transit replenishments (emergencies)
	Inbound moves	Amount in-transit inbound exclusive of replenishments
	FIFO date	Date material was received
Location/location	From location	Location to move from
	To location	Location to move to
	Intermediate	Staging location required
Work center/location	Work center	Work center number
	Location use	Location used for pick-up of drop-off
	Location	Location number

ance is reduced by the amount taken and the pending pick quantity is similarly reduced. This frees the space in the location for other uses. And, second, the work order in-transit to manufacturing quantity is increased by the quantity being moved.

At this point, the inventory is being driven down an aisle toward the elevator. The fact that the inventory exists and is in motion is recorded on the work queue. Space is reserved for it on the item/location file in a storage location associated with the receiving work center. Manufacturing knows that the material is coming because the move was recorded on the item/operation/component record. When the material arrives at the elevator, the material handler validates its delivery by scanning a bar code at the elevator staging area. The system also knows that this is not the ultimate location of the material. It looks at the plant map again to see if the next required step is another staging location or if the material can be delivered directly. It then puts another transaction on the work queue to move the material from the elevator staging area into the elevator and out again to another staging area on the assembly floor. When that move has been completed, still another transaction is generated to move the load from the second elevator staging area to the work center.

When the material finally arrives at the work center, the books must be closed on the movement. This means that the destination's on-hand balance must be increased and its inbound moves field must be decreased. It means that the work order in-transit to manufacturing field must be decreased and the work order quantity issued field must be increased. And it means that the work center's item/location record must be updated by increasing the on-hand balance and decreasing the inbound moves quantity.

Complex as this example may be, it is simple compared to real life. For instance, small parts may be moved into manufacturing by having a material handler make several picks in the warehouse and then transport a mixed pallet of material to the shop. Or, a material movement request might be canceled while the material is under way. This, of course, will require not only reversing the existing space reservation at the work center and making a new reservation (or several of them) in the warehouse but will also require the generation of the necessary transactions to move the material back. Despite the complications, there is a very strong structure involved in the control logic. When systems take advantage of this structure, programming and debugging can be manageable. And, most important, the control achieved can be tight and clean, supporting highly accurate inventories throughout the plant.

Example 9.1. All-manual data collection using central key entry. In a high-accuracy manual data collection environment, individual movements or tasks are best dispatched in writing. As each material handler completes a task list, it is turned in to a supervisor or dispatcher who replaces it with a fresh one. The dispatcher directs the inventory system in the preparation of the task lists. He or she selects the type of work to be performed (i.e., replenishments, consolidations, deliveries to manufacturing, etc.) and specifies the number of tasks to be printed on the task list. The dispatcher does this using a screen that displays the number of tasks available in each category by priority level. The inventory system prints the tasks, selecting the highest-priority ones first and the oldest ones first within a priority. Priority levels are often limited to two—regular tasks and emergency replenishments—but some businesses may see a need for more detailed priorities.

The task list is kept simple to make it as understandable as possible. See Figure 9.5 for a sample task list. It lists only those tasks that are to be done and lists them in the sequence in which they are to be done. It lists the source location, the part number to be moved, the quantity, and the destination. Space is allowed for validation information and, if necessary, exceptions.

Tasks are listed only once by the inventory system, regardless of the number of task lists printed. The task lists are serial numbered in a bar code on each list for use by the dispatcher in entering completions. The serial number is also used by the inventory system to identify listed tasks that were not performed so they can be released and redispatched the next time a list is printed.

The material handler performs the tasks shown and, for each task, validates that the task was properly performed by recording the two-character code found on each location. These codes are randomly generated and stored on the inventory system's location file, allowing the software to validate each material movement. Because the codes are complex and difficult to memorize, the temptation to "cheat" is minimal. Therefore, material handlers are likely to actually record what they see. The inventory control system tracks the number of errors made by each material handler each day, reinforcing the need to work accurately and to record information carefully on the task lists. Location "codes" are a variation on the theme of validation. For a more complete discussion of the coding concept, see Chapter 13.

As each task list is returned, the dispatcher scans its bar code and the inventory system displays an image of the task list on the screen. The dispatcher then keys the location code for each task completed. The system validates the codes and updates on-hand balances. When validation errors occur, they are brought to the dispatcher's attention. The dispatcher can check them out personally, report them to a supervisor, or add them to a list of locations to be cycle counted.

Example 9.2.   Paper driven off-line data collection. Off-line (nonradio) terminals for data collection can be used in conjunction with a printed task list (Figure 9.5). Or, some of the more sophisticated terminals are capable of accepting a downloaded electronic version of the task list from the inventory system computer. This electronic task list can then be used to prompt the material handler through each of the required tasks. In the latter case, the material handlers work much as described for a hi-tech environment in the Example 9.3 below.

Task lists, when used with nonradio terminals, are usually changed slightly from the sample in Figure 9.5. The task list bar code is no longer required, and four new bar codes are added for each task to be performed. These bar codes identify to the terminal the source location, the destination location, the quantity to be moved, and a system-assigned transaction number.

The material handler begins by identifying him- or herself to the terminal, often by scanning a bar code on his or her badge or company ID card. The terminal

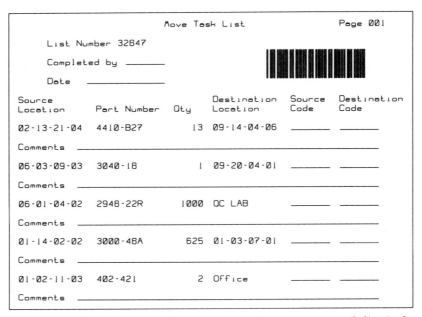

Figure 9.5. Move task list. This example of a movement task list is designed for manual (non-bar-coded) data collection.

then associates all of the work done with the employee number and, later when information is uploaded to the inventory system, the employee's ID is associated with the work he or she did.

The material handler scans all four bar codes for the first task on the task list and the terminal responds by prompting for a scan of the bar code on the source location. The material handler travels to the source location and does the required scan. The terminal compares this scan with the one found on the task list. If the two locations match, it displays the quantity to be picked. The material handler then picks the material and presses the enter key. If a problem such as an unplanned inventory shortage turns up, the material handler can key an overriding quantity. The terminal then displays the material's destination. The material handler delivers the material to the destination and scans the location label there.

If, at any time, a source or destination location does not match the one scanned from the task list, the terminal displays a warning message and makes a loud beep. The material handler must then find and scan the correct location label. Or, if the material handler for some reason cannot deliver the material as required, an override key can be used. When the override key is used, the material must be returned to the source location. The material handler cannot be allowed to select a destination because the location selected may have been reserved by the inventory system for some other use. Instead, the override is communicated back to the inventory system along with the upload of the other collected information and the inventory system selects an alternate location. The task is then printed again on another task list for another try.

Example 9.3.   Hi-tech. When radio terminals are used, the printed task list and the process of uploading collected data to the inventory system can both be done away with. Instead, the inventory system prompts and compares data directly from the master list (or queue) of tasks to be performed. Material handlers are assigned tasks by the computer, one at a time, with all material handlers assigned to making moves working out of a single queue of move transactions. Each assignment is given in the form of a source location. After the material handler has found the source location and has scanned its bar code, the inventory system validates the location and displays the item number and quantity to be moved. The material handler then takes the required material, confirms the quantity, travels to the destination, and validates the move by scanning the destination location label.

When material cannot be delivered as planned, the inventory system can assign an alternate location immediately, eliminating the trip back to the source location. The material handler can even be asked why the task cannot be completed as planned. Based on the response, appropriate action can be taken such as, for instance, disabling the location if repairs are needed or scheduling a cycle count if an inventory error is suspected.

10

Outbound Operations

The outbound side of an inventory facility is often the most complex part because material tends to be received in bulk and shipped in smaller quantities. Shipment in small quantities means relatively high picking, packing, and shipping cost and, therefore, justification for sophisticated material handling equipment. Because inventory accuracy is tightly bound to material handling, sophisticated material handling equipment means the inventory system will need to be sophisticated too.

Picking and shipping methods vary considerably from company to company, both in terms of the equipment used and the way it is used. For example, take the hardware distribution industry. All major hardware chains handle more or less the same items and all have more or less the same handling problems and more or less the same customer ordering patterns. One Midwest chain of hardware stores has a distribution center that is organized into full pallet, full case, and broken case areas with a separate area set aside for hard-to-handle items. The broken case area consists of bins of all sizes while the full cases are stored on shelving and the full pallets on racks. Each of these three areas is replenished from the previous one.

Picking of full cases and single items is done by pickers on foot. The pickers use carts, each containing up to six totes. On each pass through the warehouse, each picker picks orders that have been computer selected based on the expected cube of the shipment, to a maximum of the cube of the six totes. The walking distance and time required is minimized by subdividing the broken case and full case areas into smaller areas for fast movers, slow movers, and in-between items. Pickers, therefore, frequently skip aisles and some aisles may go unvisited for hours at a time.

Next to the shipping dock is an order assembly area, divided into cart and pallet parking spaces. Completed carts and full pallet picks made by lift-truck operators are delivered to this area and dropped in any available space. The picker tells the inventory system where the material was left, takes another work assignment, and leaves.

Shipments are made on company trucks that work regular routes. When a trailer is to be loaded, the system begins with the customer who will be unloaded last. It gives the loaders a list of the parking spaces in the assembly area where the product for that customer can be found. Loading then proceeds from the nose of the trailer to the rear on an order-by-order basis. The beauty of this system is the minimal investment in equipment and the accomplishment of sortation as a by-product of the trailer-loading process.

An east coast hardware distributor works differently. About a dozen trailers are loaded at a time. Full and broken case picking of high-volume items is done from a flow rack to a conveyor system in waves of 20 to 30 orders each. The conveyor system deposits the picks on a large, slowly rotating carousel where they are sorted out by order and placed on carts. Full pallet and hard-to-handle items are picked separately and brought to a staging area. The trailer loaders at each door again work from the nose to the rear of the trailer, loading orders in reverse stop sequence. As each order is loaded, the necessary items are retrieved from the carousel and the staging area and placed on the trailer.

The differences between these two operations are striking, particularly since their overall productivity is about equal. In effect, the Midwest company has invested in systems, while the east coast company has invested in conveyors. Because picking and shipping methods and system requirements differ so much, it is impossible to present a single best way to achieve outbound accuracy. But, there are many proven ideas that can be abstracted, described, and evaluated. The integration of these ideas into a single system for a specific business is left in the hands of the reader.

ORDER ENTRY

Outbound inventory processes are driven by orders that come from three sources: customers, manufacturing facilities within the building or nearby, and other manufacturing and distribution facilities at other sites within the company. The terms "customer order," "shop order," and "transfer order" are used to distinguish between the three kinds of orders. The entry of customer orders and either generation or entry of shop and transfer orders are not usually included in inventory systems.

Customer order entry, particularly in high-volume businesses, is a sophisticated, customer service oriented application that combines material availability with customer needs. Such functions as quotations, pricing, credit approval, shipment date forecasting, priority updating, and inquiry response are often included.

Shop orders may be generated by hand but are often created by a Manufacturing Resource Planning system. Manufacturing Resource Planning (also known as MRP II) begins with customer orders booked for future delivery or a sales forecast or a blend of the two. From this information, a master production schedule is created that determines what the shop will build in the coming time periods. Then, based on this master schedule, the Material Requirements Planning (MRP) subsystem plans and schedules the shop and purchase orders necessary to meet the master schedule.

Transfer orders, in companies that operate several plants and distribution centers, are often created by a Distribution Requirements Planning system (DRP). In a process much like MRP, DRP determines the need for replenishment of finished goods and, often, the requirements for transfer of material from one facility to another.

All three of these systems use material availability information kept by the inventory system and produce, among other things, orders that are used by the inventory system. The orders are either downloaded to the inventory system computer or are otherwise made available to it. Usually, availability of an order occurs only when the inventory system is authorized to take action based on it.

In some installations, orders are not given to the inventory system until shortly before their due date. In others, orders are passed as soon as the creating system is done with them. Delaying order downloading has the advantage of limiting the size of the inventory system's files and, to some degree, reducing the computer's workload. In addition, when downloading is delayed, order changes can be made more easily. On the other hand, when orders are sent to the inventory system immediately, the users of the inventory system gain a degree of visibility into the future, which may have significant management benefit.

Most modern inventory systems accept orders, order changes, and order cancellations from the order entry, MRP, and DRP systems. Most also include the ability to enter, cancel, and update orders directly. These abilities can be essential when communication with the order-generating systems breaks down, and they can be useful when rush orders and special adjustments must be handled. Depending on the design of the order-generating systems, it may be necessary for the inventory system to upload locally made additions and changes.

Inventory system designers should also recognize that there comes a point in the life of every order when change is no longer possible. If order changes are necessary after this point, they are made by placing a new, corrected order and advising the recipient that unwanted material received on the old order should be returned. The inventory system, at this point, is committed to the picking and shipment of the original order and cannot reasonably back out.

The selection of the point at which order changes are no longer accepted by the inventory system has a significant impact on system cost and on material handling and shipping costs. It should be a conscious decision. In some businesses, it will be an important one. At one extreme, a few companies allow orders to be changed up to the time the shipment physically leaves the plant. At the other extreme, a few companies consider orders to be final at the time they are turned over to the inventory system for shipment. Most companies, however, select a point somewhere between these extremes.

SELECTION AND ALLOCATION

Material allocation—the reservation of material for orders—is done at several levels. The order entry system allocates available inventory as commitments are made to customers. MRP and DRP allocate subassemblies, component parts, and raw materials as work orders are planned. Each system allocates on its own files based on the available quantity reported by the inventory system. The final and most authoritative allocation is the one done by the inventory system. This allocation is considered the most authoritative because the inventory system has the master inventory file and because it is the system that will actually take action based on the allocations. The other systems need to allocate to perform their functions, but actual shipments cannot occur until the inventory system does its allocation.

Allocation at the inventory system level is best delayed until just prior to picking and shipping (or delivery to the plant). This delay keeps open the company's options for use of material. The additional flexibility gained can, at times, make a great deal of difference in operational efficiency.

Order Selection

The first step in the allocation of orders by the inventory system is the selection of a group of orders to be allocated. This group of orders is usually called a "wave." The term is apt because, starting with allocation, the group of orders can move through the warehouse like a wave moves across a beach. Each warehouse area handles its part of the wave in turn, and the next wave is right on the heels of the first one.

The process of creating waves is useful for two reasons. First, it provides a point of manual control and an opportunity for a planner or supervisor to intervene. In a sense, the selection of orders for a wave is analogous to the MRP master scheduling function. And second, order selection can be used to pace warehouse operations and provide a measure of control over the workload in its various parts.

Order selection is typically done by a planner with significant help from the inventory system. The planner begins by defining selection criteria to the inventory system. Based on these criteria, the inventory system reviews open, unselected orders and makes a preliminary selection. The preliminary selection is then displayed along with summary information such as the total weight and cube of the wave (by trailer if selection is trailer based) and the number of picks in the wave by picking zone. Shortages are not known for certain at this point because allocation has not been done. But, projected shortages based on the overall quantity available and the requirements of the wave are summarized and displayed. The orders in the wave are also available to the planner with information about their potential shortages. The planner is given the choice of rejecting the preliminary wave and respecifying the selection criteria, of modifying it by adding or subtracting orders or groups of orders, or of accepting it. One design for a wave display screen appears in Figure 10.1.

```
                                    WAVE 30282
SELECTED: CARRIER    UPSZ    LIMITS:  WEIGHT    NONE    RESULTS: WEIGHT      6849
          MAX PRIOR  6                CUBE      NONE             CUBE        1947
          SHIP DATE  DUE              LINES     NONE             ORDERS      803
                                                                 SHORTAGES     13

ORDER NO.  PRI  DUE DATE  CUSTOMER  LINES  POUNDS  CUBE  SHORTAGES

 48293      2    4/20     804227      7       32     6
 48072      2    4/22     384623      3       12     4
 48254      3    3/17     385674      2        6     7
 48091      3    3/18     364512      5       22     9     1  $  146
 48440      3    3/27     374261      1        5     6
 48522      3    4/12     813409      1       19    14
 48092      3    4/21     002843      4       61    12
 48441      4    3/12     432841      3       44    10
 48442      4    3/17     846342      1       37     8
 48503      4    3/23     020042      1       11     4
 47770      4    4/18     482881      2        9     5
 48332      4    4/20     283461      3        4     1     2  $  309
 48042      4    4/20     483022     10       58     8
 48196      5    3/29     328520      1       13     2
 48202      5    4/01     230870      2       16     3

F1=ACCEPT/ALLOCATE F2=REJECT/EXIT F3=DELETE ORDER F4=DISPLAY ORDER F5=ADD ORDER
```

Figure 10.1. Order selection screen. The selection of the outbound orders that will comprise a picking wave is done through an on-line CRT using a screen similar to the one illustrated.

The order selection criteria used by the warehouse planner will depend on the business, the industry, the picking methods in use, the carriers used, and other factors. In most cases, however, the following will be adequate:

- Planned or promised order ship date. Allows orders to be picked without including those intended for shipment in the future. In some instances, the planner may also wish to build a picking wave for one or more specific days in the future.
- Order entry date. Allows orders to be selected and allocated in the order in which they were received and entered. In some businesses this is an important criteria when product shortages exist.
- Carrier. Order selection by carrier allows the coordination of picking with carrier arrival schedules. If, for instance, UPS picks up daily at 2 P.M., a 10 A.M. wave of UPS orders might be appropriate.
- Order priority. Allows selection of only the important orders for a particular wave or, conversely, allows the least important orders to be ignored temporarily.
- Order type. Allows shop orders to be picked separately from customer orders.
- Specific orders or customers. The selection of a small number of specific orders is useful in special situations where certain orders must be picked out of turn.
- Minimum and maximum order size, measured in pounds and/or cubic feet. Depending on picking and handling methods, it may make sense to pick small orders separately from large ones.

- Maximum wave size, measured in pounds and/or cubic feet. The ability to limit the total size of a wave allows the planner to schedule the picking of the right amount of product to fill a trailer or a predefined group of trailers.
- Maximum wave size, measured in number of picks. The ability to limit a wave by the number of picks involved gives the planner control over the likely amount of time that will be required to complete it.

The allocation of inventory to customer orders in a strict first-come, first-served basis is important to some businesses and can be handled by the planner in two ways. The planner can either build waves in the sequence in which the orders were received or, when certain customers simply must not be shorted, material can be "reserved" for them. Reservation facilities are described in Chapter 11.

Some inventory systems allow completed waves to be stored pending a later allocation. But, storing waves might create a problem. If new orders or important changes arrive between the time the wave is created and the time the material is shipped, there will be a need to change the wave prior to allocation. This complicates the software with little apparent benefit. Unless there are business reasons to the contrary, it is simpler to delay the creation of waves until the last minute and then carry them through from start to finish without interruption.

Allocation

During the wave-building process, the inventory system displays shortage information to the planner. But typically, this information is created "on the fly" and does not involve the actual allocation of product. In a real-time system, therefore, there is always the possibility that different shortages will be found when allocation is done. This situation can arise, for instance, if a cycle count adjustment is made between the time the planner builds the wave and the time the allocation is run. New receipts can also affect shortages. It is, therefore, important that the inventory system provide a way for the planner to "deallocate" material reserved for a wave and then delete the wave itself to start over again.

The allocation processor is normally a background task because it usually involves a significant amount of computing. It is responsible for:

- Reserving (allocating) material
- Generating picking transactions
- Identifying and reporting shortages
- Replenishing forward picking locations

The first step in allocation is usually the sorting of the order lines in the wave into allocation sequence. The allocator works item by item and order by order so the sort should be by item, priority, and order. Then, for each line on each order, the allocator decides how much of the order can be filled, selects the locations from which it will be picked, and makes the allocation. The selection of picking locations is, in itself, a complex process, described in detail in Chapter 11. Allocation is accomplished simply by adding the quantity to be picked from each location to an "allocated quantity" field on the item/location file. It is important that allocation be done on a location-by-location basis to avoid duplicating picking assignments when the next order is allocated.

For each picking location selected for each line on each order, a record is added to the picking work queue file. This record documents picks that have been planned but not yet executed. Later, when the picking is actually done and validated, the record will be removed from the file. Software must allow for instances in which a single order line is picked from more than one location. Physical handling methods must, likewise, provide a way for the picks to be merged into a single shipment or a single delivery to the factory.

In some cases it will not be possible to select picking locations for an order line because there is inadequate stock available. These shortages are usually best placed in a work file and held for either printing or display after the allocation run is complete.

And, finally, in some cases, the allocator will identify forward picking locations that require replenishment. Usually material to be picked from a forward picking location is limited to less-than-pallet quantities. If inadequate material exists in the forward picking locations and if reserve stock exists, the allocator will allocate despite the shortage and then generate an emergency (high priority) replenishment. Or, in some businesses it may be more appropriate for the allocator to direct these picks to reserve locations.

In addition to emergency replenishments, some allocators also identify cases in which picks reduce the on-hand balance below a predefined replenishment point. They then generate lower-priority (regular) replenishments. Regardless of the type (or priority) of the replenishment, the allocator must select reserve picking locations, allocate material, create transactions to do the work, and put those transactions in the replenishment queue. The handling of replenishment needs is often done by a subordinate task rather than in the allocator itself to limit the overall complexity of the software.

Replenishments are defined on an item-by-item basis, not order by order, to avoid the creation of multiple replenishment moves for a single item in a single wave. This, along with processing efficiency, is the primary reason why the allocator works in item number sequence.

The replenishment point can either be a previously established quantity or can be calculated based on the size of the item and the size of the location. In the latter case, the replenishment point is usually stated as a percentage of the location's capacity. Thus replenishment would be done when, for instance, the on-hand balance drops to 25 percent of the capacity. Percentage replenishment points have the advantage of not requiring recalculation when products are moved between locations of different sizes. Shortages found during an allocation run can be handled automatically during the replenishment run or can be presented to the planner on a screen during the run. If shortages are to be handled automatically, logic will be required within the allocator to decide how. Orders with a shortage can be dropped from the wave, single line items can be dropped, material can be allocated to the extent it is available, or a substitute item can be allocated.

Many companies simply allocate everything possible to every order possible. This avoids the additional logic required to handle the other alternatives and eliminates the need to station a planner at the screen for the duration of the allocation run.[1]

In most businesses, substitutions are straightforward: either a one-for-one substitute part is available or it isn't. In some instances, however, substitutions can assume incredible complexity. Imagine, for instance, the case where service part B can be substituted for A but only when the customer has a recent model. Or, imagine the case where there are many possible substitutions, as can occur with colors in the apparel industry. Sometimes certain customers allow substitutions and others do not. Some substitutions must be preapproved by quality control or by engineering. None of these schemes are beyond the ability of a good inventory system. But when they all come together in a single business, the complexity may be more than it is worth. In those cases, it may be best to leave substitution selections to the judgment of the planner, programming the inventory system only to implement his or her decisions.

Among other things, the allocation run results in the creation of picking transactions and their placement on the picking work queue. The handling of these transactions and the system support necessary to assure high levels of accuracy in their handling are the subjects of the next section.

PICKING

For purposes of this discussion, it is useful to divide picking operations into three categories. For lack of better terms, these categories are called "low-volume," "high-volume," and "automated." Many companies, of course, have elements of both in their operations.

Characteristics of low-volume, nonautomated picking operations include:

1. Orders are picked one at a time, usually by a single person.
2. Most pickers work part time at picking and part time on other jobs such as packing or shipping. Some may even work part time in other departments.
3. Picking, packing, and shipping are often combined into two or fewer steps. One person, for instance, might pick, pack, and ship an order.
4. Personnel productivity is not measured.

Conversely, characteristics of high-volume, nonautomated picking operations include:

---

[1]The time required to allocate a picking wave depends on the size of the wave, the number of picking locations that must be selected, the amount of replenishing that must be done, the size and speed of the computer being used, and the number of other users competing for the computer's resources. Allocation isn't necessarily a lengthy process, but it can easily involve tens of thousands of disk accesses. Elapsed times of between 10 and 30 minutes are common.

1. Orders may be picked one at a time or, to improve productivity, personnel may pick several orders at once.
2. Picking, packing, and shipping are full-time jobs.
3. Picking and packing may be combined into a single job, or packing and shipping may be combined. Often, however, all three functions are performed by different people.
4. Most picking is done from a dedicated "fast pick" zone in the stockroom or warehouse.
5. The productivity of picking personnel, and possibly packers and shippers, is measured.

Automated picking operations are those that involve the use of carousels, automated storage and retrieval machines, or picking machines to assist or even replace human pickers. In all three kinds of picking operations, systems and procedures must assure that the right parts are picked in the right quantities, that they are packed properly, and that they are shipped to the right customers. Errors are reflected not only in incorrect inventories but in unhappy customers and, ultimately, in lost revenue.

If inventory records are accurate, it is relatively easy to do the picking, packing, and shipping jobs accurately. However, complications arise as volume increases. Since low-volume picking operations are the easiest to control, they will be discussed first.

Low-Volume Picking Operations

In a low-volume picking operation, the picking transactions generated by the allocator are often assigned to pickers via printed pick lists. Electronic pick lists can also be downloaded to nonradio terminals or transmitted to radio terminals. Typically, the picks are grouped by order and sequenced by storage location within each order so the picker does not need to figure out an efficient picking sequence. A supervisor, dispatcher, or clerk distributes the work by passing out terminals or pick lists (or both). The employees pick the material and validate their work by scanning bar codes on the pick lists and storage locations. As always, the purpose of validation is to catch and correct errors at the time they are made.

When small items are being picked, counts can be verified with scales in strategic locations throughout the stockroom. In other cases, the accuracy with which pickers count product can be improved by separating full pallet, full case, and broken case picks. Suppose, for instance, that an order calls for 100 pieces of a product that is packed 12 to a case and 6 cases to a pallet. Pickers should be instructed by the computer to pick one full pallet (72 pieces), two full cases (24 pieces), and four items. The margin for error is obviously much less than were a picker expected to make the calculations by hand, or even worse, to individually count 100 pieces.

For the sake of both accuracy and efficiency, the picked order must be identified before it leaves the hands of the picker. When the picker is responsible for picking and packing, the shipping label can serve as the identifier. When someone else is responsible for packing and shipping, other methods are required.

When reusable containers such as totes are in use, they can be bar coded and the bar codes can be scanned by the pickers during the picking process. Software is then required to link the tote "license plate" to the order. If containers are not reusable, picking or packing lists or a shipping label can be left with the material. Or, in "paperless" situations, it may be necessary to find other ways of identifying the order.

High-Volume Picking Operations

In a high-volume operation, pickers are usually more specialized. Picks are frequently separated into full pallet and less than pallet groups (sometimes even into full case and less than case groups) for picking.

When case picking is done from pallet rack, picks can be sorted by order and divided into pallet loads, with one pallet load assigned to a picker at a time. The picker will then pick individual cases, building a mixed pallet in the process. When advisable, the picking of a single pallet can be done in density sequence so that the heaviest items are on the bottom, or it can be done in location sequence for picking efficiency.

When case picking is done from a flow rack, pickers are often responsible for only a small section of the rack (called a picking zone). Each picker picks his or her portion of each order and passes the order on to the next person. Zone boundaries can be dynamically recalculated for each wave based on the amount of picking do be done by each person. Dynamic rezoning helps to level the workload throughout the entire picking area. In other operations, pickers may cover larger areas but pick more than one order at a time to reduce the proportion of their time spent walking between locations.

In many high-volume picking operations, the number of picks is large enough so the cost of individually validating each pick with a bar code scanner becomes prohibitive. Even when picks cannot be individually validated, there are ways to improve accuracy. For example:

1. Intelligent design of picking documents can help a great deal. For example, Figure 10.2 shows one form of packing list, designed for efficient and accurate use in a high-volume picking operation where validation is not feasible. This particular design recognizes that, for the great majority of the work, the picker cares only about the picking location and the quantity to be picked. Therefore, these numbers are emphasized in block character form, with the supporting information in smaller type. To simplify the problem of handling the pick list, perforations are provided between each pick, making the list into tickets. As the picks are done, the picker tears off the ticket and encloses it with the material. There is, therefore, little likelihood that the picker will lose track of his or her place on the pick list and little likelihood of skipping or duplicating picks.

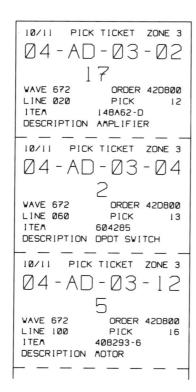

Figure 10.2. High-speed pick ticket. These pick tickets are designed for use in a high-speed picking environment where individual validation is not economical. As each pick is done, the picker tears off the corresponding ticket and encloses it with the material for later use as an identifier.

In general, a good pick list should emphasize the information most needed, should present it in the sequence needed, and should be easy for the picker to handle. Units of measure (items versus cases) should be clear. In some circumstances, a graphic display of picking locations might be useful.

2. So-called pick-by-light systems can be installed. These systems feature a miniature LED display and one or more pushbuttons at every picking location. When a picker is ready to begin picking a zone, the inventory system transmits the picks to the pick-by-light system controller. The controller then displays an order number and quantity at each location from which a pick is necessary. As each pick is completed, the picker presses an acknowledgement button and the system either displays the next pick from that location or turns off the display to signal the picker to move to the next location. Various schemes allow for the handling of quantity discrepancies.

In many instances, pick-by-light systems allow high-speed picking to coexist with high levels of accuracy. The picker works with both hands free and deals mentally only with quantities, the locations being determined by the lights.

3. Scales can be used to weigh completed picks and compare their weight with a weight calculated by the system. Weight comparisons

can catch major picking errors but, as is generally true when dealing with gross weights, small errors may get lost in the variation inherent in container tare weights.

4. Checkers can inspect, recount, and verify completed picks, either fully or on a sample basis. Checkers can catch and correct many errors, but they are comparatively costly and will not catch everything.

5. And, finally, many high-volume companies simply accept a moderate level of picking errors as a "cost of doing business." In zone picking operations, the pickers get to know their own zones very well. Even a moderately attentive person can do a reasonably high-quality job if properly motivated. In the long run, a realistic approach is likely to be the most cost effective.

High-volume pickers may also be responsible for delivering the picked product to the shipping dock or to a staging area. But, in most businesses, they simply place the product on a conveyor. In either case, some form of identification is required. The pick list (or pick ticket) can often be designed to fill this requirement. In other cases, separate labels will be required or, in still other cases, containers are used that can be labeled with permanent license plate numbers. When container license plate numbers are used, they must be identified to the inventory system during the picking process so the system can link them to the order and to the individual picks.

Automated Picking Operations

Automated picking operations are those in which the picker is assisted by a carousel, an automated storage and retrieval machine, or an automated picking machine. Carousels and automated storage and retrieval machines can be effectively operated either through an electronic interface or a paper interface with the inventory system; picking machines almost always involve electronic interfaces.

For example, one large company operates a dozen carousels in its warehouse. Its inventory system builds separate picking work assignments for each "pod" of three carousels and passes the transactions to a personal computer assigned to the pod. The personal computer works under the direction of the picker, who picks up to 16 orders at once from the carousels, with each order being sorted into a separate tote. As picks are completed, the personal computer passes commands to a programmable controller that cause the carousels to rotate as required and picking instructions to be displayed on LED displays next to the carousels and the totes.

Another company operates a single pod of three carousels without communication to the inventory system. This company defines the carousel storage locations as a single pick zone. Tickets bearing the location number are printed for each item to be picked and delivered to the carousels. The operator keys each location into the carousel's programmable controller and manages the sortation of completed picks into containers him- or herself. While this approach is less productive than the first one, there were enough programming and testing economies involved to make it attractive at the time the inventory system was installed.

Beyond a certain point, it is difficult to generalize about automated picking because the equipment used is almost always customized to the installation, the product, and management's strategies. Inventory systems, therefore, rarely approach two installations the same way. There are, however, three areas where inventory system designers should look for differences when an existing low-volume or high-volume picking operation is to be automated. First, picking transactions should be grouped by machine for distribution to pickers. This is often easily done by defining storage locations in the machine as a separate picking zone. Second, if the machine is to be interfaced with the inventory system, the interface technology itself can be an important aspect of the system. And, third, the information required by the picker is likely to differ from that required by manual pickers.

SORTATION

Whenever orders are picked by more than one person, there is a need to physically sort the material to bring together the various items for packing and shipment. Exceptions can exist when shipment is to be made via a parcel carrier because the carrier will treat each parcel as a separate shipment. Exceptions can also exist when material is picked for in-house delivery. In this case, packaging is usually not required and the recipient usually does not care if the material arrives piecemeal. But even in these two instances, there may be reason to sort. Parcel carriers will handle a 20-pound parcel for less money than two 10-pound parcels (and packaging material costs will be less). And sortation of material picked for manufacturing may reduce the number of delivery trips required, helping to limit overall material handling costs.

The number of possible sortation schemes is limited only by the imagination of the material handling engineer and the system designer. The story of the Midwest hardware distributor earlier in this chapter describes how a system design eliminated the need for physical sortation by making intelligent use of a staging area. That particular sortation method is helped by the fact that the product is packed, where necessary, by the pickers and is shipped on the company's own trucks.

Conveyor systems are one popular method of sortation. As illustrated in Figure 7.1, cartons or totes are introduced to the sortation system with bar-coded labels. A scanner reads the labels and passes ID numbers to the inventory system through a programmable controller. The inventory system decides which lane should receive the material and passes the lane number back to the programmable controller. The programmable controller then diverts the material as necessary.

In a simpler version of this system, labels are produced at the time of picking, after the lane determination has been made. The label bar code contains the lane number rather than just an identifier. The programmable controller, then, can operate independently of the inventory system, reading each label and making its own decision where to divert each item.

In other situations, it may not be possible to devote an entire lane to each order. A recirculation loop can be added to the conveyor system so that orders that do not currently have assigned lanes can be cycled back to the scanner after traveling the loop. Eventually, after several trips around, a lane will be assigned and the material can be diverted. Recirculation loops can also be used to make a second try at scanning no-read labels. When recirculation loops are used, it is important that the programmable controller (or the inventory system) track the number of times each item has gone around the loop. Material arriving late might otherwise recirculate forever.

When sortation systems are in use, careful consideration should be given to the way that picking waves are constructed. Picking should be done, to the extent possible, in loading sequence to minimize the amount of accumulation conveyor required.

Other equipment such as tilt-tray sorters, monorails, and even automated guided vehicle (AGV) systems can be used for sortation. From the viewpoint of the inventory system, there is little difference in the logic required.

Kitting is, in a sense, another kind of sortation. Kitting is the construction of "kits" of material, each of which contains a precounted number of each of two or more items that are packaged together by later assembly (maybe by the customer). Kitting is really an assembly operation in itself and should normally be treated as such. The completed kit should have a different and unique item number. Unless there is reason to the contrary, material should be delivered to the kitting operation and taken away from it as described in Chapter 9. This is usually true, regardless of whether the people who do kitting work for the warehouse or the manufacturing organization.

PACKING

The packing operation, whether or not it is preceded by a sorting step, is another source of error. Packing stations should be equipped with bar code scanners and packers should be required to scan identifying bar codes as material is packed. The inventory system should verify that the materials packed are, in fact, the items picked, that orders are properly packed together, and that everything picked is packed.

Shipping labels can be applied as part of the packing operation. They should be bar coded for use in the shipping function. Printing them on-line as the packing is done eliminates the possibility that the wrong label will be put on a shipment. Accurate shipping weights can also be captured by an electronic scale as part of the packing process.

SHIPPING

Once the material is packed and a shipping label is properly applied, the shipping function is reasonably foolproof from an inventory accuracy point of view. Shipments accidentally given to the wrong carrier or loaded into the wrong truck will eventually be returned or redirected. However, in some businesses, the delays and extra costs involved may justify the validation of truck loading.

Loading validation is done either by bar-coding trailers (if company owned) or loading doors (if common carriers or parcel shippers are used). Rail car loading can be validated by bar coding the loading positions. Loading personnel are then equipped with portable bar code scanners and required to scan both shipping labels and either trailer or door labels as material is loaded. The inventory system validates proper loading and handles error correction.

Loading validation requires that a supervisor or clerk define which orders are to go into which trailers (or through which doors). Or, in some cases, it may be possible for the system to make the determination automatically. Such cases might include companies that ship carriers through the same doors on a regular basis or those that extend their inventory system to control the "inventory" of empty trailers in the yard.

Another highly productive and highly accurate way of shipping product depends on radio-linked terminals and is applicable only to businesses that ship in pallet quantities. In this method, picking is not done until the trailer has been spotted at the door. A supervisor or clerk then decides which orders are to be loaded. The system assigns pickers and transmits picking transactions to them. The pickers pick the required pallets, apply shipping labels , and move the material directly to the floor of the trailer. Labels can be printed on board the lift trucks or in a convenient location near the shipping doors. Bar codes are used to validate the work as it is done.

Example 10.1.   All-manual data collection using central key entry. Accuracy can be reasonably assured in a manual picking environment (one in which portable terminals are not used) through proper design of facilities and documents. For instance, a small, high-volume forward picking area might be laid out as shown in Figure 10.3. Pickers (A, B, C, and D) each pick from a flow rack zone and place completed picks in totes. The totes are on skate wheel conveyor, making it easy for the pickers to pass orders among themselves. Printed pick lists are distributed to the pickers for each wave, with each picker getting those orders that start in his or her zone. Following the pick tickets for each order, and printed on the same form, are several shipping labels. These shipping labels show the usual names and addresses but also include the carrier's name and a bar code that identifies the order. In addition to being a shipping label, they separate and identify orders for the pickers, provide routing information for the checker and the packers, and tell the inventory system that the order has been picked and shipped.

As picker A finishes each order, the picking list is placed in the tote. Then, if there are further picks to be made, the tote is pushed along to picker B. Picker B adds more items if necessary and continues the process by pushing the order around the end of the conveyor to picker C. If an order requires more than one tote, additional empty ones can be put on the line. Since the pick tickets are perforated (as in Figure 10.2), they can be torn apart with completed ones on top

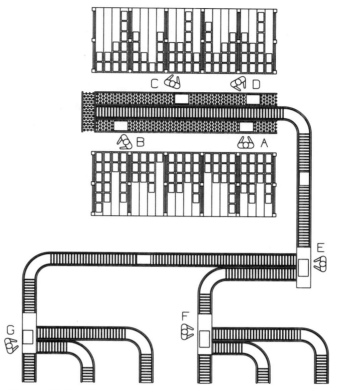

Figure 10.3. Simple manual picking area. In this illustration, A, B, C, and D are pickers, E is a checker, and F and G are packers. The system is designed for a manual data collection environment.

of the tote containing the material and the remaining ones in the last tote. Completed orders are pushed back to the center powered conveyor. Material is stored in the flow racks in such a way as to even out the workload among the four pickers. Fast-moving items are placed at the best picking height, about 40 inches above the floor. Slow movers are below, with the remaining items above.

The powered conveyor takes completed orders to the checker (person E). The checker verifies the content of each tote, counting parts and assuring that the right items have been picked. The checker also distributes work to two packers (F and G) by placing the checked totes on the appropriate conveyor.

The packers begin packing each order by verifying that the checker has properly sent it to them. They then pack the order, apply the shipping labels, remove the totes, scan a shipping label bar code, and put the completed material on one of three outgoing conveyors. The outgoing conveyors carry the material to a staging area where it is accumulated by carrier. Truck loaders (not shown) handle the material from the staging area into trailers as the carriers arrive, making one final check that it is being loaded into the correct trailer as they do so.

The inventory system is responsible for sorting the orders and picks in a wave, printing the combined pick lists and shipping labels, and accepting scans from the packer's scanners. When the scans are received, the system relieves inventory and allocations and posts completions to the outgoing orders. Manifests and bills of lading are printed on request at the time of loading.

When problems occur (such as an unplanned shortage), they are reported to a supervisor or clerk who makes adjustments to the order on the inventory system before the packer reports it as complete.

This design provides for a reasonable level of accuracy. It organizes the operation so that all work is, in one way or another, checked by someone else before shipment is made. And, the checking has been accomplished with a minimum of additional labor and a minimum of investment in systems.

Example 10.2. Paper-driven off-line data collection. Off-line data collection terminals can be used to validate picking by downloading picks to them and using their on-board computer power to catch and correct errors as they occur. The process begins with the division of a wave into work assignments, each consisting of a number of picks spread across a number of orders. Work assignments can be either order based or zone based, depending on the needs of the business. If items are to be consolidated for shipment, zone-based order picking requires that the mixed material be sorted by order after it is picked. Order-based picking, however, raises the possibility that several pickers may simultaneously need to work the same aisle, sometimes an impossibility. Order-based picking also tends to involve additional travel time for pickers and, therefore, can be less efficient.

The picking cycle begins with the downloading of a work assignment to a portable terminal. For each pick, the information downloaded includes the picking location, the item number, the quantity to be picked, the order number, and the line number. Other information that may be of value to the picker might include a customer name or number, the item's description, and, in some cases, lot or serial numbers. Once downloading is complete, the terminals are distributed to pickers and work begins.

The terminal starts by displaying a picking location. The picker travels to this location and scans the location bar code with a wand attached to the terminal. The terminal verifies that the correct location has been found and displays the item number and quantity to be picked. The picker does the picking and either enters a corrected quantity or simply confirms that the full quantity required was picked. The terminal then displays the next location.

On completion of an order (this example assumes order picking), the terminal displays the staging location to which the material should be taken. The picker takes the completed material to the staging location and scans its bar code, verifying proper delivery. The terminal then displays the first picking location for the next order and the process continues.

If, at any time, the picking container (tote, pallet, or other container) becomes full, the picker can press a function key. The terminal then displays the staging location and validates proper staging before returning to the next pick in sequence.

Containers are either serial numbered or the picker applies temporary serial number labels as the picking is done. The terminal collects the serial numbers (via bar code) and keeps a record of the material in each container. When the containers are staged, the serial numbers are stored along with the staging information for later use.

On completion of the work assignment, the picker returns the terminal to a clerk, who uploads the collected information to the inventory system. The system relieves inventories and allocations and sets up transactions to destage, pack, and ship the material.

At a later time, a shipper receives a terminal containing pack-and-ship transactions for a specific staging area. Along with the terminal, the clerk gives the shipper a stack of shipping labels that the inventory system printed at the time the work was downloaded to the terminal. The shipper selects a container to be shipped (probably the first one found in the staging area) and scans the container's bar code. If other containers exist in the staging area for this order, the terminal informs the shipper and the shipper locates and scans them. If the container selected is part of an order that is still being picked, the terminal instructs the shipper to select another container.

Once all of the containers for an order have been identified, the shipper packs the material, applies the shipping labels, and stages the completed work for later loading. When the shipper's terminal is uploaded to the inventory system, the orders are tagged as having been shipped and the corresponding records are removed from the staging area file.

This system can function with extremely high levels of accuracy because every step in the process is validated with bar codes. However, there can be significant timing problems. Shippers cannot ship product until it has been staged, the picker's terminal has been uploaded to the inventory system, and shipping transactions have been downloaded to the inventory system. If terminals are typically loaded with 2 hours of work, this could mean a 4-hour delay between picking and shipment. And the shipment staging area will be crowded with work that cannot be shipped, even though it has been completely picked. In some businesses these problems are minor and the lower cost represented by off-line portable terminals easily justifies dealing with them. In other businesses, the delays may virtually rule out off-line terminals.

Example 10.3. Hi-tech. The most important justification for radio terminals is the fact that they are on-line devices. As one example of the value of on-line control over material handlers, imagine a business that ships exclusively (or almost exclusively) in full pallet quantities. In this business, the planner generates picking waves by carrier, limiting each wave to the capacity of a single trailer. The waves are allocated and picking transactions are stored, but no picking is done until the carrier arrives.

On arrival of the a carrier's trailer, the shipping supervisor assigns a shipping door and "releases" the wave by entering the door number. This release makes the picking transactions available to the material handlers. Each material handler is given a picking location on the screen of his or her radio terminal and is required to scan that location's bar code. At this point, the material handler does not know whether the pick is for shipment or for some other purpose. Upon validation of the pick, the radio terminal tells the material handler to deliver it to a specific shipping door. The pallet is driven to the door and directly loaded onto the trailer. As the material handler enters the trailer, a stop is made at a printer located at a convenient height by the side of the shipping door. While the pick was being done, a shipping label was being printed on this printer. The material handler takes the shipping label, scans its bar code to assure that the right label is being used, and applies it to the pallet.

By picking and shipping in a single motion, no staging or sortation is required and significant labor is saved without sacrificing accuracy.

11

Locations

A "location" is simply a place where inventory is kept. It can be a pallet position in a rack structure, a bin, a place on the floor, a drawer in an automated storage and retrieval machine, or even a trailer sitting in the yard. Locations can be intended for temporary or long-term storage. They can be designed for bulk material movement, as is often the case with reserve stock, or for the fast movement of smaller parts, as in forward picking. Locations can be in a frozen food freezer or behind a security fence. They can be accessible to only certain types of material handling equipment or to all. The variations are nearly endless.

Because accurate inventory systems are closely tied to material handling, a structure is needed to define the storage locations. This structure must cover not only the identity of each location but also the characteristics of it that are important to the storage and retrieval of material in it. This chapter describes one such structure.

DEFINING AND CHARACTERIZING LOCATIONS

An inventory location has been defined as a place small enough to make it practical for employees to thoroughly search it for parts every time a pick or a cycle count is to be done. This definition leaves open the physical size of a location, the number of different item numbers that can be stored in it, and the quantity of each that it can handle. Although there are exceptions, most locations can be modeled by specifying the value of the 15 variables shown in Table 11.1. The meaning and use of these variables is described below. Depending on the nature of the product and the business, few inventory systems need all of these variables.

TABLE 11.1. STORAGE LOCATION DEFINITION DATA

Item	Comment
Location number	Uniquely identifies the location
Height	Inside measure of height
Width	Inside measure of width
Depth	Inside measure of depth
Weight capacity	Weight limitation, if any
Environment	For use in storing product
Function	What the location is used for
Device	The storage device used
Demand	Controls storage of fast vs. slow-movers
Pick zone	For use in selecting picking locations
Pick subzone	For use in assigning pickers
Dedication	To a specified item number
Material handling class	Material handling equipment that can be used
Mode	The way the location is or can be used
Mix	Allows or disallows mixing item numbers

Location Numbers

Locations must be numbered so the computer and people can deal with them. (Despite the use of the word "number," most location numbering schemes are actually alphanumeric to make it easier for people to read and remember them.) Unlike item numbers, which are often purposefully not significant, significance in location numbers has great value. It enables employees to find locations quickly and easily with a minimum of training. Gridbased systems are popular. In these systems, location numbers are not actually *x-y-z* coordinates but are nearly so. Coordinates are restated in terms of the facility layout, in a fashion that makes sense to both people and the inventory system.

In one reasonably complete system, the location number consists of six subfields that alternate between alphabetic and numeric characters to enhance readability. In most facilities, two characters are adequate for each of the subfields, making the entire location number 12 characters long. The subfields are often defined as listed below. Refer to Figure 11.1 for a picture of how these subfields can be used.

- Area. The first subfield of the position number is called "area." It is often used to denote buildings within a complex and areas within the buildings, as in Figure 11.1. Inventory facilities are usually divided into areas with parallel aisles. There need not be any requirement that an area consist of only one kind of storage device or be used for only one kind of product.
- Aisle. Some companies prefer to number rows rather than aisles. (One row of storage devices appears on each side of an aisle.) From the point of view of the people working in the warehouse, the difference is minimal. But, from the point of view of the inventory system, aisle num-

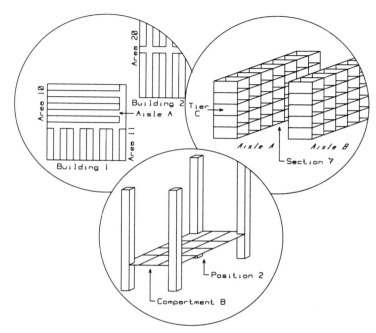

Figure 11.1. Location numbers. One commonly used location numbering system consists of 12 digits representing, in pairs of digits, the area, aisle, section, tier, compartment, and position. The illustration shows this numbering scheme applied to shelving, but it can equally well be applied to other material storage devices.

bers are more convenient because processing is sometimes done by aisle and almost never by row. Numbering aisles saves the need for a row-to-aisle conversion table.

- Section. A section is a vertical stack of locations, each separated from the next by a post or divider. When aisles are numbered, section numbers are usually odd on the left and even on the right or vice versa.
- Tier. Tier is the height of the location from floor level, measured in storage locations. The floor is tier 1, not tier 0.
- Position. Within a pallet location, shelf, or bin, it is possible to store many items. The position parameter is used to designate the left-to-right position of the material.
- Compartment or subposition. Similar to position, the compartment parameter designates the front-to-back position of material.

While a 12-position location number is manageable, shorter numbers are easier to use, remember, and key correctly. The inventory system should be smart enough to print and display only the significant portion of the location number and to accept key entry of only that portion. For instance, if rack locations exist that are not divided into positions and compartments, the inventory system should let users deal with only area-aisle-section-tier. Likewise, if there are 32 aisles lettered from A to AF, the system should handle either the single or the two character form.

Height, Width, Depth, and Weight Capacity

The height, width, depth, and weight capacity of a storage location are often grouped under the term "dimensions." Units of measure are normally inches and pounds, with fractional amounts rounded down to the next lowest whole number. Many companies understate their physical location dimensions, particularly height and width, to provide maneuvering room for material handlers.

Environment

The environment parameter is intended for use when material is put away. The term originated with systems built for the food industry. It first addressed the need to keep certain foods within certain temperature ranges. Ice cream had to be stored in the freezer, fresh meat in the cooler, and so on. The concept of an environment, however, is not limited to the food industry. As an example, a computer manufacturer wishes, for management reasons, to store printers in one section of the warehouse and disk drives in another. In this case, there can be a printer environment and a disk drive environment. The logic is identical to that used by the food industry.

Environments need not be contiguous and can overlap geographically. The top tier of a pallet rack, for instance, might be a different environment from the other tiers because the warehouse is hotter near the ceiling. Or, for security reasons, the top three tiers might be used as a high-value environment to minimize pilferage.

Function

The function parameter defines the way the inventory system treats each storage location. There are four basic functions: reserve, forward picking, staging, and cross-docking. Variations on these four themes are, of course, possible. Reserve storage locations are used for larger quantities of either unitized or loose materials that are put away with no immediate plans for their withdrawal. A forward picking location is a location that is intended to be picked in the near future. Forward picking locations are designed to hold product for only a few days and often contain less than one or two unit loads of product at a time. There are usually no more than two forward picking locations for a single item, while there can be as many reserve locations for each item as needed.

Staging locations are locations that are used to hold material on a temporary basis. Material is not put into a staging location unless there already exists a plan (and probably a transaction) to move the material out. Staging locations are needed when material is transferred between some kinds of material handling devices. One example of a staging area might be the place in front of an elevator where material is left when the elevator is at another floor. Staging areas are also used to hand material off between high-rise and conventional lift trucks, between lift trucks and AGVs, and in other instances.

Staging areas are considered to have infinite capacity and the ability to handle many different items at once. They give the inventory system a way to account for material that is not currently in motion but is also not in any other recognizable location.

Cross-dock locations are locations that, like forward picking locations, are reserved for inventory that is to be allocated, picked and shipped in the near future. Unlike forward picking locations, however, cross-dock locations are limited to the storage of material that has already been assigned to an existing order. Intended for high turnover, these locations should be close to the shipping dock and may actually be part of the shipping area.

Device

The device parameter defines the kind of storage device used for each storage location. It is used primarily by the system logic that searches for storage locations.

As described in more detail in Chapter 13, the list of possible storage devices is nearly endless. It includes floor storage, single and multideep pallet racks, drive-in pallet racks, pallet and carton flow racks, cantilever racks, shelving, bins, drawers, carousels, automated storage and retrieval machines, storage conveyors, and even custom-made equipment designed for a specific business.

Demand

The demand parameter describes the intended use of each storage location in terms of its turnover. Using the demand parameter, the inventory facility can be divided into areas for slow movers, for fast movers, and for in-between items. Most inventory systems use the demand parameter only to prioritize location search logic. They do not insist that an item defined as slow moving be stored only in a location intended for slow movers.

The demand parameter is particularly important to productivity. If intelligently used, it, alone, can reduce material handling labor by as much as 30 to 40 percent compared to a facility that stores material entirely at random. The savings are achieved by putting the high volume items in the most accessible locations and keeping the slow movers out of the way. This reduces employee travel times and increases the amount of productive work that each employee can accomplish in a day.

As an example of the use of the demand parameter, look at Figure 11.2. It shows one side of an aisle in a high-rise reserve storage area that is serviced by a wire-guided turret truck. Like most of these vehicles, this truck moves faster horizontally than it does vertically. The dividing line between the fast-, medium-,

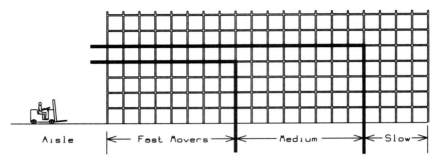

Figure 11.2. Use of the demand parameter in high-rise storage areas. Because material handling vehicles move at different horizontal and vertical speed, the access time to different locations in a row of pallet rack depends on both the location's height from the floor and it's distance from the main aisle.

and slow-moving zones is L-shaped to account for the difference in access time between the top and bottom tiers.[1]

Pick Zone

The pick zone parameter lets the inventory system divide picks into consistent work assignments that can be given to pickers without requiring them to constantly switch between methods. Reserve storage areas should be in a separate zone from the forward picking areas (in addition to being a different function). Both the reserve and forward areas should be subdivided as necessary. For example, locations that are picked into totes on a conveyor should be separated from those that are picked to pallets or totes on pallets. Locations in which picking is validated should be separated from those in which no validation is done. The pick zone parameter is also the key to a pick zone table, which details picking methods.

Pick Subzone

In a location where zoned picking is done, a pick subzone is the portion of a pick zone that is to be assigned to a single picker. Pick subzones can either be specified as fixed location parameters or can be dynamically changed by the inventory system as part of the creation of work assignments.

---

[1]The exact shape of the lines dividing fast, medium, and slow-moving areas in high-rise storage depends on the details of the equipment servicing the area. Figure 11.2 assumes a truck that travels horizontally 3 times as fast as it travels vertically and one that operates at half speed in all directions above tier 5. The affects of acceleration and deceleration are ignored. A 20-30-50 percent split between fast, medium, and slow moving items is assumed. Readers should determine their own demand parameters in a three step process: (1) Calculate the access time for each opening in the rack, (2) Sort the rack positions into ascending access time sequence, and (3) Assign demand codes to the locations in fast-medium-slow sequence.

Dedication

Storage locations can either be dedicated to a single item number or can be allowed to float. When the location is dedicated, the item number to which it is dedicated is entered in the dedication parameter field. Location dedication implies that the inventory system will not store any other item in it, even when it is empty. A floating location is one that the system may reassign to any other item when the location is empty.

Material Handling Class

The material handling class parameter is the key to the material handling class file. The material handling class file defines, for each class, which types of material handling vehicles can access a location. For instance, one class might limit access to people on foot. Another class might permit a mixture of high-rise turret trucks (for pallet moves) and order pickers (for case moves). A third class might permit either conventional lift trucks or pallet jacks (for floor storage under racks), while the tiers above might be limited to lift trucks.

The material handling class table describes only the types of vehicles that can directly access a location. It does not describe how hand-offs are made between vehicle types. That function is filled by the plant map, which is a separate file not directly related to location parameters. Additional limitations to vehicle classes exist on the item master file, requiring, for instance, that only clamp trucks handle unpalletized rolls of paper, regardless of where they are stored.

Mode

Some locations can be used in more than one way. For instance, a 120-inch-wide pallet opening can be used to store three 36-inch-wide pallets, two 48-inch-wide pallets, or one pallet of each size. Most systems faced with controlling the storage of multiple-sized pallets use a system-controlled mode parameter on the location file. The opening is initially defined as three locations and established with the mode parameter at a null value. When the first item is stored, the mode parameters for all three locations are set to the size of that load. All subsequent putaway transactions are limited to pallets of that size and, if the mode setting indicates that the pallet was a 48-inch one, the third location is not used. As pallets are removed, the system checks to see whether or not the other two locations in the opening are empty. If they are, it returns the mode parameter to the initial null value, letting the location be reused with any size pallet.

Mix

The mix parameter controls whether or not the inventory system should allow more than one item to be stored at a time in a location. The mixing of material in a storage location is further controlled by another parameter kept on the item master file. Mixed storage will occur only if permitted by both parameters.

LOCATION LABELING

Many of the concepts in this book are based on the validation of material movements using a bar code scanner and a bar-coded label on each storage location. Because these labels are central to achieving accuracy, their design and use deserve comment.

A sample of one location label design appears in Figure 5.3. While other designs are feasible, it is important that the label be clear and easily understood and that there be no ambiguity about the storage location to which it refers. Putting labels on the beam between two locations may leave doubt as to which locations they refer to.

When labels are inconveniently placed, there is an increased likelihood that validation scans will be done incorrectly. So, it is also important that the labels be conveniently located. Good label locations can be hard to find when several different kinds of vehicles will be using them because the vehicle drivers will be in different positions relative to the storage location and will require different label placement. In the more complex cases, it may be a good idea for a supervisor or system designer to experiment with the vehicles personally to arrive at a satisfactory compromise. Or it may be necessary to mount two or even three labels on each location to accommodate the needs of everyone. When multiple labels are used, a color coded border will help the material handlers know which ones they are supposed to use.

LOCATION SEQUENCING

It is usually best to assign location numbers in a logical sequence for work. This lets the system sort transactions by location number and end up with a reasonable and efficient picking sequence. It is also possible, however, to define a database field called "pick sequence" on the location file. This field can carry a number by which the system can sort to arrive at an efficient picking sequence. The pick sequence field lets the location numbering scheme be devised without regard to picking sequence. However, assignment of location numbers in a logical picking sequence is usually easy, so relatively few systems include pick sequence numbers.

Pick sequencing sometimes includes the need to sort into an S pattern to direct the picker up one aisle and down the next. S-pattern sorting is easily done in a three step process:

1. Make a pass through the file of picks to be performed by a single picker. Every time a new aisle is encountered, switch a variable between the values $+1$ and -1. Multiply the section subfield of the picking location by this variable.
2. Sort the file by picking location.
3. Make a second pass through the file, multiplying all negative section numbers by -1.

The result is an S pattern that accounts for aisles skipped as well as those visited.

SELECTING STORAGE LOCATIONS

The automatic selection of storage locations for incoming material is an important feature of most modern inventory systems. Under most circumstances, a properly programmed system can do a better job of selecting locations than a material handler because:

1. The system can do a structured search, following management's strategies to the letter without taking unauthorized short cuts.
2. The system can use information that is not readily available to a material handler. This information makes possible:

    Accurate, reliable placement of material in the required storage environment, using the right storage device

    Stratification of inventory by demand class (velocity)

    Automated cross-docking

    Direct storage from receiving to forward picking, eliminating some replenishment moves

    Direct movement from receiving to the smallest available opening that is capable of handling the material

    Reliable segregation of product by FIFO date and, if necessary, by lot number

    Accurate control over the mixing of product in a storage location
3. The system can find locations in places that are not readily visible to material handlers, such as the higher levels in racking.
4. The system does not have to travel into the stockroom to find a location. It is much faster.

However, there are some conditions under which the inventory system cannot reliably select locations. One example is the floor storage of items with uncertain stacking characteristics. Only the material handler can know for sure the capacity of these locations because it may be possible to stack three pallets high in some cases, but only two high in others. So, in these instances the inventory system must let the material handler override a system assigned storage location. And, in some businesses, the material handler can even be allowed to select a storage location without a system recommendation. However, complete elimination of computer selection eliminates the benefits of computer selection as well.

When automated selection of locations is mixed with manual selection or override, the system must verify that the location has not been reserved for another item before allowing the material handler to complete the put-away.

Typical Logic

The selection of storage locations for incoming product is often based on a concept called a storage class. A storage class is a prioritized list of sets of criteria for storing product. Every item belongs to a storage class. When a receipt occurs, the first set of criteria for the storage class associated with the item is retrieved. A search is made for a location that fits the criteria of that class and that has adequate cube and weight capacity available. Other considerations may also be applied. If a suitable location is found, it is used. If no suitable location is found, the next set of criteria is retrieved and the process repeats.

The location selection logic is executed one time for each unit load to be stored or one time for each item on each mixed-item unit load to be stored. It is as follows:

1. The first step in selecting a storage location is often to determine whether or not the item is authorized for cross-docking. Cross-dock authority is kept in a flag on the item master file. If this flag is on, the inventory system reviews outbound orders (customer and manufacturing orders) to decide whether or not there will be a need for the material in shipping soon. If so, and if the orders on file will at least cover the quantity in this unit load, a flag is set for use in step 5, below.

2. Next, the inventory system decides whether or not the product may be stored in a location that already contains a quantity of the same lot number of the same item with the same or almost the same FIFO date. Again, the decision is based on an item master flag called the store-to-existing-lot flag.

3. Another flag is examined to decide whether or not the product may be stored in a location that already contains a quantity of the same item with the same FIFO date but of a different lot. This flag is called the store-to-existing-item flag.

4. If FIFO dates differ, the system checks the FIFO window field on the item file to determine whether or not product can be mixed in storage. This field specifies a maximum number of days difference allowed between the FIFO date of the material in storage and the material to be put away. If the difference fits within the window, the material may be mixed in storage, with everything in that location assuming the older of the two FIFO dates.

5. And, finally, one more flag, the store-mixed flag, is examined to decide whether or not the product may be stored in a location that already contains other products.

6. The system now retrieves the first record on file for the storage class indicated on the item master. This record contains values for the environment, function, device, and demand storage parameters.

7. If the cross-docking flag is on, the function code on the storage class record is replaced with the cross-dock function code.

8. Two searches are now made through the location file, looking for a location that matches the specified environment, function, device, and demand storage parameters. The details of how these searches are performed will depend heavily on the database manager used and on the design of its data dictionary. It is usually best to provide separate retrieval paths for empty and partly full locations to avoid the need for a full-file sweep. (There is, of course, no need to retrieve full locations.) It is assumed here that the database manager is able to

return only records with the defined values of environment, function, device, and demand.

The first search is for partly full locations. It is made only if one of the three store-to-existing flags (steps 2, 3, and 4) are on.

The second search is for empty locations. It is made only if a suitable location was not selected in the first search.

9. For every record retrieved from the two searches, the following checks are made (assuming that environment, function, device, and demand already match specification):

If the location contains product, does the product in the location meet the criteria of item number and lot number established by the three store-to-existing flags?

If the location contains product other than the product being stored, is the flag on the location file which permits mixed items on?

Does the location have adequate remaining space (cube) and capacity (weight) to accommodate the material to be put away? Depending on the kind of material being handled, it may also be smart to verify that the item's largest dimension is smaller than the location's largest dimension. This check prevents fishing poles with a volume of 40 cubic inches from being assigned to a 12- by 12 by 12-inch bin.

10. When the first location is found with positive answers to all three of these checks, it is assigned as the storage location. The inventory system records the assignment on the material handling transaction and reserves the space by increasing the location's pending-inbound-move field. The system then exits from the location search process for this particular unit load.

11. If a storage location is not found and if another storage class record exists in the item's storage class, the system retrieves that record and returns to step 6.

12. If all records for the storage class have been exhausted, the cross-docking flag is examined. If it was on, the implication is that there is no suitable location in cross-dock storage. The cross-docking flag is then turned off and the process returns to step 5 to start looking for a space elsewhere in the warehouse.

13. If ultimately no location can be found, most systems hand the problem to the user. The material handler or a planner is allowed to choose between making a temporary change to the search parameters for one more search, and manually entering a storage location.

Variations

This logic has been designed to structure the warehouse according to management's strategies while maximizing space utilization to the degree possible. Because each item is associated with a prioritized list of storage specifications in the storage class table, great flexibility is provided. Cube, weight, and the maximum dimension are checked for every item, as are the device and environment. As a result, virtually all computer location selections will be feasible and a substantial increase in warehouse utilization and productivity can be expected.

Although the logic described above has broad application, it is not truly universal. For example, there are chemicals that cannot be stored in proximity to each other, often because of possible fire hazards. Another exception occurs when some kinds of special storage devices are used. One good example is a drive-in rack that can be accessed from both ends. Each end of the rack represents a separate location, but the dividing line between them is flexible. Storage devices are described in more detail in Chapter 13.

SELECTING REPLENISHMENT LOCATIONS

Replenishment is the transfer of stock from a reserve area to a forward picking area. The need for replenishment is defined based on a comparison of the available inventory in the forward picking area with a replenishment point. Or, in some cases, replenishment is based on an actual or pending stock-out in forward picking. The quantity required is usually based on the amount that can fit into the forward picking location. That is, at the time the need is identified, the replenishment quantity is the difference between the available, unallocated quantity and the capacity of the location. Replenishment quantities are often rounded or truncated to the nearest case quantity for handling convenience.

The quantity available is used rather than the on-hand balance because picking is an ongoing, high-volume operation, while replenishment is slower and may be intermittent. In such a situation, the odds are good that allocated material will have been picked by the time the replenishment arrives.

The selection of picking locations for replenishment is, of course, limited to reserve storage and to locations and product that are not on hold. The logic has three goals:

- First-in, first-out use of stock, assuring product turnover and minimizing the losses associated with obsolescence, shelf life, and other age-oriented problems
- Minimizing the number of partial pallets in reserve (and thereby maximizing space utilization) by picking less-than-pallet quantities from less-than-full locations
- Minimizing the number of moves and the cost of replenishment

In some cases these goals conflict or can even be mutually exclusive. For the purposes of many businesses, the logic outlined below represents a reasonable balance:

1. The system starts by dividing the replenishment into a quantity of full pallets and a quantity of cases. In FIFO sequence, it allocates full pallets from reserve against the full pallet quantity until either

the full pallet quantity is fully subscribed or until all full pallets in reserve have been allocated. Each successful allocation results in the creation of a replenishment record in a work queue.

2. After allocating full pallets to the extent possible, an unsatisfied balance can remain. This balance is then converted to an equivalent case count and added to the case quantity calculated in step 1.

3. Because replenishments need not always be made in the exact quantity specified, the system next compares the case quantity to a prespecified minimum replenishment. The minimum replenishment quantity is often stated as a percentage of either the original replenishment quantity, the forward picking location's capacity, or the full-pallet case quantity. Or it may be stated as a combination of these factors. If the case quantity exceeds the minimum, the system then selects additional picking locations using the process described in steps 4 through 6, below.

4. If cases are to be picked for replenishment, the system makes another pass in FIFO sequence through the reserve locations that contain partly full pallets of the product to be replenished. As each pallet is found, it is allocated and the quantity contained on it is subtracted from the open case quantity to be picked. After each subtraction, the balance open is again compared to the minimum to decide whether or not to continue the process. Again, each successful allocation results in the creation of a replenishment record in a work queue.

5. If, at any point in this scan of the partly full pallets, a pallet is found that contains more product than required by the open case quantity balance, the difference is compared to a preestablished maximum to determine whether or not the entire pallet should be used. Like the minimum replenishment quantity, this maximum can be stated as a percentage of either the original replenishment quantity, the forward picking location's capacity, the full-pallet case quantity, or a combination of these factors. If the pallet quantity is less than the maximum, the entire pallet is allocated to free a storage location. Otherwise, only the quantity required is allocated.[2]

---

[2]Since the original replenishment quantity was calculated to entirely fill the forward picking location, one might wonder how an increase in the quantity can be physically handled. Where, after all, can it be put when it arrives in forward picking? The answer is that the replenishment quantities cannot be absolutely precise because they are established based on the assumption that all allocated material will be picked before the actual delivery occurs. Uncertainties in the availability of people and the time it takes to perform a replenishment will always hold out the possibility that the material will arrive too early and will not physically fit when delivered. One solution to this problem is to understate the physical capacity of the location to provide "insurance." Another solution is to provide manual procedures for placement of the material on the floor until space appears in the picking location. In either case, the picking of a few extra units is generally unlikely to make much difference, so the maximum replenishment factor can be of value if it occasionally results in additional empty reserve locations. Users, however, should limit themselves to small factor values until it is known that larger values are workable.

6. Only if, after completing the scan of partly full pallets, an open case quantity balance remains, will the system create a partly full pallet from a full one. All remaining cases are then allocated against the oldest full pallet in reserve.

7. And, finally, if reserve inventory is inadequate to make up the complete replenishment quantity, the replenishment quantity is reduced to the quantity actually available.

SELECTING PICKING LOCATIONS

The selection of picking locations works with the same goals as the selection of replenishment locations and, consequently, uses similar logic. But, the logic must now encompass both reserve and forward picking locations and can no longer be allowed to change the quantities to be picked.

Typical Logic

Picking locations are selected for an entire picking wave at one time, usually in a background process. The steps involved are:

1. First the wave is sorted into allocation sequence. The sequence varies from business to business but often involves some combination of customer priorities, promised shipment dates, and/or order values. Allocation then proceeds one order and one line at a time.

2. The first step in allocating a line is to look for inventory in cross-dock storage. If inventory is found there that has been preallocated to the order, it is deducted from the open order balance and a pick record is created in a work queue. If the line is completely satisfied from the cross-dock area, the system proceeds with the next line. Otherwise, it continues with step 3.

3. The system divides the line into a quantity of full pallets and a quantity of pieces. (Some systems further split out full-case quantities.) In FIFO sequence, it allocates full pallets from reserve against the full-pallet quantity until either the full-pallet quantity is fully subscribed or until all full pallets in reserve have been allocated. Each successful allocation results in the creation of a picking record in a work queue.

4. After allocating full pallets to the extent possible, an unsatisfied balance can remain. This balance is then converted to an equivalent piece count and added to the piece quantity calculated in step 2.

5. The unsatisfied balance remaining after step 4 is then compared to the inventory in the forward picking area as follows:

   If a forward picking location exists, its entire available quantity is allocated up to the quantity required. If two or more forward picking locations exist, the material in them is allocated as necessary to make up the entire required quantity. Since FIFO is not a consideration in forward picking, allocations may be evenly distributed over the locations or may be concentrated on the smallest possible number of locations. The needs of the business will dictate the best method.

At each forward picking location, if the available quantity is greater than the quantity needed, then the quantity needed is allocated. If, however, the available quantity is less than the required quantity, an emergency replenishment transaction is generated and picking locations are selected for it as described earlier in this chapter. So long as inventory exists, even in reserve, the required quantity is allocated against the forward picking locations. This may result in an allocation temporarily greater than the available quantity but the over-allocation will be resolved as soon as the emergency replenishment move is completed.

When emergency replenishments are generated, some systems check to see if a previous emergency or regular replenishment exists. If one exists in a state in which it can be upgraded to include the new requirements, it may be advantageous to do so.

Some systems also define regular replenishments during allocation by comparing the remaining available quantity with the location's replenishment point. These systems usually defer selection of the replenishment location until later. Others identify regular replenishments and allocate material for them as part of a separate process.

6. If, after allocating from both reserve and forward picking, a quantity remains unallocated, it is because the warehouse is out of product. Shortages are usually printed on an allocation exception report but can reported on-line if a planner is available to take note of them.

Variations

Many variations exist in picking location selection methods. Depending on the needs of the business, it may be necessary to work special considerations like the ones listed below into the logic:

1. Some businesses have more than one forward picking line to increase the number of orders that can be picked each day. In these situations, each order must be allocated to a single line and the total workload must be reasonably balanced across the lines.

2. When picks are made for delivery to manufacturing, many companies prefer that reserve picks be in pallet quantities only. The quantity requested by manufacturing is then rounded up to the next full pallet when necessary. The idea is that it is not possible to predict the exact quantity that manufacturing will use. Therefore, there is no justification for the cost of picking and counting individual units. There will

always be leftover parts to put away after a work order is complete and the person delivering the material might as well move the maximum possible quantity. This feature is often controlled by a flag on the item file that enables and disables the rounding.

3. Substitutions (either automated or manual) are sometimes made when the inventory system is unable to allocate the quantity required. Substitution logic significantly increases the complexity of location selection.

4. Some businesses let sales people or customers reserve product for orders that have not yet arrived. Reservations are usually made by entering a reservation number. Material is allocated but only at the item level. Picking locations are not assigned. The location selection routine must recognize the reservation quantity and allocate only unreserved material. When an order arrives for reserved material, the system must be capable of decrementing the reserved quantity, allocating the material, and selecting picking locations.

12

Cycle Counts and Physical Inventories

The fact that paper-driven inventory systems are far from accurate has been known for a long time. Over the years, a variety of things have been tried to improve accuracy while still keeping costs at a reasonable level. Two methods are commonly used today: cycle counting and the "full" physical inventory.

Cycle counting is a process by which portions of the inventory are selected for counting on a regular basis. People, called cycle counters, are sent into the warehouse to physically view and count the material actually on hand. The results of these cycle counts are then used to make corrections to recorded inventory levels and are often used for other purposes.

The full physical inventory is, in a sense, a simultaneous cycle count of every location and every item in inventory. The scope of the full physical inventory is much greater than that of a cycle counting program. And, for a variety of reasons, the financial and auditing staff is more likely to be involved in a full physical inventory than in a cycle count. Therefore, the systems and procedures used to support full physical inventories are significantly different from those used to support cycle counting.

Inventory systems, with few exceptions, are called upon to support both cycle counting and physical inventory processes. Some businesses will provide all or part of the required support by integrating the inventory system with other, existing software. Other businesses either do not have or do not choose to use existing software and will require full support for these functions within the inventory system. The descriptions that follow assume that complete support must be provided by the inventory system.

CYCLE COUNTING

Cycle counting, according to the American Production and Inventory Control Society, is:

> An inventory accuracy audit technique where inventory is counted on a cyclic schedule rather than once a year. For example, a cycle inventory count is usually taken on a regular, defined basis (often more frequently for high-value fast-moving items and less frequently for low-value or slow-moving items). Most effective cycle counting programs require the counting of a certain number of items every workday with each item counted at a prescribed frequency. The key purpose of cycle counting is to identify items in error, and trigger research, identification, and elimination of the cause of errors.[1]

In practice, cycle counting often involves counting the product in specific locations and comparing quantities found with the records. Errors are usually brought to the attention of supervision and attempts are often made via historical records to locate the source of the errors. Management reports and summaries can also serve to measure actual inventory accuracy levels.

REASONS FOR CYCLE COUNTING

Cycle counting is an often-misunderstood activity. Cycle counters are in a position to achieve four separate goals as they work their way through the inventory. These goals are to:

1. Catch and correct inventory errors, thereby improving accuracy
2. Double-check the corrections that result from inventory errors found by others
3. Validate the proper use of procedures for recording and handling of inventory transactions and identify procedural problems
4. Measure the accuracy of the firm's inventory records

To put the cycle counting function in its proper perspective, and to show how an effective cycle counting program can be constructed, it is best to examine each of these goals separately.

Error Correction

Cycle counting, by itself, cannot turn inaccurate inventories into accurate ones. Cycle counters do, on occasion, find inventory record errors. They are in a position to correct the errors they find and should be charged with doing so. But the percentage of the errors that a reasonable level of cycle counting will correct is

---

[1]Reprinted with permission, The American Production and Inventory Control Society, Inc., *Dictionary*, 6th ed., 1987, p. 7.

too small have a significant impact on the overall level of accuracy in most businesses.

To understand why this is so, consider an inventory system as containing its own "inventory" of errors. Figure 12.1 illustrates the inflow of errors made as material is moved through the plant and the outflow of errors made by cycle counters as they locate and correct them. Accurate inventories are achieved by keeping the level of "water" in the "container" low.

The rate of flow out of the container is a function of the number of cycle counters employed and the frequency with which they can find and correct errors. Assuming that errors are randomly distributed through the inventory and that the cycle counters check locations selected at random, the frequency with which errors will be found and corrected is a function of the overall level of accuracy and the rate at which they work:

$$R_{EC} = N_{CC} \times R_{LC} \times (1 - IA)$$

In this equation, R_{EC} is the rate with which errors are corrected, N_{CC} is the number of cycle counters employed, R_{LC} is the rate at which each cycle counter checks

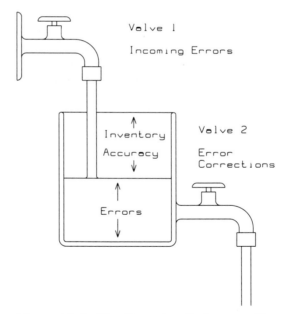

Figure 12-1. The "inventory" of errors. Errors are received and dispensed within an inventory facility much like the product itself. The key to accurate inventories is to minimize the introduction of new errors while maximizing the rate at which existing errors are found and corrected.

locations, and IA is inventory accuracy. So, if a business has four cycle counters, if they each check six locations an hour, and if 10 percent of the locations are incorrect (i.e., inventory accuracy is 90 percent), they will find an average of 2.4 errors per hour.

Similarly, the rate of flow into the container is a function of the number of material handlers, the rate at which they work, and the accuracy of their work. Because some errors are posted to already-incorrect inventories and should not be counted, the rate at which errors flow into the container is also a function of the overall accuracy:

$$R_{\text{EI}} = N_{\text{MH}} \times R_{\text{MH}} \times R_{\text{TE}} \times \text{IA}$$

In this equation, R_{EI} is the rate at which errors are inserted into the inventory, N_{MH} is the number of material handlers, R_{MH} is the rate at which material handler work, and R_{TE} is the rate at which material handlers make mistakes. If the same business employs 20 material handlers, if each material handler does 12 moves per hour, and if the movements are performed and recorded with a 2 percent error rate, 4.8 errors per hour are generated. If the inventory accuracy is 90 percent, then 10 percent of these errors don't count and the net rate of errors created is 4.32 per hour.

Over a period of time, assuming no outside influences, the overall inventory accuracy will stabilize. The rate of errors being inserted into the inventory will equal the rate at which they are discovered and corrected. We can, therefore, combine these two equations and solve for the resulting level of inventory accuracy.

$$\frac{(1 - \text{IA})}{\text{IA}} = \frac{N_{\text{MH}} \times R_{\text{MH}} \times R_{\text{TE}}}{N_{\text{CC}} \times R_{\text{LC}}}$$

A new term can now be defined: the ratio of the rate at which material handlers move material to the rate at which cycle counters check locations. This term, R, is defined as:

$$R = \frac{N_{\text{MH}} \times R_{\text{MH}}}{N_{\text{CC}} \times R_{\text{LC}}}$$

Substituting it into the equation for inventory accuracy:

$$\frac{(1 - \text{IA})}{\text{IA}} = R \times R_{\text{TE}}$$

or

$$\text{IA} = \frac{1}{1 + (R \times R_{\text{TE}})} \tag{12.1}$$

So, inventory accuracy is a function of the amount of cycle counting done in comparison to the amount of material handling done and is a function of the accuracy with which movements are recorded. This relationship is graphed in Figure 12.2. It is important to remember that it represents only a steady state level of accuracy and that it assumes random cycle counting and a random distribution of errors in the inventory. Also, the equation and graph are a little optimistic because they assume that the cycle counters themselves do not make errors.

The two keys are the ratio of the speed of material handling to the speed of cycle counting and the accuracy with which transactions are recorded. If transaction accuracy is 99 percent, then to achieve a steady state of 75 percent inventory accuracy, Equation 12.1 implies that one cycle count must be performed for every three material movements. If the plant employs 15 full-time material handlers

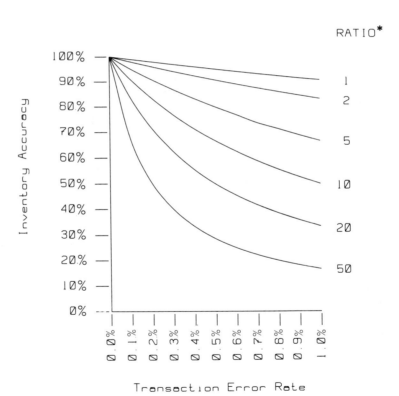

Figure 12.2. Inventory accuracy function. Mathematically, inventory accuracy is a function of the rate at which material handlers make mistakes and the ratio of the amount of material handling done to the amount of cycle counting done. This figure shows the theoretical accuracy level that will be achieved for various combinations of those two factors. (*, See text for definition.)

and if a cycle count can be performed in the same amount of time as a typical material movement, a staff of five cycle counters will be required.

This high ratio is based on the important assumptions that cycle counters must search (either at random or in a planned fashion) to find errors and that there is no other mechanism in place for finding and correcting errors. Clearly, no sane cycle counting program, by itself, can turn inaccurate inventories into accurate ones.

On the other hand, the equations above can also mean that, given enough time and labor, inventory accuracy can result from cycle counting by itself. Businesses that have a small number of highly critical items can assure accuracy for those items through intensive cycle counting. If the number of items is small and if the number of movements made is also small, the cycle counting labor required may be an acceptable alternative to a complex and expensive inventory system. At least one major pharmaceutical company once tried this approach on a large scale. They literally cycle counted every storage location every time material was moved into or out of it. The problem then became one of finding a way to check the checkers.

Double-Checking

Material handlers will, from time to time, find that the amount of material in inventory does not appear to be what it should be. Some of these exceptions will, in fact, be instances in which the records are incorrect. Others will be instances in which the records are correct, and the material handler is wrong. As inventory accuracy increases, the second cause becomes more important. The number of errors put into the inventory by erroneous corrections then becomes a significant concern.

Some protection against erroneous corrections can be gotten by requiring that a second person confirm the need before applying a correction to the inventory database. For instance, when a material handler finds an error such as a shortage or material in a location that is supposed to be empty, he or she should be required to determine and enter the correct on-hand quantity on the spot, but the correction should be posted to the database only after a cycle counter has visited the location and agreed with the material handler's adjustment. The protection can be extended one step further if the system is designed so that only cycle counters can make inventory adjustments. Even the plant manager, then, must enlist the aid of a cycle counter to post an adjustment. By creating people who are specialists in verifying and correcting inventory balances, fewer errors are created and overall inventory accuracy levels are enhanced.

Procedure Validation

From time to time in even the most accurate inventories, the people doing cycle counts will encounter real errors. If the inventory system keeps adequate historical records of the movement of material, it should be possible to track down the reason why the error occurred. Once the source of the problem has been located, management has an opportunity to prevent future occurrences.

Although the validation of procedures is a reasonable goal for cycle counting, it is a difficult one, even with the best audit trails. If, for instance, an inventory is incorrect because an unrecorded withdrawal was made, how is the cycle counter to trace the lack of a transaction to its source? Or if, for instance, a quantity was incorrectly picked, how can we take action to prevent recurrence if the error was random and the person who made it is otherwise a valuable employee?

Further, the tracing of errors through history files and other records requires a great deal of time and effort. Often the people who physically perform cycle counts are trained only for the counting process and the tracing job falls to salaried people. When many transactions affect an inventory over a short period of time, the workload can be enormous.

Still, at least to some degree, cycle counting can help ensure that proper procedures are being followed and that the best possible job is being done to keep the inventories accurate.

Accuracy Measurement

Knowledge of a firm's actual level of inventory accuracy is important. It serves as a management guide and provides the accountants and auditors with assurance that the books properly reflect the actual value of the company's investment in inventory. Representations to the stockholders, the government, and management must be accurate.

Inventory accuracy is also important to the inventory manager because inaccuracy can cause material shortages, unneeded expediting, production delays, and wasted labor. Inaccuracy can also result in a decision to increase safety stocks, consuming both valuable storage space and investment capital.

Operating a shop without a measure of the accuracy of the inventory records is like flying a plane without instruments or driving country roads without a map. The results are hit-and-miss. Inefficiency, poor customer service, and, in a competitive environment, even business failure can result.

Chapter 4 is devoted to the mathematics of measuring inventory accuracy.

STRUCTURING A CYCLE COUNTING PROGRAM

Cycle counting is most effective when the program is steady and regular, but modest. If inventory accuracy is relatively good, it does not take much work to prove that accuracy has remained good, and few errors will be found to be investigated. If accuracy is poor, it doesn't take much work to prove that either.

Cycle Counting Methods in an On-Line Environment

The basic cycle counting method is simple: employees are sent into the warehouse with instructions to visit preselected locations, identify and count the material found in them, and report the results back for comparison with the inventory records. The results are then used to measure accuracy, maintain audit trails, and make adjustments to the records.

For example, in an on-line, radio controlled environment, a cycle counter might carry a hand held radio terminal. The terminal begins the cycle counting routine by specifying the location number to be counted first. The cycle counter walks to that location. Since there is a possibility that he or she might select the wrong location, the terminal requires that the location label bar code be scanned.

Next, in an environment where product is stored in unit loads, the cycle counter is prompted to scan the bar code on one of the unit load labels in the location and then identify and key (or scan) the part number. The system verifies that the unit load does belong in the location counted and that it does contain that part number. Finally the counter is required to count the number of pieces of that particular part number on that unit load and the system verifies the quantity. If everything checks out, the system prompts for the next unit load label. When the counter indicates that the location is complete, the system verifies that its records show no uncounted product in the location and then displays the next location to be counted.

Exceptions will be found from time to time. Unit loads will be found that are not supposed to be there and some that should be present will be missing. Items will be found that do not belong on the unit load and other items that should be there will not be. And quantities will be incorrect.

When unit load numbers are found to be incorrect, the system should revalidate the location number and then search for the unexpected unit load in its database. If the unit load is recorded as being elsewhere, the system should add it to the location being counted, remove it from its recorded location, and put its recorded location on the list for cycle counting. Serious errors such as this should also be brought to management's attention for further investigation.

When item numbers are found to be incorrect, the system should revalidate the location number and display descriptions of the item number found by the cycle counter together with the descriptions and item numbers of the items that are on file as being in the location. The cycle counter should then be allowed to confirm the item number or change it. If the item number is confirmed, the system should record the existence of that item in the location being counted and put all locations containing the item on the list for cycle counting.

When quantities are found to be incorrect, the system should prompt for a recount. If the cycle counter confirms his or her count, an adjustment should be posted to make the recorded quantity match the quantity actually found. Or, if the recount results in a number that matches neither the recorded on-hand balance nor the first count, several actions are possible. Some systems will ask for another recount, some will plan the location for counting by another cycle counter, and some will simply accept the second count, regardless.

Cycle Counting in Other Situations

Those inventory facilities that do not use or number unit loads can modify the cycle counting methods described above by simply eliminating input and verification of unit load numbers. When lot numbers and/or serial numbers are tracked as product moves through the warehouse, they should also be verified during the cycle counting of a location.

In some businesses it may be difficult for the cycle counter to determine the item numbers for the products found in a location. Many distributors, for instance, handle products that are clearly marked with the vendor's item number but do not bear the company's own item number. These businesses will often compromise by displaying the item number and description to the cycle counter and asking him or her to verify the number rather than requiring that it be independently determined. Some companies will even go so far as to assume that item numbers are correct and verify only quantities. Their argument, often, is that if the item is wrong, the quantity will almost certainly also be wrong.

Cycle Counting Methods in an Off-Line Environment

Cycle counting in an off-line environment involves some significant complications relating to the timing of the cycle counts and other activities that are going on in the warehouse. Imagine, for instance, an inventory facility in which the various tasks required are printed on worksheets and distributed to employees to be done. The employees check off the work as it is done and return completed worksheets to a clerk for key entry. When a cycle counter verifies the content of a location, there is no way for the system to know which of the outstanding picks and put-aways were complete and which were still pending at the time the count was done. Therefore, it has no way of knowing whether the quantities found by the cycle counter are right or wrong.

Cycle counting in an off-line environment can only be done by freezing locations, counting them, and then releasing them. Freezing is usually done by setting a flag on the location record to prevent new transactions from being generated for that location. Once the existing open transactions have been completed and confirmed back to the system, the cycle count can be done and the results entered. Then and only then can the system be allowed to create new material movement transactions for that location.

Some companies with off-line inventory systems create a priority scheme that the system uses to determine the relative importance of transactions. When, for instance, material arrives in receiving and is to be put away, the system might recognize the put-away transaction as less critical than the cycle count. It would, therefore, hold the putaway transaction until the cycle count was complete. On the other hand, if a customer order requires picking from a location to be cycle counted, the cycle count would be canceled to allow the pick to take place immediately.

These complications apply just as much to locations that are partly serviced by on-line and partly by off-line material handlers. They are one of the most important justifications for on-line, radio-based inventory systems.

Basic Principles

Regardless of the situation, several basic principles are important to the design of an effective cycle counting system. To be effective, cycle counting employees must count locations, not items. It is far from simple for a counter to reliably locate all of the places where an item can be stored. Finding and counting all of the items in a location, on the other hand, is easy. However, when an item (or a specific lot of an item) must be counted, the inventory system can determine which locations are involved and the cycle counter can count all of those locations. Don't forget that cycle counting accuracy is as important as transaction accuracy.

The use of the computer to select the locations to be counted removes normal human biases and allows more sophisticated item selection methods. Methods used to select locations for counting are described in more detail in the next section.

Whenever a location is picked to a zero balance, some businesses with on-line inventory systems ask their material handlers to verify that no material remains. This is a very cheap and accurate way of getting one more cycle count done.

Audit trails should consist of two parts. The date, time, and transaction number of the last cycle count and of the last material handling transaction should be stored on the location record and updated as work is done. In a separate audit or history file, every material movement and every cycle count should be recorded. These records should specify the location affected, the date and time the work was done, the identity of the person who did the work, the type of work done, and the before and after on-hand balances.

Some businesses store the identity of the person who did the last material movement on the location record. When locations are assigned to people for counting, this allows them to assign someone else to do the count, eliminating, or at least minimizing, the temptation to cheat.

Cycle counting can be done either by dedicated cycle counters or by existing material handlers as part of their normal workload. Using existing material handlers saves labor (travel time into and out of the stockroom or warehouse). More important, the impact of being required to clean one's own house will motivate better performance in the recording and performing of transactions. Using dedicated cycle counters, on the other hand, allows for more detailed training and reduces the likelihood that cycle counts will suffer when the workload increases elsewhere. Productivity and error rate measures should be provided for cycle counters as well as for material handlers.

Planning Cycle Counting

When a material handler finds an inventory error, good practice specifies that the location should be frozen and a cycle counter should be brought in to verify that an error exists and make the actual correction. Many businesses prefer to make these kinds of cycle counts on a priority basis to assure that working locations are tied up as little as possible. Part of the cycle counter's day, therefore, is spent reacting to problems found by the material handler.

The majority of the cycle counter's time, however, should be spent counting in a planned and orderly fashion. To achieve this, each day's cycle counting should be preceded by a planning process. In the planning process, a supervisor or planner uses the inventory system to determine the amount of cycle counting that should be done and to select the locations to be counted. The planning process results in a work queue of locations to be counted. The work queue can be either transmitted to the cycle counters via radio or can be printed and handed out in the form of a worksheet.

The cycle count planning process typically begins with a supervisor or planner entering the number of cycle counters who will be working and the number of counts that should be generated for each. Based on this information, the system will select the locations to be counted and will display them for approval.

The locations to be cycle counted should be selected using a combination of several methods, with the number selected by each method either predetermined and stored in a system table or specified by the supervisor or planner. The selection methods are:

1. Randomly selected locations. The selection should be truly random, without bias for inventory value, ABC code, or the number of pieces on hand.
2. Locations that have gone the longest since last being cycle counted.
3. Locations that have had the most activity since last being cycle counted.
4. Locations specified by a supervisor or by the planner.

PHYSICAL INVENTORIES

The original idea behind the physical inventory was financial. Its primary goal was and is to provide a fair and unbiased count of the dollars invested in inventory so the company can give stockholders an accurate picture of profitability.

The advent of computer-run inventory systems created a second use for the physical inventory—that of recording the quantity on hand for each part to verify the inventory records. But, since the original concept was designed only to provide an accurate overall total, the second use has not worked well. Most physical inventories result in error rates between 10 and 40 percent by location. So long as these errors are unbiased—that is, so long as they are equally divided between too high and too low—the resulting inventory is accurate enough for accounting purposes. But, there are obvious consequences for material planning. Problems inherent in most physical inventories include:

1. Their temporary nature. An entire organization is often built for physical inventory taking, complete with titles and lines of authority. But, since everyone in the organization knows that it is temporary, there is little loyalty or dedication.
2. Pressures to get done and get back to work. The people doing the physical inventory know that the main business of the company is not to count inventory. They are often anxious to get back to their normal jobs. Pressures from management and customers to keep the plant on schedule can result in sloppy work and inaccurate results.
3. Lack of training. The people who do the counting and recording of physical inventories are usually taught how they should do their jobs

but are rarely taught why. As a result, they do not often appreciate the consequences of failure and the importance of the physical inventory in total.

4. Inadequate performance measurements. In many cases, the only measure of performance that emerges from a completed physical inventory is the financial one: the size of the inventory write-down. Sometimes location accuracies are also measured. But, if individual inventory takers were measured on the speed and accuracy with which they worked, there would be a significant improvement in the amount and quality of work done.

5. Inadequate auditing. The auditing of physical inventories is almost always done by financial auditors who are interested only in dollars. Rarely are these inventories audited by personnel with concern for individual location accuracies.

The net result is that physical inventories often insert more errors into the inventory records than they remove. The most successful companies no longer do physical inventories. Instead, they use cycle counters to demonstrate that their inventory records are accurate. Auditing firms are increasingly willing to accept existing records based on an audit of the effectiveness of a company's cycle counting program.

Some years ago a firm in the upper midwest installed the systems they needed to achieve highly accurate inventory records. Later, the company's parent corporation found itself in bankruptcy, complete with indictments against the parent's management for fraudulent inventory records. One day, the subsidiary company was paid a surprise visit by three teams of auditors representing the court, the parent company's board, and the original auditing firm. The visitors were prepared to close the company down to take a complete inventory, but they chose to look first at a sample of the company's cycle counting records. When they found that the company was keeping records that were more than 99 percent accurate, they agreed to accept the inventories as recorded and, within a matter of hours, were gone.

Planning a Physical Inventory

A well-run physical inventory meets two sets of requirements: those of the company's auditors and those of the inventory control organization. The requirements imposed by auditors can be hard to predict in a book such as this one because auditors vary in expertise and experience. However, the basic concerns involved should include (1) assurance that the business' assets are properly represented in the financial ledger, (2) assurance that management information generated by the inventory system is accurate, and (3) detection of any possible instances of theft or fraud.

The inventory control organization needs precise knowledge of the part number, quantity, lot number, and serial number on hand at each location. Inventory control needs this information to support high levels of customer service and operating efficiency at the lowest possible level of inventory investment.

Physical inventories are expensive exercises that are not always necessary and need not always be done annually. Before a physical inventory is started, a conscious decision should be made based on the costs and benefits involved. First, the cost of running the physical inventory should be estimated including both labor cost and the opportunity cost of being essentially out of business while the count is being done. Then inventory accuracy should be measured (see Chapter 4). With this information in hand, two informed decisions can be made by management and the auditing staff: (1) Is a physical inventory really necessary and (2) must it cover the entire operation or can selected areas be isolated for counting?

The physical inventory requires more than software. Organization, training, and supervision are also important parts of the process. The planning process should begin several months in advance of the scheduled inventory date with the creation of a cross-functional committee. The committee should usually be made up of representatives from finance, manufacturing, warehousing, inventory control, purchasing, data processing, and auditing. It should be charged with complete responsibility for planning and executing the physical inventory.

The committee's work is divisible into tasks, described here in approximately chronological order:

1. One of the committee's first jobs should be to create a list of the tasks that must be done and the events that will occur. This list will undoubtedly grow and change over time and should be reissued several times to a wide distribution.

2. Inventory methods must be determined and instructions must be written covering counting and count recording procedures, unit-of-measure problems and their resolution, location numbering methods, item and lot number identification techniques and methods for identifying and counting company owned off-site material. Off-site material includes material in-transit as well as material temporarily off-site for other reasons.

3. Data processing requirements must be defined including both software specifications and the computing resources and support that will be required during the physical counting.

4. Equipment and labor must be scheduled. Equipment requirements may include additional scales, forklifts and computer terminals that must be purchased or leased. Personnel must be scheduled for counting, writing, auditing, and reconciliation.

5. Cutoff dates and times must be established for receipts, issues, shop movements, shipments to customers, shipments to other plants and warehouses, and scrap processing.

6. A fresh standard cost buildup should be done shortly before the inventory takes place. This requires verification of labor rates and a freeze on routing and vendor price changes.

7. Shortly before the physical inventory begins, counting responsibilities must be defined and supervisors and auditors must be trained. On the day before the count begins, or on the first morning of the

count itself, counters and writers must be trained and given an opportunity to ask questions. The value of training cannot be overemphasized. Some companies even set up miniature stockrooms in the training area to allow hands-on demonstration of the required methods and procedures.

Physical Inventory Methods

Many businesses, even those that control material movements and cycle counts with on-line radio based systems, run off-line physical inventories. There are often many more counting teams than radios, and the cost of purchasing additional radios is simply not justified for an activity that takes place infrequently. Further, there is little need for on-line database updating during a physical inventory.

Physical inventory taking methods differ significantly from one business to another based on the products and facilities involved and the requirements of both management and the auditors. The sample method described below will support high levels of accuracy in the completed inventory but may not meet the needs of all companies.

Assuming that radio terminals are not to be used, a physical inventory system can be based on clerks working at on-line CRT workstations with attached bar code wands. The clerks are responsible for distributing the counting work to two-person counting teams. The counting process begins after all material movement in the facility has ceased. Clerks scan the bar-coded employee badges of the counting team members, one team at a time. The inventory system then prints count sheets like the sample in Figure 12.3 for each team. It also records the identity of the people who are to count each location for future reference.

Count sheets are usually constructed by the inventory control system to provide approximately 2 hours of work for a team. Factors involved in estimating the workload for a group of inventory locations can include the accessibility of locations, the nature and quantity of items stored in the locations, and the necessity for special equipment such as lift trucks or scales. Each count sheet can consist of several pages.

Along with the count sheets, the system prints a group of simple count identification labels as shown in Figure 12.4. These labels simplify some aspects of the auditing function and also provide a measure of motivation to counters by labeling each location with their names. The count sheets and the count identification labels are given to the team. The team proceeds into the warehouse and begins counting.

Counting is done location by location, with each team responsible for the identification and counting of all the material in a location. As items are identified and counted, one member of the team records item numbers and quantities on the count sheet, while the other does the physical counting. Upon completion of each location, a count identification label is applied to the material. Upon completion of the count sheet, the team returns to the office and turns in the sheet.

In the office, a clerk rescans the team's employee badges to produce new count sheets for them. Then the clerk keys the information on the completed count

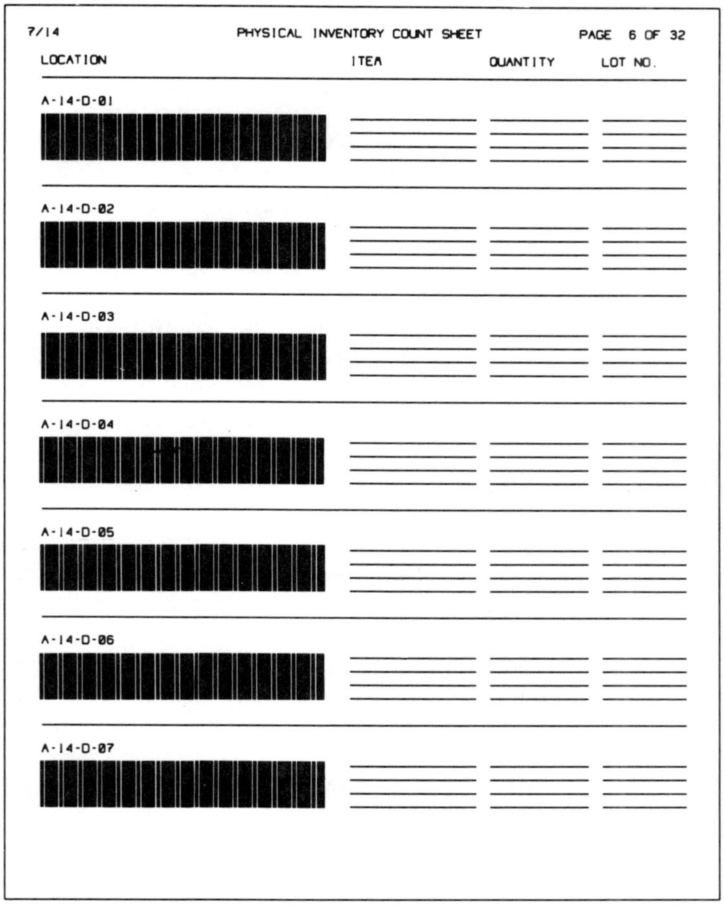

Figure 12.3. Physical inventory count sheet. This design is intended for use in a manual data collection environment. The bar codes shown are for data entry after the counts have been completed.

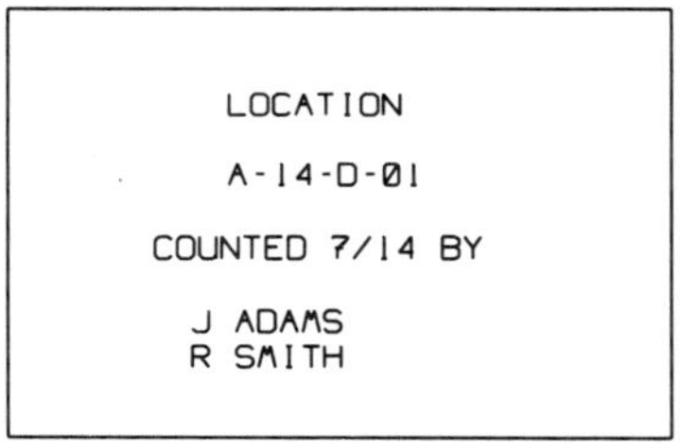

Figure 12.4. Count identification label. The count identification label is used as part of the count auditing process.

sheet. Bar codes are provided to assure accurate entry of location numbers. The system verifies the correctness of the item number, quantity, and lot number information as it is keyed and gives the clerk an opportunity to correct keying errors as variances are found. When a variance is found that is not due to a keying error, the location is added to a file of pending recounts. When the results of the inventory match the system's records exactly, the system logs the count in its history file, updates the date of last count on the location file, and continues to the next location.

This process differs markedly from most of the ones described in previous chapters. Bar codes are not used by the counting teams because the objective is to collect item numbers, quantities, and lot numbers without reference to existing records. The absence of bar codes on the floor, however, does not mean that the principle of validation has been abandoned. Validation, in this procedure, comes from the comparison of the physical count with the system's records. The location is bar coded on the count sheet not only to improve key entry productivity but also because the location number itself isn't otherwise validated and must be entered accurately.

After the last count sheet has been printed and issued to a counting team, the inventory control system begins printing recounts. Recounting procedures are identical to the initial counts, except for a restriction that the recounting team cannot be the team that performed the initial count. If a recount does not match the recorded on-hand value but does match the first count, an inventory variance is recorded for later posting to the inventory file. If the recount matches neither the recorded on-hand balance or the original count, the location is added to a problem list.

As the counting and recounting processes near completion, the auditing function comes into play. Both the accumulated variances and the problem list can be displayed on a terminal and printed in the form of count sheets as necessary. Auditors and supervisors can recount locations and enter or adjust the count results. The system tracks and can report the number of instances in which a count made by a counting team is adjusted by an auditor or by a supervisor.

Eventually it will be decided that the inventory is adequately complete to allow the facility to resume work. At this point, the system will post the accumulated variances to the inventory records and will place holds on the locations that remain on the problem list. These holds can be released one at a time or in groups by auditors or supervisors as the problems are resolved.

Following completion of the physical inventory and any final adjustments, the inventory control system reports:

- Inventory value
- Value of adjustments made during the inventory
- Recount listings by part number, location, and team
- Inventory accuracy as measured by the physical inventory.

This procedure assumes that the count teams are required to verify item numbers, quantities and, where they exist, lot numbers. In some businesses, item identification is more difficult and therefore more expensive than in others. If it is unreasonable to expect a counting team to determine item numbers by looking at the product, count sheets can include item number and descriptions. However, the teams should be specifically instructed to verify part numbers in addition to counting and recording quantities.

13

Material Handling Considerations

Inventory accuracy results from accuracy in individual material movements. The simultaneous achievement of both accuracy and productivity requires a system that fits the methods and procedures used in the business. These methods and procedures, in turn, are often dictated by material handling and storage equipment. Inventory systems, therefore, must be designed to accommodate a variety of equipment and a number of ways of using it.[1]

MATERIAL HANDLING DEVICES

The basic material handling device is the lift truck. Available everywhere, easily repairable, and inexpensive, few businesses can operate without at least one lift truck. Much of this book has assumed the use of lift trucks for material movement. But, even the basic lift truck is not as simple as it may sound. And many other kinds of material handling devices exist. The most important of these are discussed below with emphasis on their impact on an inventory system.

Lift Trucks

A lift truck is an operator-controlled vehicle capable of moving a unit load either horizontally or vertically. Lift trucks usually handle material on pallets but also come with clamps for handling paper rolls, rams for steel coils, grabs for slip

---

[1]For those who wish a more detailed physical description of some of the material handling and storage devices described, the following book is recommended: Tompkins, James A., and Jerry D. Smith, *The Warehouse Management Handbook,* New York: McGraw-Hill Book Company, 1988.

sheets, and many other special-purpose devices. Lift trucks also vary in the size of aisle they require. Some trucks can reach higher than others. Some can handle heavier loads than others.

The counterbalance lift truck suspends its load in front of the front axle. The straddle truck carries its load between the axles, with the front axle split so the truck can straddle the load to pick it up and put it down. While the straddle truck needs more side-to-side clearance to handle a load, it is shorter overall than the counterbalance truck and can work in narrower aisles. There are also side-loading lift trucks, swing mast lift trucks, and turret trucks. All are designed to work in very narrow aisles since they do not have to turn into the rack to pick up or put down a load.

Some high-rise lift trucks are supported from the top as well as from the bottom or can even be exclusively supported from the top. These devices are often called cranes but are the equivalent of lift trucks in the areas that matter to inventory systems. This book, therefore, lumps them into the general lift truck category. Other lift trucks are capable of "reaching" into a two-pallet-deep rack to extract a pallet, while others are not. While most lift trucks raise and lower loads with the driver stationary, some also raise and lower the driver along with the load, providing better visibility at higher levels.

Productive use of lift trucks requires that the truck be properly matched to the load in terms of its weight and size and to both the source and destination locations.

Order Pickers

The term "order picker" is usually applied to vehicles designed for moving material in less-than-pallet quantities. These vehicles vary greatly in their sophistication, ranging from simple four-wheel carts, to sophisticated high-rise powered trucks.

Order pickers vary not only in height and width but also in the way in which they handle material. Some order pickers, for instance, are equipped with bins or shelving so several orders can be picked at once and easily kept separate. Others consist only of a single place to put material and require the operator to keep track if more than one order is being picked.

Some order pickers are not equipped to handle pallets. Therefore, when an order picker is used to pick the last carton from a pallet in storage, provision must be made for removal of the empty pallet. And a similar circumstance arises when an order picker is used to put away cartons in an empty pallet storage location: An empty pallet must be provided.

Automated Equipment

More and more inventory facilities are using automated and semiautomated material handling equipment. For the purposes of an inventory system, there are two major categories: conveyors and automated guided vehicles (AGVs).

Conveyors are continuously operating devices capable of both horizontal and vertical movement. They can be used for sorting or for carrying or can do both. Conveyors come in many varieties: rollers, belts, skate wheels, and monorails, to name a few. Unpowered conveyors are generally not of interest in the design of an inventory system since they only assist people and can be controlled by controlling the people. Powered conveyors, however, are different because they work unattended. If control is to be exercised, it must be through a different mechanism than that used to control the people.

Conveyors have two basic characteristics that distinguish them from lift trucks. First, they can handle many loads at once. And second, they follow a strict first-on, first-off rule, although this rule can be affected by diverging and merging routes.

Some inventory systems work with material coming off a conveyor. For instance, they may manage the transfer of the material to another conveyor or issue instructions to a person receiving the material. In relatively simple conveying systems it is often practical to track loads as they are introduced to the conveyor so the system knows the identity of the material as it comes off. In more complex systems it may be simpler to reidentify the material through a bar code reader as it comes off the conveyor.

The identity of individual AGV carriers is normally tracked by the AGV controller and is not of consequence to the inventory system. Logically, therefore, most AGV systems differ from conveyors only in added flexibility. Like conveyors, they handle many loads at a time and usually operate without human supervision.

Vertical Movement Devices

Ramps connect floors or levels and need no special consideration unless they are so steep that only some types of lift trucks can negotiate them. Vertical conveyors are logically no different from horizontal ones. But, elevators handle loads in batches and the unloading sequence may bear little relationship to the loading sequence.

Special Considerations

Sometimes, lift trucks or other devices are used to handle two, three, or even more unit loads in a single movement. Double length pallet jacks can be bought for just that purpose. Tuggers (devices that pull a train of cars) can handle dozens of pallets in a single move. The job of tracking and controlling material movement can become extremely complex if each of the pallets in a movement has a different source and a different destination location.

Other equipment, notably high-reach lift trucks, moves very slowly when going from aisle to aisle. The well-designed inventory system must, in these cases, take steps to minimize the amount of aisle changing. And, in some instances, safety considerations demand that vehicle access be limited by the vehicles already working in or around a location. For instance, some kinds of high-rise lift trucks carry the operator up with the load. While this gives excellent visibility for material handling purposes, it reduces floor-level visibility to near zero. These lift trucks, therefore, cannot be safely operated in aisles together with other vehicles. If the inventory system is directing material movement, it must consider and accommodate this situation. Responsible system design allows no compromise where safety is concerned.

MATERIAL STORAGE DEVICES

Material storage devices are more varied than material handling devices. The pallet rack is the device most often used and is usually the simplest to control. Many other devices exist and most have unique characteristics that affect inventory systems.

Pallet Rack

As the lift truck is the fundamental material handling device, so the pallet rack is the most common material storage device. Pallet racks come in many shapes and sizes. The differences between most kinds of pallet rack can be adequately expressed by the dimensions and weight limitations assigned to each opening. But other important factors can arise. Modern inventory storage facilities seem to rise higher and higher each year. Ceilings of 40 and 50 feet are no longer rare. When high-rise racking is used, special equipment is needed to reach the top tiers.

Two-deep racks can be handled by "reach" lift trucks. Each opening in a two-deep rack is usually represented within the inventory system as a single location with the ability to handle two pallets. Unless locations are limited to a single item, the system should keep track of which pallet is in front and which is in back. It should also take steps to assure that the front pallet is properly handled (i.e., relocated) if access to the pallet in back is necessary.

Drive-in and drive-through racks provide an opportunity for very high density storage. When lanes can be limited to a single item, each can be considered a single location. Capacity, however, can no longer be stated in cubic measure but must be stated in the number of unit loads that can be handled, with each unit load meeting maximum length, width, and height limits.

The situation quickly gets more complex as the methods of use of the drive-in and drive-through rack get more sophisticated. A rack, for instance, that is accessible from both ends can be considered to be two locations, capable of handling two items. But, the capacity of either location then depends not only on the amount stored in the other location but also on how far back into the location it was placed.

Even more complex, some businesses attempt to use drive-in and drive-through racks to store single pallets, each pallet independent of the others and each, potentially, carrying a different item. In these cases, it is generally thought that each pallet position in the rack should be designated as a separate location. Access to the locations, however, depends on the state of the locations in front, whether they are empty or full. Often the situation becomes logically so complex that the value of high-density storage is more than nullified by the cost of the system needed to control it.

Other Rack-Like Devices

Other devices are logically similar to the pallet rack but have their own unique characteristics. A cantilever rack, for instance, is designed for the storage of pipe and other long slender products. When selecting storage locations, the inventory system must be able to differentiate between a cantilever rack and a pallet rack, assigning each item to the proper device.

Shelving and bins are also similar to pallet racks, but do not involve the use of pallets. Containers must be provided along with a way of removing them after product is stored and a way of introducing them as product is picked. The inventory control system, however, need not necessarily be involved in container handling.

Both shelving and bins are typically used for the storage of less-than-pallet quantities. Both can occasionally be found in high-rise versions that need special handling equipment. Bins are like shelving in that several locations exist on each tier in a section. Bins differ from shelving, however, by the existence of physical dividers between these locations. When inventory systems select locations, shelving is normally treated like bins. Each location is assumed to have a fixed width, so cube and maximum dimension can be used to decide whether or not product will fit. If business needs dictate that shelving locations must be flexible, the computer selection of locations becomes much more complex. In such cases it may be best to leave the selection of locations up to the material handler.

Drawer storage differs from bins and shelving primarily in the number of locations that typically appear in each foot of aisle. Very high-density drawer storage can also present special problems. For instance, because locations are so small, material handlers working in a single aisle can interfere with each other, affecting both productivity and accuracy.

Mezzanines

High-rise bins and shelving units are often accessed using mezzanines. The mezzanines themselves rarely present problems to the inventory system. But, they must be set up as separate picking and put-away zones and location numbers must be established in a sensible working sequence. If, for instance, a bin area is reached through a three-level mezzanine, each level of the mezzanine should probably be a different series of location numbers (a different "area"). Tier numbers will normally begin with one in a separate series at the floor level of each mezzanine.

Flow Rack

There are two kinds of flow racks: carton and pallet. Both are physically similar to a rack (or, in the case of a carton flow rack, to bins) but are logically quite different. First-in, first-out turnover is virtually assured with a flow rack, but like the drive-in and drive-through pallet rack, capacity is most accurately stated in loads.

Because locations are filled from one end and emptied from the other, it is possible that they will be accessible by one kind of material handing device for putting away and by a different kind for picking.

Floor Storage

Floor storage is also a commonly found storage "device." Floor storage areas are usually divided by aisles and the area between aisles is usually divided into lanes. The dividers are often simply lines painted on the floor. Lanes are usually one pallet wide but can equally well be small rectangular areas. Each lane is usually considered to be a separate location.

Sometimes single locations are restricted to the storage of a single item and, when lot control is of importance, to a single lot. In other cases, however, locations can be configured that will store multiple items or even multiple lots of multiple items.

Location numbers are usually made up of an area number, an aisle number, and (in place of the section number found in rack areas) the lane number. The division of lanes into sublocations is rare. Location numbers are best assigned to make it easy for a lift truck operator to find a location. Usually they are in sequence within an aisle and cross-aisles are sequential along a main aisle.

Compared to a rack, floor storage allows higher storage densities at a lower cost. However, for the system designer, floor storage creates a problem because there is no place to put a bar-coded location label. One validation technique for floor storage requires a modest amount of key entry, but it is actually little slower than bar coding and is very nearly as effective.

As part of the process of adding location numbers to its database, the inventory control system generates a "random" two-position alphanumeric location code. Since a two-position alphanumeric code only allows for 1296 values (36 squared), location codes will not be unique in a large warehouse. So, before assigning a code to a location, the system should verify that it is not duplicated nearby on the same aisle, in the same position on another aisle, or in the same position in the same aisle in another warehouse area. Such duplication might measurably compromise the validation process.

At least one sign is made for each location. The sign must be large enough, when mounted, to be easily read by the lift-truck operator. These signs bear the location number and the location code. They should be durable enough to withstand occasional bumps from a lift-truck mast and remain legible for a number of years.

The signs are then mounted over or adjacent to each location. The preferred method is to hang them from the ceiling on chains directly over the entrance to each lane. However, they must be hung high enough to clear lift truck masts and, in some warehouses, readability becomes a problem. In extreme cases, both the location number and the location code can be painted on the floor, but maintenance (repainting) costs will be high.

Location codes are used as follows:

1. An operator, for instance, is told by the computer to move a load to location 3-A-17 (the seventeenth lane in aisle A in warehouse area 3).
2. Upon arrival at 3-A-17, the operator finds a sign over the lane that reads "3-A-17/R8." 3-A-17 is, of course, the location number and R8 is the location code.
3. The operator drops the pallet in the lane and keys the location code, R8, into a terminal. Since the system knows that the operator was destined for 3-A-17 and since it knows that R8 is the code for 3-A-17, it can validate the transaction.

Absolute code uniqueness is not needed for validation to function effectively. If, for instance, a large warehouse has 13,000 floor locations, each location code will be repeated an average of 10 times. But, validation is only concerned with catching errors. If location errors occur in 1 percent of all material movements and if the probability of catching a random error is 1295 / 1296 (i.e., the probability that the error will not involve a duplicated location code), only one movement in 129,600 will result in an undetected error. Most companies would prefer this error rate to the labor involved in keying a longer location code.

Floor storage validation choices exist. In one example, RF tags can be buried in the floor and RF antennas mounted under the lift trucks to read the tags' serial numbers. The lift trucks, however, must somehow be guided to assure that material handlers do not cut corners and actually pass over the right tag as they enter and exit the lanes.

In a business where unit loads are identified with bar codes, validation of floor storage can sometimes be done by scanning the unit load label on a unit load in the lane to the material handler's right. The inventory system can look up the location of that load and verify that the load being stored is, in fact, being put in the correct lane. Rules must be established to cover instances when the lane to the right is empty or when there is no lane to the right.

Like the drive-in and drive-through rack, floor storage lanes are sometimes accessible from both ends. When the two ends are treated as separate locations, the same complexities arise with the assignment of locations.

Automated Equipment

Vertical and horizontal carousels can be treated much like bins, with the exception that only one person can work an aisle at a time. Carousels, in fact, are often grouped with a single material handler working two or more at once. In this arrangement, each carousel is usually considered to be an aisle and the single-person limitation is modified to apply to the carousel group.

The sequencing of transactions in a carousel environment can be important to productivity. Typically, when several carousels are used by a single operator, transactions alternate among the carousels and those for a single carousel are sorted by section. This allows some carousels to be rotating while others are being used. It also limits the rotation time required for each carousel to move from one pick or put-away transaction to the next.

Productivity and accuracy considerations often require that the inventory control system be directly connected to the programmable controller that operates the carousels. The link is used to pass transactions to the carousel controller in real time, rotating them automatically as needed. The inventory system must also be able to communicate the exact picking location and quantity to the material handler. It must be able to receive a signal from the material handler denoting the completion of each transaction. And, there must be a means by which the material handler can enter exceptions such as unplanned shortages or incorrect carousel rotations as they occur. A translation table is often needed to convert between the location numbers understood by the inventory system and those understood by the carousel controller.

Real-time communication between the carousel and the inventory system can be handled by an intermediate computer. Personal computers have been successfully used for this. Batches of work, such as a picking wave, are downloaded to the PC. The PC manages the carousels and the picking process. Validated results are uploaded to the inventory system on completion of the wave.

Automated storage and retrieval systems (AS/RS) are similar to carousels except that the mechanism for moving the load to the operator is different. While a carousel rotates the entire "aisle" until the appropriate bin is in front of the operator, an AS/RS extracts individual bins or unit loads and carries them to the operator. Most automated storage and retrieval systems are capable of moving one load while the operator is working on another.

Like carousels, automated storage and retrieval systems are often interfaced with the inventory system to reduce key entry requirements. Like carousels, the interface is almost always done through a programmable controller to handle the digital to analog conversion. And, in many cases, a personal computer is placed between the programmable controller and the main inventory control system to assure fast real-time response.

Moveable aisle systems consist of high-density storage in which an entire row of locations is mounted on wheels and can be moved laterally. When an operator needs access to a location, rows are moved until an aisle is created. Moveable aisle systems are often best suited for slow-moving items in long-term storage and, therefore, are not often found in inventory facilities with sophisticated control systems. They can be useful, however, in instances where physical security is a concern.

The rack and flow rack can be semiautomated with the addition of a pick-by-light system. These systems include small LED displays at each location that are used to display a picking quantity and, sometimes, an order number. They often enhance picking productivity by eliminating paperwork. Accuracy is also improved because the pick quantity is displayed at the picking location and the picker does not need to figure out which location to pick from.

Pick-by-light systems require a significant degree of integration with the inventory system. As always, the picker must have the ability to signal completion of a pick or a group of picks, often by pressing a button. Methods of recording and acting on exceptions are also needed.

The term "pick-by-light" implies that these systems are intended for picking. While they are most commonly used to control pickers, they can also be used for storing material and for other tasks. In the case of a put-away, for instance, a material handler could scan a bar code on a pallet of mixed items to be put away. The inventory system could determine the location for each of the items and signal the location by displaying the put-away item number and quantity on each one.

CONTAINERS

Containers are also important to the smooth integration of systems with the working environment. Most people think of a pallet as a wooden device consisting of planks nailed across three or more risers. Pallets, however, are actually much more varied. They can be made from wood, plastic, wire, corrugated cardboard, or other materials. Some have sides and even tops, although most do not. Some kinds of pallets, notably shipsheets, need special equipment. Totes and cartons of various kinds are logically equivalent to pallets for purposes of the inventory system.

When designing inventory systems, the key considerations relating to containers are their dimensions and the kind of equipment needed to handle them. More specifically, each type of container has associated with it:

- An interior height, width, and depth
- An exterior height, width, and depth
- A weight capacity
- A tare weight
- A transportation class
- A stacking or loading pattern

In rare cases, containers may also be limited to specific materials or kinds of materials, or their weight capacity may differ depending on the material placed in them. For example, a cardboard box may be able to handle four 1-gallon milk bottles but would split if loaded with the equivalent weight in loose sand.

Interior dimensions and the weight capacity can normally be used by the inventory system to determine what may be put in the container. When containers have sides, the exterior dimensions, the weight of the contents, and the tare weight determine where they can be stored. When the containers do not have sides, the height of the load can sometimes be calculated from the content, but many systems request the height of the completed load from the person who put the material on the container. This avoids the complexities associated with multiple-item stacking and nesting patterns.

The transportation class, as described earlier, defines the material handling devices needed to move the loaded container. In some instances (totes and cartons), handling methods will also be a function of the gross weight. Totes, for instance, below a certain weight can be handled by operators alone; those above the limit require mechanical assistance.

Stacking or loading patterns are often tracked by inventory systems. Generally, however, the pattern information kept is limited to the quantity per tier and the number of tiers to be used when stacking a single item on a standard pallet. The information is most often used to guide material handlers as pallets are built in receiving and is rarely used to predetermine the items and quantities that will fit.

Systems that use container tare weights can be successful, but reusable containers are a point of concern, particularly if the tare weight is expected to be accurate within a few percentage points of the actual weight. Wooden pallets for instance, are often green when new and lighten considerably as they dry. Then, later, they may have absorbed enough oil and waste to make them heavier again, or pieces may have been broken off, making them lighter. When reusable container tare weights are an important part of an inventory system, the system should track the date on which each container was last weighed and should prompt operators to reweigh each one on a regular basis.

TRAILERS

Some companies store material in trailers or other vehicles. Telephone company service trucks, for example, are usually equipped with an inventory of parts and materials. In other cases, an over-the-road trailer may be loaded with an outbound shipment and spotted in the parking lot pending actual shipment some time in the future. Or, in still other cases, trailers may simply be used as an extension of the warehouse. They can be filled and parked, and when the material is needed, they can be moved back to a dock and unloaded. Inefficient as this may seem, there can be times when there is little choice. Businesses that find themselves using trailers for storage often (and businesses that have mobile service inventories) may find that controls are necessary and justifiable.

Over-the-road trailers can be tracked as containers, as locations, or as an entirely different entity with an entirely different data structure. The decision among these alternatives is best made based on how the data will be used. When trailers are treated like containers, the parking lot can be established in the system's location file. Each parking space becomes a storage location and each dock door is a staging location used for the transfer of material between trailers and other material handling devices. Since trailers can contain containers that, themselves, can contain several items, a multilevel, bill-of-material-like structure is needed to track inventories in detail.

When trailers are treated like locations, they themselves cannot logically be placed in a location. One implication is that the placement of the trailer in the parking lot and its retrieval cannot be controlled by the system. In modestly sized parking lots, this should not present a problem. But, in larger lots it may be unworkable. The U.S. Postal Service, for example, handles large numbers of trailers at its bulk mail centers and tracks them into and out of its yard. Incoming trailers are assigned to parking spaces, then to dock doors for unloading, back to parking spaces when empty, and then to another door for loading before being dispatched on the next trip.

Company trailers can be usefully bar coded. Bar codes are often best applied to the inside of the rear doors to protect them from the weather and covered with transparent tape to protect them from abrasion. The bar code can contain a serial number that can be the key to a trailer file containing, among other things, the inside dimensions and weight capacity of the trailer. Trailers belonging to carriers are harder to handle because only standardized measurements can be used. When the trailer delivered by a carrier varies from the expected measurements, the system must be able to compensate.

Service truck inventories are often handled as forward picking areas. Picks, however, are not order controlled but occur at the discretion of the service person and are accompanied by the entry of a job, order, or customer number. Off-line hand-held portable terminals can be ideal for recording these numbers together with the identity and quantity of the material withdrawn from stock. At the end of each day, when the service person returns to the warehouse, the terminal can be uploaded and a replenishment cycle can be initiated to restock the service truck.

CONTROLLING MOVEMENT

The productive and safe operation of an inventory facility requires that material handling equipment be properly matched to its loads. The matching involves both the container used and the load's weight and size. Both the container and the material handling equipment must also be matched with both the source and destination locations. Considerations include the location's height above the floor, the load's weight and the capacity of the material handling vehicle, aisle size and overhead clearance, load clearances, source and destination storage devices, and the route to be taken from the source to the destination (including staging areas). Efficient dispatching requires that task priorities be observed and that supervisory controls be in place to limit material handlers to the work assigned to them.

As inventory facilities grow and as they are automated in an effort to improve productivity, there is a tendency toward increased diversity in all of these factors. The dispatching job thus becomes more and more complex and, soon, the point is reached where human dispatchers can no longer juggle all of the factors accurately and reliably. Automated dispatching is often the solution.

Automated, real-time dispatching can be effectively done with radio terminals, either mounted to lift trucks or hand carried by material handlers. The inventory system communicates with the material handlers through these terminals. It uses them to present tasks to the material handlers and receive either validation or exception information as the work is completed. On completion of each task, the inventory system then selects another task and presents it.

Task selection is most easily done if the tasks themselves are represented by data records in a work queue. Work queues are usually independent files in the inventory system's database. The structuring of these files depends on the database manager in use but, in many cases, access paths are maintained by vehicle and task types. Records are arranged in the queue by priority and in location sequence within priority. When multiple, identical vehicles are assigned to work a queue, conflicts can arise with many of them attempting to work simultaneously in a single aisle. The solution is often to subdivide the queues into individual work assignments and to limit work assignments to one vehicle at a time.

UNITIZATION

Unitization is the prepackaging of product in standard quantities on standard containers into unit loads. The value of unitization in a modern inventory facility is easily seen: It eliminates the need to count product as movements occur. Instead, by scanning a unit load bar code, the material handler informs the inventory system of both the identity of the product and the quantity being handled.

Unitization should be evaluated in terms of costs and benefits, as should all changes to handling and storage methods. But, when the evaluation is done, care should be taken to assure that all of the potential benefits are accounted for. Included are productivity improvement, loss and damage reduction, and improved inventory accuracy.

14

Management

Like "The best laid schemes o' mice and men . . ." (Robert Burns), even the best-designed inventory systems will fail to produce accuracy and high levels of productivity unless they are well managed. The system designer builds for the present and for the future, to the extent it can be anticipated. The manager works with the present and the future, both now and in the future. As business conditions change, as staff turns over, and as volume climbs (or drops), it is the manager who must compensate and adapt. While some changes in climate must be addressed with changes to the inventory system, others cannot. The manager's challenge is to identify problems, select the best solution, and see that the chosen solution is properly implemented and effective.

The system designer, however, is not left entirely out of the management picture. In order for the manager to do his or her job well, the designer must plan a manageable system. The system must measure its performance and the performance of the people and equipment that work under its control. And it must provide the data platform on which other management decisions can be built. This chapter discusses these and other management concerns.

ORGANIZING FOR ACCURACY

The topic of organization can be approached from several angles. The division of responsibilities among managers and supervisors and the structuring of reporting relationships are important to success in any business. But before responsibilities can be divided and structured, they must be identified. A discussion of the things that must be organized, particularly those that relate directly to inventory systems, divides easily into two areas: preinstallation and postinstallation.

Preinstallation Organization

The management of the system development project is described in Part 3 of this book. However, Part 3 does not address some proper concerns of the inventory manager who will take over the system after it is completed and installed. That person has several subjects to consider.

First, it is important that the inventory manager and staff recognize the magnitude of change involved in the installation of systems such as the ones described in this book. Some businesses move directly from an all-manual environment to a sophisticated on-line inventory system. In these cases, it is obvious that the degree of change is great. Other businesses simply move up from off-line, batch oriented systems to an on-line environment. The inventory managers of these businesses may be the ones most likely to underestimate the degree of change involved.

When systems are off-line, whether computer driven or manual, the consequences of an error are often hidden from the person who made the error. Someone else suffers the consequences but not immediately and the error may not be traceable back to the person who made it. In an on-line system, consequences are more immediate and people will find that they are making more errors than they had realized. Being human, many employees will fail to understand that they are now being held to a different and more exacting standard. They will, instead, blame their problems on the system.

The solution, of course, is training. Employees, and especially supervisors, must know the new systems well. They must understand not only how to do their jobs but also how to recover from virtually every possible error. And they need enough visibility into the overall scope of the system to understand the consequences of what they do and how they do it. It is very difficult to provide too much training or to provide it in too much detail.

Training cannot be limited to a presentation of the new system and a description of how employees are to use it. Training cannot even be limited to hands-on practice on the system. Training sessions must also be designed to produce a change in attitude. Slogans such as "the customer comes first," and "quality is job number one," must be joined with "accuracy is critical," and "do it right the first time." An appropriate balance between these responsibilities is the key. Customer service, quality, accuracy, and productivity can and must coexist.

Bank tellers, in one often-repeated example, are the material handlers of the banking industry. They receive, store, count, pick, and disburse the bank's inventory of currency. It is hard to imagine a successful bank that would allow tellers to perform transactions without keeping accurate and current records. In a similar way, the material handlers in warehouses and stockrooms must adopt the "bank teller" attitude. Work must proceed one task at a time and no task can be started until the previous one has been fully and properly completed. It must be generally known that sloppy work is detectable and intolerable.

Training should not be limited to supervisors and material handlers. The inventory manager and staff must also be trained. It is difficult to effectively manage the use of a sophisticated, on-line system without a fundamental understanding of computers and how they work. Even a little programming experience can have value.

Management training should include not only the functional aspects of the system but also introductions to the hardware and operating system used. The system's database manager should be reviewed and the database manager's query and reporting language should be covered in detail. It may be a good idea to place a systems person on the inventory manager's staff, even in businesses where a corporate data processing staff has responsibility for operations and technical support. This person can assume responsibility for a number of tasks, not the least of which might be advising the inventory manager in the use of the tools at his or her disposal.

Before training is even considered, the inventory manager should assume responsibility, unofficially if necessary, for supervision of the design process. It is, after all, going to be the manager's system when complete.

The inventory manager need not chair the design committee or even take part in all of its meetings. The inventory manager should, however, assure that the design committee is properly composed and that the people on the committee are competent. As design work progresses and the system takes shape, the inventory manager should be involved in reviews. He or she should take or make time to read and comment on all documents created by the committee. Ultimately, only the inventory manager can decide whether or not the design provides all of the needed function in a way that will be useful and productive.

Another major preimplementation concern for the inventory manager is the transition from the existing to the new system. These transitions are critical and can be the most difficult part of an inventory system development project. And, since the regular business of serving customers cannot be halted during the transition, the work ends up on top of existing jobs. The inventory manager is the one who must make sure that resources are available and that the work will get done properly and on time.

Modern on-line inventory systems use a great deal of information that older systems do not require. The collection and verification of this information can be an immense task. The amount of work involved is often underestimated, resulting in budget overruns at best and complete system failure at worst.

Data maintained by the new inventory system can be divided into "static" and "dynamic" categories. Static data is information that changes relatively slowly and, therefore, can be gathered, entered, and verified in advance. Dynamic data, however, changes much more rapidly. If entered in advance of the start-up date, it will be obsolete before it is used.

Static data may be available from an existing system. If so, a program can be written to transfer it to the new system. If not, however, it must be manually collected by people, entered, and verified. Temporary and part-time employees can sometimes be hired for this purpose, but knowledgeable supervision is required. Information that often must be collected manually includes:

- Location numbers, dimensions, and capacities
- Item dimensions and weights

- Vehicle numbers, capacities, and types
- Employee numbers, passwords, and access levels

The first two items on this list, location and item information, often involve hundreds or even thousands of hours of work, particularly if items must be measured and weighed, one at a time. This process alone can be a major management challenge.

Plans must be made to gather and enter the dynamic data at the last moment. Dynamic data may be available from an existing system or it may be necessary to close the facility for the time required to do a full physical inventory. Dynamic data required includes:

- On-hand balances by item and location
- Existing unit load numbers by item and location
- Existing lot and serial numbers by item and location
- Open customer, shop, and outbound transfer orders
- Open purchase and inbound transfer orders

Postinstallation Organization

The wise inventory manager will recognize that training and data collection activities do not end with the installation. Personnel turnover and growth both result in new employees who must be given at least as much training as the old employees received prior to the installation. Products and processes also come and go. Each requires the collection and verification of new information. Training and data collection activities must be ongoing.

In addition, the inventory manager will find that he or she has assumed a new responsibility for identifying system problems. These problems can be left over from the original installation, or they can be the result of business or personnel changes. System problems should be classified into two groups: those that can be solved with procedural improvements and those that require system change. The Inventory Manager will most likely be the focal point for these problems and for the management of the actions required to resolve them.

PRODUCTIVITY MEASUREMENT

The achievement of an efficient, productive organization can only occur when people are equally efficient and productive. The inventory manager, therefore, needs a measure of the productivity of the people who work in the inventory facility, both as individuals and in groups.

When systems direct people, as do modern inventory systems, it is relatively simple for the system to keep track of the tasks it has assigned and the time spent on each. A report based on the file of completed transactions can summarize these tasks by shift, supervisor, work group, and employee. With appropriate logon procedures and passwords, the resulting information can be both accurate and revealing (see Figure 14.1).

SHIFT	DEPT	EMPLOYEE	FUNCT	PER	STD	ACT	VAR	INDIR	EFF	PRO	UTIL
1	12	0611 WEST	RECVE	WTD	8.8	8.4	.4		104		
				MTD	30.2	30.3	.1-		100		
				YTD	782.7	744.6	38.1		105		
			STORE	WTD	2.9	2.8	.1		103		
				MTD	11.0	10.5	.5		105		
				YTD	292.8	289.6	3.2		101		
			REPL	WTD	1.6	1.7	.1-		95		
				MTD	1.8	1.8			100		
				YTD	68.5	69.0	.4-		99		
			COUNT	WTD	.3	.3			99		
				MTD	1.1	1.1			104		
				YTD	41.0	41.4	.4-		99		
			OTHER	WTD	.8	.8			99		
				MTD	1.8	1.3			101		
				YTD	245.4	234.4	12.0		105		
			TOTAL	WTD	14.4	14.1	.4	1.8	103	80	88
				MTD	45.8	45.0	.4	2.5	101	78	87
				YTD	1431.4	1279.0	52.5	80.5	104	88	85
1	12	3985 PENN	RECVE	WTD	6.5	6.6	.1-		98		
				MTD	20.3	20.1	.2		101		
				YTD	788.0	757.8	30.2		104		
			STORE	WTD	1.9	1.8	.1		105		
				MTD	5.6	5.5	.1		102		
				YTD	192.4	201.0	8.7-		96		
			REPL	WTD	2.3	2.2	.1		106		
				MTD	6.7	6.4	.3		104		
				YTD	223.7	216.5	7.2		103		
			OTHER	WTD	4.3	4.1	.2		104		
				MTD	14.2	13.7	.5		104		
				YTD	355.1	371.2	16.1-		96		
			TOTAL	WTD	15.0	14.8	.3	1.2	102	94	92
				MTD	46.8	45.7	1.1	14.3	102	78	76
				YTD	1559.2	1546.5	12.7	73.5	101	96	95
1	12	TOTAL	RECVE	WTD	15.3	15.1	.2		102		
				MTD	50.6	50.5	.1		100		
				YTD	1570.7	1502.4	68.3		104		
			STORE	WTD	4.8	4.6	.2		104		
				MTD	16.5	16.0	.6		104		
				YTD	485.2	490.6	5.5-		99		
			REPL	WTD	4.0	3.9	.1		101		
				MTD	8.4	8.2	.3		103		
				YTD	292.3	285.5	6.8		102		
			COUNT	WTD	.3	.3			100		
				MTD	1.1	1.0			104		
				YTD	41.0	41.4	.4-		99		

10/11   15:38   EMPLOYEE PRODUCTIVITY   PAGE 1

Figure 14.1. Productivity report. This sample productivity report shows efficiency, productivity, and utilization measures week to date, month to date, and year to date for each employee, with detail by transaction type and totals by department and shift (not shown).

If engineered time standards exist and if the inventory system is able to record time spent on nonproductive tasks, the amount of work done can be expressed on the report in standard hours, and utilization, productivity, and efficiency ratios can be calculated. On the other hand, if no engineered time standards exist or if nonproductive time is not collected, the report can be expressed in transaction counts, with different kinds of work shown separately. For experienced supervisors, transaction counts are usually adequate to determine which employees are accomplishing the most. The inventory system can also capture and report instances in which employees make certain kinds of errors.

It is these productivity and error-rate measurements that motivate employees to work accurately as well as quickly. If an employee is inaccurate, assignment of the next task will be delayed by the need to validate the last one. The employee is therefore affected not only by the nuisance of having to correct the work done but also by the resulting impact on productivity measurements.

MANAGING PILFERAGE

Inventory pilferage is a significant problem for some businesses, particularly those with small, marketable products and those with consumer-oriented products. While no inventory system can prevent an employee from walking out with something in a pocket or purse, most pilferage is based on impulse. The inventory system can help reduce the rate of pilferage by limiting both opportunity and temptation. Here are several ways this can be done:

1. A fenced and locked security area can be created and, for selected items, the inventory system can be instructed to select only storage locations in this area.
2. Or, almost as effective and much more flexible, items requiring secure storage can be limited to locations that are beyond a normal person's reach. Employees who do not regularly work on high-rise equipment will then rarely see or handle them.
3. The system can limit the people who handle vulnerable items to a select few. This further limits both opportunity and temptation.
4. Security items can be picked last, possibly only minutes before shipment. This limits the time these items spend in the shipping area and limits the opportunity for pilferage.
5. Security items can be picked to special, sealable containers. If the containers are sealed and marked by the picker as part of the picking process, the opportunity for pilferage is further reduced.
6. Conveyor systems can be used to handle security items rather than entrusting employees with them. Both opportunity and temptation are reduced because fewer people handle the material.

Sometimes pilferage costs are higher than necessary simply because management lacks a measure of the size of the problem. The inventory system can, and in appropriate businesses should, prepare a report of net inventory adjustments (see Figure 14.2). While this report will include losses for reasons other than pilferage, those that are known can be filtered out and the remainder used as an indication of pilferage. Items that show the largest downward adjustments over a significant period of time are candidates for some form of protection. The total facilitywide adjustment is a measure of the total pilferage rate.

UTILIZATION

Another significant concern of the inventory manager is the rate at which assets are utilized. In an inventory facility, the assets of greatest concern are personnel, space, and equipment. Personnel utilization is measured by the productivity re-

```
10/11  15:38                        NET ADJUSTMENTS                          PAGE  1

                                 FROM  01/01 TO 10/01
```

ITEM	SHIPMENTS	TOTAL NET ADJUSTMENTS	PERCENT	KNOWN REASONS	NO KNOWN REASON	PERCENT	DOLLAR VALUE
151019	8361	1313	15.7	721	592	7.1	26432.80
409519	10027	385	3.8	241	144	1.4	12336.48
157305	2019	151	7.5	71	80	4.0	10640.80
187841	2261	65	2.9	38	27	1.2	9580.14
243298	21316	64	.3	40	24	.1	8948.40
229485	9498	66	.7	10	56	.6	8028.72
532002	19848	70	.4	11	59	.3	7849.95
184966	6301	57	.9	34	23	.4	7710.75
513274	17868	37	.2	1	36	.2	6835.32
260497	74	59	79.7	38	21	28.4	6665.40
541138	13677	493	3.6	311	182	1.3	6490.12
476039	9388	31	.3	6	25	.3	6332.75
309613	11128	123	1.1	23	100	.9	5804.00
487815	18982	23	.1	6	17		5878.26
135384	17141	28	.2	14	14		4925.06
490898	24688	64	.3	40	24		4827.12
499042	19408	245	1.3	69	176	.9	4581.28
342501	12848	30	.2	16	14	.1	4305.56
427207	10671	58	.5	36	22	.2	3725.70
171593	24963	73	.3	47	26	.1	3638.44
411671	7231	35	.5	12	23	.3	3106.61
365477	14651	23	.2	14	9		2735.64
200685	15644	69	.4	46	23	1.5	2517.81
448938	10147	33	.3	22	11	.1	1827.10
411300	7623	16	.2	7	9	.1	1651.68
496595	1925	20	1.0	11	9	.5	1591.34
542317	19769	18	.1	8	10	.1	1467.62
344083	6176	41	.7	17	24	.4	1308.15
590733	574	19	3.3	12	7	1.2	1091.23
488691	11214	35	.3	21	14	.1	962.96
599841	8729	18	.2	9	9	.1	708.86
195071	20064	363	1.8	232	131	.7	711.24
592091	22858	4	.0	0	4		676.41
446656	8773	2	.0	0	2		391.54
464839	4071	2	.0	0	2		334.10
552121	9022	20	.2	13	7	.1	285.90
491490	17522	2	.0	1	1		280.12
180555	7347	4	.1	2	2		221.56
172516	13659	8	.1	4	4		104.45
549373	250	2	.8	1	1	.4	94.09
374704	503	2	.4	0	2	.4	67.06
374756	11852	1	.0	0	1		62.00
415220	14918	6	.0	3	3		12.40

Figure 14.2. Net adjustments report. This report lists inventory losses by item, separating out those with a known cause from those with no known cause. In some businesses it can be used to identify items that are most prone to pilferage.

port, described above. Space utilization can be reported by the inventory system (see Figure 14.3). The report should be available with summaries by warehouse area and such location characteristics as environment, demand, device, function, size, and weight capacity. In addition, it can be useful to know the utilization of locations dedicated to an item versus those that are allowed to float and by single-item versus multiple-item locations. With an on-line system, the utilization of equipment operated by the system can also be measured. When radio terminals are in use, lift truck utilization can also be measured (see Figure 14.4).

REPLENISHMENT

The idea of replenishing forward picking was discussed in Chapter 9. In some businesses it can be taken one step further: the "replenishment" of the entire

```
10/11  15:38                                                        Page  1
                              SPACE UTILIZATION
                                                                UTILIZ
  AREA   TOT OP   TOTL CUBE    TOTL WT  OP USED  CUBE USED    WT USED   OP  CU  WT

    1     2544     140251     6360000    1832      84158     3797672    72  60  60
    2    12603     694803    31507500    8696     432215    15946600    69  62  51
    3    13984     770938    55936000   11327     618485    38227868    81  80  68
    5      292      13797      730000     111       4976      226716    38  36  31
    6      227      12515      567500     143       7727      215619    63  62  38
    8     6003      14227     6003000    5583      12220     4528167    93  86  75
   11     5742      62530     5742000    5283      46728     4961889    92  75  86
   14      783      17398      548100     611      13506      380463    78  78  69

         42178    1726459   107394100   33586    1220015    68284994    80  71  64
```

Figure 14.3. Space utilization. Many different space utilization reports are possible. This sample reports openings (locations), cubic capacity, and weight capacity by area. For each, the total available, the total used, and the percent utilization is listed.

warehouse (see Figure 14.5). Based on a user-maintained order point and order quantity, the inventory system can create purchase and shop requisitions. After approval, purchase requisitions can be forwarded to the purchasing system for vendor selection and order placement. Manufacturing orders can likewise be sent to the production control system for scheduling. This process can be further supported by the accumulation of usage information and the periodic recalculation of order points and order quantities. Normal practice would require human approval of the recalculated order points and order quantities prior to use.

This method of replenishment assumes that past demand rates will continue into the future unchanged. Since all products experience changes in demand sooner or later, blind use will eventually result in either shortages or excess inventories. Other techniques (namely, Manufacturing Resource Planning and Distribution Requirements Planning) do consider demand forecasts and, therefore, are

```
10/11  15:38                                                    Page  1

                        LIFT TRUCK UTILIZATION

          ( -------- WEEK ------- )  ( -------- MONTH ------ )  ( --------- YEAR ------ )
  TRUCK  HOURS USED  UTILIZATION   HOURS USED  UTILIZATION   HOURS USED  UTILIZATION
     8       17         35.9          41         32.1          1324        41.8
    12       23         48.1          52         40.7          1286        40.6
    15       15         32.0          35         27.4           830        26.2
    30       16         34.1          57         44.5          1419        44.8
    44       13         27.0          34         26.3           897        28.3
    46       44         90.7         126         98.3          2648        83.6
    49       40         83.4          91         71.3          2018        63.7
    57       15         30.7          33         25.4           941        29.7
    60       35         73.9          98         76.8          3130        98.8
    82       13         26.3          36         28.2          1147        36.2
    84        9         19.3          31         24.0           855        27.0
    87       13         28.1          38         30.0          1023        32.3
    89       21         44.5          57         44.5          1555        49.1
    90       33         68.7         113         88.6          2648        83.6
    91       20         42.1          52         40.7          1283        40.5
   103       26         53.8          63         48.9          1296        40.9
   111       13         28.1          33         25.6           995        31.4
   115       27         55.5          83         65.2          2135        67.4
   124       21         43.2          68         52.8          1359        42.9
   126       17         35.5          54         42.5          1765        55.7
   135       43         88.7         115         89.6          2984        94.2
```

Figure 14.4. Lift-truck utilization. Material handling equipment utilization can be reported in instances in which the equipment is controlled by the inventory system. This example presumes that the lift trucks are not in use if they are not logged on through a radio terminal.

superior. However, MRP and DRP are complex and can be hard to implement. So, intelligent use of a simple replenishment method may be better for some low-cost, easily available products in some companies.

COST MANAGEMENT

The employee productivity database contains a record of every material movement made in the facility and, for each, the amount of time spent on it. In addition to employee productivity, this database can be used to report warehouse labor cost by function as shown in Figure 14.6. If budget information is made available to the inventory system, a budget versus actual comparison can be added to the report.

```
 10/11  15:38                                                    Page  1
                        INVENTORY REPLENISHMENT

         ITEM      ON-HAND     AVAILABLE    ORDER POINT    ORDER QTY
         111801      2065         1102         1400          1800
         119704       340          196          200          1000
         122624        91           78          100           500
         124932      3568         3194         3800         18500
         126353      3465         2866         3300          6800
         131531      1258          655          800           900
         138908       775          713          900          1300
         161808      1149          796          900          1900
         162946      4080         2786         2900          9200
         207712      2751         1700         1900          7600
         231389       650          548          600          2200
         243884      2834         2362         2600          2700
         255448       624          398          500          1700
         290257       585          374          400           500
         301591      1639         1293         1600          4400
         307008      4236         2700         3200         14900
         310000      2112         1306         1500          4300
         321430      2260         1875         2400          3300
         332771      1419         1178         1300          5500
         334071       436          255          300           900
         334962      1465          997         1300          6200
         354824      1649          992         1100          2500
         379914      3166         2696         3500          8400
         407657       978          806          800          2700
         408059      1283          655          800          3300
         440563      3393         3141         3200         12200
         441251      4290         2371         2800         12000
         441350      1746         1243         1500          4200
         453937       920          768         1000          3200
         455336      4174         2279         2800          7900
         456187      3969         3645         4100         12200
         456378      2172         1512         1900          8400
         461025      2364         2133         2700          5500
         470815      1628         1385         1600          6500
         471403      2937         2500         2800          9800
         494471      1431         1032         1300          4500
         498785      3941         2227         2800         11900
         520953      4364         2207         2300         10300
         527816      4386         2920         3700          7000
         542890       170           93          100           200
         563646      3984         2730         3300          3400
         576875      3289         1829         1900          5500
         579323      2706         2017         2200          3000
         581927      3344         2104         2300         10100
         590656      1176         1111         1300          4700
         597131      1529          986         1000          1900
```

Figure 14.5. Inventory replenishment. This report lists items that are below their order point and should be purchased or ordered from the shop. (It does not relate to the replenishment of a forward picking area from reserve.) This replenishment technique is generally inferior to Manufacturing Resource Planning techniques but may still be applicable in some businesses.

CUSTOMER SERVICE AND QUALITY

A variety of reports (not illustrated) can be created from the inventory system's database to measure quality and customer service. Inbound quality can be measured from the results of incoming inspections and from the frequency of rejections resulting from those inspections. Outbound quality can be measured from customer returns. Both reports are likely to be approximations, but in businesses where no other information is available, they are much better than nothing. Those businesses that have sophisticated quality systems should rely on them rather than the inventory system's database.

Customer service can be measured in a variety of ways depending on the data available in the inventory system. On-time shipments can be reported by compar-

```
 10/11   15:38                                                    Page   1

                              WAREHOUSE  LABOR

               (----------HOURS-----------)    (----------DOLLARS-----------)
FUNCTION       STANDARD    ACTUAL   VARIANCE    STANDARD    ACTUAL    VARIANCE

RECEIVE          518.1     522.7      4.6       7382.93     7448.48     65.55

PUT  AWAY        435.5     422.6     12.9-      4681.63     4542.95    138.68-

REPLENISH        668.0     641.7     26.3-      7181.00     6898.28    282.72-

MOVE              88.2      91.0      2.8        948.15      978.25     30.10

PICK            4841.3    4647.7    193.6-     44782.03    42991.23   1790.80-

SHIP             693.2     690.4      2.8-      9878.10     9838.20     39.90-

CYCLE  COUNT     437.9     440.1      2.2       6240.08     6271.43     31.35

INVENTORY          0.0       0.0      0.0          0.00        0.00      0.00

INDIRECT         202.0     202.0      0.0       1737.20     1737.20      0.00


TOTAL           8084.2    7658.2    226.0-     82831.12    80706.02   2125.10-
```

Figure 14.6. Warehouse labor. Tracking warehouse labor by function provides management with visibility into costs and cost variances.

ing requested or promised shipment dates with the actual dates. Another useful customer service report is the fill rate report. Fill rate reports generally cover the orders shipped in a single day and report the percentage of lines that were filled, as opposed to being back ordered. Variations on this report will consider not only whether a line was completely shipped but also whether part of an order line was shipped. Measurements can be made as a percentage of either units or dollars or both.

OTHER MANAGEMENT REPORTS

The list of possible management reports is limited only by the designer's imagination. A few additional ones deserve brief comment:

1. The labor forecast considers pending inbound and outbound orders and estimates warehouse or stockroom labor requirements based on

the volumes found. This report often requires sophisticated logic to compensate for the fact that orders are continuing to arrive for shipment during the forecast period.

2. A replenishment frequency report can be used to assure that forward picking locations are correctly sized. This report should separately summarize emergency and regular replenishments by picking zone and item.

3. The consolidation opportunity report (discussed in Chapter 9) identifies opportunities to increase warehouse utilization by combining partly filled locations.

4. An inventory value report describes the present investment in inventory either at standard cost or at actual cost or both.

5. The inventory turnover report calculates turns per year for each item in inventory based on the current inventory level and the historical sales or usage rate. The report is a handy way for management to identify opportunities to reduce inventory.

6. The inventory accuracy report tells management how accurate inventory records are (see Chapter 3). Inventory accuracy, of course, affects the believability of all other information coming from the inventory system.

In addition to these management reports, many modern inventory systems include database management systems with flexible ad hoc query capabilities. While the truly user-friendly query language has yet to be invented, managers who invest the time to learn to use the one available to them will be paid back many times over. The ability to build subsets of the inventory system's database and move them to spreadsheet and statistical analysis programs is particularly valuable.

15

Just-in-Time and Other Special Considerations

Because successful inventory systems deal with real life, the forces that shape them are not always easily categorized and arranged in neat rows. Several important subjects remain that do not easily fit into any of the previous chapters.

THE IMPACT OF JUST-IN-TIME

Just-in-Time (often abbreviated JIT) is an approach to business operations that has the objective of eliminating waste by having material arrive just in time to be used. Close synchronization of all material flow is necessary to achieve this goal. The result, particularly in manufacturing organizations, can be a drastic reduction in inventories and a corresponding increase in productivity.

While Just-in-Time reduces inventory, it does not reduce the need to control inventory that remains nor does it reduce the need to have accurate inventory records. In fact, close synchronization of operations requires even higher levels of accuracy than does the traditional job shop. Unplanned shortages, should they occur, will affect more than just one work center and more than just one operation. In short order, the entire plant could be shut down.

The Just-in-Time concept primarily affects production and process planning and material handling methods in the shop. It is, therefore, important to the designers of inventory control systems. However, its importance is more a matter of degree than of fundamental principle. The ideas in this book are applicable to both the Just-in-Time shop and the traditional shop. Only the application is affected. For instance, compared to traditional shops, Just-in-Time shops:

1. Have many more storerooms. To the greatest possible extent, Just-in-Time shops move material directly from the receiving dock to the

point of use and store it there to save material handling costs and delays.

2. Make more frequent and smaller receipts of purchased items into the plant and of finished goods into the warehouse. The philosophy of small lot sizes keeps inventory down and allows close coordination of vendors with the operations that use their parts. Similarly, withdrawals from inventory tend to be smaller and more frequent.

3. Have much less inventory in total. Work-in-process, raw material, and parts inventories are reduced dramatically by the introduction of Just-in-Time. Finished goods inventories will be similarly reduced in some businesses but will be relatively unaffected in others. (Build-to-order businesses are affected; build-to-stock businesses are less affected, depending on their stocking policies.)

4. Part demands from the shop may, in some instances, not take the form of work orders. Instead, they may simply be withdrawal requests. A work order specifies the part number being built, the total quantity to be built, the schedule, and a complete list of parts and quantities required. A withdrawal request, on the other hand, simply lists a part number and a quantity along with the parent part number and, possibly, a manufacturing order or account number. From the viewpoint of the inventory system, the most important difference is the immediacy of the withdrawal request. Just-in-Time is, in effect, often implemented as a pull system rather than a push system.

5. In some environments, when major production facilities like assembly lines are converted from one product to another, the Just-in-Time shop may place very heavy short-term demands on the inventory system. All remaining floor stock and point-of-use inventories must be brought into the stockroom and put away. Simultaneously, and as quickly as possible, an entire new inventory of parts for the next job must be picked and moved into the shop.

6. And, the introduction of Just-in-Time and the storage of materials at the point of use may greatly increase the number of people who create inventory transactions. The result is a significant increase in the importance of inventory system training.

The introduction of Just-in-Time to a business, therefore, affects inventory control systems by simplifying operations in the warehouse or stockroom and by complicating operations elsewhere in the plant. The requirements for keeping accurate inventory and the basic techniques used for achieving accuracy, however, are not affected.

INTERLEAVING

Figures 15.1 and 15.2 show two warehouse designs. In Figure 15.1, the shipping and receiving docks are located next to each other at one end of the building. The warehouse in Figure 15.2, however, is of the "flow-through" type, designed with

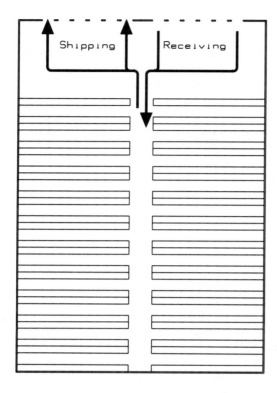

Figure 15.1. One-ended warehouse. When shipping and receiving doors are side by side, there is opportunity for reduced labor cost if movements into and out of storage can be interleaved to allow lift trucks to travel loaded both ways.

the shipping and receiving docks at opposite ends of the building. Most modern warehouses follow one or the other of these patterns.

Flow-through warehouses simplify some aspects of material handling because the basic material flow is in a single direction. In addition, flow-through warehouses provide separate facilities for receiving and shipping. One-ended warehouses, on the other hand, offer the ability to operate lift trucks loaded in both directions as they travel into and out of the storage area. In some businesses the productivity gains achieved can be important. One-ended warehouses also offer the opportunity to have dual-purpose docks that can be used for either shipping or receiving, depending on need.

Two-way, loaded travel of material handling vehicles is an important inventory system function that comes into play in one-ended warehouses and in other situations. For example, Figure 15.3 illustrates a high-rise area serviced by turret trucks in a flow-through warehouse. In this example, counterbalance lift trucks move material between receiving and turret truck staging locations and between the staging locations and shipping. The counterbalance lift trucks offer little opportunity for two-way handling of loads, but the turret trucks can and probably should alternately carry loads into and out of the aisles.

The alternation of put-away and pick transactions is often called interleaving. From the viewpoint of the inventory control system, interleaving is primarily a concern of dispatching and, therefore, a matter of work queue design. But, it is

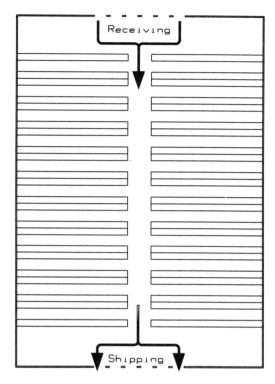

Figure 15.2. Flow-through warehouse. The flow-through warehouse provides (almost always) unidirectional material movement.

not often just a matter of assigning transactions alternately from the two work queues.

The design of interleaving involves two conflicting considerations. Work queue priorities must be observed while simultaneously minimizing the material handlers' travel time between transactions. The minimization of travel time is particularly important when turret trucks are involved because aisle changes are slow and costly.

Some systems, often ones that involve high-rise storage and slow aisle changes, work by segregating all transactions for an aisle and arranging them in priority sequence within the aisle for execution. When aisle-change times are not significant, other systems work in a similar fashion by zone. In either case, the systems dispatch transactions within a group until all work has been completed for that group. The final transactions for a group, then, often involve a few trips in or out without matching loads going the other way. Only after a group of transactions is complete does the system form and dispatch another group.

The organization of transactions within a group usually assumes that picks are more important than put-aways, so picking transactions are arranged in priority sequence and put-aways are done in whatever sequence is convenient. In some systems, however, an attempt is made to select each transaction based on the travel distance from the ending point of the previous one. When a single aisle

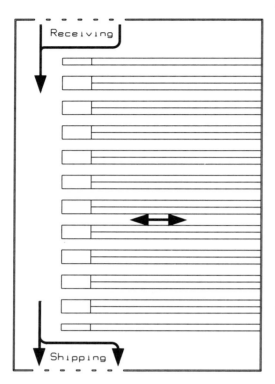

Figure 15.3. Flow-through warehouse with interleaved high rise. Some warehouses are a combination of the one-ended and flow-through designs. In this example, the basic warehouse is flow-through, but the high-rise storage area is one ended.

is being worked, the distance calculation can be simple: It can be calculated by subtracting one location's section number from the other's. But, there are complications. Sometimes vehicles travel at different horizontal and vertical speeds. Since the objective is to minimize travel time, the problem becomes three-dimensional. Further, when a zone is being worked, the distance calculation can be much more complex.

Consider, for instance, Figure 15.4. In this figure, a load has just been put away in location 4–12–5 (represented by the round dot). Picks must be made from 4–11–10, 4–13–5, and 4–14–6 (each represented by an X). Which is closest? By inspection, we can see that 4–14–6 is closest to 4–12–5, but an algorithm capable of calculating this is harder to come by. A straight-line distance calculation would select 4–11–10; a scheme that works by aisle might select either 4–11–10 or 4–13–5.

Attempts to handle pick and put-away transactions in a logical geographic sequence must also consider transaction aging. It is possible to imagine a case in which one transaction is never performed because it is simply too far from all the others to ever be selected as the next one. In addition to making physical sense, the program that organizes and selects interleaved transactions must be fast or response times will be unacceptable. No universal algorithm for this purpose is known. The best solution may be either the development of a unique algorithm based on the geometry of a company's particular warehouse or the subdivision

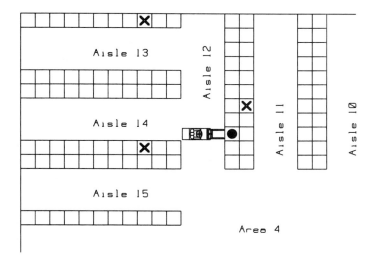

● Completed Put-Away

✖ Picks Awaiting Action

Figure 15.4. Difficult distance calculation. This figure illustrates one of the difficulties in automatically sequencing material movements based on the distance between them. The operator has just completed a put-away. The three Xs denote picks that must now be made. Which should be done next? How can an algorithm be written to make this decision?

of the warehouse into picking zones that are small enough so that distance calculations are no longer important.

Systems that interleave transactions should also consider the possibility of adding cycle counts to the interleaving pattern. The working pattern would then begin with a put-away followed by a cycle count followed by a pick.

OBSOLETE AND EXCESS INVENTORY

Obsolete and excess inventories are important concerns for the inventory manager. To the extent that such material exists, investment money is tied up, available warehouse space and flexibility are reduced, and labor is consumed when it is necessary to move the material about.

Causes of Excess and Obsolete Inventory

An understanding of the causes of excess and obsolete inventory is helpful to the inventory manager who must identify and control the material. To the extent that these causes can be controlled, the overall amount of excess and obsolete inventory can be reduced, making the inventory operation that much more productive. Factors that contribute to the amount of excess and obsolete inventories created by a business include safety stock levels, lot sizing techniques, forecasting methods, lead times, and engineering changes.

Safety stock

Safety stock is inventory carried solely to protect the business against unanticipated changes in supply and demand. If, for instance, a market forecast predicts that 100 units of product will be sold in the coming period, a company could plan to make 110, just in case the forecast turns out to be low. The extra 10 units are considered safety stock. Then, if each unit of product requires a unit of raw materials, it might be decided to purchase 120 units of raw material, just in case a vendor is unable to deliver or an inventory error is found. The extra 10 units of raw material are also safety stock.

In businesses that use material requirements planning or distribution requirements planning, safety stocks are automatically maintained by the computer. In other businesses, buyers and planners tend to cover themselves with a little extra here and a little extra there. While these safety stocks are less formal and may not even be acknowledged, the effect is the same as when the formal planning systems calculate safety stock quantities.

Safety stock levels directly and intentionally inflate inventory levels over the quantities actually required. Safety stocks become excess and obsolete inventories as product designs and customer demands change. Increased inventory accuracy reduces demand variability for raw materials and component parts and supply variability for finished goods and assemblies. It, therefore, reduces the need for safety stock and the cost of excess and obsolete inventory.

Lot sizing

Both material requirements planning and distribution requirements planning use lot sizing techniques to determine lot quantities when material must be bought or made. The idea behind lot sizing is to take advantage of the possibility of spreading setup and ordering costs over a large number of pieces to reduce unit costs. While lot sizing has merit as a concept, the potential exists for significant excess inventory. This is particularly true in businesses where lot sizes are informally determined by people who may or may not appreciate all of the risks involved.

Forecasting

The forecasting of demand for a company's products is, at best, an art. When forecasts run out of control, the result can be substantial overproduction and the purchasing of unneeded raw materials and supplies.

Lead times

Excessive planning lead times cause material requirements planning to recommend manufacturing and purchase orders earlier than necessary. The result is that inventory arrives too soon and stock levels are inflated. Distribution requirements planning suffers from the same phenomenon when purchasing lead times are too long.

Engineering changes

Uncontrolled engineering changes are a major cause of obsolete inventory. A proper engineering change control system will take existing inventories into account and will schedule engineering changes based on an economic balance between the cost of delay and the cost of obsolete inventory disposition.

Identification

A company in the publishing industry outgrew its warehouse. At significant expense, a second warehouse was built and product was moved into it. Soon thereafter, the complexity of operating in two buildings prompted the company to upgrade its inventory control systems. The new software included excess inventory identification features that soon revealed the fact that almost 40 percent of the material in the original warehouse had not had even a single transaction posted against it for almost a year and was, therefore, presumably either excess or obsolete. Had this information been available earlier, the entire new warehouse project could have been shelved, saving the cost of the inventory system several times over.

Excess inventory is most easily identified by assigning a FIFO date to every pallet, tote, and carton of material as it is received. The FIFO date is usually the date of receipt in the warehouse but can also be a date of manufacture or a date on which shelf life expiration is calculated. It should not be the shelf life expiration date itself because that date tells the system nothing about how long the material has been in inventory. If a shelf life expiration date is required, it should be stored in a separate field, either as a date or as an offset from the FIFO date.

Although the primary use of the FIFO date is to assure first-in first-out rotation of inventory, it can also be used to produce inventory aging reports like the one shown in Figure 15.5 and excess inventory reports line the one shown in Figure 15.6. These reports are the primary tools used to identify excess and obsolete inventories. The inventory aging report is simply a listing of the inventory control system's location file sorted in ascending FIFO date. Only items with a FIFO date more than a specified number of months in the past are included. Quarterly subtotals and a grand total (not shown) are included.

The excess inventory report is slightly more sophisticated than the inventory aging report. Material requirements planning provides a projected usage figure. In the figure, projected usage is stated in average monthly units over the coming 12 months, but different systems will provide projections differently. For each

```
11/03                              INVENTORY AGING                          PAGE   1

ITEM                    FIFO      LAST                    HOLD    HOLD    ON
    DESCRIPTION         DATE      MOVED     LOCATION    REASON   RESP    HAND    VALUE

A14B1758              04/12/88   09/10/88   2-D-15-E                      22     913.44
    BEARING. ROLLER
R32D14A               06/03/88   06/03/88   2-A-22-B                       4     194.20
    TACHOMETER

    SUBTOTAL - QTR 02/88                                                 26    1107.64

N14B0042              08/18/88   09/12/88   1-F-15-A     14     OC       144     269.50
    INSULATION. FIBREGLASS

    SUBTOTAL - QTR 03/88                                                144     269.50

D14317A8              10/11/88   10/11/88   1-D-12-C                       9     608.25
    WINCH SUBASSEMBLY
43704576              10/14/88   03/02/89   2-C-4-D                        2     214.26
    BAR STOCK BRASS SOFT
E142F                 10/21/88   10/21/88   3-B-2-B                       12      84.57
    CLEVIS PIN
R02734X               10/21/88   08/25/89   3-F-12-C     21     ENGR      41     124.50
    SILICONE SEALANT
C40A4854              11/03/88   11/03/88   4-C-1-B                       30     964.20
    OIL. CUTTING
T21414T3              11/05/88   11/05/88   2-A-2-6                      125     803.40
    TAPE. SEALING
B004D21               11/11/88   04/02/89   2-D-18-A     26     ENGR      19     184.40
    ANGLE IRON
E1432                 11/19/88   11/19/88   2-B-7-B                       21     643.55
    TORSION ROD
S40241                12/04/88   02/02/89   2-E-3-C                       47    2914.83
    BRAKE SHOE
A40C10                12/12/88   12/12/88   4-C-12-E                       1      18.55
    CONNECTOR

    SUBTOTAL - QTR 04/88                                                298    5952.26

P205C956              01/05/89   01/05/89   3-A-1-B                        4       3.57
    GASKET
S205C75N              01/06/89   11/14/89   1-C-1-E      03     OC        27     337.50
    CASTER. SWIVEL
S852C                 01/11/89   08/03/89   1-E-21-B                     113     741.70
    INSULATOR
G99G1                 01/21/89   01/21/89   2-B-14-D                     100    1853.00
    CASTING
```

Figure 15.5. Inventory aging. The inventory aging report lists inventory by age and shows its location and dollar value. Control over obsolete inventories is essential to an efficient warehouse operation.

item, the total inventory across all storage locations is calculated and standard costs are used to calculate the total inventory value. The total on-hand balance is divided by the projected usage to arrive at the number of month's supply on hand. An index is calculated by multiplying the number of month's supply on hand by the inventory value and dividing by 100. The report is sorted in descending index value and limited to items with either zero projected usage or an index value greater than a preestablished figure.

Control

Control over identified excess and obsolete inventory should be exercised by a committee representing the engineering, quality control, production control, purchasing, finance, and warehousing functions. Much as the material review board controls out-of-specification material, this committee should be charged with identifying and disposing of obsolete and excess inventories. It has three choices when it comes to material disposal: The material can be used or scrapped; if scrapped, it can be sold, or thrown out. The use of excess or obsolete inventory

```
11/03                        EXCESS  INVENTORY                       PAGE    1

    ITEM              FIFO    PROJ    ON      MONTHS
    DESCRIPTION       DATE    USE     HAND    SUPPLY    VALUE      INDEX

    E1432            11/19/88   0      21       -       643.55       -
      TORSION ROD

    D1431748         10/11/88   0       9       -       608.25       -
      WINCH SUBASSEMBLY

    437D4576         10/14/88   0       2       -       214.26       -
      BAR STOCK BRASS SOFT

    R32D14A          06/03/88   0       4       -       194.20       -
      TACHOMETER

    B004D21          11/11/88   0      19       -       184.40       -
      ANGLE  IRON

    M40C10           12/12/88   0       1       -        18.55       -
      CONNECTOR

    P205C956         01/05/89   0       4       -         3.57       -
      GASKET

    S40241           12/04/88   2      47      23.5     2914.83     684
      BRAKE  SHOE

    G99G1            01/21/89   3     100      33.3     1853.00     617
      CASTING

    C40M4854         11/03/88   2      30      15.0      964.20     144
      OIL. CUTTING

    T21414T3         11/05/88   7     125      17.8      803.40     143
      TAPE. SEALING

    S852C            01/11/89   6     113      18.8      741.70     139
      INSULATOR

    A14B1758         04/12/88   2      22      11.0      913.44     100
      BEARING. ROLLER

    N14B0042         08/18/88   4     144      36.0      269.50      97
      INSULATION. FIBREGLASS

    S205C75N         01/06/89   1      27      27.0      337.50      91
      CASTER. SWIVEL
```

Figure 15.6. Excess inventory. The excess inventory report calculates the months of supply of each inventory based on projected use. The index shown is a measure of the value of the excess inventory.

may require rework or reprocessing in the plant. In some cases, even scrapping may require rework, possibly in the form of disassembly.

Regardless of the method of disposal, the inventory control system should continue to track excess and obsolete inventories so long as the material remains on company property. Procedures for the handling and tracking of this material as work progresses are essentially identical to those employed by the material review board.

LOT AND SERIAL NUMBER TRACKING

The tracking of lot and serial numbers as they move through an inventory facility is necessary in many businesses. The drug and food industries commonly collect lot control information, for instance, while the automotive and computer industries are concerned with serial numbers. In both cases, the objective is (1) to maintain records that will support product recalls, should a quality problem develop and (2) to provide traceability to allow analysis of failures when necessary. Other reasons for serial and lot numbering can exist. Guns, for instance, are serial numbered by law.

Lot numbering involves the separation of product into homogeneous groups by manufacturing batch, by date of production, or by some other criteria. The assumption is that all material within a lot is identical for traceability purposes. Serial numbering, on the other hand, assumes that every item is unique and different from every other one. Lot numbering is necessarily applied to all fluids and items that are produced in such large quantities that serial numbering would be uneconomic. Serial numbering provides a greater degree of control but at the added cost of assigning and tracking unique serial numbers.

Some businesses produce a lot-numbered or serial-numbered product that involves no lot-numbered or serial-numbered components. These companies simply assign their own numbers and, at shipment time, record which numbers were sent to which customers. Other manufacturers may have multiple levels of serialization or lot numbering (i.e., serial numbers on both the air conditioner and on its compressor) or may have purchased parts or materials that bear important serial or lot numbers. If, in these latter cases, complete traceability is required, every movement of product throughout the facility must be accompanied by a record of the individual serial numbers involved. And, at every work station in which serial-numbered or lot-controlled components are handled, data must be recorded to track the individual components of each finished item. In effect, the inventory control system must generate an as-built bill-of-material for every product manufactured. Obviously the processing can get complicated, particularly when one considers the possibilities inherent in rework (which may involve disassembly and reassembly).

The most commonly used method of tracking lot movement through a manufacturing operation is to maintain physical segregation of material on a lot-by-lot basis. The inventory control system prevents lots from being mixed in a storage location and tracks their identity. In most businesses, serial numbered product is best handled by applying bar-coded serial number labels to each item. Labels should be applied to purchased items by the vendor or, if necessary, on the receiving dock. Labels for manufactured items should be applied at the point in the manufacturing process where the serial number itself is determined. When serialized products are moved into or out of the warehouse or between work centers, the inventory control system should require that all serial number labels be read with a bar code reader.

The labor cost involved in reading a large number of labels can sometimes be reduced by defining serialized unit loads (i.e., pallets) and reading the product serial numbers as these pallets are built. Any future reference to the unit load would then be applied to all of the items on it.

WORKING WITH FLUIDS AND FRACTIONAL ITEMS

This book assumes that the products in inventory are discrete and can be counted and moved about in individual units. It also assumes that materials cannot exist in fractional quantities. Some products, however, do not lend themselves to this model. The two major classes of products that do not are fluids and fractional items.

Fluids are products that will flow and can be most economically stored in tanks and moved with pumps or pneumatic systems. Liquids, gasses, and powders are all included. Packaged fluids, such as cans of motor oil or bags of flour, however, are discrete and are not usually considered to be fluids. Fluids are subject to handling losses as they are moved. Material sticks to the inside of pipes, pumps, and tanks, and leaks may occur. The effects are not precisely predictable. Further, the instruments used to measure inventory levels always involve a degree of error. For all of these reasons, extremely accurate inventory levels of fluids are much harder to achieve than for discrete products.

Happily, most businesses that handle fluids deal with large quantities of a relatively small number of items. Because the quantities are large, the need for high-precision inventory accuracy is reduced. Because there are relatively few item numbers to keep track of, manual control and frequent review are simplified. So, except for the most valuable fluids, sufficiently accurate records can be kept using flow meters to record the amount and direction of movement.

This, however, is not to say that a properly designed inventory control system cannot or should not contribute to accuracy and productivity. As a first step, valves, flow meters, and pumps are often operated by programmable controllers. These programmable controllers can be interconnected with the inventory system to report material flow. While the programmable controllers often do not "know" the identity of the material being moved, they do know the source and destination tanks (locations). From this information, the inventory system can deduce the identity of the material and can keep accurate records.

As a second step, the inventory control system can use the information contained in its database to verify, authorize, and even direct the movement of material. While human error in the setting of valves and the operation of pumps may be rare, even a single error can have expensive consequences if incompatible materials are pumped together. A double-check performed by the inventory system can be valuable if no other checks exist.

The second major class of products that does not fit the normal inventory model is the group of items known as fractionals. Fractional items are those items that are discrete for handling purposes but that can exist in fractional quantities. One example is the meat in a grocer's display case. Ground beef, for instance, is a single item for most purposes, but each package has an individual weight and differs from all other packages of ground beef in that respect. Fractional items normally differ from each other in weight, but some may have other units of measure. Electrical cable, for instance, is sold by the foot.

Good management of inventories of fractionals depends to a great degree on how the material is bought and sold. In the simpler cases, it may be enough to simply allow fractional on-hand quantities to exist in the database. In the most complex cases, it may be necessary to consider each unit of product as a separate entity with an associated length or weight. When this level of detail is needed, the database size will increase and the computing "horsepower" needed to support the facility will increase with it. In the most complex case, since every unit of product is unique, each will have to be identified every time it is to be handled.

SAMPLES AND MISCELLANEOUS WITHDRAWALS

Some legitimate uses for inventory can not be predicted by planning systems, and they are not often represented by orders. These uses are typified by, but not necessarily limited to, engineering and sales samples. They are generally called "miscellaneous withdrawals."

Typically, miscellaneous withdrawals involve small quantities and an immediate need. They are generally—but not always—charged to an internal account, rather than being billed. Unauthorized and unrecorded withdrawals are common in situations where the inventory system does not make it easy for the requester get the needed material. Therefore, the inventory system must provide fast service while also protecting existing commitments for the material.

The problem of unauthorized or unrecorded withdrawals is partly solved by inventory control systems that dynamically assign storage locations. The person who urgently needs a part will find it easier to go through the inventory control system than to walk the stockroom looking for the part. However, discipline also plays a part. Unrecorded material movements always create inventory errors and must be absolutely forbidden to all personnel.

The inventory control system should support a miscellaneous withdrawal screen. This screen should allow a user to enter an item number, a quantity, an expense charge number, and the location to which the material should be delivered. After editing the information entered, the inventory control system should allocate the material and print a withdrawal ticket bearing the picking location, the item and quantity, and the delivery location. (When radio terminals are in use, the ticket need not be printed but can be transmitted instead.) A material handler can then be assigned to retrieve the material, validate the pick, and make the delivery.

MISCELLANEOUS ITEMS

Miscellaneous items are nonproduct items stored in the warehouse. Examples include financial records, furniture, office supplies, marketing supplies, and obsolete tooling. While miscellaneous items are not part of the mainstream business, they are part of almost every business and storage for them is necessary. It is almost always cheaper to store them in the warehouse than to rent outside space or build a separate storeroom. So most inventory managers find themselves with responsibility for anywhere from a few to several dozen pallets of miscellaneous items.

One way to handle miscellaneous items is to store them in dedicated space outside the control of the inventory system. The top tier of a row of racking, for instance, could be reserved for miscellaneous items. If this tier were removed from the inventory system's location file, the system would not be aware of it and would not attempt to store product there. Movements into and out of the dedicated miscellaneous item space would then be manually controlled and manual records would be required to keep track of the items and their locations.

Since miscellaneous items are usually slow moving, this approach can work, but it has several limitations. First, the space consumed by the miscellaneous items is inflexible and fixed. When additional space is required, the locations available are not likely to be contiguous with the original ones, resulting in a patchwork of locations, some under system control and others outside of it. And, when space requirements are reduced, people must remember to return the excess locations to system control by reestablishing them on the system's location file. Second, the movement of miscellaneous items can be done only by removing people and equipment from system control. This requires supervisory time, eliminates some of the benefits of automated dispatching, and reduces the effectiveness of productivity measurements for the people and the inventory facility. And, third, because the movement of miscellaneous items is not done under system control, validation cannot be done and inventory records are likely to be less than completely accurate. There is, therefore, a case for the control of miscellaneous items by the inventory system.

In view of the low volumes involved, miscellaneous item control need not be a complex or sophisticated part of the inventory system. Most systems provide a simple screen that allows the entry of basic information about newly received miscellaneous items and initiates a search for a suitable storage location. The information keyed can be as simple as a description of the material, its dimensions, and its weight. The location search is usually simplified by restricting it to empty reserve locations of the lowest possible demand classification. Some systems simply present the user with a screen of empty locations and force a manual selection.

During the miscellaneous item receipt process, most systems assign a control number to each pallet. The pallet can then be added to the item file under that control number or can be added to a separate miscellaneous item file. When identical miscellaneous items are handled frequently (i.e., photocopy paper), the former method may be preferred because one item record can cover many movements and many pallets in the warehouse. However, when items tend to be unique, the latter method may be better because records can be easily deleted as the items are withdrawn. Once the miscellaneous item has been identified and a location has been selected, it can be treated as just another unit load. Existing procedures can then be used to put it away and to validate that it has been properly stored.

The withdrawal of miscellaneous items can be even simpler than receipt and storage. In many systems a screen is available that displays the miscellaneous items in the warehouse together with their locations. The user is allowed to select items for withdrawal. As each is selected, a transaction is created and queued for movement of the material from its storage location to a user-specified destination.

The picking and validation of the material releases the location for reuse and, where a separate miscellaneous item file is used, causes the associated item record to be deleted from the file.

Most companies exclude miscellaneous items and the space they consume from warehouse utilization reports and inventory valuation reports but include the labor required to handle them in personnel productivity reports.

16

Grote Manufacturing Company—An Example

Other chapters of this book have described a variety of techniques for obtaining the ultimate in productivity and accuracy in every nook and cranny of an inventory facility. They have not, however, considered the investment cost involved. In real life, companies must pick and choose the techniques that offer the best payback in their individual situations. Few, if any, can or should do everything.

Probably the best way to illustrate this is with a case study. The case presented here is the story of a company that has successfully made a major investment in its inventory system. The work done does not represent the ultimate inventory system nor does it represent the end of the line for systems development at this company. But, it is an example of a successful project that is paying for itself on a daily basis.

The Grote Manufacturing Company makes lighting, signaling, and mirror assemblies for the automotive, bus, truck, and trailer markets. Founded in 1901, the company established the nation's first plastic injection molding shop in 1922. Grote sells in volume to customers like Ford, Kenworth, and Fruehauf and also sells blister-packed items to the replacement parts market. Their displays can be found in larger auto parts stores nationwide. Grote remains privately held.

Grote works out of a 390,000-square-foot plant in southern Indiana. The plant does plastic molding, metal stamping, painting, and assembly. Connected to the plant through two passageways is a new 143,000-square-foot warehouse used for storage of all raw materials, component parts, and finished goods. Grote employs 800 people, with 60 assigned to the warehouse. The plant works two shifts; the warehouse works three, with the third shift reserved for put-away of newly received materials and for cycle counting.

Material is handled in the Grote facility almost entirely by a combination of automated guided vehicles (AGVs) and conventional lift trucks. The AGVs run from the warehouse to the manufacturing floor, while lift trucks perform local service chores within each of the two facilities.

Grote's products are, with a few exceptions, small enough to fit into a briefcase and weigh, at most, a few pounds each. Although there are finishes to be protected, the nature of the product imposes no special material handling problems. Many raw materials and in-process parts are handled in welded wire containers. Most other product is palletized for movement.

Grote operates a mainframe computer for both business systems and material requirements planning. When Grote's new warehouse was built, it was recognized that the inventory control features of the material requirements planning system were not sophisticated enough to achieve the levels of accuracy, productivity, and space utilization required and a separate inventory control system would be needed. Grote was particularly interested in a system that would maximize the utilization of space in the new warehouse, assure FIFO turnover of all materials, improve the productivity of warehouse personnel, and provide individual work measurements for material handlers.

Grote chose to purchase a customized version of a turn-key warehouse control system from Catalyst USA, Inc. Grote's management opted for the purchase mostly because the resources and experience required to do the development work were not available internally. Further, construction of the new warehouse had already been started, imposing a fixed deadline on the completion of the system. The risk of taking on a large and complex systems project with inexperienced personnel in the face of a firm deadline was believed to be significant.

The initial system planning project, including vendor selection, took 6 months to accomplish. Working with Catalyst, the software design, development, and installation took another 6 months. The project came in on time, concurrent with the move into the new warehouse.

The inventory system project, after a few teething problems, has been successful. The new warehouse is more fully utilized than would have been possible with the previously existing manual locator system. Inventory accuracy, which had stood at about 99.5 percent by item, is now measurable at 99.8 percent by location. The shift from accuracy measurement by item to measurement by location is significant because measurement by item allows the plusses and minuses in individual locations to cancel each other, while measurement by location does not. With the new system in place, Grote has weeks in which no cycle counting errors are found. And, as a bonus, cycle counting productivity is improved by allowing counters to work in a single aisle, rather than making them search the entire facility for an item.

MAJOR DESIGN CONSIDERATIONS

On average, Grote receives 40 purchase orders, starts 150 manufacturing orders, and ships 750 customer orders per day. The company has 15,000 item numbers and 9000 locations on file in its inventory system. Most shipments arrive and leave by truck, but about 15 percent are handled by parcel carriers, primarily UPS.

Grote's new warehouse is divided into four areas: raw materials, work-in process (semifinished items), packaging, and finished goods. Areas are set aside for receiving and shipping, an office, and a packaging area. The packaging area is not considered part of the warehouse for inventory control purposes.

Three carousel units are used for high-volume small parts. A consolidation area next to the carousels is used to accumulate material to be sent to manufacturing. Accumulated materials are loaded onto the AGV system and routed through one of the two passageways into the plant. A similar return-to-stock area is used to stage and organize materials coming back from manufacturing.

In each row in the finished goods area, the rack section closest to the shipping dock is equipped with a carton flow rack. These sections, together with the pallet flow rack, make up the finished goods forward picking area. This arrangement keeps order pickers close to the shipping area and minimizes the distances they have to travel while still keeping reserves as close to forward picking as possible.

Early in the system design process, Grote recognized that time and funding limitations would control the scope of the system. Since "The reasonable man adapts himself to the world" (George Bernard Shaw, *Maxims for Revolutionists*), four "short cuts" were taken:

1. Off-line portable terminals were used in place of on-line radios. Although the principles of Just-in-Time are important to Grote, system costs were reduced and manual procedures could compensate, at least for a period of time.
2. The system's scope was limited to the physical boundaries of the warehouse, leaving the manufacturing system to control shop floor inventory. While it would be convenient and probably more efficient to have a single system with complete responsibility for inventory, Grote was willing to live with two systems sharing the job.
3. The new warehouse project included a network of automated guided vehicles and three carousels. Direct interfaces between these systems and the inventory system could have been included, but Grote felt that the simplicity of a manual interface was, at least temporarily, preferable. Therefore, carousel operators now key picking locations from pick lists printed by the inventory system. And loads are similarly dispatched on the AGV by key entry.
4. The initial system concept called for the tracking and control of inventory by engineering change level. On further investigation, however, it was decided that the inventory system only had to enforce FIFO turnover and that the details of change management could be controlled elsewhere.

On the other hand, Grote felt that some system features were indispensable. Therefore, the completed design did include:

1. Bar coding of material handling transactions and storage locations, together with validation of material movements.
2. System selection of storage locations using logic much like that described in Chapter 11.

3. Control over the release of newly arrived material to prevent its use prior to approval by quality control.
4. System selection of picking locations for both replenishments and shipments to assure FIFO inventory rotation.

HOW THE SYSTEM WORKS

Grote's inventory system operates on an IBM minicomputer located in the warehouse. Communication between the mainframe business computer and the inventory system is interactive, managed on both ends by continuously operating programs that monitor both the line and transmission data files. When an application program wants to communicate with its opposite number, it does so by putting a record in the transmission file. The communication program detects the presence of the record, verifies that the line is not in use, transmits the data, and removes the record from the transmission file. The business computer downloads customer, purchasing, and manufacturing orders. It receives back actual shipments, actual receipts, and inventory adjustments.

Receiving

The material handling cycle begins, as always, in receiving. As shipments arrive, receiving personnel log onto the inventory system to establish their starting time for productivity measurement purposes. Then, working one trailer or one shipment at a time, they unload the material, compare the bill of lading with the receipt, note external damage, and release the driver.

The packing list and freight bill are taken into the receiving office. The order number, items, and quantities shown on the packing list are keyed, as are the carrier code, shipment weight, freight charges, number of damaged pieces found, and other information. The system prints a receiving worksheet that lists information from the packing list and also identifies hot and hazardous items, items that must be repacked prior to storage, and items that require inspection before they can be used. The worksheet is taken back to the receiving floor, boxes are opened, product is counted, and the counts are compared against those found on the worksheet. The receiver repackages the material for storage if necessary and draws a sample for QC. Finally, the receiver records the types of containers or pallets used and the quantities of material on or in each one.

Information from the worksheet is then keyed and storage locations are selected. The system is usually allowed to select locations based on existing storage parameters, but options exist to allow the user to enter storage locations or modify storage parameters before the system selects a location. Storage parameters available for modification include function, device, demand, environment, a location range limitation, maximum quantity in the location, dimensions, and the maximum number of locations containing the item. If locations are selected by the operator, the system verifies that they are available before using them. If the system selects the location, the operator can specify whether an empty location is to be used or whether the receipt is to be combined with existing stock of the same item. Inventory listings for items and empty locations are available.

Upon completion of the location assignment process, the system prints barcoded store tickets for each pallet or container. A sample store ticket is shown in Figure 16.1. These tickets include the item number, quantity, and storage location in human-readable form and both the transaction number and the storage location in bar code form. The printing of a store ticket locks the affected location so no other transactions can be scheduled until the put-away has been validated. Issue tickets are also printed for QC samples. Then the tickets are taken onto the receiving floor and applied to the material.

QC samples are not included in inventory. They are received and immediately issued, with the balance of the receipt for that item automatically placed on hold. On completion of the QC tests, the sample is received back into the warehouse and the hold is released. When material is scrapped or returned to the vendor, it is removed from the inventory by an issue transaction.

Issues are done by entering the item number and an account number. The system displays locations containing that item. The key operator selects the issue location, enters the quantity to be issued, and indicates the place to which the material should be delivered. The system then prints an issue ticket, much like the store ticket shown in Figure 16.1.

Material that is urgently needed in manufacturing is cross-docked by storing it to a pseudo-location on the receiving dock and immediately picking it. Picking procedures are described below. The pseudo-location is a real location that exists on the location file but is specially coded to have infinite cubic capacity.

Completed work and unused parts are received from the factory using a similar but much simpler process that eliminates freight bills and quality inspections.

Figure 16.1. Grote store ticket. The store ticket is indicative of the techniques used by Grote to control material movements into, within, and out of the warehouse.

(Inspections are done in the shop before the material reaches the warehouse.) In all cases, order numbers, item numbers, and quantities received are captured and transmitted to the mainframe business computer.

Put-Away

The put-away process is done by a material handler using an off-line portable terminal with an attached bar code scanner. The terminal is capable of reading bar codes, making relatively simple comparisons between pieces of information, and storing the results in memory for later transmission to the inventory system. It includes a keyboard for quantity entry and for instances when bar codes prove to be unusable. It also includes a small display for error messages and prompts.

The put-away process begins with the assignment of a portable terminal and bar code scanner to a material handler. The material handler scans the bar code on his or her ID badge, selects a pallet or container to be put away, reads its storage location from the store ticket, and moves it to that location. As part of the process of putting the material away, the material handler scans both of the bar codes on the store ticket and the bar code on the location. The terminal compares the location from the location label with the location on the store ticket and, if they match, prompts the operator to proceed with the next transaction.

If the locations do not match, the material has been incorrectly stored, so the terminal prompts the operator to try again. If the operator, for some reason, is unable to place the material in the correct location, the transaction is bypassed and turned over to a supervisor for resolution. When a group of put-away transactions has been completed, the material handler plugs his or her terminal into the inventory system and instructs it to upload the work completed. The inventory system then closes out the transactions and credits the material handler for the work done.

Inventory Management

Grote's system includes a variety of inventory management tools. Holds and releases may be applied to a single location or to all locations containing a specified part number. These holds are separate from the hold that is automatically applied as material requiring inspection arrives and is put away.

Storage locations can be added and deleted, allowing the system to adapt to change in the warehouse layout without requiring modification to the inventory system software. Location labels can be printed in either of two sizes, employee badges can be printed, locations can be dedicated to items, and dedications can be removed. Grote has adopted the practice of dedicating all forward picking locations to specific items, while allowing reserve locations to be assigned freely by the system. This provides manual control over picking efficiencies without affecting the system's ability to maximize the utilization of space in reserve.

To protect the system against instances in which scanners or bar codes fail, supervisors are given the ability to override validations, manually complete transactions, and unlock the affected locations. To cover special circumstances and provide the maximum amount of flexibility, the system allows authorized users to issue material without a corresponding order and to make adjustments to the inventory in a location.

Replenishment and Moves

The replenishment of forward picking locations is controlled by a planner at a system terminal. The planner keys a range of location numbers to be replenished, the system determines the required replenishment quantity, selects picking locations in reserve, and allocates the material. A report of locations requiring replenishment is available to help the planner predict the volume of work that will be generated. Replenishments do not lock either the reserve or the forward picking location.

On request, the system prints a consolidation opportunity report. Both consolidations and miscellaneous moves between inventory locations are specified by the planner, who keys item number, source location, quantity, and destination location. Moves and consolidations lock both the source and destination locations. Additional transactions cannot be scheduled against them until the moves are validated.

Whether the work is a move, a consolidation, or a replenishment, the system then prints two tickets, one to be used when picking the material, the other for put-away. The material handler picks up the material and uses a bar code scanner attached to a portable terminal to scan the source location's label and the bar code on the move-pickup ticket. The material is moved and the same scanner is used to scan the destination location's label and the bar code on the move-store ticket. In both instances, the terminal matches location labels with the location numbers found in the ticket bar codes, warns the material handler if an error has been made, and allows the error to be corrected. Transaction numbers are saved and transmitted to the inventory system later to allow the system to close out the transactions and adjust on-hand balances in the two locations. The system considers the move-pickup and move-store transactions to be separate entities, allowing material handlers to make several pickups before putting material away.

Inventory Counting

Cycle counts are also planned in advance through a system terminal. The user keys either a range of location numbers or a range of part numbers. Part numbers, if specified, are converted by the system into a list of locations. The system then checks each location to determine whether or not there is activity pending and, if not, locks the location and prints a cycle count ticket.

Cycle counts are done using the same portable, off-line terminals used for validating other material movements. The operator scans the bar code on the cycle count ticket and the bar code on the location and keys the on-hand quantity. The terminal compares the on-hand quantity keyed with the quantity found in the bar code and requests a recount if they differ.

When the off-line terminal is connected to the inventory system, it uploads cycle count results. These results are not directly posted as adjustments to the on-hand quantity but instead are held for a supervisor's review and approval.

Grote, as a matter of practice, does most cycle counting work on the third shift to avoid conflict with other work.

Full "annual" physical inventories used to be done between Christmas and New Year at a cost of 3 days of production and 700 to 1000 labor hours each year. Because Grote's inventory records are more accurate than any physical inventory could be, the company has not done one for 7 years.

Customer Orders

As customer orders are entered and credit is approved, they are downloaded from the mainframe business computer to the inventory system. Sold-to names and addresses are maintained in a file in the inventory system; ship-to names and addresses are downloaded with each order along with item numbers and quantities, carrier information, and a priority. Priorities escalate automatically each day to assure that no order is forgotten for long.

From time to time during the day, a warehouse planner builds picking waves. The orders to be included in each wave can be selected from the pool of open orders by specifying a latest planned shipment date and/or minimum priority. Special circumstances may be handled by entering individual order number and carrier restrictions. The planner also enters an upper limit to the total number of orders to be selected for the wave.

Orders may be coded on the mainframe as "emergencies", which will assure that they are selected for picking in the next wave, regardless of the criteria entered by the planner. Grote uses this facility rarely, reserving it primarily for instances when customers need extremely fast service.

Following the creation of each wave, the inventory system prints a brief statistical report. The planner may "deselect" the orders and try again or may commit them to picking. Once the wave is committed, the system allocates the required material, identifies any emergency replenishments needed, and prints replenishment tickets. When allocation is complete, it prints an allocation report, sorts the picks into picking sequence by zone, and prints picking documents and packing lists. Depending on the pick zone and the type of order, picking documents may consist of a combined ship-to stencil and pick list, picking labels, and/or shipping labels.

Picking work is assigned to employees by supervisors who manually distribute the picking documents. The methods used vary from zone to zone. Carousel operators work from pick tickets that specify the picking location (i.e., carousel number and bin number) and the quantity to be picked. The inventory system does not directly interface with the carousel, so operators must key each location number into the carousel controller, picking the material after the carousel has stopped rotating. Exceptions, if any, are marked on the tickets. Although bar code validation is used throughout the warehouse, it is not used at the carousels.

Pickers working the work-in-process and raw materials zones also use tickets. Unused tickets and quantity exceptions are noted and left with the material. Finished goods pickers work from a pick list, noting exceptions on the pick list if necessary.

Completed picks are delivered to the shipping area. In the shipping office, picker ID numbers, the number of pieces to be shipped, freight charges, and shortage information are keyed into the inventory system. The system prints bills of lading, closes out the picking transactions, and reports shipments and exceptions to the mainframe business computer. The completed order is then staged, loaded, and shipped.

Manufacturing Orders

Like customer orders, manufacturing orders originate on the mainframe and are downloaded to the inventory system. Unlike customer orders, however, they are not selected for picking until the shop needs the material. They are then selected and allocated, one order at a time. The process is similar to that used for customer orders.

While customer orders are always allocated as specified on the orders (assuming availability), the planner is given more flexibility with manufacturing orders. He or she can specify that the system allocate all components or only specific ones and can limit allocation to a percentage of the ordered quantity. Picking, of course, is limited to the quantities allocated. In addition, some items are identified as "bulk issue" items through a flag on the item file. When these items are allocated for manufacturing use, the system always allocates everything in the location, regardless of whether or not the quantity exceeds the order quantity. The theory behind "bulk issue" is that it is less expensive to return unused stock to inventory than to count a precise quantity when picking.

As with customer orders, picks for manufacturing are controlled with tickets printed by the inventory system in an efficient picking sequence and distributed to pickers by a supervisor. Completed picks are delivered to the AGV staging area rather than to shipping. An employee in the AGV staging area assembles orders, scans pick labels, and keys exceptions using an off-line portable terminal. The completed orders are then placed on the AGV pickup conveyor and the destination is keyed into the AGV system. When the content of the terminal is uploaded to the inventory system, the pick transactions are closed, inventory and allocations are relieved, and the mainframe is notified.

Management Reports

While the Grote inventory system is primarily an operational system, a variety of reports are available, including some management analyses. Table 16.1 lists the most important ones.

IMPORTANT PRINCIPLES

The Grote story illustrates a few important principles:

1. By careful attention to detail during system design and by strict adherence to operating procedures, extremely high levels of inventory accuracy can be obtained in a very productive environment.

TABLE 16.1. GROTE MANUFACTURING INVENTORY SYSTEM REPORTS

Report	Use
Part Descriptions and Storage Parameters	File listing
Parts Requiring Dimensions	Trigger action of obtaining dimensional data
Parts Statistics	File listing
Part Activity	Activity by part number
Warehouse Demand Analysis	Compares actual demand with expected
Parts by Location	File listing
Parts/Locations on Hold	Lists non-QC holds currently in effect
Standard Pallets/Containers	File listing
Storage Locations	File listing
Miscellaneous Items by Location	Lists miscellaneous items in the warehouse
Picking zones	Pick zone file listing
Empty Locations	Assists when locations are manually selected
Quality Control Holds	Lists QC holds currently in effect
Quality Control Receipts	Lists product issued to QC
Anticipated Receipts	File listing
Receiving and Inspection	Lists recent receipts
Receipt Exceptions	Lists exceptions taken on recent receipts
Freight Bills	Shipping document
Vendors	File listing
Customer Orders	File listing
Customer Order Waves	File listing
Manufacturing Orders	File listing
Customer Names and Addresses	File listing
Locations Requiring Replenishment	Triggers replenishment
Consolidation Candidates	Triggers consolidation
Part/Location Parameter Exceptions	Triggers warehousing
Cycle Counts	Recent cycle counts
Inventory Transactions	Incomplete inventory transactions
Transaction Audit Trail	Recently completed transactions
Transaction Log	Offloaded transactions from disk
Shipments	Recent shipments
Employees	File listing
Employee Statistics	Productivity report
Employees Logged On	Employees currently logged on
Work Assignments	Incomplete work assignment list

2. Bar code validation of material movement is the most important single key to accuracy.
3. However, validation need not necessarily be used everywhere. Accurate receiving, storing, and replenishment are most important and should come first.
4. Sometimes the ultimate system is not the best. Grote's warehouse could be made more productive with, for instance, the use of radio terminals, the installation of a data link between the carousels and the inventory system, and the ability to pick batches of manufacturing orders. For the time being, Grote is far better off with a working system that includes short-cuts than they would be with nothing.

Part 3

SYSTEM DESIGN AND IMPLEMENTATION

17

Conceptualization

In many respects, the project work required to implement an inventory system differs little from that required for other modern software, therefore we will not rehash the basics of project management. However, inventory systems do involve some unique issues and some that, while not unique, stand out as frequent problem areas. These issues are the focus of this chapter and the succeeding ones.

COMPARISON TO OTHER KINDS OF SYSTEMS PROJECTS

One might reasonably draw a parallel between the installation of an inventory control system and a manufacturing planning system. The software required to fill these two functions is of the same order of magnitude both in complexity and in size. Both systems involve human interfaces with people whose job is directly related to the processing or handling of material and to whom the computer may be a strange and somewhat forbidding tool of questionable necessity.

But, from the viewpoint of the project manager, there are some major differences between manufacturing planning systems and inventory control systems. For instance:

1. Material requirements planning, a major element of most manufacturing planning systems, has a theoretical and mathematical underpinning that can be learned in a classroom and separately applied to the job. Inventory control systems, on the other hand, are based on practice and common sense, involving almost no "science" whatever.
2. The American Production and Inventory Control Society (APICS) has done an excellent job of educating users and system vendors in

manufacturing planning technologies over several decades. As a result, it is relatively easy to hire expertise in manufacturing planning. But, neither APICS nor any other society has done significant inventory control system education. The only people available who understand inventory control, therefore, are the ones who have learned it from experience.

3. There are many commercially available, standardized manufacturing planning systems. Competition and repeated sales have worked together to reduce software prices to the point at which there is almost never justification for a do-it-yourself, in-house development project. Inventoɪy control systems, however, are harder to standardize and fewer have been sold. Therefore there are few, if any, truly general purpose commercial inventory control systems, and inventory control system projects almost always involve a make-versus-buy decision.

4. Manufacturing planning systems lend themselves to standardization because they deal with the logic of the manufacturing and distribution processes while inventory systems, on the other hand, tend to deal with physical aspects. This means more variation from plant to plant, business to business, and system to system. Increased variability means that the designers can rely less on software written for other companies and must exercise more ingenuity and inventiveness to reach their goals.

REQUIREMENTS DEFINITION

Inventory systems projects often do not have a well-defined starting point. A conversation in a staff meeting, a speaker at a professional society dinner or a visit to a supplier may trigger an idea. Discussion of the idea within the company can result in an informal consensus that it ought to be looked into. Eventually someone will either be assigned to make an initial investigation or will decide to do so on his or her own volition.

At this stage, the project can take many forms, but several questions are likely to be uppermost in the minds of the people involved:

1. What is technically possible?
2. What have other companies done?
3. What are the benefits that can be achieved?
4. What are the costs involved?
5. What steps will be required to see the project through to completion?
6. What staff is available to work on the project?
7. How long is the project likely to take?

The answers to these questions form the Requirements Definition. The steps involved usually include:

1. Review of existing systems and documentation.
2. Interviews with management and supervisory personnel to determine problems and needs. The people interviewed can also serve as sounding boards to help determine the feasibility of ideas and their potential benefits.
3. Making contact with other firms to determine what they have done and the degree to which their ideas and concepts are applicable.
4. Searching the literature for additional ideas and concepts.
5. Making contact with hardware and software vendors, both to obtain the benefit of the work they have done and to obtain contacts in other businesses.

In most businesses, the requirements definition takes the form of a written document and, most likely, a presentation to management. Assuming a forecast surplus of benefits over costs, the presentation will probably also include a request for funding to continue with the next step.

In-House Requirements Definition Projects

Because the technology that makes real time inventory control systems possible is relatively new and because requirements definitions are frequently done by in-house personnel, many are done by people with little experience in the field, even though they may have a great deal of experience with other kinds of systems. Several classes of errors are often made. Awareness of these classes of errors can help designers avoid them.

System objectives and scope are always difficult to establish accurately in the early phases of any project. It is important, however, that the subject be broached during the requirements definition phase and that both objectives and scope limitations be proposed. If the subject is ignored, different people will have different perceptions of the system and it will be more difficult to reach a consensus on the features and functions to be included.

The people doing requirements definition should either have or, as part of the project, should develop a good understanding of the material handling methods in use in the business and those that are projected for the future. The interdependencies between material handling and inventory systems can easily escape the attention of people without cross-disciplinary training in both data processing and either manufacturing or distribution.

The design of systems to accommodate expected future business growth is often wise. The purchase, for instance, of a computer somewhat larger than immediately necessary can handle increased future volumes without incurring upgrade costs. However, during the requirements definition, costs are not well known and it is easy to go too far. Systems built to accommodate growth that never occurs are not economical. Likewise, systems that are replaced because of technical obsolescence before the projected volume levels are reached have, in effect, wasted funds by providing capacity that is never used. And, finally, systems that provide capacity that simply sits unused for several years represent a waste of investment funds, even if only temporarily. Somewhere there is a middle ground. Although the requirements definition phase may not be the right place to find it, it is a good place to start looking.

Interfaces with existing systems and equipment should be considered during the requirements definition. If, for instance, automated truck routing is to be part of the scope of the system, the people doing the requirements definition should ask whether or not the data required is available or can be created and maintained at reasonable cost. If the data already exists, interfaces are indicated to make it accessible to the inventory system and their feasibility should be verified. If feasibility is a problem, the choice may be between altering the inventory system's scope to eliminate automated truck routing and either modifying or replacing the system that has the required data.

Dependencies, assumptions, and anticipated problems should be itemized as part of the requirements definition. For example, a major portion of the benefits that justify a system may depend on the introduction of a new product, entry into a new market, or reaching a new level of growth. Anticipated problems, for instance, might include the firm's ability to staff the development project with people experienced in the programming of real-time applications.

At the level of the requirements definition, a range of possible solutions should be considered and the people involved should be careful to avoid assuming the use of a particular technology. Bar codes, for instance, are a means and not an end. Further, nonautomated solutions should not be ignored. The inclusion of people with nonsystems backgrounds in the requirements definition will often tend to remind others that the computer is not the only possible answer.

It should be remembered that requirements are functional. The requirements definition should consider only the information that users need to do their work or to do their work better. Involvement, at this stage, in the amount of memory required, the type or model of disk drive to be used, or even the type of computer is counterproductive.

Arguments for additions to the system's scope and objectives will almost certainly arise later in the project. There may also be disagreements on the requirements that were initially established. The requirements document serves as a reference for resolving these disputes and allows team members to identify and record changes. Time invested in the requirements definition document is almost always time well spent.

Usually, while requirements are being defined, everyone involved has ideas and concepts in mind and is eager to see their concepts adopted by the group and developed. There is, therefore, a tendency to overdesign and overdevelop. This work, both unplanned and unfunded, can go on almost indefinitely if management fails to make clear the level of detail desired in the requirements definition and fails to monitor the progress of the work.

Using Consultants for Requirements Definition

Some companies prefer to use outside consultants either to perform or to assist in the performance of the requirements definition. Consultants with experience in inventory systems can provide quick and easy answers to many questions. They can be of great help in avoiding pitfalls and can use their experience to move directly to good solutions without wasting time on technical deadends. Consultants can also, in the process of consulting, provide a significant amount of rub-off training to the company people who work with them.

However, there are two disadvantages to the use of outside consultants. First, depending on how the company evaluates the cost of its people, consultants may cost more than employees. And second, their motivations may be different from those of employees. Consulting firms are companies that sell consulting. They have a built-in bias toward doing additional work and may recommend continuing with a project, even in cases where an informed insider would hesitate. And where alternatives exist, consultants sometimes lean toward the alternative that maximizes their own revenue and earnings.

FUNCTIONAL DESIGN

The requirements definition roughly defines the project, identifies major costs and benefits, and describes the resources required to bring it to fruition. While the requirements definition is not detailed, it does allow management to decide whether or not a formal project should be established to arrive at a complete system design and accurate pricing.

The design, if done, is usually best divided into two steps. The first step is called the functional design. It focuses on the wants and needs of the users, differing from the requirements definition primarily in the level of detail. The second step, often called a technical design, begins with the functional design and adds data processing specifications. The hiatus between the two design steps is often a convenient and appropriate time to approach vendors and obtain bids for the proposed system. See Chapter 18 for a discussion of the make-versus-buy decision and the process of obtaining and evaluating bids. Chapter 19 covers the technical design effort and subsequent tasks.

Separation of the design process into a user-oriented phase and a technical, data-processing-oriented phase is generally best because few data processing decisions can be finalized until all of the functional design work is complete. When internal, technical decisions are made too early, the result can be excessive backtracking and reworking, which wastes time and money. Premature technical decision making can also result in systems that are driven by computer technology when they should be driven by business needs.

Often, the hardest part of a functional design project is finding the appropriate level of detail. For instance, while most system internals are avoided during the functional design, some elements of logic are key to the system's function and should be included. For example, a functional design can reasonably specify the algorithm to be used to sort packages on a conveyor and the one used to select picking locations. Both affect the way the system will meet business needs. On the other hand, the algorithm to be used to retrieve records from the database is purely a technical matter and should be left out of the functional design.

Functional Design Methods and Common Pitfalls

Functional designs are usually best done by a small team of data processing and operations people. Their purpose is to provide a complete and consistent description of the proposed system from the viewpoint of the users. Table 17.1 lists the major elements that should be covered. Similar tables (19.1 and 19.2) describe topics that should be designed later and, therefore, are excluded from the functional design.

The first and most time-consuming step in a functional design is the description and analysis of existing and planned work flows. Detailed procedural descriptions should be written for each process. Then the design team should imagine how each process could be improved with computer support and write new descriptions. Work volumes, timing constraints, and the physical layout of the inventory facility should be considered. Possible problems and alternative solutions should be cataloged and evaluated. A refined cost and benefit estimate should be made. And a preliminary delivery schedule for the system should be developed. The functional design should culminate in a detailed report with a brief management summary.

Users (even technically oriented ones) should not be presented with massive reports for their approval. Instead, summaries and excerpts should be prepared as each process is described. These summaries should be reviewed by users and technical people with knowledge of and concern for the topic who are both within and outside the design team. Because they are brief, summaries can be reviewed and assessed quickly, promoting fast turn-around and full comprehension.

Equipment requirements should be listed in the functional design to establish needs but not to specify makes or models. It is reasonable, for example, to state that the supervisors will each need a workstation and a printer and that certain features will be required. But the functional design should not specify the communications protocol to be used between the workstations and the inventory control computer. Later, a specialist can perform the detailed work of equipment specification, evaluation, and selection.

A report summary should list all reports, screens, and other output (such as labels) that the system is to produce. The summary can be in the form of a table of reports showing the information contained in each. Users may wish to specify additional details such as record selection criteria and report sequence. In some cases, it may be wise to include complete layouts and mock-ups. Or, in other cases, report specifications may be limited to a statement of intent such as, "An item file listing will be required to display all fields on the file in a single, comprehensive report."

Measurable performance objectives should be included in the functional design when they are important to the success or failure of the system. For example, one performance objective might specify that the system allocate product at the rate of 50,000 lines per hour based on a business need to allocate 200,000 lines in a daily 4-hour window. On the other hand, a blanket specification that workstation response times must not exceed 2 seconds might be counterproductive unless it is backed up by reasons why the limit is necessary.

TABLE 17.1. TOPICS TO INCLUDE IN A FUNCTIONAL DESIGN

Topic	Coverage

Operational functions
  Receipt order management
  Receiving
  Quality control
  Put-away
  Order management
  Allocation
  Picking
  Shipping and issuing
  Miscellaneous movements
  Rewarehousing
  Physical inventories
  Cycle counts
  Productivity measurement
	All operational functions should be described in detail. Descriptions should include step-by-step procedures for users but should include only those elements of the system logic that are necessary from a business standpoint. The functions to the left should all be considered for inclusion.

Technical matters Validation	A description of validation should cover all methods used, all imaginable problems that users might encounter and the methods to be used to recover.
Equipment	Equipment should be described generically in terms of what must be done and, where capacity requirements are known, they should be specified.
System start-up	Known constraints and limitations should be described. Known tasks should be listed and, where possible, the amount of work should be estimated.
Reports	Reports and the information they contain should be listed. Report layouts and mock-ups should be made only where it is important to the users.
Screens	Selected screens, the information they contain, and the information that may be entered into them should be listed. Layouts and mock-ups should be made only where it is important to the users.
Symbology	A symbology should be selected and the selection should be justified.
Labels	Labels should be defined and listed. Because label design often involves critical tolerances, most labels should be laid out and mock-ups should be part of the design.
Performance objectives	Where possible, system performance objectives should be specified. If numeric goals cannot be defined, the areas for goal-setting should be delineated.
Reliability	System reliability objectives should be specified. Numeric goals should be used where possible. All goals, whether numeric or not, should be backed up with the reasoning behind them.
Security	Users should be grouped by access level and the functions accessible at each level should be defined.

Users can be legitimately concerned about detecting malfunctions in equipment, highlighting abnormal activity, or preventing unauthorized data access. Even though these topics border on the technical specification, they can be included in a functional design, providing the methods are left as open as possible.

DESIGN VALIDATION

A completed functional design is a cohesive, consistent set of ideas intended to reach one or more business-oriented goals. It explains what must be done, without getting too involved in how it should be done. It also estimates the benefits of reaching the goal and the costs that will be incurred along the way.

However, as first compiled, most functional designs are unproven. The ideas and concepts contained in them appear workable to the design team but have not been tested. Before proceeding to the next step, it is wise to validate the concepts and verify, in one way or another, that they are indeed workable and, more than workable, that they are the best possible way of achieving the goals.

Validation of the functional design is important for three reasons. First, new ideas can be uncovered, leading to a better design. Second, the experience of others improves the ability of the design team to plan the remaining steps in the project. Third, the added confidence gained through validation improves the chances of funding approval.

There are five ways to validate a design. Several should be used; there is no harm in doing all of them. They are:

1. An outside consultant can be employed to review and comment on the completed design document. Even if the initial design was created by or with the help of consultants, the use of a second consulting firm to validate the design could be worthwhile. The consultant should, of course, be experienced in the design and implementation of similar systems.

2. If software purchase is a realistic alternative, system integrators and hardware and software vendors with inventory system experience can be invited to comment on the completed design. Their comments, while colored by their desire to make a sale, can contain new ideas. Most vendors will be happy to comment at no charge so long as the scope of their involvement is limited and so long as they understand that they will be given a chance to bid on the work later. Unvalidated concepts should not be given to vendors for bidding.

3. Design committee members can and should visit other companies who have solved similar problems with similar systems. Contacts with such companies can usually be made through trade associations, professional societies, or hardware and software vendors.

4. Additional in-house personnel—ones not heavily involved in the functional design process—can be asked to review and comment on the design. In particular, if one or more capable hourly people can be found, their comments are worth soliciting. Sometimes the view from

the bottom is equally valid but significantly different than from the top.

5. Members of the design committee should wait a week or so and then should walk the warehouse and shop floor with a copy of the design in hand. They should review each procedure in the design as though they were the person doing the work, again as though they were that person's supervisor, and once again as though they were an industrial engineer. The objective is to verify reasonability and look for better ways. This is also a good time to check the design for physical hazards such as sometimes occur with high-rise vehicles, chemically incompatible products, and unit loads that do not always stack well.

18

Commitment

The functional design defines what it is that should be done. The decision to commit funds to the project depends on the cost-benefit analysis that logically occurs after the functional design has been completed. The cost-benefit analysis determines whether:

1. Funds should be committed to create and install the system
2. The effort should be abandoned as unproductive
3. The functional design should be revised to achieve a better cost-benefit ratio

Two activities are thus indicated: one directed at cost and one at benefits. Either can be done first, or both can be done at once. They can be done as a single effort but are often best divided into two separate tasks. Of course, when the cost and benefit analyses are done separately, coordination is required to assure that each cost element is included in one and only one place.

Ideally, the cost analysis will result in a single figure representing the new costs that the business will incur to implement the system described in the functional design. Similarly, the benefits analysis should arrive at a single figure that represents the net change in existing costs if the system is implemented. Although it is desirable to reduce both costs and benefits to single numbers, the process is rarely that simple.

Since both costs and benefits will occur over time, present value calculations should be made to compensate for the effects of inflation and for the unspoken alternative of investing the funds in other projects. Costs and benefits in the distant future, in particular, should be estimated recognizing the uncertainties of life in a highly technical world. Items more than 2 or 3 years away, therefore, should be heavily discounted.

Cash flow analysis is also required for businesses that have limited investment capital available. The cash flow analysis should determine the net amount of funding required as a function of time to assure that funds will be available when needed.

DETERMINING COST

High-accuracy inventory systems can be expensive. Compared to traditional inventory control systems, hardware requirements are extensive and logic is complicated by special considerations and exceptions to the considerations. And the entire project can be made still more difficult by the timing requirements that are often inherent in real-time systems.

Cost overruns almost universally result from one of two things: either a cost element was missed in the budgeting process or an unexpected technical difficulty changed specifications. Overruns can be eliminated by providing sufficient contingency funds. But large contingency budgets imply less-than-thorough analysis and, therefore, greater than necessary risk. Contingencies, therefore, require their own justification.

There are two phenomena that tend to obscure the overall cost picture and lead toward inaccurate estimates. First, at the point in the development of an inventory system when the cost and benefit analyses are being done, many people are anxious to see the system implemented. Enthusiasm and optimism can lead to understated contingencies in an unconscious effort to assure that benefits exceed costs.

Other people, particularly those responsible for programming and delivering the system, will be measured on the degree to which their cost estimates come true. These people often tend to build contingencies into their budgets without specifically identifying them as such. As the costs are passed up through the organization, each manager is prone to add his or her own cushion, burying it in the accumulated total and duplicating the contingencies already there. The result can be a cost estimate that includes more contingency than actual cost.

In reality, modest contingency funds make good sense, but detailed and thorough planning is also necessary. The cost estimating process must be done as carefully as possible by experienced people working in a "do it right" atmosphere. And care must be taken to assure that all contingency funds are listed separately and clearly labeled for what they are.

Outside resources are easily assigned cost values because they are priced by the vendors. In-house costs are more difficult to value. The cost of items such as management time may not be available. Indirect costs such as the delays imposed on other projects can be difficult to pin down.

Specific project costs are sometimes buried in overhead. For instance, the addition of a distributed processor to run the inventory system will cause more electricity to be consumed. This electricity is a real, if minor, cost of the project. More significantly, some businesses account for their software maintenance personnel as overhead. If the inventory system requires, for instance, support on the second shift where none was required before, the cost can be important, but easily over-looked. There are also secondary effects. For example, the installation of a new inventory system may alter career paths and lead to unforeseen personnel changes. How far should one go in detailing costs?

In many companies, corporate policies provide guidance on what should be included in the cost analysis and what should not. The analyst must assume that policy writers knew what they were doing. In addition, adherence to corporate policies makes possible a fair and reasonable comparison between competing investment proposals. Analysts should also remember that a large scale cost analysis is expensive, time-consuming, and disruptive to the normal flow of work. In addition, results can be misleading and difficult to apply if decision-making criteria are not well defined. The middle ground is often the best course.

Major elements that should be considered in developing the cost of a proposed inventory system are listed below. Because the definition of "cost" varies from company to company based on management's policies and on bookkeeping methods, the list is not definitive, but it can serve as a guideline.

1. One-time software costs
   Purchased application software cost
   In-house written software cost including design, programming, and testing of programs, systems, and communications
   Documentation cost
   Development management cost
   Consultants assisting in decision and design
   Modifications to existing systems as necessary to communicate with the new inventory system
   Systems software cost including operating system, database manager, telecommunications manager, and others
   Training for users, software maintenance personnel, and computer operators
   Start-up costs including file conversions and new data collection and entry

2. One-time hardware costs
   Site preparation including power, power protection, air conditioning, furniture, and cables
   Computer hardware and peripherals
   Computer and peripheral equipment installation
   Installation of data communications lines between the inventory system and other computers (as necessary)
   Physical warehouse preparation including reorganization, application of location labels (including the labels themselves), and performance of an initial physical inventory if necessary

3. Recurring costs
   If required, labor costs for additional computer operators, supervisors, planners, clerks, and data entry personnel
   Supplies including paper, forms, ribbons, and labels

Data communications line charges
Computer and peripheral equipment maintenance
Purchased software maintenance
Utilities costs
Depreciation on hardware and facilities

4. Other costs
Cost of capital required to undertake the operation
Cost of management and staff time for planning
Costs associated with the disruption of normal activities

In some instances, shortages of staff, skills, and other resources may require that inventory system software be purchased. In other instances, the situation may rule out software purchase. For most inventory system projects, however, the make-versus-buy decision should be addressed as part of the costing effort. Even if it is a foregone conclusion that the system will be written internally, cost analysis should be done because it will help measure success and keep priorities straight when conflicts occur.

DETERMINING BENEFITS

Benefits always tend to be overestimated. The benefits analysis will best serve the company when it is done with an unbiased view toward practicality. In general, benefits are best estimated by the users who, presumably, have a detailed understanding of current operations and know better what the impact of the new system will actually be.

Because so many different business systems depend on inventory accuracy and because inventory data is used by so many people, the benefits of most inventory systems are scattered and some may be hard to identify. For the sake of discussion, benefits can be separated into those attributable to improved inventory accuracy and those attributable to improved productivity. Tables 18.1 and 18.2 list possible benefits and can function as a checklist for the analyst.

Sometimes other benefits exist that are less obvious and harder to measure. These so-called intangibles often present a problem for the analyst because they, by definition, cannot be accurately quantified. But, the fact that intangible benefits are hard to express in numbers does not make them less important. They can, in fact, be crucial to the justification of an inventory system. For example, some intangible benefits which are often associated with inventory systems are listed below.[1] In the right situation, any of them could be the make-or-break difference.

- An organized, consistent way of controlling and operating inventory reduces time spent fire-fighting.
- Management strategies are implemented on a consistent and error-free basis.

---

[1] Adapted from an unpublished document by Catalyst USA, Inc. Used with permission.

TABLE 18.1ᵃ. SAVINGS ATTRIBUTABLE TO IMPROVED ACCURACY

Benefit	Savings
Elimination of time looking for lost material.	Labor cost
Elimination of the annual physical inventory saves not only the labor required to count but also avoids the need to close the business while counting is in progress.	Labor cost Customer service
Reduced safety stocks. When inventory is accurately known, safety stocks are needed only to cover variability in supply and need not allow for inventory surprises.	Inventory Space costs Inventory losses Labor cost
Debt service costs. When inventory is reduced, a one-time favorable cash flow occurs, which can be used to retire outstanding debt.	Management cost
Reduced purchasing activity. Accurate inventory eliminates surprises and therefore the need for emergency purchase orders and change notices.	Management cost
More accurate customer promises because of more accurate inventory information.	Customer service
More accurate inventory records and more accurate customer promises reduces the need for premium-rate shipments (both incoming and outgoing).	Transportation cost
More accurate shipments. Reduced returns, happier customers, and fewer losses.	Labor cost Inventory losses Customer service
More accurate bills of lading and invoices.	Labor cost Customer service

ᵃAdapted from an unpublished document by Catalyst USA, Inc. Used with permission.

- More detailed and more complete audit trails are available for improved analysis and security.
- Software tools offer the ability to aggregate large amounts of information for planning purposes.
- Management information is more detailed, more accurate, and more timely, leading to better decision making.
- Improved inventory record accuracy can often make the difference between success and failure with MRP and JIT.
- Reduced losses and the resulting improved quality can reduce the size of the quality organization.
- Employee morale is improved when systems actually work the way they are supposed to.

Intangible benefits can be ignored if the proposed inventory system shows clear tangible benefits. In this case, the intangible benefits might be the "icing on the cake" for the proposed system. But it often happens that tangible benefits

TABLE 18.2[a].   SAVINGS ATTRIBUTABLE TO IMPROVED PRODUCTIVITY

Benefit	Savings
Faster receiving of incoming material with on-line order access and automated assistance in counting.	Labor cost
Automatic identification of hot back orders needing immediate access to incoming materials.	Labor cost Customer service
Faster storing of incoming material because storage locations are preassigned and employees do not have to search for an appropriate opening.	Labor cost Equipment costs
Reduced employee travel within the warehouse or stockroom because product is dynamically organized by demand.	Labor cost Equipment costs
Picks and stores can be interleaved.	Labor cost Equipment costs
'Forward' or 'fast-pick' zones supported.	Labor cost
Picking performed on multiple orders at once and in an efficient sequence.	Labor cost
Automated replenishment assures that pickers never run out of material.	Labor cost
Reduced paperwork, elimination of inventory bin cards, pick lists, etc.	Clerical cost
Automatically prepared reports including shipping paper, inventory status reports, scrap reports receipt and shipment logs, warehouse utilization reports, etc.	Clerical cost
Use of bar codes to eliminate or minimize handwriting, copying, and key entry.	Labor cost
Direct operation of automated equipment.	Labor cost
Avoidance of the need for automated equipment.	Equipment costs
More effective use of space, for instance, by managing openings sized for several different pallet heights and using the computer to assure that small pallets are not stored in large openings.	Space costs
Complete use of all existing openings through computer search and assignment.	Space costs Labor cost
Consolidation of like inventories.	Space costs
Identification of old and obsolete material for proper disposition.	Space costs Inventory losses
Enforcement of proper stack heights.	Space costs Inventory losses Safety
Ability to build truckloads and picking waves inside the computer system to minimize picker travel and maximize cube and axle loading utilization in the trailer.	Labor costs Transportation cost Shipping damage
Ability to substitute products in the event of a shortage.	Customer service

(Continued)

TABLE 18.2ª.   (CONTINUED)

Benefit	Savings
Automatic FIFO picking.	Inventory losses Customer service
Elimination of staging and sortation by picking and loading in the proper sequence.	Labor cost
Reduced safety stocks. When inventory is accurately known, safety stocks are needed only to cover variability in supply and need not allow for inventory surprises.	Inventory Space costs Inventory losses Labor cost
Reduced purchasing activity. Accurate inventory eliminates surprises and therefore the need for emergency purchase orders and change notices.	Management cost
More accurate customer promises because of more accurate inventory information.	Customer service
More accurate inventory records and more accurate customer promises reduces the need for premium rate shipments (both incoming and outgoing).	Transportation cost
Faster shipments and invoices.	Customer service Cash flow
More accurate shipments. Reduced returns, happier customers, and fewer losses.	Labor cost Inventory losses Customer service
More accurate bills of lading and invoices	Labor cost Customer service
Automatic task assignment and follow-up. Assurance that no task is forgotten or unduly delayed.	Labor cost Supervision cost
On-line productivity and error-rate reports.	Labor cost Supervision cost

ªAdapted from an unpublished document by Catalyst USA, Inc. Used with permission.

are so close to costs that intangibles must be considered. A few techniques exist that can simplify the consideration of intangible benefits and make them more palatable to senior management.

First, with the tangible and quantifiable benefits firmly established, best-case and worst-case limits can be set on what the intangible benefits might add, allowing a bottom-line range of predicted benefits to be considered. For instance, in a particular project if enforcing first-in, first-out stock rotation is expected to reduce customer returns, the amount and value of the reduction may be hard to estimate. Research, such as a brief customer survey or a sample inspection of returned items, might lead the analyst to believe that return rates will be reduced by 5 to 15 percent. If the cost of handling returns is known to be, say, $200,000 per year, most managers would accept a claimed benefit of $10,000 to $30,000 per year and few would demand that it be pinned down to a single number.

Or, in some circumstances intangible benefits can be aggregated to reduce perceived risk. Suppose past experience indicated that picking and shipping errors have also been a cause of customer returns. If the proposed system is expected to reduce the incidence of this problem, the analyst might claim a $30,000 per year benefit for stock rotation and use the incorrect-item benefit as reinforcement. In effect, the analyst would be saying that enforcement of rotation is worth $30,000 per year in reduced returns but, if that estimate doesn't come completely true, the reduction in incorrect shipments, which has not otherwise been claimed as a benefit, will make up the difference.

Third, a sensitivity analysis can be conducted using best-guess values for the intangibles. Suppose the inventory system costs $900,000 and will produce $800,000 in tangible benefits and $200,000 in intangibles. A sensitivity analysis would then note that the decision to commit funds to the project will be the wrong decision only if the estimate of intangible benefits is wrong by $100,000, or 50 percent.

Or, a break-even analysis can determine the value that must be attributed to intangible benefits for a project to be viable. Break-even analysis differs from sensitivity analysis mostly in the way the information is presented. In the same example, a break-even analysis would list the intangibles and note that if they are valued at $100,000 or more, the project should be undertaken. The break-even point, then, is $100,000. The list of intangibles can be given tentative values by the analyst, or some might be valued and others listed without values. When intangible benefits are listed without values, each manager is free to assign his or her own values to them.

Finally, intangible benefits can be recognized for their contributions to the realization of tangible benefits, with or without assigning actual values to them. Reduced customer returns, for instance, might be only one of the reasons why stock rotation would contribute to reduced cost. Another reason might be reduced need for quality inspection, a very tangible benefit in some businesses. If incoming inspection costs are known to be $400,000 per year and if a more efficient inventory system will reduce those costs by $80,000, it might be pointed out that the intangible benefit of reduced returns will contribute further to the productivity of the inspection department.

All of these techniques work best when benefits can be quantified, even if they cannot be valued in dollars. The truly intangible benefits—those that cannot be quantified in any way—should be mentioned in the benefits analysis but should not be given major emphasis unless decision makers are known to value them highly.

MAKE OR BUY

Comparing vendor proposals with in-house development is not just a matter of dollars. Businesses buy inventory systems rather than writing them for a variety of reasons. Systems vendors usually have a larger staff dedicated to the specialized area of inventory control. Within that area, their experience is both broader and deeper than an internal staff is likely to have. The result can be faster delivery, better quality, fewer bugs, and better support. The vendor, having done dozens of similar systems, can contribute valuable ideas and concepts to a design effort. When the resulting software is at least partly taken from "the shelf," costs can be significantly lower. And, with a proper payment schedule built into the contract, the buying organization can wield the "club" of nonpayment should things go wrong. This club is often more powerful than any that can be used on internal developers.

On the other hand, there are also reasons why development should be done internally. An internal "vendor" will not go out of business, leaving behind software that cannot be supported. Internal development also gives the business more control over the quality of the work done and the timing of its completion. It allows more flexibility for last-minute changes. And, internal development is usually done at lower hourly rates because no profit margin is involved.

Writing a Request for Proposal

The objective of a request for proposal is to obtain a price and delivery schedule from several potential system suppliers. This goal requires communication of the system specification to bidders. Because ground rules for bidding are rarely the same from one company to the next, it also requires supplementary information about the bidding process.

A request for proposal (RFP) for an inventory control system should be structured in six sections: introduction, business background, system specification, information requirements, bidding requirements, and statistical information. A table of contents and tabs at the major section headings will help vendors understand the requirements completely and quickly.

The request for proposal introduction should indicate the purpose of the request for proposal and the conditions under which it has been issued to prospective vendors. Some of the topics that should be covered are listed below.

- An invitation to vendors to submit proposals and an assurance that proposals will be held in confidence and not shared with competitors.
- A request that the vendor acknowledge receipt of the RFP and indicate within a few days whether or not it will propose.
- A statement that the issuer assumes no obligations by issuing the RFP or receiving a vendor's response.
- A statement reserving the right to accept or reject any or all responses.
- A statement that any costs incurred by the vendor in the preparation of a proposal will be borne solely by the vendor.
- A requirement that vendors take specific exception to requirements that they are unwilling or unable to accept.
- The date by which the vendor's proposal must be received. For com-

plex inventory systems, this date should be at least three weeks from the mailing date of the RFP.

- A definition of whether a fixed-price, an estimated price, or a time-and-materials price is desired. Unless the functional design has been exceptionally well done, many vendors will object to quoting a fixed price and will prefer to quote only a design project in preparation for setting a fixed price for the job.

The business background section should briefly describe the company's current business and its plans for the future at a strategic level. This description places the inventory system specification in context and helps prospective vendors understand it more quickly and more thoroughly.

The system specification must carefully explain each technical issue in sufficient detail to ensure the vendor's understanding. The explanation should cover both specifications and expected results. Great care should be taken to avoid overspecification because the result will almost certainly be a corresponding increase in the vendors' quotations. Essential and desirable requirements should be stated separately. Technical descriptions should carefully avoid (or clearly define) terminology unique to the issuer's business.

The system specification section should be divided into subsections addressing the topics listed below.

- Existing hardware and software environment.
- Desired hardware and software environment including a list of terminals, printers, and other peripherals specifying where each item is to be placed and what function it will fulfill. The volumes to be handled by each peripheral should be specified, if known.
- A description of the desired system functions. This subsection usually consists of a copy of the completed functional design document. It is often the longest and most complex part of the RFP.
- Operational considerations including staff availability and daily operational schedules.
- Backup and recovery requirements.
- System benchmarks and acceptance test criteria and procedures. Proposals should specify what happens if the system does not meet a mutually agreeable acceptance test.
- Software and hardware communications capabilities and other interfacing requirements.
- Desired maintenance and enhancement responsibilities and procedures.
- Training requirements.
- Product reliability measurements and goals.
- Required adherence to industry standards.
- Site specifications such as air conditioning, electrical power, signal wiring, and cables.

The information requirements section of the request for proposal should contain a list of special points and questions that vendors should answer in their proposal. Some suggestions for this list appear below.

- Brief historical and financial information about the vendor's businesses including bank and trade references.
- A list of customer references including an indication of which references will be available for future telephone contact or an on-site tour. The RFP should recognize that many vendors prefer to withhold references until the bidding process is complete to avoid overusing them.
- A statement of the warranties offered.
- An implementation schedule showing significant milestones.
- A description of the vendor's project management techniques.
- A statement of the work that the vendor will subcontract.
- Leasing options, if desired.
- Options for emergency substitute equipment and/or system fault-tolerance.
- Copies of the vendor's standard contract form.
- Specification of the amount and type of training included in the proposal.
- The vendor's assumptions concerning taxes, transportation charges, and employee's travel expenses.
- A statement of the proprietary rights to the software subsequent to purchase. Most vendors do not sell software but only license it, retaining resale rights themselves. In most instances, this is acceptable but additional fees may be involved if the system is to be installed at or moved to another site.
- The availability of source code, either to allow the purchaser to upgrade and maintain the system itself or in an escrow account or lockbox arrangement to provide protection in the event that the vendor should become unable or unwilling to support it.
- A statement of the vendor's ability to offer ongoing support, maintenance, and modification services. Vendors should describe the size of their support organizations, response times, preventive maintenance requirements, and the availability of upgrades written for other customers.
- Résumés of senior members of the development team. The RFP could require that the vendor agree contractually not to reassign key individuals to other projects during the life of the development effort.
- A list of customer-furnished equipment required to complete the project.
- Information about hardware and software expansion paths and the related costs.
- A description of the vendor's documentation standards and a sample of existing documentation.

The bidding requirements section should tell the vendors what ground rules will be in force. Explicit ground rules make it much easier to treat bidders fairly.

In addition, this section helps assure that proposals will be as easy as possible to compare to one another and offers some degree of protection to the requesting company. The bidding requirements section should cover the topics listed below.

- An outline of the company's acquisition procedure to familiarize vendors with the steps involved. This description should include a list of the major criteria that will be used to select a vendor. The list need not be detailed or definitive but should inform vendors about the relative importance of, for instance, price, delivery, reliability, maintainability, and other factors.
- The expected format and organization of the proposal. If many bids are to be received, the evaluation process is made easier if the bids are similarly organized. In particular, it is often smart to require that one-time, recurring, and optional costs be listed in a standard form.
- To whom the proposal should be delivered and the date on which it is due.
- The minimum acceptable period through which proposals must remain valid; 60 to 90 days is usual and acceptable to most vendors.
- The procedure for handling vendor's questions should be described. Most RFPs name a person as the vendor's contact; some name separate people for technical and bidding questions. Other RFPs call a bidder's conference and ask that the bidders attend. Bidder's conferences have many pros and cons. Most vendors dislike them but find that they are an effective way of answering questions, particularly when the RFP does not do a good job of describing the application.
- Whether the required equipment must be new or can be used. Significant savings can sometimes be had by accepting used, but guaranteed, equipment.

The final section of the request for proposal lists statistics that communicate to vendors the size of the business and the level of activity that must be supported by the system. Information that can and should be included follows.

- Company name and address
- Parent corporation name
- Location of the inventory facility
- Expected system delivery date
- Desired system acceptance date
- Contact person name and phone number
- Start and stop time for each shift
- Number of employees by function and shift
- Size of the inventory facility in square feet
- Maximum storage height of the inventory facility in feet
- Current and maximum future number of item numbers in inventory
- Current and maximum future number of storage locations broken down by function (reserve or forward picking) and device type
- Current and maximum future quantity of material handling devices in use broken down by type

- Current average and maximum future number of receipts and returns (in trailers or deliveries) per day and per month, broken down by shift
- Current average and maximum future number of line items, item numbers, full pallets, and loose cartons per receipt
- Current average and maximum future number of outbound orders per shift, day, and month
- Current average and maximum future number of line items, item numbers, full pallets, loose cartons, and loose pieces per outbound order
- Current average and maximum future number of picking waves built per shift, day, and month, broken down by order selection method (i.e., by delivery route, carrier, ship date, etc.)
- Current average and maximum future number of picks per shift, day and month, broken down by picking method (batch pick, zone forward pick, carousel pick, etc.)
- Current average and maximum future number of orders, lines, and pieces shipped per shift, day, and month, broken down by shipment method (company-owned trailer, common carrier trailer, contract carrier trailer, rail, UPS, air freight, etc.)
- Types of containers used (i.e., pallets, totes, cartons, etc.) in receiving, storage, and shipping, for each, the relative frequency of use
- For each specified report, projected average and future maximum volumes in lines or pages per shift, day, and month
- For each specified label, projected average and future maximum volumes per shift, day, and month
- For all automated material handling devices (such as carousels, automated guided vehicles, etc.), projected average and future maximum number of transactions per shift, day, and month
- For each radio-controlled function, projected average and future maximum number of transactions per terminal per hour

The topic lists presented here are not exhaustive. Request for proposal issuers should review their situation in detail to assure that important topics have not been omitted. The more information given to bidders, the more accurate the resulting bids will be. Issuers should also consult legal counsel to assure that no necessary provisions or qualifications have been forgotten.

Evaluating Proposals

The evaluation of vendor proposals necessarily begins with an attempt to compare and rank them based on price and delivery dates. One frequent problem, especially with complex inventory systems, is that different proposals will make different assumptions and offer different features and functions. The first step is to read the proposals carefully and list the areas where they differ. Contact the vendors, where necessary, to make sure that each proposal is fully understood. The vendor's assumptions, promises, guarantees, and conditions of sale are important.

For each proposal, evaluate the cost and feasibility of using internal program development to replace functions that were excluded. If necessary, determine the viability of the system without the exclusions. Consider, also, the value of features and functions that are provided beyond the functional specification. All costs and benefits must be identified before comparisons can be made among proposals and between the vendor proposals and the cost of internal development.

In discussions with vendors, give emphasis to subjects that may eliminate a vendor from consideration. For example, most inventory systems require an interface with existing customer order entry, manufacturing and financial systems. If a vendor's products are constructed so that the existing systems will require extensive rework to accomplish the interface and if personnel are not available to make the required changes in the required time, the proposal can be considered unworkable. The vendor should be informed and asked if alternatives can be made available.

Next, look at the vendor's proposed delivery schedule. Has the vendor promised to meet the dates given? What conditions have been placed on the vendor's promises? Are they reasonable? Does the vendor appear able to meet the schedule? Is the schedule requested in the RPF really necessary?

Then call (or even visit) the references provided by each remaining vendor. The reference checks will almost universally be complimentary, or the vendors would not have proposed them. Nevertheless, quite a bit can be learned by asking the right questions. Quality of product, quality of service, and promptness of delivery are the key issues.

Then ask to see each vendor's offices. Assess each company's size, professionalism, and ability to do what they say they will do. Meet the individuals proposed by the vendor as the project managers. Assess the professionalism and degree of experience of these people. The project will actually succeed or fail based on their abilities. Determine whether these people will be assigned to the project full time or part time and the number of people who will be working on the project under them.

The actual selection of a vendor is often best done in three steps. First, eliminate vendors who have not offered valid, workable solutions and those who appear unable to deliver on their promises. Then, assuming several are left, eliminate any that stand out as being significantly more expensive than the others. Finally, among the remaining vendors, select the one that has best demonstrated the ability to deliver a workable solution on the promised dates.

19

Delivery

The completion of the functional design and the cost-benefit analysis are almost always necessary precursors to a commitment to build or buy an inventory system. Once that commitment is made, much work remains to be done. The next step is the technical design of the system.

TECHNICAL DESIGN

There is a tendency to begin work on the technical design too early. The project team is likely to be eager to begin detailed planning, but major changes can occur during the review of the functional design, particularly as the costs for developing and operating the new system become apparent. If the technical people are too far ahead of the rest of the team, their efforts must be thrown out and other plans unnecessarily revised. In addition, the senior people who help prepare functional specifications are not necessarily the best ones to work out the detailed implementation plans. In fact, no work on the technical design should be done until the functional design has been approved and a management commitment has been made to the project.

Table 19.1 lists topics that should be included in most technical designs for inventory systems. Some of the items in this table are self-explanatory or are well covered elsewhere in the project management literature. Others require some additional comment in the special case of inventory systems.

Function

During the functional design some details may be overlooked. File purges, for example, are frequently not of concern to users and may not have been specified.

TABLE 19.1.   TOPICS TO INCLUDE IN A TECHNICAL DESIGN

Topic	Coverage
Function	Only where necessary; in playscript form
Auditability	Logging requirements, activity, and performance statistics
Security	Access control
Recovery plan	Methods for backup and restart from a software failure
Reports, labels, screens	Layouts, text, and messages where required; identify program that produces each; source of each data element
Input editing specifications	Data field, cross-checking, and completeness requirements
Response times	
Database design	Files, records, and fields; field sizes and precision
User interface design	
System architecture	Structure of programs required and methods of communication between programs
Program design	Program objectives, methods, division into tasks
Test plan	List of tests and acceptable results for each
Bar code specifications	Code used, internal standards to be met
Hardware specifications	Processor and peripherals; manufacturer, model, and quantity of each
Communication specifications	Cable specifications, protocols used, records passed, record layouts
Reliability	Methods for recovery from a hardware failure
Development schedule	Milestones and dates

Function should be detailed where necessary but should not be changed where the functional design provides adequate depth unless absolutely necessary.

Auditing

Auditing specifications should be determined. Every material movement should be recorded in a log file and the record retained for anywhere from 1 to 30 days, depending on the needs of the business. Log records should contain the type of transaction (i.e., pick, put-away, etc.), the name or number of the person who did the work, the date and time the work was done, and the item number and quantity of pieces involved. The log should also note when a terminal becomes active and should record security and privacy violations.

The need for system activity and performance monitoring should also be investigated. Control over response times and the identification of bottlenecks that lead to improved response times often depend on the ability of the system to report appropriate statistics.

Security

The inventory control system should, at a minimum, include a password-and-ID security system limiting access. Separate levels of access should be provided for hourly employees, supervision, plant management, system management, and quality control. A hard-coded "secret" ID that allows access to everything is useful for debugging and may be essential if the security file is lost and must be rebuilt.

Systems are best designed so that users have no visibility into the functions that they are not allowed to use. Menus, therefore, should not display options that the user cannot select.

If telecommunications via public lines are included in the system, further security concerns arise. If only occasional dial-up communications are involved, the best solution may be to simply leave the modems disconnected and require that an operator plug them in before use. If telecommunications use is more extensive, other measures may be required such as call-back modems or more extensive data encryption and decryption. There have been instances where outside agents have attempted to sabotage inventory control systems.

Output

Output includes reports, labels, and screens. Ideally, most output requirements are defined in the functional design. Any remaining work must be completed as part of the technical design. A sample copy of the required report is the best way to define these specifications. The programmer must then write code to generate identical output. Explanatory text may be necessary, but the picture tells most of the story. In addition to cleaning up work left over from the functional design, the technical design should identify the program that produces each output and the source of each element of data. Where appropriate, it should also specify calculation equations.

Input Editing

The technical design should specify the editing that will be applied to each element of data input including (1) value, range, and type checking, (2) cross-checking with information supplied previously, and (3) verification that input, once entered, contains all necessary information and is logically valid. The conditions under which programs verify the validity of input data should also be listed.

Response Times

Important response time requirements should be listed together with the reasons why each is significant. This includes both user-requested response times and those that are technically required.

Database Design

Database design includes the layout of all files, tables, and parameters that will be shared by two or more programs. The technical design must include a description of the logical database as it will appear to the project's application programmers and systems analysts. Records are best diagrammed on traditional forms showing data fields, types, lengths, and precisions. Field characteristics should be crosschecked with output designs for consistency.

User Interface

Systems that are intended for direct use by hourly personnel require design to more exacting standards than those that interface only with salaried workers. In particular, menus, prompts, defaults, and error messages must be crystal clear. Helps should be context-sensitive and should specify exactly what the user should do. Existing shop language should be used. If, for instance, material handlers call pallets "skids," the system should use that specific term.

Interfacing with a user through the small displays found on radio terminals and portable off-line bar code readers involves different techniques than those used with full-function CRT workstations. The specific techniques used will depend on display unit size and other features of the terminal such as function keys, cursor movement keys, and bar code scanner types. Although techniques may differ, the basic objectives of clarity and brevity remain important.

System Architecture

System architecture is the structure of programs required and methods of communication between programs. The technical design should list all of the programs that will be required, what function each will perform, and how they will communicate with each other.

Program Design

Individual programs must be designed within the context of the system architecture. Program designs should include both objectives and methods. More specifically, for each program the technical design should specify:

1. Required output, by reference to report formats and screen layouts, communications records, and protocols and by other means as necessary
2. Input by reference to data entry screens and other sources of data
3. Files and tables to be used
4. Programs that invoke this one and any programs or tasks that should be invoked by this one
5. Processing requirements including any necessary actions and calculations
6. Error detection methods and actions to be taken
7. Standard installation utility programs or subroutines to be used
8. Installation standards that specifically have been waived for this application
9. Requirements for unit testing
10. Memory or performance requirements, where applicable

This book assumes that existing programming standards will be used to guide the technical design. These standards should specify file, field, and program naming conventions, program and system documentation standards, methods for passing condition codes, language usage techniques, and other routine matters.

Test Plan

The test plan portion of the technical design should specify the list of tests that must be performed and the results that will be found acceptable. These criteria are used to determine whether the inventory system is ready to become operational. In total, they should comprise a revision of the criteria set forth in the functional specification.

The document can also set criteria for the abandonment of testing. While this subject is likely to be unpopular with team members, it can prevent tests from dragging on indefinitely while the project bugs are worked out. Tests can be resumed when the system is in better shape or when the user can better support the testing effort.

Bar Code Specifications

If user considerations have not resulted in specification of the bar code symbology to be used, the technical design should. In addition, relevant internal and industry standards should be examined and the technical design should specify which will be adhered to.

Hardware Specifications

Some hardware specifications may have been established in earlier phases. During the technical design, these specifications should be reviewed and any missing specifications should be supplied. The technical design should specify both the processor and peripherals including the manufacturer, the model number, and the quantity of each item required, including spares. Configurable items like the processor, should be spelled out in detail.

Operation of the inventory system on a dedicated distributed processor may be a good idea. A corporate host computer can run order entry, material requirements planning, financial systems, and other applications. Purchase orders, work orders, and customer orders can be passed to the inventory system for execution. Order completions and inventory adjustments can be passed back.

The idea of distributing the inventory system is valuable for three reasons. First, it isolates factory and warehouse operations from mainframe downtime (and vice versa). Second, it allows inventory system response times to be independent of host workloads. And third, it simplifies the inventory system and, in some ways enhances it, by "licensing" it to take over an entire machine without concern for other applications. However, distributed computing is achieved at some additional hardware cost, requires some additional support effort, and involves some potential loss of control for the data processing organization.

The specification of radio terminals should involve calculation of radio channel utilization. Because radio frequencies are shared by several terminals and because rapid response times will be important, most designs should call for channel utilization of 35 percent or less. Additional frequencies can be provided as necessary to meet this goal.

The specification of bar code equipment can also be tricky, particularly for first-time users. Analysts should not rely on industry standards or sales people's promises to assure that the selected printers will produce labels that can be read by the scanners. To the degree possible, test all unfamiliar equipment before making commitments and remember that many factors are involved in bar code readability including printer and scanner quality and compatibility, employee training, ambient lighting conditions, label stock, and printer ribbons.

Communication Specifications

Compared to some software, inventory systems tend to involve large numbers of remote devices. Portable off-line bar code readers tend to communicate infrequent bursts of information. Other devices, such as radio terminals, programmable controllers, and scales communicate more often, but individual transmissions tend to involve short messages. The resulting low communications line utilization factors may make these devices candidates for networking.

Multiplexers, line sharing devices, local area networks, and other sophisticated communications equipment can solve individual problems and reduce costs. However, communications and equipment interfaces may be the most difficult part of an inventory control system from the viewpoint of the programmer, particularly in view of the need to maintain acceptable response times. Analysts without significant expertise in communications should be wary. Communications line utilizations should be calculated for lines that carry time-sensitive information to assure that communications traffic does not significantly affect the responsiveness of the system.

The technical design should include the manufacturer, the model number, and the quantity of each piece of communications equipment required, including spares. It should also include a list of necessary cables with specifications for each, a description of the protocols used over each cable, and layouts for the records passed.

Reliability and Recovery

The ability to restart the system is critical. A power, processor, disk, or software failure at any point cannot be allowed to cause significant lost data. Fully or partially redundant hardware is also important, as is software designed for recoverability. Remember that the plant and warehouse will grind to a halt within minutes of a failure. However, the degree to which the inventory system needs to be failure-proof is a matter of judgment. Redundancy and reliability cost money.

The first and most important point of concern should be data loss. Databases must be backed up and provision must be made for the reconstruction of a database from the most recent backup and the log records that have accumulated since that backup was made. Disk drives and peripherals represent the second most important concern. Disk mirroring or shadowing is a software technique that copies all information to two physical disk drives, detects drive failures, and automatically switches the system to the surviving drive. With mirroring in place, users should be unaware that a failure has occurred.

Backup equipment should include one spare radio base station for each frequency in use. The spare units should be prewired so they can be brought on-line quickly and easily. Other peripherals, such as terminals, printers, and bar code scanners should be backed up with spare units so that a failure can be replaced in a matter of minutes. The computer itself should be powered through an uninterruptable power supply (a UPS) to protect against power failures. The provision of a generator is usually not necessary because the warehouse and shop will be unable to work during a power interruption, but if the computer can continue online for a few minutes after the power goes off, an orderly shut down can be accomplished, eliminating the possibility of data loss and database damage.

Development Schedule

The final step in the technical design is the creation of a detailed development schedule: a list of milestones and the dates on which each will be achieved. The milestones themselves will vary from situation to situation but should, at a minimum, include the dates on which work will start and end for programming and unit testing of the software, hardware purchasing and delivery, software integration tests, computer-to-computer communications tests, the writing of documentation, the training of users, preparation of the site, the physical installation of the hardware and software, the conversion of the database, and the start of productive use of the system.

PROGRAMMING AND TESTING

The programming of complex, real-time systems is an art that is markedly different from the art of programming efficient batch systems. Businesses with little or no experience in real-time systems should consider either the use of a consultant or the hiring of people with the required experience. Real-time operating systems and database management systems, which purport to handle all real time issues, may contribute substantially but are not likely to be an effective substitute for experience.

At a minimum, the software should be tested at three points during its development:

1. The individual programs should be separately tested after they have been completed.
2. Groups of programs, subsystems, and the entire system should be tested as the individual programs become available.

3. And the completed system should be fully tested after installation onto the actual hardware on which it will run.

These tests should be run by someone other than the people who wrote the programs. The tests should conform to a plan that was thought out prior to the start of programming. All functions in the system should be exercised at least once during the testing process. While the discovery of all errors will not be guaranteed, this method is a practical, effective way to systematically analyze the software and locate the great majority of the problems.

A conference-room pilot may be a good way for the users to take a final look at the system before committing to its use. This involves setting up the system in a single room—probably a conference room. At least one unit of each kind of peripheral should be included in the test. A test database is developed and selected users and managers are trained in the use of the system. These users are then presented with a test scenario and asked to simulate a day's worth of processing on the system. There are several advantages to the conference-room pilot:

1. Key users get a chance to learn the system and practice on it under nonthreatening, noncritical conditions. They also get the opportunity to perform hourly work that, under more normal circumstances, they would only observe.
2. The software receives a thorough test, operated by at least some of the people who will actually operate it in the real world. Additional bugs and, possibly, design flaws will be brought to light while there is still time to correct them in a measured and reasoned way.
3. The system supplier (whether internal or external) gets the opportunity to demonstrate that it has delivered the agreed-upon specification and can enter the implementation phase of the project with confidence that the system will meet the user's expectations.

DOCUMENTATION

Inventory system users differ significantly from the users of many other kinds of computer systems. They are typically nontechnical people who have little interest in the computer or what it can accomplish. Sometimes, depending on the labor environment in which a business operates, the users of an inventory control system will lack sympathy for the its goals or even be hostile to its implementation. Some may have poor educations and modest reading skills. Others may not even communicate well in English. These factors place special demands for clarity, accuracy, and conciseness on the documentation.

But documentation covers more than just users. As with most other major systems, inventory system documentation can be viewed as supporting three separate functions: system users, technical support personnel, and operations personnel. Each of these groups needs different information and has different ways of looking at the same system. Each, therefore, must be supported by different documentation.

This is not to say that there must be three physically separate manuals documenting an inventory system. The physical division of the documentation into manuals should, rather, be governed by the format in which the material is presented, the way in which it will be used, and security considerations. Program listings, for instance, may not fit into the same binder as narratives. Similarly, instructions for updating passwords should not be distributed to everyone. Physically, the documentation should be written as a series of subject modules that can be combined into manuals in whatever manner makes sense to the people who are going to use it. After the modules are combined into manuals, a "shell" consisting of a table of contents, an index, and other materials can be built to make the modules into a cohesive whole.

Documentation has two separate uses: as a reference work for the experienced and as a training tool for new people. One of the hallmarks of bad documentation is ignoring one or the other of these two types of use. In general, documentation should be targeted at the least experienced. However, writers must take care to assure that the experienced user can quickly and easily find the material needed. A thorough index is critical. A different typeface can be used to separate the more sophisticated features of a system from the basics, allowing first-time users to concentrate on their needs, while more experienced users can go directly to the material they want.

Documentation drafts should be developed during the final stages of the programming and testing phases. Writers should work closely with the system designers and programmers to assure that all relevant details have been covered. The completed draft should then be critiqued by the users as part of system training.

User Documentation

Because inventory systems deal with two distinct classes of users—the salaried and hourly workforces—user documentation should consist of two parts: a manual, and a set of procedures or methods. The purpose of the user manual should be to teach salaried personnel (including supervisors, managers, and clerical people) how to perform the functions of the inventory system. It should provide step-by-step narratives and include illustrations and examples in a clearly organized manner.

Some manuals include tutorials. If classroom training is provided by the developers, documentation tutorials are optional. If they are present, the tutorial should be conversational in tone, clearly stating the objectives of each section or exercise while highlighting the information that tells users what they need to know in order to perform the exercise. Frequent practice exercises should be interspersed at logical places, and examples should be used to illustrate important points.

In general, the manual should contain the following information:

1. An introduction that describes how to use it.

2. An overview of the system's purpose and how it fits into the general scheme of the business and other systems.

3. A simplified overview of the database, describing in nontechnical terms what data is stored and how it is arranged.

4. A detailed description of each function. The description should include all user options and all normal responses from the computer. The most common errors should be described together with actions that the user can take to resolve them. Less common errors can be relegated to an appendix. Examples, drawings, and tables should be used liberally.

5. An explanation of how certain data elements are calculated (e.g., replenishment quantities).

6. A detailed listing of all error messages describing possible causes and actions that the user can take to recover from each condition.

7. A compilation of other reference documents that may help the user answer questions that are not answered in the manual.

Documentation writers should consider including a quick reference card with the manual. The card should include references to the full descriptions contained elsewhere.

Quick reference cards can be particularly useful to material handlers since they spend most of their time moving about the facility and do not always have convenient access to the manuals. A special reference card for RF terminal users should be considered.

Hourly procedures typically differ from the user's manual in two ways. First, they are more focused on the job at hand and less concerned with the context of the business. Second, they are not limited to system functions but include all of the elements needed to accomplish a task. For instance, as written in the salaried manual, the description of the work required to put away newly received material would cover the interaction of the forklift driver with the system via his or her radio terminal and bar code scanner. The same description in the form of an hourly procedure would include instructions on how to select the lift truck to be used, safety instructions, and similar material. Because hourly procedures cover the total business system, they are generally not provided with purchased software but must be written by the system buyer using the functional design, the vendor's manual, and existing procedures as sources.

There is, of course, no reason why selected hourly personnel should not be given a copy of the salaried worker's manual nor is there a reason why procedure distribution should be limited to the hourly workforce. Documentation writers, however, should be sensitive to differences in the needs of these two groups.

Technical Support Documentation

The structure and content of technical support documentation will vary with the structure of the system and with the tools and techniques used to create it. At least four elements, however, are critical and should not be eliminated without good reason.

First, the functional and technical design documents, the installation plan, test plans and results, and copies of all training materials should be retained and updated as the system changes and evolves. Second, all hardware documentation should be retained in a library along with the documentation provided with all software tools used in the writing of the system. Third, a technical system manual should be created to record the details of the construction of the system and to provide the technical staff with solutions to problems likely to be encountered. And fourth, program listings must, of course, be retained. It is a fact that listings and file and record layouts are the only items of documentation that maintenance programmers really use. Herein lies the reason why structured programming and complete commenting are so important. Although flowcharts are effective in theory, they have a poor performance record, are only rarely used, and therefore are only rarely updated when systems change.

Operations Documentation

Operations documentation for inventory systems differs little from that which should be maintained for other systems. It should include:

1. Instructions for starting up and shutting down the inventory system together with a schedule defining when the system should be started and when it should be shut down.
2. Backup requirements and a description of backup and restore methods.
3. A list of program messages including the text of the message, a statement of the problem, and instructions on how to correct the condition.
4. To the extent the system is designed to accommodate it, a description of the configurability of the system, telling the operator how to manage the system's storage and how to reassign terminals and printers as necessary.

TRAINING

Inventory system training should be provided for shop and warehouse supervision and management. Each supervisor should then be responsible for training the hourly and clerical people, with project personnel present in the supervisor-run training sessions to assist with technical questions. This procedure is generally preferred for two reasons. First, supervisors are motivated to learn the system thoroughly and accurately when they know they will be required to pass their knowledge along to their employees. And second, the supervisors can tune the training to meet the exact needs of the hourly and clerical employees.

When systems include bar coding and particularly when bar codes are being introduced into a business for the first time, training should include at least one segment on bar coding. In addition to explaining what bar codes are and why they are valuable, the instructor should demonstrate the use of the readers and each student should be given a hands-on opportunity to practice scanning a bar code. Wand readers, in particular, require a modest amount of manual skill on the part of the user; the wand must be held at an appropriate angle, started in the right place, and moved at a reasonably consistent speed past the end of the bar code. While the skill is not hard to learn, practice in the training room will make implementation day that much easier.

In addition to user training, project personnel and/or the software vendor should, of course, be responsible for training operations and support personnel. Operations training should include a thorough review of the daily procedures required plus a "tour" of the documentation so they will be able to locate reference materials easily and quickly when necessary.

If implementation plans allow, training is best done on-site in the inventory facility after physical installation of the system's hardware and software. Classroom work is, of course, a necessary part of the training. But, hands-on training conducted in the warehouse lends realism to the entire proceeding and brings home the lessons with much-improved retention. A special database should be designed and created specifically for use in these hands-on sessions. It can be replaced with the real database after the classes are over.

INSTALLATION AND SUPPORT

The installation plan should be created along with the system's technical design. Elements of it may even be considered during the functional design. A list of topics for an inventory system installation plan appears in Table 19.2. The plan should, of course, define what will be done under each topic, who will do the work, and when the work will be completed.

Phased Installation

The inventory system project manager should look for ways to subdivide the system and should pursue the idea of a phased implementation. While it can be difficult to phase the implementation of a tightly integrated inventory system, the reduction in risk associated with phasing makes the idea worth investigating.

Generally it is not possible to phase in inventory system installations on a product line basis because the inventory control system must have up-to-date knowledge of the complete contents of all storage locations. However, phasing may be possible in other ways:

1. If material is stored in several stockrooms, it may be reasonable to implement one stockroom at a time. The raw materials and purchased parts stockroom might be first, for instance, together with the receiving department and incoming inspection operations. Next,

TABLE 19.2.   TOPICS TO INCLUDE IN AN INSTALLATION PLAN

Topic	Coverage
Installation plan	Milestones and dates; phasing
Site plan	Hardware locations, cable requirements
Conversion of files	Download or special conversion program
New file loading	Who, how, when
Physical inventory	If necessary
Hardware installation	Who, where, when
Software installation	Who, how, when
Cables	Specifications, routing, and methods
Telephone lines	Specifications and schedules
Site preparation	Requirements and schedules
Training plan	Why, where, what, when
Workload management	Make first day a light one
Contingency plans	For system failure; criteria for activating them
Short-term support	Who, when
Long-term support plan	How, who

the work-in-process stockroom and the factory floor might come under control, with the finished goods stockroom and the shipping department being the final phase.

2. Or, depending on the flexibility of the inventory recordkeeping methods being replaced, it may be possible for the new system to manage stockroom receipts and the put-away function only, passing inventory transactions to the old system and allowing it to continue to manage picking, delivery to the factory, and shipment to the customers. An interim way of relieving inventory as stock is picked will, of course, be required.

3. Or, based on the layout of the plant, the materials handled, and the existing systems, there may be other ways in which the inventory control system can be segmented to allow a phased implementation.

The primary disadvantage of a phased implementation is, of course, project cost. Special, temporary-use software will be required. The project will take longer to complete, and more hours of work will be required. In addition, some benefits of the system will not be received as soon as they would be if it were implemented at once. The project manager and the project team must weigh the risks and costs and select the best course for the business.

Site Plan

The site plan determines where each piece of system hardware will be located upon delivery. It also identifies requirements for power, air conditioning, data communications and telephone lines, and the cables that will run between the computer and the peripherals. And, finally, the site plan identifies who will be responsible for preparation of the site and when each element of work will be done.

Most distributed inventory system processors are best located in the factory or warehouse rather than in a separate facility. On-site location of the computer minimizes communications costs and business exposure when communications lines go down. It also tends to make system operations more responsive to the needs of the users.

Database Creation

The creation of a starting database for a new inventory system usually involves three steps. First, existing files must be converted to the new format, either through a download from a host computer or through special file conversion programs. Often distributed inventory systems are designed to accept host-based and transmitted maintenance of several key files, usually including the item, vendor, and customer master files. When this is the case, file conversion is simple.

Second, there will be files and tables in the inventory system that contain data that is currently unavailable in previously existing systems. These files and tables must be manually loaded. Control tables, in particular, demand close attention. The information to be put into them should be reviewed by the project team to assure its consistency with the intent of the software.

Finally, the item/location file—the actual inventory file—must be considered. If the previous inventory system contains location-by-location records, a file conversion program can load the new system's files. If not, however, it may be necessary to schedule a physical inventory as part of the start-up process. Physical inventories are major undertakings (see Chapter 12) and demand a great deal of planning. They can significantly complicate the start-up of the new inventory system.

Installation planners and users should remember that the benefits of an inventory system may not appear immediately if the system is started up with old, inaccurate records. It will take the new system a period of time to work out the erroneous inventories and replace them with accurate data.

The ideal situation occurs when a new system is started in a new warehouse or stockroom. Materials can simply be received and stored under the new system as they are moved in from the old warehouse. No initial physical inventory is required. And high levels of accuracy can be achieved from the start. The money saved can be large enough to justify delaying either the system introduction or the move into the new warehouse if they cannot be completed simultaneously.

Workload Management

To the extent possible, the first day of use of the new inventory control system should be a light day. It should involve the minimum possible amount of material handling, possibly even deferring the introduction of some functions to the second day. There are at least two ways of doing this:

1. If ordering and scheduling systems permit, a day can be scheduled

on which the plant concentrates on relatively large jobs with a small component of material handling. The receiving department can be closed, or at least noncritical receipts can be rescheduled to another day. It may also be possible to defer the picking and shipment of selected customer orders. And some material can be preissued to the shop.

2. Or, if necessary, a Saturday can be selected for start-up using only a skeleton workforce. If the day can be used to get a head start on Monday's work, two light days result. While overtime operations are expensive, the opportunity for users to learn and work at the same time, together with the opportunity for the project team to correct problems while the system is running at less than full capacity may well justify the cost. The difference could be one of success versus failure in the implementation.

Despite all the work done and all the effort put in, the installation plan should include contingency plans for returning to the old inventory system with a minimum loss of efficiency if all else fails.

Short-Term Support

The project team and/or the system vendor should plan on providing personnel to work in the factory and the warehouse for at least a week after implementation of the inventory system. The people doing this work should be charged with responsibility for responding to user questions, in effect continuing the training with additional on-the-job learning. They should also be charged with the identification and investigation of the problems that are almost certain to arise.

Project personnel should be present on all shifts in which the factory or warehouse is working, should be knowledgeable in the use of the system, and should have the investigative skills required to run problems to ground. System designers, trainers, and systems analysts are all candidates for this temporary duty. Those not actively working should be on call, including all of the programmers who contributed to the system.

Long-Term Support Plan

And, finally, the installation plan should include a plan for long-term support of the inventory system. This plan should identify how support will be provided, who will make emergency fixes, and how needed improvements will be logged, estimated, authorized, and accomplished. In addition, the long-term support plan should describe how vendor support services will be used and how the quality of their support will be judged so that future support purchases can be wisely made.

Appendix I

Bar Code Standards Organizations

Adherence to bar code standards can be important for three reasons. First, whenever bar codes are received from vendors, the possibility exists that they can be used to eliminate data entry in receiving. Second, if internally printed bar codes meet industry standards, it may be possible to satisfy customer demands for bar coding on shipments without additional cost. And third, to the extent that standard bar codes are used, the likelihood is increased that purchased software and hardware will work without modification.

Some of the organizations that maintain and distribute general-use standards are:

American National Standards Institute (ANSI)
1430 Broadway
New York, NY 10018
212-354-3300

Computer Identics Corp.
5 Shawmut Rd.
Canton, MA 02021
617-821-0830

Federation of Automated Coding Technologies (FACT)
1326 Freeport Rd.
Pittsburg, PA 15238
412-963-8588

Industry Bar Code Alliance
24 Far View Rd.
Chalfont, PA 18914
215-822-6880

Intermec
4405 Russell Road
Lynnwood, WA 98036
206-348-2600

Material Handling Institute
Automatic Identification Manufacturer's Product Section
1326 Freeport Rd.
Pittsburgh, PA 15238
412-963-8588

Uniform Code Council, Inc.
7051 Corporate Way, Suite 201
Dayton, Ohio 45459
513-435-3870

In addition, there are literally hundreds of industry associations, many of which are involved in bar code standards specific to the needs of their members. The list below is only a sampling. Some of these organizations have published standards; others are working on them. Businesses in industries not listed here can probably locate one or more associations for their specific industry in the *Encyclopedia of Associations;*[1] a copy should be available in most libraries.

Aluminum Association, Inc.
900 19th St. NW
Suite 300
Washington, DC 20006
202-862-5116

American Paper Institute
160 Madison Ave.
New York, NY 10016
212-340-0660

Automotive Industry Action Group (AIAG)
26200 Lahser Rd.
Suite 200
Southfield, MI 48034
313-569-6262

Association of Home Appliance Manufacturers
20 N. Wacker Dr.
Chicago, IL 60606
312-984-5800

Book Industry Study Group, Inc.
160 Fifth Ave.
Suite 604
New York, NY 10010
212-929-1393

Chemical Manufacturer's Association
2501 M St. NW
Washington, DC 20037
202-887-1100

Department of Defense
DARCOM Packaging, Storage and
Containerization Center
Attention: SDSTO-TP
Tobyhanna Army Depot
Tobyhanna, PA 18466
717-894-7146

Electronic Industries Association
2001 I St. NW
Washington, DC 20006
202-457-4900

---

[1]Gruber, Katherine, Ed., *Encyclopedia of Associations,* New York: Gale Research Company, published annually.

The Fiber Box Association
Distribution Symbol Study Group
5725 East River Road
Chicago, IL 60631
312-693-9600

Health Industry Business
Communication Council
5110 N. 40 St.
Suite 120
Phoenix, AZ 85018
602-381-1091

National Electrical Manufacturer's
Association
2101 L St. NW
Suite 300
Washington, DC 20037
202-457-8400

National Office Products Association
301 N. Fairfax St.
Alexandria, VA 22314
703-549-9040

North American Heating &
Airconditioning Wholesaler's
Association
1389 Dublin Rd.
Columbus, OH 43216
614-488-1835

Software Publishers Association
1111 19th St. NW
Suite 1200
Washington, DC 20036
202-452-1600

Grocery Manufacturers of America,
Inc.
1010 Wisconsin Ave., NW
Suite 800
Washington, DC 20007
202-337-9400

National Association of Music
Merchants
5140 Avenida Encinas
Carlsbad, CA 92008
619-438-8001

National Forest Products Association
1250 Connecticut Ave. NW
Washington, DC 20036
202-463-2700

National Wholesale Druggists'
Association
105 Oronoco St.
Alexandria, VA 22313
703-684-6400

Power Transmission Distributor's
Association
100 Higgins Rd.
Park Ridge, IL 60068
312-825-2000

Tile Council of America
Box 326
Princeton, NJ 08542
609-921-7050

Appendix II

Glossary

It seems that terminology is always a problem. Specialized technologies and disciplines need specialized terminologies to allow communication to occur rapidly and accurately. Medicine, law, and the computer industry are good examples. Therefore, when a new subject is to be learned, terminology should be a consideration. This glossary explains the terms used in this book. It is presented to promote understanding of the meanings behind the words more than for the sake of any particular rigor.

ABC Classification. Classification of the items in decreasing order of annual dollar volume or other criteria. This array is then normally split into three classes, called A, B, and C. Class A contains the items with the highest annual dollar volume and receives the most attention. The next grouping, Class B, receives less attention, and Class C, which contains the low-dollar volume items, is controlled routinely. The ABC principle is, that effort saved through relaxed controls on low-value items will be applied to improve control of high value items. The ABC principle is applicable to inventories, purchasing, sales, etc.[1]

Accuracy. The percent of locations in a facility for which the computer's inventory record exactly agrees with the kind and quantity of material stored in that location.

Adjustment. To the on-hand balance. Accounting conventions usually dictate that adjustments are added to the on-hand balance. When it is necessary to reduce the on-hand balance, a negative adjustment is added.

AGV. See Automated guided vehicle.

AIAG. See Automotive Industry Action Group.

Aisle. In an inventory facility, the space between storage devices that is used by material

---

[1] Reprinted with permission, the American Production and Inventory Control Society, Inc., *Dictionary,* 6th ed., 1987, p. 1.

handlers for access. Aisles are sometimes numbered in place of row numbers, with the aisle number being part of the location number.

Allocation. The reservation of material for a specific use, usually an out-bound order. Material is usually allocated or reserved in a specific location. Note: the word "reservation," itself has a slightly different meaning.

Analog to digital converter. A circuit board that reads electrical signals (voltages or current flows generated by a machine), converts the signals into digital values, and places the digital values in memory for access by the processor.

Anker code. A variation on the Plessy code.

Annual physical inventory. See Physical inventory.

Anticipated receipt. A record of material expected to be received into inventory in the future. Anticipated receipts are often purchase orders but can also include manufacturing orders, transfer orders, and customer return authorizations. Information contained on the record usually includes vendor or source name and number, purchase order number, date, product number, quantity, and expected arrival date.

Architecture. For a computer system, the structure of programs required and methods of communication between programs.

Area. A major subdivision of an inventory facility, usually consisting of numerous aisles. The areas are generally numbered (or lettered) and the number is usually made part of the location number.

ASCII. A method of binary encoding for alphabetic and numeric characters. The ASCII code is used by almost all computers except for some large IBM models and certain plug-compatibles. ASCII computers cannot communicate with EBCDIC computers without a character translator.

AS/RS. See Automated storage and retrieval.

Assembly. (1) The process of combining component parts to create a new part or item, usually with a new item number. (2) In the context of inventory facilities, the process of bringing together the components of an order prior to shipment.

Assembly schedule. A plan for the assembly of product. It defines the products that will be made and the quantity of each to be made in each time period.

Asterisk (*). In Code 39, the start-stop character. This character is displayed as an asterisk by convention.

Audit trail. A computer file that contains a record of every transaction processed by the system or of every record of a specified type. Audit trails are used primarily as problem-solving tools since they can explain why a database field has a certain value. Audit trails are also known as history files.

Auditing. The business function of verifying that procedures and practices are being properly followed. Auditing usually involves random and preplanned checks over a period of time. Audits often, but not always, concern financial matters.

Autodiscriminate. The ability of a bar code reading system to attempt to decode a symbol using the rules of more than one symbology. In effect, the ability to scan multiple symbologies and determine which one is being used.

Automated guided vehicle. A horizontal transportation system using individual vehicles that follow a previously installed guide path. Many of these vehicles are capable of loading and unloading themselves and can communicate with a host computer to determine destinations. Some are capable of vertical movement.

Automated storage and retrieval system. A device that automatically moves product between storage locations and a workstation at the end of the aisle, completely eliminating travel time.

Automatic identification. Any of a group of technologies that allow a computer to identify products, locations, people, or equipment presented to it. Automatic identification technologies include bar coding, optical character recognition (OCR), radio frequency identification (RFID), and others.

Automation. The application of computer-based systems and/or intelligent devices to improve productivity and accuracy. (cf Mechanization.)

Automotive Industry Action Group (AIAG). An organization originally formed by members of the automotive industry for the purpose of establishing bar code labeling standards for use between businesses. AIAG standard labels are now used in many manufacturing businesses.

Availability. The difference between the quantity of a product that is on hand and not subject to a hold and the quantity of that product that has been allocated to orders.

Background. A program or task that is executed by an on-line computer system that takes advantage of the fact that the computer is far faster than its peripheral devices. The background program is run using time such as that between a user's keystrokes or while waiting for a disk drive to respond.

Back order. An order with a past-due shipment date.

Bar. In a bar code, a dark area.

Bar code. A series of light and dark printed bars. The pattern of the bars is preestablished to represent alphabetic and numeric characters in any of a number of standard schemes. When a light pen or a laser beam is run across the bars at a constant velocity, light is reflected from the bars and spaces in a series of pulses that can be electronically detected and converted into the appropriate characters for use by a computer.

Bar height. The height of the bars in a bar code, assuming picket-fence orientation.

Bar ratio. The ratio of the width of wide to narrow bars and spaces in a bar code.

Batch. (1) Batch inventory system. A system in which material handlers manually record receipts and shipments for central processing at another time. (2) A group of tasks to be performed or, sometimes, a group of orders to be picked and shipped. In this case, synonymous with wave.

Batch pick. A group of pick transactions to be performed by a single order filler that cover several customer orders. The batch is picked by the order filler in a single pass through the picking area.

Beginning balance. The on-hand balance at the beginning of a time period. Usually established when a physical inventory is taken.

Bidirectionality. The ability of a bar code symbology to be scanned in either direction.

Bill of lading. A document that accompanies a shipment. The bill of lading covers the pieces shipped to a single destination. It summarizes the piece count and weight by freight class and lists both the shipper's and consignee's name and address.

Bill of material. A listing of all the subassemblies, intermediates, parts, and raw materials that go into a parent assembly showing the quantity of each required to make an assembly. There are a variety of display formats of bills-of-material, including single level bills of material, indented bills of material, modular (planning) bills of material, transient bills of material, matrix bills of material, costed bills of material, etc. May also be called "formula," "recipe," or "ingredients list" in certain industries.[2]

Bin. A storage device designed to hold small, discrete parts. A shelving unit with physical dividers separating the storage locations.

Blind count. An inventory count performed by a person who does not know in advance what the result should be.

Break-even analysis. A financial analysis technique in which uncertain variables can be tested to determine the value that they must assume to make the final decision a toss-up.

Broken case. A carton of product that has been opened. By association, product in less-than-carton quantities.

Cantilever rack. Rack designed for the storage of pipe and other long slender products. Pallets are not used.

Carousel. A device that automatically moves an entire row of storage past an operator, stopping at key points to allow picking and put-away. The row is generally arranged in a circle, hence the name. Carousels can move either vertically or horizontally.

Cart. A horizontal transportation device pushed by a material handler. Carts may or may not have shelves on them.

Carton. A material container, often of corrugated cardboard. Cartons are sometimes designed for specific items and contain a preestablished quantity.

Carrier. The trucking line, parcel delivery service, airline, or railroad responsible for delivering incoming material to the plant or for delivering shipments to other plants, warehouses, or customers. As used here, the term includes company-owned trucks.

Cash flow analysis. A financial analysis of a series of receipts and disbursements that determines the net amount of funding required over time.

Cauzin strip. A two-dimensional bar-code-like printing technology that encodes bits in pairs of black and white boxes. The Cauzin strip is capable of information densities between 150 and 1000 characters per square inch but requires that the symbol be removed and placed in a scanner to be read.

CCD scanner. See charge-coupled diode scanner.

Charge-coupled diode scanner. An optical bar code scanner that records an image of the bar code in pixel form and analyzes the image to decode the code.

---

[2]Reprinted with permission, the American Production and Inventory Control Society, Inc., *Dictionary*, 6th ed., 1987, p. 3.

Check character (check digit). A character included in a data transmission or bar code symbol to enable the detection of errors. The check character is determined by the system that originates the transmission or prints the symbol based on the characters that are to be checked. Often the determination is done with a mathematical equation or logical algorithm. The receiving (or scanning) system uses the same equation or algorithm to recalculate the check character and then compares the one received with the one calculated to verify correctness of the message.

Checker. An individual responsible for verifying the quality (and sometimes the quantity) of the work done by others.

Check-in. The process of receiving a tool or other loaned or leased item from the person to whom it was loaned or leased. Part of the process involves removing the data link between the item and the person who had it.

Check-out. The process of delivering a tool or other loaned or leased item to a person with the expectation that it will be returned and, if the return does not occur, with the responsibility to take action in some form. Part of the process involves establishing a data link between the item and the person who has it.

Clerk. An individual responsible for recordkeeping and data entry. Clerical functions vary widely from business to business; the definition is imprecise. In some businesses clerks also act as dispatchers (cf).

Codabar. A symbology originally designed to accommodate the inaccuracies inherent in early printers. Each character consists of four bars and three spaces; a single narrow space separates characters.

Code 2 of 5. (non-interleaved.) A symbology that encodes all information in the width of the bars, using narrow spaces to separate all bars. It produces relatively less dense symbols than some other codes and it is not often used.

Code 11. A symbology that uses three bars and two spaces for each character, separating the characters with a single narrow space. Code 11 therefore carries the density of Interleaved 2 of 5 without its requirement that an even number of digits be encoded.

Code 39. A bar code symbology that represents characters with nine bars and spaces, three of which are wide with the remaining six being narrow. Code 39 can encode numerics, alphabetics, and a limited number of special characters. It is often used in inventory control and other business applications.

Code 49. A stacked bar code symbology, consisting of between two and eight rows, each composed of 18 bars and 17 spaces. All 128 ASCII characters are represented.

Code 93. A high-density alternative to Code 39. Code 93 uses three bars and three spaces with a total width of nine elements to encode the same 43 characters as in Code 39. Code 93 uses two check characters.

Code 128. A more recent and more dense symbology, able to encode all 128 ASCII characters. Characters in Code 128 consist of three bars and three spaces, with their widths distributed to encompass a total of 11 elements. Code 128 is not self-checking.

Common carrier. A firm selling transportation services to the public. Company-owned vehicle fleets are not normally considered common carriers.

Company identifier. (UPC). A five-digit preassigned number that appears as part of a Universal Product Code.

Compartment or subposition. Similar to position, the compartment parameter designates the front-to-back position of material.

Completion. The release of a unit load of product from a production group for transportation to another material handling group or to storage.

Component item. An item that is to be assembled into another item, losing its identity in the process.

Conference-room pilot. A system test performed by users, nominally in a conference room setting but more importantly with time to discuss test results and review system output compared to both the design specification and to expectations.

Consignee. The person or company who is to receive a shipment. Usually the ultimate recipient when freight is handled by several carriers.

Consignment. A shipment, usually when sent by common carrier.

Consolidation. (1) The process of determining all the partially filled locations containing the same item so that they can be brought together into one location, freeing up storage space. (2) The process of combining orders from a single customer at the time of picking to improve picking efficiency. (3) The process of combining several orders from a single customer to make a single shipment, thus reducing freight costs.

Contact scanner. A bar code scanner that must be used in contact with the symbol.

Container. (1) A large (20 to 50 feet long) box-like device intended for unit movement of one or more shipments over long distances by a variety of carriers. Most containers are designed to be moved, interchangeably, by truck, rail, or water transportation, eliminating the need to unpack and repack as the shipment moves from one carrier to the next. (2) A generic term used to denote a material handling device such as a pallet, a tote, or a carton.

Control chart. A plot of measurements taken over a period of time. Control charts usually define a point beyond which the measurements are considered out of control and require management attention. The control limit is generally established using statistical calculations.

Control limit confidence factor. A mathematical factor used in calculating the space between the expected value and the control limit on a control chart.

Control limit spacing. The space between the expected value and the control limit on a control chart. The control limit is a function of a confidence factor and the precision with which the measurement being plotted is made.

Conveyor. Any of a group of devices for the horizontal or inclined movement of material. Conveyors take many forms and can be built into systems with significant capacity and flexibility.

Cost-benefit analysis. The cost-benefit analysis determines whether funds should be committed to create and install the system, the effort should be abandoned as unproductive, or the functional design should be revised to achieve a better cost-benefit ratio.

Counterbalance truck. A lift truck that carries its load in front of the front axle, using the truck body to counterbalance the load.

Counting scales. Scales that are capable of counting a group of parts by measuring the weight of the group and comparing that weight to the weight of a single part. These scales are usually able to communicate the resulting count to a computer over a data cable.

Crane. (1) A vertical lifting device, usually employing cables. (2) A synonym for high-rise truck.

Credit approval. An order-entry function. Credit approval consists of the decision to extend or not extend credit to a potential customer.

Cross-docking. Movement of material directly from the receiving dock to the shipping dock without putting it away. The intent is to reduce material handling labor and cost and to improve customer service by shipping more quickly.

Customer. A consumer of the company's product. Customers are generally distinguished from other users of product by the degree of formality involved in the order acceptance and shipping processes. A remote warehouse or distribution center, therefore, can be considered a customer if it is required to submit purchase orders prior to the shipment of material to it.

Customer order. A document issued by a customer requesting shipment of material and promising payment in exchange. Customer orders always specify the customer's name and address and the items and quantities to be shipped. Many other data elements can appear.

Customer return. Product sold and shipped to a customer that is returned for either replacement or reimbursement.

Customer service. (1) The degree to which a business meets the expectations of its customers. (2) More particularly, the degree to which shipping commitments are met. (3) Sometimes, a numeric measure of the degree to which shipping commitments are met.

Cycle counter. An employee who does cycle counting either full or part time.

Cycle counting. A process by which the contents of inventory locations are counted and the counts compared with the inventory records. Cycle counting has several purposes including (1) the measurement of inventory accuracy, (2) the detection through examination of historical material movement records of the underlying problems that cause inventory inaccuracies (thereby enabling the correction of these problems) and, in isolated cases, (3) the direct support of accurate inventory records by the detection of errors and correction of the records. According to the purpose being served, the locations cycle counted may be selected randomly or may follow a fixed pattern.

Database. An organized collection of computer files, designed to be used together by one or more application systems.

Deallocate. To remove an allocation, freeing product for other use.

Decoder. In a bar code reading system, the decoder converts the signal received from the scanner to digital form if necessary, determines which symbology is in use (many decoders "autodiscriminate" between several symbologies), detects errors in the scanning of the symbol, determines which characters it contains, and passes the resulting character string to the terminal or computer to which it is connected.

Dedicated location. A storage location that remains logically assigned to a single product even when empty. Locations that are not dedicated are called "floating" and are eligible for reassignment to another product when they become empty.

Default. The value assumed by a computer system in the absence of user entry. Defaults are usually invoked by pressing the return (or enter) key.

Demand. A parameter used to describe a storage location. Using the demand parameter, the inventory facility can be divided into areas for slow movers, fast movers, and in-between items.

Demand storage. The division of storage areas into segments, each reserved for items with a similar material handling frequency. Demand, in the context, is not necessarily related to the quantities ordered by customers.

Density. (1) A measure of the amount of information that can be encoded in a given space. Density can be measured in characters per linear inch, or (with two-dimensional technologies) in characters per square inch. (2) In a more general sense, density refers to the narrow bar width of a bar code: Low density bar codes are normally considered to be those with narrow bar widths greater than 0.012 inch. Medium-density codes are those with narrow bar widths between 0.008 and 0.012 inch. And high-density codes are those with narrow bar widths less than 0.008 inch.

Depth. A parameter used to describe a storage location. Usually the inside measure of the depth available for storage.

Depth of field. The difference between the closest and the farthest possible distance between a noncontact bar code scanner and the symbol to be read.

Destage. To physically take product from a staging location and move it elsewhere.

Destination location. The inventory storage location to which a material movement is directed.

Device. A parameter used to describe a storage location. The device parameter defines the kind of storage device used for each staging location. It is used primarily by the system logic that searches for storage locations.

Dimensions. The height, width, depth, and weight capacity of a storage location are often grouped under the term "dimensions."

Direct thermal printer. See Thermal printer.

Dispatch. The function of assigning tasks to employees, often including material handlers. Dispatching functions are usually concerned with the achievement of schedules and the simultaneous maintenance of high levels of productivity. Dispatchers are considered clerical in some businesses and salaried in others.

Dispatcher. The person or system that does dispatching.

Disposition. The determination of what is to be done about rejected material. Typically disposition is one of four possibilities: (1) Use as is (which implies that the rejection was erroneous or of a minor nature), (2) rework (which implies correction of the problem within the facility), (3) return to vendor, or (4) scrap (which implies physical destruction). Disposition can also be made to sort the product, with portions of it being disposed of in various ways.

Distributed processing. A computer system architecture in which two or more computers each support different functional areas, with communication between the computers as appropriate.

Distribution Requirements Planning (DRP). The function of determining the need to replenish inventory at branch warehouses. A time-phased order point approach is used where the planned orders at the branch warehouse level are "exploded" via MRP logic to become gross requirements on the supplying source. In the case of multilevel distribution networks, this explosion process can continue down through the various levels of master warehouse, factory warehouse, etc., and become input to the master production schedule. Demand on the supplying source(s) is recognized as dependent, and standard MRP logic applies.[3]

Distribution Resource Planning (DRP). The extension of distribution requirements planning into the planning of the key resources contained in a distribution system: warehouse space, manpower, money, trucks, and freight cars, etc.[4]

Diverter. A device capable of altering the path of a carton or other item on a conveyor. Diverters may take the form of swing-arms controlled by air cylinders, but many other designs exist.

Dot matrix printer. A printer that uses a "head" containing anywhere from 9 to 24 pins and a mechanism for firing and retrieving each of them separately from the others. The head is moved across the page and the pins are fired as each crosses a point on the page where ink is required.

Download. The act of transmitting information from a superior computer to a subordinate one.

Drawer. A storage device that allows storage in compartments arranged in two dimensions. When drawers are stacked in a cabinet and arranged to pull out for access, the result is three-dimensional storage. Drawer storage is usually limited to small parts.

Drive-in rack. A pallet rack that stores pallets with zero aisle space but without stacking.

Drive-through rack. Similar to a drive-in rack but accessible from both ends.

Drop-off. The act of yielding control over a unit load of material. Involves placement of it in a storage location.

Drum printer. See Formed character printer.

DRP. See Distribution Requirements Planning and Distribution Resource Planning.

Dynamic rezoning. The recalculation of zone borders with each wave or group of orders. The purpose of dynamic rezoning is usually to even out the workload between a group of pickers.

EAN. See European Article Numbering.

EBCDIC. A method of binary encoding for alphabetic and numeric characters. The EBCDIC code is used primarily by large IBM computers and by certain plug-compatibles. EBCDIC computers cannot communicate with ASCII computers without a character translator.

---

[3]Reprinted with permission, the American Production and Inventory Control Society, Inc., *Dictionary,* 6th ed., 1987, p. 9.

[4]Reprinted with permission, the American Production and Inventory Control Society, Inc., *Dictionary,* 6th ed., 1987, p. 9.

EDI. See Electronic data interchange.

Efficiency ratio. On a productivity report, the ratio of the standard time for the work done by a person or group to the actual time used for those tasks alone.

Electronic data interchange (EDI). The transmission of data between computers belonging to different companies. Standards are maintained by the American National Standards Institute. Documents supported by the standards include purchase orders, invoices, remittance advices, price lists, quotations, shipping schedules, shipment notices, receiving advices, and more.

Electrostatic printer. A printer that uses a transfer drum to capture an image. The drum passes under a toner (ink) applicator and picks up ink only in those places required for the image. The drum then carries the ink to the paper where it is deposited and fixed with an application of heat. Electrostatic printers place the image on the drum using a character generator.

Element. A bar or space in a bar code. Sometimes used to denote a narrow bar or space.

Elevator. A vertical movement device that handles larger quantities of material in a single movement than do vertical conveyors. Some elevators handle lift trucks and operators in addition to loads, but most must be loaded on one floor and then separately unloaded on another.

Emergency replenishment. The movement of material from reserve storage to a forward picking area in response to an out-of-stock condition.

Engineering. (1) The business function that designs and specifies the product itself. (2) The business function that designs and specifies processes and methods.

Engineering change. A revision to a parts list, bill of materials, or drawings, authorized by the engineering department. Changes are usually identified by a control number and are made for "safety," "cost reduction," or "functionality" reasons. In order to effectively implement engineering changes all affected functions such as materials, quality assurance, assembly engineering, etc., should review and agree to the changes.[5]

Environment. A subdivision of a stockroom or warehouse intended for specific types or categories of material.

Error. In context, any action made by a person or a device that can lead to an incorrect entry in inventory files.

European Article Numbering (EAN). A symbology like the Universal Product Code but developed for use in Europe.

Excess inventory. Usable inventory that exists in quantities beyond that reasonably necessary for use in the near future. For this purpose, the "near future" is sometimes considered to be between 100 and 200 percent of the lead time required to obtain replacement stocks.

Expediting. The business function of detecting problems relating to the flow of materials, making short-term plans for the resolution of these problems, obtaining agreement to the plans, usually from supervisory personnel, and then verifying that the plans are

---

[5]Reprinted with permission, the American Production and Inventory Control Society, Inc., *Dictionary,* 6th ed., 1987, p. 10.

followed. The level of authority carried by expediters and the degree to which they are permitted to control the flow of material varies from business to business.

Expiration date. The date beyond which a lot or unit load of material cannot be used because of its advanced age. Paint, foods, and photographic film are all products that have expiration dates.

Field. An element of data. When fields are stored, they are generally kept on records in a file.

File. An organized collection of data concerning a single subject. Files usually consist of records, one for each occurrence of the subject.

Fill rate. The percentage of the lines on an order or a group of orders that can be filled (i.e., picked and shipped). For some businesses, particularly those that sell relatively undifferentiated products, the fill rate is a key customer service indicator.

FIFO. See First-in, first-out.

FIFO date. A date associated with inventoried material, used by inventory systems to control first-in, first-out flow. The FIFO date is usually the date the material was received in inventory.

Finished goods. Inventoried material that has no use other than shipment to customers. Replacement parts generally have use as components in the company's product and are thus not considered finished goods. In some cases, however, separate inventories of parts are kept for the replacement market. These separate inventories can be considered to be finished goods because they have no purpose other than shipment to customers.

First-in, first-out. The rotation of inventory, usually based on (1) the date received into the inventory facility or (2) for product manufactured in-house, the date of manufacture.

First time read rate. The percentage of correct scans achieved in a single pass of a scanner over a bar code symbol.

Fixed-beam laser scanner. A hand-held bar code scanner with a beam that does not oscillate. The operator uses wrist action to pass the beam over the symbol.

Fixed-location laser. An moving-beam laser scanner designed for unattended operation in a fixed location. Fixed-location lasers are similar to hand-held lasers but are packaged in a box designed to be bolted or clamped beside a conveyor to read bar codes as objects pass.

Flag. An indicator, usually a single bite or bit on a data file, that carries the value of a single attribute. For instance, a flag on an inventory location record could indicate that the location is on hold.

Floating location. A storage location that is eligible for reassignment to another product when it becomes empty. Locations that are not floating are called "dedicated" and remain assigned to a single product even when empty.

Floor stocks. Stocks of inexpensive production parts held in the factory from which production workers can draw without requisitions.[6]

---

[6]Reprinted with permission, the American Production and Inventory Control Society, Inc., *Dictionary,* 6th ed., 1987, p. 12.

Floor storage. A material storage "device." The storage of material directly on the floor without use of a device.

Flow rack. A storage device, usually made from a skate wheel or roller conveyor. Product is loaded into one end of the device and flows by gravity to the other. A flow rack is usually designed to handle either cartons or pallets.

Flow-through warehouse. A warehouse designed for one-way movement of material. Receiving and shipping docks are usually at the opposite ends of the building.

Fluid. A product that will flow and can be most economically stored in tanks and moved with pumps or pneumatic systems. Liquids, gasses, and powders are all included. Packaged fluids, such as cans of motor oil or bags of flour, however, are discrete and are not usually considered fluids.

Forecasting. The business function that attempts to predict sales and use of products so they can be purchased or manufactured in appropriate quantities in advance of receiving orders.

Formed character printer (drum printer). A printer that consists of a drum with raised characters (and bars) around its edge. The drum is rotated and a hammer mechanism is used to force the ribbon and paper against it as the appropriate character passes the trigger point.

Forward picking location. A storage location from which broken case or full case picks are made. Forward picking locations are usually replenished from reserve locations but may be resupplied directly from receiving.

Four-wall inventory. An inventory that records only the on-hand balance within a building or a department within a building. Therefore, it is one that tracks inventory only "within the four walls."

Fractional. A product that is discrete for handling purposes but that can exist in fractional quantities.

Freight bill. A freight carrier's invoice. Freight bills usually specify an identifying number (PRO number, airbill number, etc.), the origin and destination points of the shipment, the shipment's weight, and the amount due.

Freight claim. A claim for reimbursement filed with a freight carrier when shipments are lost or damaged in transit. Freight claims may also be filed in the event of billing errors or duplicate payments. Also, the document on which the claim is recorded and transmitted.

Freight class. A standardized method of classifying freight, maintained for the trucking industry by the American Trucking Association of Alexandria, Virginia.

Function. A location parameter that defines the way the inventory system treats each storage location. There are four functions: reserve, forward picking, staging, and cross-dock.

Function key. A special key on a workstation or terminal. Pressing this key invokes a software function. Function keys are controlled by the application software and, therefore, they do not necessarily have a fixed use.

Functional design. A study project performed to determine the user's requirements for a system. The functional design usually avoids specifying technical and data processing details that are of no interest to users.

Hand-held laser. A hand-held noncontact device for scanning bar codes.

Height. A parameter used to describe a storage location. Usually the inside measure of the location's height. Height measurements are often understated to allow maneuvering room for lift-truck drivers.

High-reach truck. See High-rise truck.

High-rise truck. A lift truck with the ability to reach higher levels than usual. High-rise trucks are often automatically guided and usually move the operator vertically with the load to provide improved visibility when pallets are picked or put away.

High-volume picking. A situation in which (1) orders may be picked one at a time or, to improve productivity, personnel may pick and pack several orders at once. (2) Picking, packing, and shipping are full time jobs. (3) Picking and packing may be combined into a single job, or packing and shipping may be combined. Often, however, all three functions are performed by different people. (4) Most picking is done from a dedicated "fast pick" zone in the stockroom or warehouse. (5) Picking may involve opening cartons to pick single units. (6) The productivity of picking personnel, and possibly packers and shippers, is measured.

History. See Audit trail.

Hold. A logical restriction enforced by the system that prohibits activity against a location or product or against any or all of the locations containing a product. There are several kinds of holds. See also Release, Receiving hold, Incoming inspection hold, In-process inspection hold, Inventory accuracy hold, and Shelf-life hold.

ID badge. A security device that identifies an employee. Usually about the size and shape of a credit card, ID badges are sometimes encoded with magnetic strips or bar codes to simplify identification to a computer system.

Impound. To place material on hold. To prevent material from being used or shipped, usually because of a quality concern.

Inbound side. In an inventory facility, the functions of receiving, inspecting, and putting material away.

Incoming inspection. The inspection of newly arrived material at an inventory facility. Incoming inspection can be formal or informal. In most larger facilities it is performed by a separate quality control organization using a predetermined set of methods and procedures.

Incoming inspection hold. A specialized hold designed to restrict the use of material until the inspection department has tested and approved it.

Ink jet printer. A printer that forces liquid ink under pressure from a nozzle through a charging tunnel that gives it an electrical charge. The droplets then pass through deflector plates that are also electrically charged. The plates, in effect "steer" the droplets onto a path that puts them in the right place on the paper.

In-process inspection hold. A specialized hold designed to restrict the use of material until it can be inspected or until existing doubt about its quality can be removed.

Inspection. The business function responsible for measuring product quality, determining whether or not specifications have been met, and exercising control as necessary to assure that out-of-specification material is not used.

Installation plan. A list of the activities required to install a system, together with the dates on which they will be completed.

Intangible. A cost element or system benefit that cannot be accurately valued.

Interleaved 2 of 5. A symbology that encodes numeric characters in a pattern of five bars or spaces, two of which are wide and three narrow. The code is interleaved because characters are encoded in pairs, with one character occupying the bars and the other occupying the spaces.

Interleaving. The alternation of picking and put-away tasks with the objective of minimizing unloaded travel for lift trucks. Cycle counts are sometimes included in interleaving.

In-transit. The quantity of an item that is in transit to a specific place or storage location. The term can be applied to either intraplant or interplant shipments but is not usually applied to both at the same time.

Inventory. The items stored in the warehouse. Inventory may consist of finished goods, parts or raw materials, or work-in-process. In some facilities, the term is also used to include indirect materials such as supplies. See Miscellaneous item.

Inventory accuracy hold. A specialized hold designed to restrict the use of material until the actual quantity on hand can be determined and corrections can be made to the records.

Inventory balance. The current on-hand balance.

Inventory classification. See ABC classification.

Inventory control. The business function responsible for maintaining inventories at acceptable levels. The inventory control function is usually also responsible for maintaining inventory records.

Inventory control system. The methods and procedures through which a company keeps track of how much inventory it has of each part and where that inventory is currently located. Inventory control systems can be either automated (computerized) or manual.

Inventory facility. A distribution center, warehouse, stockroom, tool room, or other place where inventory is kept. Inventory facilities are usually, but not always, confined to a single building and a single manager.

Inventory manager. The person with management responsibility for all aspects of the completed inventory system. Also has organizational reporting responsibility for the people who direct and are directed by the system.

Inventory stratification. See ABC classification.

Issue. A shipment that is not based on an order. Issues are usually informal and unplanned. In the absence of an order, the material issued is generally charged to an account number.

Item. Something inventoried. The quantity inventoried can be greater than one. Items are usually represented by an item number (which may be alphanumeric). All units of an item are, by definition, completely interchangeable. Synonymous with part.

JIT. See Just-in-Time.

Just-in-Time (JIT). A logistics approach designed to result in minimum inventory by having material arrive at each operation just in time to be used. The implication is that each operation is closely synchronized with the subsequent ones to make that possible. In the narrow sense, Just-in-Time refers to the movement of material so as to have only the necessary material at the necessary place at the necessary time. In the broad sense, it refers to all the activities of manufacturing which make the Just-in-Time movement of material possible.[7]

Kanban. (1) Japanese for "visible record." (2) The card that Toyota attaches to containers to document a requirement. (3) By extension, in a "pull" system of supplying manufacturing, the method by which requirements are communicated to the inventory system.

Key. Relating to computer data storage, the element(s) of data that provide(s) access to a record. The key, for instance, to a part file is usually the part number. The key to an inventory locator file may be the part number together with the location ID.

Kitting. The construction of "kits" of material, each of which contains a pre-counted number of each of two or more items that are packaged together by later assembly (maybe by the customer). Kitting is really an assembly operation in itself and should normally be treated as such.

Label. A device for identifying an object such as an inventoried item or a storage location. Labels can be paper, metal, plastic, or even cloth. Labels may or may not have adhesive applied to them. Typically, in inventory control systems, labels carry information about the object to be identified (such as its identifying number and a description), with some of the information in bar-coded form and some of it in human-readable form.

Ladder orientation. The display of a bar code so that the bars are horizontal (appearing like the rungs of a ladder) and scanning is done vertically.

Lane. (1) In a conveyor sortation system, one of the "fingers" to which product is directed. (2) In an area of floor storage, a subdivision usually one pallet wide and several pallets deep marked on the floor with paint. Equivalent to a section in a pallet rack area.

Laser. (1) A device for producing coherent light. (2) In context, a device that transmits a beam of coherent light and detects the reflection of that light from objects. When the light beam is swept across a bar code, the detector is able to read it and communicate the information to a computer.

Laser printer. A printer that uses a transfer drum to capture an image. The drum passes under a toner (ink) applicator and picks up ink only in those places required for the image. The drum then carries the ink to the paper where it is deposited and fixed with an application of heat. Laser printers place the image on the drum using a laser and a rotating mirror.

Lead time. A span of time required to perform an activity. In a logistics context, the time between recognition of the need for an order and the receipt of goods. Individual components of lead time can include order preparation time, queue time, move or transportation time, receiving and inspection time.[8]

---

[7]Reprinted with permission, the American Production and Inventory Control Society, Inc., *Dictionary,* 6th ed., 1987, p. 16.

[8]Reprinted with permission, the American Production and Inventory Control Society, Inc., *Dictionary,* 6th ed., 1987, p. 16.

License plate. License tag. Bar-coded tag or label that serves as a unique identifier to the warehouse control system. The term is usually restricted to use when the label is applied to a unit load of inventory.

Lift truck. A material handling device that moves palletized material horizontally and vertically. The term is generally applied to vehicles that are operator guided, at least part of the time. There are many subclasses. See also Straddle truck, Counterbalance truck, Pallet jack, Order picker, and High-rise truck.

Location. A storage place small enough to make it practical for employees to thoroughly search it for parts every time a put-away, an issue, or a count is to be done. It is often assumed that a location also has a fixed capacity (stated both in weight and in cubic measure) and is limited to a single part or item number. These limitations, however, are not universal and, while they are often useful, they are not necessary.

Location code. A randomly selected code assigned to storage locations. Location codes can be used in validation in some situations that preclude automatic identification.

Location number. A location identifier. Often nonnumeric.

Log file. A computer data file on which is recorded every movement of material and every significant event in the warehouse. The records are generally used for audit and recovery purposes.

Logging on or off. (1) The process of an operator signing on to the system (or a particular job) by identifying him- or herself (and the job) through a terminal. (2) The logoff function is the disassociation of an operator from a system or job, the release of system resources for other purposes, and, usually, the crediting of work performed to the operator.

Logmars. A bar code standard adopted by the Department of Defense, based on Code 39.

Losses. (1) Inventory lost by virtue of destructive testing such as that done by quality control. (2) Inventory lost in shipment or in handling. (3) Inventory lost as part of a production process. Losses are sometimes difficult to capture for inventory control purposes.

Lot number. An identifying number that designates a group of related items. Often used to designate items manufactured in a single run or received from a vendor in a single shipment. Lot numbers, when carefully tracked, can assist in the tracing of quality problems to their source.

Lot sizing. When a product is to be purchased or manufactured, lot sizing is the determination of the quantity to be bought or made. The objective is to spread setup and ordering costs over a large number of pieces, reducing unit costs.

Lower control limit. The line or point on a control chart below which a measurement represents a problem with a specified probability. See Control chart.

Low-volume picking: A situation in which (1) orders are picked one at a time, usually by a single person. (2) Most pickers work part time at picking and part time on other jobs such as packing or shipping; some may even work in other departments. (3) Picking, packing, and shipping is often combined into two or fewer steps. One person, for instance, might pick, pack, and ship an order. (4) Personnel productivity is not measured.

Magnetic ink character recognition (MICR). An automatic identification technology in which data is stored in printed form using magnetic ink. MICR is widely used by the banking industry to identify and sort cancelled checks.

Magnetic strip. An automatic identification technology that encodes data in magnetic strips, much as data can be encoded on magnetic tape.

Mail room. A facility or function for the receiving, sorting, and distribution of arriving mail. Because some material is shipped by mail, the mail room may become involved in the receiving process.

Manifest. A document that lists the pieces in a shipment. A manifest usually covers an entire load regardless of whether the load is to be delivered to a single destination or many. Manifests usually list the piece count, total weight and the destination name and address for each destination in the load.

Manual system. A system that does not use a computer.

Manufacturing order. See Work order.

Manufacturing Resource Planning (MRP II). A method for the effective planning of all resources of a manufacturing company. Ideally, it addresses operational planning in units, financial planning in dollars, and has a simulation capability to answer "what if" questions. It is made up of a variety of functions, each linked together: business planning, sales and operations (production planning), master production scheduling, material requirements planning, capacity requirements planning, and the execution support systems for capacity and material. Output from these systems would be integrated with financial reports such as the business plan, purchase commitment report, shipping budget, inventory projections in dollars, etc. Manufacturing resource planning is a direct outgrowth and extension of closed-loop material requirements planning.[9]

Map. See Plant map.

Margin. See Quiet zone.

Mark-sense. A technology in which printed forms are used for data entry. A grid of boxes is printed on the form, usually in gray or blue ink. Each row of boxes represents one character of the alphabet or one numeric digit; each column represents one character in a message. The characters that will make up the message are indicated by blackening the appropriate boxes with a pencil. Completed forms are then passed through a reader, which optically senses the blackened boxes and deciphers the data.

Material. The things stored in an inventory facility. The term generally applies to both direct and indirect materials and often includes miscellaneous items as well.

Material handler. A person who physically handles material. Loosely used to represent all hourly employees in a warehouse or stockroom and those who move material throughout a facility as part of their jobs. Usually paid on an hourly basis rather than being salaried.

Material handling class. A data element that defines the types of material handling vehicles that can access a location.

Material handling device. Any of a number of kinds of equipment for the horizontal or vertical movement of material.

Material Requirements Planning (MRP). A set of techniques which uses bills of material, inventory data, and the master production schedule to calculate requirements for mate-

---

[9]Reprinted with permission, the American Production and Inventory Control Society, Inc., *Dictionary*, 6th ed., 1987, p. 18.

rials. It makes recommendations to release replenishment orders for material. Further, since it is time-phased, it makes recommendations to re-schedule open orders when due dates and need dates are not in phase. Originally seen as merely a better way to order inventory, today it is thought of as primarily a scheduling technique, i.e., a method for establishing and maintaining valid due dates (priorities) on orders.[10]

Material review board (MRB). A group of people who have been given formal responsibility for reviewing materials rejected for quality reasons and determining the best disposition for these materials. Material review boards differ greatly in their formality and in the degree to which they exercise control over rejected material. They are often composed of representatives from product engineering, process engineering, quality control, and production.

Mechanization. The application of nonintelligent devices (machinery) to improve productivity and accuracy. (cf Automation).

Merge. (1) The act of combining two separate flows into a single flow. (2) The device that does this combination. The flows may involve the movement of physical items like cartons on a conveyor or of information like records on a tape.

Mezzanine. A method of reaching higher levels of bins, shelving, or a flow rack. Mezzanine upper levels are generally accessible only to material handlers on foot.

MICR. See Magnetic ink character recognition.

Mirroring. A software technique (sometimes implemented in firmware) that copies all information to two physical disk drives, detects drive failures, and automatically switches the system to the surviving drive.

Miscellaneous item. An item that consumes space in an inventory facility and must be received, put away, and withdrawn but is not represented by an item or stockkeeping unit number and thus does not appear on the item file. Such items as historical records, office supplies and furniture, and obsolete tooling are typical miscellaneous items stored in inventory facilities.

Miscellaneous withdrawal. The withdrawal of small quantities of product, usually on short notice and usually for internal company use. Miscellaneous withdrawals generally are charged to an internal account but can sometimes be billed.

Mode. Controls the method of use of a storage location when they can be used in more than one way.

Module width encoding. The use of bars and spaces of varying width to encode information in a bar code. Bars and spaces alternate with each other.

Monorail. A horizontal transportation device that uses carriers hung from an overhead rail. Monorails may, at times, use more than one physical rail to support the load.

Move. The movement of inventory from one location to another within an inventory facility. Movements are usually made under the direction and control of the inventory system.

---

[10]Reprinted with permission, the American Production and Inventory Control Society, Inc., *Dictionary*, 6th ed., 1987, p. 18.

Moveable aisle system. High-density storage in which an entire row of locations is mounted on wheels and can be moved laterally. When an operator needs access to a location, rows are moved until an aisle is created.

Moving-beam laser scanner. A hand-held or fixed-location bar code scanner with a beam that oscillates, scanning the symbol without operator effort beyond alignment.

MRB. See Material review board.

MRP. See Material Requirements Planning.

MRP II. See Manufacturing Resource Planning.

MSI code. A variation on the Plessy code.

Nesting. The factor by which products stack together, making the cubic volume of the stack less than the unit cubic volume multiplied by the number in the stack.

Noncontact scanner. A bar code scanner that must be supported some distance from the symbol to be used.

Nonreturn to zero (NRZ) encoding. The use of bars and spaces of unvarying width in a bar code. Bars and spaces do not necessarily alternate; the information is encoded in the pattern of the bars and spaces. Visually, NRZ symbols appear to have wide bars and spaces, but they are actually several regular bars and spaces next to each other.

Notification. The act of notifying interested people of the arrival of material that has been on order.

NRZ encoding. See Nonreturn to zero encoding.

Obsolete inventory. Inventory of acceptable quality that is no longer usable or salable. Inventory often becomes obsolete because of changes in specification.

OCR. See Optical character recognition.

Off-line. When two devices interact off-line, information is passed between them in batches. Usually used in reference to a person and a computer but also applicable to other devices and to devices other than humans.

Omni-directional scanner. A laser bar code scanner that has a beam that oscillates in a two-dimensional pattern.

One-ended warehouse. A warehouse that locates the shipping and receiving docks near to each other, providing for two-way material flow into and out of the storage area and the opportunity for interleaving tasks.

On-hand balance. Properly, the amount of material physically present in an inventory location. In some inventory control systems, on-hand balances include in-transit inventories and/or exclude materials that have been designated to be picked, but this is normally considered bad practice.

On-line. When two devices interact on-line, information is passed between them one transaction at a time rather than in batches. Usually used in reference to a person and a computer but also applicable to other devices and to devices other than humans.

Operation. A single production step. Usually, but not necessarily, performed by an individual employee on one part at a time.

Optical character recognition (OCR). The direct interpretation of human-readable characters by a scanning device. The most popular method uses one of several type fonts designed specifically for OCR use. Scanners also exist that can read typeset and ordinary computer-printed pages and even hand printing. Read rates are lower than most bar codes because reader-to-code alignment requirements are hard to meet and because OCR does not contain the redundancy of bar codes.

Optical scanner. See Charge-coupled diode scanner.

Optical throw. The optimum distance between a noncontact bar code scanner and the symbol to be read.

Order assembly. The gathering of the several parts of an order prior to shipment. Order assembly is necessary when several pickers are involved in its picking.

Order entry. The business function of interpreting incoming orders and entering them into a computer system (usually not an inventory control system). Separate order entry processes may exist for customer orders and internal (manufacturing) orders. The function of customer credit approval is sometimes included in the definition of order entry.

Order management. The inventory system function of receiving orders from an order entry system, modifying them as necessary, forming them into waves, allocating inventory, and creating work assignments for the material handlers. The term is usually applied only to outbound orders. (See Receipt order management.)

Order picker. A transportation device intended for the movement of less-than-pallet quantities of material. Order pickers usually provide both vertical and horizontal movement and usually move the operator vertically with the load to allow the picking of individual items from above-ground pallets. They are often guided automatically.

Order picking. The picking of orders, often of one order at a time, for shipment.

Order point. An inventory balance that is compared to the sum of the on-hand and on-order balances. When the order point is found to be less than on-hand plus on-order, a new order (either manufacturing or purchase) is indicated. This method of reordering stock has been discredited in many situations in favor of Material Requirements Planning and/ or Distribution Requirements Planning but is still in broad use in manufacturing, distribution, and other industries.

Order selection. The business function of selecting outbound orders for inclusion in a picking wave.

Order type. A database field that distinguishes between customer orders, shop orders, and transfer orders.

Outbound side. In an inventory facility, the functions of order selection and allocation, picking, packing, and shipping.

Packing. The function of packaging inventory items for shipment.

Packing list. A shipping document that describes the content of the shipment, usually listing individual items, quantities, and descriptions. The name and address of the shipping and receiving companies is usually included.

Pallet. (1) A material handling device that allows material to be handled in unit loads. (2) By extension, a unit load.

Pallet jack. A horizontal transportation device for palletized material. The pallet jack has no vertical movement capability beyond that required to gain clearance for horizontal movement. Its use, therefore, is restricted to floor locations.

Pallet rack. A material storage device designed for material on pallets.

Parcel. A package containing one or more products of a size appropriate for shipment by a parcel carrier such as UPS or RPS. The various parcel carriers each have size and weight limitations that restrict parcels. Parcels are always smaller than pallets and normally are much smaller.

Parcel carrier. A freight carrier that deals primarily in parcels and either does not handle pallets or handles them at premium cost. Parcel carriers usually limit the weight and size of the materials they will take. The hallmark of the parcel carrier is that each parcel is treated as a separate shipment and there is no assurance that parcels shipped together will be delivered together. The category includes overnight delivery services such as Federal Express and Emery as well as standard parcel services such as United Parcel Service (UPS) and Roadway Parcel Service (RPS).

Parity checking. A data verification technique in which a single bit is added to a string of bits. The value of the added bit is set to either 1 or 0 so that the entire string, when summed, results in either an even (even parity) or an odd (odd parity) number.

Part. Something inventoried. The quantity inventoried can be greater than one. Parts are usually represented by a part number (which may be alphanumeric). All units of a part are, by definition, completely interchangeable. Synonymous with Item.

Password. A sequence of randomly selected characters that an individual memorizes and uses to authenticate him- or herself to a computer system at logon time.

Performance objective. A numeric goal for a system project. Performance objectives usually relate to speed of operation but can also relate to capacities and other requirements.

Perpetual inventory. A bookkeeping system in which new inventory levels are determined by adding receipts to and subtracting withdrawals from an existing inventory level. Adjustments can also be made to the inventory.

Physical inventory. The process of completely recounting the inventory in a facility or in a major portion of a facility. All movement is usually halted during the counting process. Most physical inventory counts are accompanied by an audit conducted by professional auditors.

Pick-by-light system. A system in which each picking location is accompanied by a computer-operated display unit, usually mounted immediately above or immediately below the location. At the start of a wave, the displays are used to show the quantity to be picked from each location for the first order. Pickers then pick the material required and confirm each pick by pressing a button on the display. When the last pick has been completed, the computer then displays the picking quantities for the next order and the cycle continues until the wave is complete. Pick-by-light systems are most applicable to high-volume situations in which picking is being done from bins, a flow rack, or shelving with the individual locations between 4 and 48 inches wide.

Pick list. A document (which may be electronic) that tells the picker what to pick for an order or customer. The pick list usually shows the picking location, the identity of the item to be picked, and the quantity to be picked. Many pick lists are arranged in an efficient picking sequence to minimize the time the picker spends moving from one location to the next. Depending on use, pick lists also may show the customer's name and address, the method of shipment, and other information.

Pick sequence. This field can carry a number by which the system could sort to arrive at an efficient picking sequence.

Pick subzone. A group of storage locations that are picked by a single person. Usually a subdivision of a pick zone.

Pick-up. The act of assuming control over a unit load of material. Involves removing it from a storage device for transport elsewhere.

Pick zone. A group of storage locations that are picked by a common method.

Picker. A person whose primary job is picking.

Picket-fence orientation. The display of a bar code so that the bars are vertical (appearing like a picket fence) and scanning is done horizontally.

Picking. The process of selecting inventory to fill an order and physically removing it from its storage location. Picking operations usually feed other downstream processes and do not directly result in reducing the inventory facility's total on-hand balance. (They do, of course, result in reducing the on-hand balance and the allocation amount for the picking location).

Piece. A single package or unit load, ready for shipment or currently in-transit. A shipment, for instance, may consist of several pieces. Each piece has a specific destination but may contain several items or parts and can even contain more than one customer order.

Pilferage. Premeditated theft of product or supplies, usually accompanied by an attempt to avoid detection. The term implies relatively small quantities taken by employees rather than outsiders.

Plant map. A computer file that defines material movement requirements between locations. Specifically, the plant map lists staging areas and facilitates hand-offs between different kinds of equipment.

Plessy code. A symbology that encodes each character in four bars and four spaces, with each bar and space pair being either wide, narrow or narrow, wide to encode a single bit.

Point-of-use store. Inventory stored near the production facilities that will use it. The objective of point-of-use stores is quick access.

Portable transaction terminal. A device, usually with a bar code scanner attached, which can be used to gather both scanned and keyed information for later transmission to the inventory system. Also called a portable terminal. Unless otherwise specified, portable transaction terminals are assumed to be nonradio.

Position. In a single rack or bin structure, at a specific level above ground there may be space for storage of more than one item, pallet, or load. These spaces are separated by considering them to be different positions and giving them numbers. The position number is usually made part of the location number.

Present value. The value, as of the present time, of a cash flow occurring at a different time. Present value accounts for the effects of inflation and the time-value of money.

Pricing. The business function through which selling prices are determined for a specific customer order. Usually not a function of an inventory system.

Priority. The relative importance of jobs or tasks. Used in an inventory system to assure that the most important work is done before other work is assigned.

Product identifier (UPC). A five-digit user-assigned number that appears as part of a UPC code.

Production control. The organizational component responsible for determining what products should be produced at what times and for tracking actual production and taking action to eliminate variances. Production control is often also responsible for defining (or requisitioning) the direct material purchases required to support production.

Production plan. A factory schedule that defines the shop or manufacturing orders that must be started and the dates, items, and quantities to be built under each.

Production schedule. A plan for the production of product. It defines the products that will be made and the quantity of each to be made in each time period.

Productivity. (1) Broadly, the ratio of output to either input or time for a process. For instance, the productivity of a machine is the number of pieces completed in an hour or a day. The productivity of a refining process is the amount of completed product received in comparison to the amount of raw material used. (2) More specifically, the amount of work completed by an employee in a specific amount of time. Employee productivity is often gauged against a standard level of productivity, the standard being different for different types of work to allow the comparison of individual productivity measurements from time to time and between one employee and the next.

Productivity ratio. On a productivity report, the ratio of the standard time for the work done by a person or group to the actual time worked, including time spent on unmeasured tasks.

Programmable controller. A general-purpose computer that has been modified for process control use. In this book the abbreviation PLC, for programmable logic controller, is used to avoid confusion between PC as an abbreviation for personal computer and for programmable controller.

Promotion. A marketing activity that can cause dramatic changes in the velocity of a small number of items in a short time.

Prompt. A message sent by a computer system to elicit a response from a user.

Public warehouse. A storage facility that rents space to other companies. Charges are usually based on the square footage used and the length of time that it is used. The public warehouse operator generally supplies the labor and equipment required to move material into, through, and out of the public warehouse.

Pull distribution. The movement of material in response to a request from the recipient. The term can be applied either to the distribution of finished goods or to in-house distribution of parts to the manufacturing facilities.

Purchase order. A document issued by a business requesting shipment of material from a vendor and promising payment in exchange. Purchase orders always specify a delivery name and address and the items and quantities to be shipped. Many other data elements can appear.

Purchased parts. Items purchased from a vendor for assembly into a company's products. The term usually implies (1) discrete items, (2) manufactured items, and (3) items that have received processing beyond the state of a raw material.

Purchasing. The business function that is responsible for the selection of vendors and the placement and management of orders on those vendors.

Push distribution. The movement of material in response to a predefined plan. The term can be applied either to the distribution of finished goods or to in-house distribution of parts to the manufacturing facilities.

Put-away. The act of moving material to a storage location.

QC. See Quality control.

Quality control (QC). The organization or function responsible for monitoring and evaluating product quality.

Queue. A line or group of sequenced transactions waiting to be processed by the computer or an operator. Transaction sequence may be first-come, first-served, may be based on a priority scheme, or may be in any of a variety of other sequences.

Quiet zone (margin). An area on each end of a bar code symbol that contains no printing. Quiet zones assist scanners in locating the start of the symbol.

Quotation. The business function through which company selling prices are communicated to potential buyers, often along with terms and conditions of sale and other information. Usually not a function of an inventory system.

RA. See Return authorization.

Rack. A storage device for handling palletized material. A rack usually arranges pallets in vertical sections with one or more pallets to a tier. Some racks accommodate more than one-pallet-deep storage.

Radio frequency identification (RFID). An automatic identification technology that uses devices called RF tags. The tags communicate via radio waves with a transceiver and thence to the inventory system.

Radio frequency (RF) tag. A silicon chip that can absorb energy from a radio field and use that energy to make a low-power radio transmission of, for instance, a serial number. Part of an RFID system.

Radio frequency (RF) transmission. The movement of information over radio waves.

Radio terminal. A battery powered, portable, on-line device that acts as a computer terminal and communicates with the computer via radio frequency transmission. Radio terminals usually feature a keyboard, screen, auxiliary RS232 port, and a port for a bar code scanner.

Random. Without plan or logic. Selected in such a way that it is impossible to predict what the next selection will be until it has been made.

Random storage. The storage of inventory without restriction as to its location except for restrictions imposed by the physical characteristics of the storage device and the items to be stored. Use of the word "random," in this context, is a corruption since random storage need not be truly random but only be unrestricted.

Raw material. Items purchased from a vendor for assembly into a company's products. The term usually implies items purchased from material converters or refiners and not from fabricators or assemblers. Raw materials usually require some manufacturing operations to be performed on them before they can be assembled with other items.

Real time. Systems that operate interactively with other systems, with external hardware, or with humans. A real-time system processes inputs and produces outputs on an ongoing basis rather than in batches.

Receipt. A group of material that is ready for introduction into the inventory control system or that has been introduced into the system and is ready to be put away.

Receipt order management. The inventory system function of receiving inbound orders from an order entry system, modifying them as necessary, and maintaining them on file pending receipt of the material. The term can also be used to include the maintenance of open back-order quantities following receipt of a partial shipment and the preparation of various analytical reports.

Receiver. (1) A person who's primary job is the processing of receipts. (2) In some businesses, a document that records the content of a receipt or a form that is used to record the content of a receipt.

Receiving. The business function responsible for examining arriving materials and preparing them for put-away. Receiving verifies that the materials were ordered and that they have not been shipped too far ahead of schedule. It identifies and counts the material and causes it to be added to the company's inventory. Finally, receiving is responsible for preparing the material for put-away by repalletizing or repackaging it as necessary.

Receiving dock. The area in an inventory facility that is used for identification and counting of newly arrived material. Truck docks are usually part of this area.

Receiving hold. A specialized hold designed to restrict the use of material until the shipment in which it was received can be completely reconciled.

Recirculation loop. In a conveyor sortation system, the portion of the conveyor that can return material to the introduction point. Recirculation loops are most often used to recycle labels that could not be read, but then can also be used as a way of temporarily holding material.

Record. An organized collection of data concerning a single occurrence of a subject. Records are normally divided into fields, each containing a single piece of information about the occurrence of the subject.

Regular replenishment. The movement of material from reserve storage to a forward picking area in response to the stock falling below a predefined replenishment point.

Reject. An item that is of doubtful quality but that has not yet been given a disposition. Rejects are not immediately shippable but may become shippable in the future. Their movement is usually restricted by a hold.

Release. The act of removing a hold or restriction. Material that is released is available for allocation and use.

Reliability. The percentage of availability of a system or of a component in a system. The term can be applied to hardware, software, or the system as a whole.

Reorder. (1) An order (either a purchase order or a manufacturing order) for the replenishment of inventory. (2) The placement of a duplicate order when the original order has been lost or cannot otherwise be filled.

Repackaging. The removal of inventory from one package and placement of it in another. Repackaging can be done for convenience or economy in shipment or can be done to convert items from one stockkeeping unit to another. The latter case, for instance, might occur when a surplus of items packed in dozens exists along with a shortage of the same item in single packs.

Repalletizing. The restacking of merchandise on a pallet of a different size or shape or the replacement of a damaged pallet. Repalletizing is most often done to meet standard pallet sizes, either within an inventory facility or as required by a customer.

Replenish. The movement of material from reserve to forward picking to resupply the forward picking locations. Replenishments are usually divided into two subtypes: (1) Emergencies are those replenishments that are caused by the quantity available in the location going negative because of order demand. Timing of these replenishments can be important since the product needs to be in the location before the picker arrives. (2) Regular replenishments are those brought about by the quantity available in the location going below the replenishment point.

Replenishment point. A preestablished inventory value that is compared to the current on-hand quantity to determine when product should be moved from reserve to replenish forward picking. Some systems compare available quantities to the replenishment point rather than on-hand balances. Some replenishment points are stated in pieces and others in percentage of location capacity.

Replenishment quantity. When material is moved from reserve to forward picking (i.e., when a replenishment is done), it is the quantity that is moved. The replenishment quantity is usually the difference between the available quantity and the capacity of the forward picking location, but it can be altered as part of the process of selecting the locations from which the replenishment will be picked.

Request for Proposal (RFP). A document that describes a required system and requests proposals from vendors.

Request for Quotation (RFQ). Identical to Request for Proposal.

Requirements definition. A preliminary study project performed to give shape to a potential system design. The requirements definition answers seven questions: (1) What is technically possible? (2) What have other companies done? (3) What are the benefits that can be achieved? (4) What are the costs involved? (5) What steps will be required to see the project through to completion? (6) What staff is available to work on the project? (7) How long is the project likely to take?

Reservation. The reservation of material for a specific use. As compared to material allocations, reservations may be made for orders that have not yet arrived, specific sales people or territories, specific industry groups, or other entities. Reservations can be made at the individual storage location level or only in total. When specific orders are on hand, the reservation is usually replaced with an allocation prior to shipment.

Reserve location. A storage location generally intended for product in large or full pallet quantities. Normally, product is kept in the reserve location until it is needed in a forward location or for shipment. See Replenish.

Resupply. To reorder. See Reorder.

Return authorization (R/A or RA). A document (which may or may not exist in printed form) that authorizes a customer to return inventory that has been shipped and for which the customer would otherwise be obligated to make payment. The return authorization is usually used in the inventory facility as authority to receive the material when it physically arrives and also can serve as the source document for the credit posted to the customer's account.

Return to stock. Material that was delivered to production for use but was not actually used and is, therefore, being put back into storage.

Rewarehousing. The movement of material within an inventory facility to improve efficiency.

Rework. The process of correcting defects in material. Rework may involve any degree of remanufacturing from a simple repackaging job to complete disassembly and rebuilding of the product.

RF. See Radio frequency transmission.

RFP. See Request for Proposal.

RFQ. See Request for Quotation.

RF Tag. See Radio frequency tag.

RFID. See Radio frequency identification.

Route. The list of customers (or stops) to which a driver makes deliveries in a single run. The term is usually limited to delivery runs that involve more than one customer. A route may be regular (in which case it does not change frequently) or dynamic (in which case it changes with every run).

Routing. A set of information detailing the method of manufacture of a particular item. It includes the operations to be performed, their sequence, the various work centers to be involved, and the standards for setup and run. In some companies, the routing also includes information on tooling, operator skill levels, inspection operations, testing requirements, etc.[11]

Row. In an inventory facility, the rack or other storage device on one side of an aisle. Rows are often numbered, with the row number being part of the location number.

Sabotage. The intentional degradation of inventory record quality.

Safety stock. (1) In general, a quantity of stock planned to be in inventory to protect against fluctuations in demand and/or supply.[12] (2) In practice, safety stock also protects against inaccuracies in inventories.

Sample. The units selected for testing from among a group of similar units.

---

[11]Reprinted with permission, the American Production and Inventory Control Society, Inc., *Dictionary,* 6th ed., 1987, p. 27.

[12]Reprinted with permission, the American Production and Inventory Control Society, Inc., *Dictionary,* 6th ed., 1987, p. 28.

Scan. To read and decode a bar code symbol, an OCR character string, an RF tag, or other automatic identification symbol.

Scanner. (1) A device used to read bar codes. The term scanner includes both wands and lasers. The function of the scanner is to detect the presence of a symbol and to capture the pattern of bars and spaces in the form of an electronic signal. Some scanners (analog scanners) pass the electronic signal to the decoder with amplification but without other processing. Others (digital scanners) convert the signal from an analog wave form to a digital signal before passing it to the decoder. (2) A reading device for other automatic identification methods such as OCR and RFID.

Scrap. Material determined to be unusable and cannot be returned to the vendor or re-worked. Scrap is inventory, as it has value. However, it cannot be used in normal channels and will eventually be sold to a scrap dealer or thrown out.

Section. In an inventory facility, a single rack or bin structure on one side of an aisle. Sections are either numbered within an aisle (even numbers on one side, odd on the other) or within a row. Section numbers are then made part of the location number.

Security. The function that limits system access to authorized personnel and keeps records of activity by person. The objective of security is to prevent theft and destruction of information. Security concerns are usually divided into two areas: logon access and telecommunications.

Self-checking. The ability of an automatic identification technology to identify errors made during the scanning process. Self-checking capabilities are usually achieved through parity bits and/or check characters.

Sensitivity analysis. A financial analysis technique in which uncertain variables are tested to determine the degree of error in their estimation that would be necessary before the final decision would be affected.

Sensor. A device that senses the presence of an item. Sensors, for instance, are used on conveyor systems to detect the presence of cartons arriving at a particular point or on an AGV system to detect the presence of an obstruction in the vehicle's path. Sensors take many forms including photocells, mechanical switches, ultrasonics, infrared lights, and more. They are usually connected to and read by programmable controllers.

Serial number. An identifier that is unique to a single piece and will never be repeated for that piece. Serial numbers are usually applied by the manufacturer but can be applied at other points including the distributor or wholesaler.

Shadowing. See Mirroring.

Shelf. A storage device for smaller parts. When storage locations on a shelf are physically divided with barriers, the locations are called "bins."

Shelf-life hold. A specialized hold designed to restrict the use of material that has exceeded its shelf life.

Shipment promise. A shipment date quoted to a customer or, in some instances, internally to a production controller or expeditor.

Shipper. The person or firm who originates a shipment, often via common carrier.

Shipping. The business function of transferring possession of material to a carrier for delivery to a customer. Also used to denote the delivery of material from an inventory facility to another organization within the business (such as manufacturing).

Shop floor control system. A system for using data from the shop floor to maintain and communicate status information on shop orders (manufacturing orders) and work centers. The major subfunctions of shop floor control are: (1) assigning priority of each shop order, (2) maintaining work-in-process quantity information, (3) conveying shop order status information to the office, (4) providing actual output data for capacity control purposes, (5) providing quantity by location by shop order for work-in-process inventory and accounting purposes, and (6) providing measurement of efficiency, utilization, and productivity of manpower and machines. Syn.: production activity control.[13]

Shop floor data collection system. A system designed to capture, store, and forward the activities taking place in a manufacturing facility. Data gathered generally includes work order completions and may include timekeeping information. Shop floor data collection systems use data similar to inventory control systems at many points and portions of the two are, therefore, often integrated.

Shop order. Synonymous with work order.

Shortage. An instance in which product is not available to meet a requirement. Shortages can occur (1) at the time an inventory allocation is attempted or (2) at the time a picker attempts to pick the material. The latter case, known as an unplanned shortage, implies that inventory records are in error.

Skate wheel conveyor. An inexpensive, lightweight type of conveyor that supports items on wheels. The wheels often look much like roller skate wheels.

Skew angle. The angle between the light beam generated by a laser scanner and the plane of the symbol.

SKU. See stockkeeping unit.

Side-loading lift truck. A lift truck that moves at a right angle to the direction in which it picks and places loads.

Slot scanner. A device that allows bar-coded documents such as employee ID badges to be read by passing them through a slot. Most slot readers are electrically equivalent to wands.

Sortation. Sorting. The act of reorganizing a group of materials into some new sequence. Sortation machines or systems exist that can, for instance, sort incoming material by carrier for delivery to a truck door.

Source location. In a movement of inventory, the location from which the inventory is taken.

Space. In a bar code, the light space between bars.

S pattern. A travel pattern for material handlers working in two-ended aisles. The material handler moves up one aisle and down the next in an S-shaped pattern.

Speaker dependent. A method of voice recognition. Speaker-dependent recognizers require that each user record samples of his or her voice speaking each of the messages to

---

[13]Reprinted with permission, the American Production and Inventory Control Society, Inc., *Dictionary,* 6th ed., 1987, p. 29.

be recognized. These samples are stored and used as the basis for recognition. Vocabularies are generally limited only by storage space for the stored patterns.

Speaker independent. A method of voice recognition. Speaker independent recognizers are capable of recognizing the voices of most people by comparison with standardized voice prints. Vocabularies, however, may be limited compared to speaker-dependent recognizers.

Speech synthesis. A technology that converts computer-generated characters to audible human speech.

Stacking pattern. The pattern used for stacking objects in a container. Usually expressed as a quantity per tier and a number of tiers.

Staging. The temporary placement of material in a work area for a succeeding process (e.g., for put-away or shipment).

Staging location. A physical, geographic area in an inventory facility that is reserved for staging. Material is only put into a staging location when a plan exists to move it out.

Start character. A special pattern of bars and spaces placed at the beginning of a bar code symbol to notify the scanner that it should begin scanning.

Start-up. (1) The routine function of turning on the computer and initiating programs and files. (2) The one-time function of beginning beneficial use of a new system.

Stockkeeping unit (SKU). (1) An inventoried item. The term is intended to be broader than "part" or "item," encompassing kits, supplies, and all other regular inventory items. As normally used, however, SKUs do not include miscellaneous items. (2) By extension, the identifying number of an inventoried item.

Stockroom. An inventory storage facility. Synonymous with warehouse.

Stop. A customer in a delivery route. More precisely, a delivery point since some customers may have multiple addresses.

Stop character. A special pattern of bars and spaces placed at the end of a bar code symbol to notify the scanner that it has reached the end and should cease scanning.

Storage class. A prioritized list of sets of criteria for storing product.

Storage device. A physical device for the storage of inventory. Examples include a rack, shelving, bins, carousels, etc. Open floor space used for palletized material storage is usually considered to be a specialized type of storage device, even though there is no actual device involved.

Storage location. See Location.

Storage location selection. The process by which storage locations are selected and reserved for material that is to be put away. Storage location selection is often automated but can be manual.

Storage parameters. A set of data elements that define to the system the physical and logical characteristics of a part or storage location. Storage parameters thus establish the criteria used by a system to select storage locations.

Store (v.) The movement of material into a storage location. This process also updates the inventory of record with the quantity stored.

Store-mixed flag. Used to determine whether or not product may be stored in a location that already contains other products.

Store-to-existing-item flag. Used to determine whether or not product may be stored in a location that already contains a different lot of the same item.

Store-to-existing-lot flag. Used to determine whether or not product may be stored in a location that already contains the same lot of the same item.

Straddle truck. A lift truck that carries its load between the front and rear axles. The front axle is usually split, allowing the truck to "straddle" the load to pick it up.

Sub position. See Compartment.

Substitution. (1) An item shipped to a customer in place of the item ordered. Substitutions usually occur because the item ordered is out of stock. (2) The process by which an item is shipped in place of another because the item ordered is out of stock or obsolete.

Supervisor. The individual responsible for direct supervision of hourly employees. The supervisor's responsibilities usually include training, motivation, and performance measurement. In some instances they can also include work assignment and follow up.

Swing mast lift truck. A lift truck that can pick or place loads on either side by rotating its entire mast.

Symbology. A scheme for the arrangement of bars and spaces in a bar code. The symbology connects the bars and spaces themselves with their meaning.

Tare weight. The weight of an empty container.

Task. In the context of inventory systems, an individual material movement from one point to another in the facility.

Technical design. A study project performed to add technical design information to the functional design. The technical design work is usually done by data processing or by an outside vendor with the user's review and approval.

Telepen. A symbology that encodes the full 128-character ASCII set. Telepen consists of two separate character sets and includes special characters used for switching between the sets in mid-symbol.

Terminal. A device for two-way communications between a human and a computer. Terminals usually consist of a display screen and a keyboard, but any of a wide range of other devices may be included.

Test plan. A list of tests that must be performed and the results that will be found acceptable.

Thermal printer. (1) Direct thermal printers use a special paper stock that darkens when heat is applied. The paper is passed under a print head that applies hot wires to the paper, darkening the paper in the appropriate places to produce an image. (2) Thermal transfer printers are similar except that the ink is carried in a separate temperature-sensitive ribbon and normal paper stocks can be used.

Thermal transfer printer. See Thermal printer.

Tier. In a single rack or bin structure, the level above ground of the pallet beam, shelf, bin, or drawer. Tiers are usually numbered beginning with 1 at ground level and going up. Tier numbers are usually made part of the location number.

Tilt-tray sorter. A device for physically sorting small products. The tilt-tray sorter conveys product on tray-like platforms mounted on a conveyor mechanism. As the trays pass the locations where the product is to be unloaded, they are tilted and the product slides off. Tilt-tray sorters are capable of sorting very high volumes of material but are not applicable to some delicate products.

Time standard. The predetermined times allowed for the performance of a specific job. The standard will often consist of two parts, that for machine setup and that for actual running. The standard can be developed through observation of the actual work (time study), summation of standard micro-motion times (synthetic time standards), or approximation (historical job times).[14]

Tool. An inventory item (often one of a kind, at other times one of several similar items) that is checked out to an individual employee with the expectation that it will be returned.

Tote. A container, usually of 5 cubic feet or less. Totes may or may not have covers. They are usually arranged to allow stacking without damaging the product and can also nest for storage when empty.

Touch screen. A computer input device that reacts to the physical touching of the screen on which options are displayed.

Trailer. The back half of a tractor-trailer rig.

Training. The activity through which material handling, supervision, and management personnel learn how to use a system. Training should be an ongoing effort that includes refresher and update courses.

Transaction. (1) Any movement of material. (2) The record of a material movement or a pending material movement in written or printed form or in a database.

Transfer order. An order, similar to a manufacturing order, for the shipment (or transfer) of material from one inventory facility to another.

Tugger. A device that pulls a train of cars, with each car capable of handling one or more unit loads of product.

Turnover. Also turns. The inverse of velocity. That is, the amount of time it will take to completely ship the entire current inventory of an item or group of items. Turnover is usually measured in turns per year.

Turret truck. A lift truck that can pick or place loads on either side by rotating its forks and backplate but not the entire mast.

Two-deep rack. Pallet rack capable of holding two pallets in each location, with one pallet in front of the other.

UCC. See Uniform Code Council.

Unidirectional scanner. A laser bar code scanner that has a beam that oscillates in one dimension only.

---

[14]Reprinted with permission, the American Production and Inventory Control Society, Inc., *Dictionary*, 6th ed., 1987, p. 32.

Uniform Code Council. The governing body for the Universal Product Code (UPC) symbology.

Uninterruptable power supply (UPS). A device that compensates for power failure by automatically switching to battery power.

Unit. One inventoried piece such as, for instance, a single bolt or washer. Units are usually identified by a part or item number (which may be alphanumeric). All units of a part are, by definition, completely interchangeable.

Unitization. The packaging of material in standard quantities, usually called "unit loads." When a tote, box, or pallet contains a known quantity, material handlers can simply count the unit loads and multiply by the unit load quantity. This is much faster and much more accurate than counting by hand.

Unit load. A grouping of material packaged for handling as a single unit. Unit loads are normally precounted. Their packaging is often designed to prevent disturbance of the material without leaving obvious traces so the quantity contained on them is reliable. Examples of unit loads include stretch-wrapped, palletized material and material in closed, sealed totes.

Universal Product Code (UPC). A symbology designed specifically for the retail industry and its suppliers. UPC symbols consist of two parts: a preassigned supplier number and a supplier-assigned product number.

UPC. See Universal Product Code.

Upload. The act of transmitting information from a subordinate computer to a superior one.

UPS. (1) The United Parcel Service, a parcel carrier. (2) An uninterruptable power supply.

UPS manifest. (1) A parcel manifest for the United Parcel Service. (2) A document that lists parcels shipped by UPS. (3) By extension, the process by which the UPS manifest is created. This process often involves the processing of large numbers of parcels. It demands that the shipper weigh and identify each parcel and calculate the shipping charges associated with each. Because manifesting is more efficient than the alternatives, many volume shippers have systems that fill this function.

U.S. Postal Service (USPS). The government agency responsible for the mails. The USPS is also a parcel carrier.

USPS. See U.S. Postal Service.

Utilization. The degree to which effective use is made of something. In particular: (1) Space utilization measures the proportion of the space in an inventory facility that is in use at a point in time. Space utilization can be measured in locations, cubic feet, or units of weight. (2) Equipment utilization measures the number of hours in a period of time during which a piece of equipment was in use. Both space and equipment utilization are usually expressed as a percentage.

Utilization ratio. On a productivity report, the proportion of an individual or group's time devoted to measured activities.

Validation. (1) The process of confirming that the various activities of the warehouse or stockroom are performed correctly and accurately. Validation usually involves the collection of independent confirming data for each activity and a method of displaying errors and obtaining corrections. (2) The verification that a design is feasible and practical. Design validation is usually done at the functional level by comparison with existing systems in other companies or through expert review.

Velocity. The "speed" with which an item moves through inventory. Velocity can be measured in units per period of time or, less useful for inventory control purposes, in dollars per period of time.

Vertical conveyor. Conveyor designed for the vertical movement of material, usually between floors.

Vision system. A technology by which computers can use the sense of vision. A video camera produces an image that is digitized and analyzed to produce data on which a computer can form decisions.

Voice recognition. A technology that converts audible human speech to character strings recognizable and usable by a computer.

Wand. A device shaped like a thick pencil that can be used to scan and interpret bar codes. Wands are used by bringing them into contact with the bar code and moving them across it.

Warehouse. An inventory storage facility. Synonymous with stockroom.

Wave. A group of orders chosen to be released together for picking and shipment. Waves may consist of orders selected for a single carrier or a group of carriers, for a specific types of picking, or for certain types of customers. Other wave-selection criteria also exist based on a particular facility's physical layout and organization.

Weight capacity. The weight limitation of a storage device, if any.

Width. A parameter used to describe a storage location. Usually the inside measure of the location's width. Width measurements are often understated to allow maneuvering room for lift truck drivers.

Withdrawal. The act of removing material from inventory so that the inventory control system no longer has records of the material's current location. In the context of an inventory control facility, the term sometimes is restricted to use when material is being withdrawn for internal use. In many instances in which that is the case, the terms "pick" or "ship" are used when withdrawing material for shipment to customers.

Work assignment. A group of tasks to be done by a single person. Work assignments are often limited to a single type (i.e., picking, put-away, etc.) but can be of mixed types.

Work center. A specific production facility, consisting of one or more people and/or machines, which can be considered as one unit for purposes of capacity requirements planning and detailed scheduling.[15]

Work-in-process. (1) Material that is being processed or assembled. (2) Material that is under the control of the operating departments and not currently under the control of the inventory facility. (3) Material that has been partly processed or assembled (i.e. that material that is neither in the state in which it was purchased or is ready for shipment to

---

[15]Reprinted with permission, the American Production and Inventory Control Society, Inc., *Dictionary*, 6th ed., 1987, p. 34.

customers). (4) Inventory that must be controlled outside the stockroom. Can be inventory that is being processed or assembled or can be inventory that has been shipped to an outside vendor for processing.

Work-in-process system. A system that tracks work-in-process materials, usually by location. See also Shop floor control system.

Work order. A document authorizing the manufacture of a part, subassembly, or finished item. Work orders must, at a minimum, specify (1) an identifying order number, (2) the item to be made or assembled, (3) the quantity to be made or assembled, and (4) either a start date or a due date. Synonymous with manufacturing order and shop order.

Work queue. A data file containing records of material handling tasks to be performed. Work queues are normally kept in sequence by priority.

Zone. A subdivision of a warehouse or stockroom. In this book, specifically used to denote a subdivision of a forward picking line that is assigned to a single individual to pick.

Zone pick. (1) The concepts and methods that group and process picks with specific characteristics according to a series of picking locations (the zone) having a complementary set of characteristics. The prime goal is to enhance the efficiency and control of the picking process. (2) By association, a pick made under the zone picking method.

Index